San Francisco For Dummies, 5th Edition

Cheat Sheet

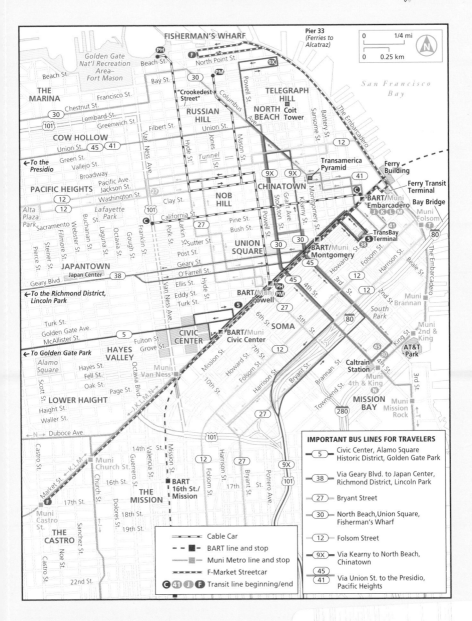

IMPORTANT BUS LINES FOR TRAVELERS

- **5** — Civic Center, Alamo Square, Historic District, Golden Gate Park
- **38** — Via Geary Blvd. to Japan Center, Richmond District, Lincoln Park
- **27** — Bryant Street
- **30** — North Beach, Union Square, Fisherman's Wharf
- **12** — Folsom Street
- **9X** — Via Kearny to North Beach, Chinatown
- **45 / 41** — Via Union St. to the Presidio, Pacific Heights

Legend:
- Cable Car
- BART line and stop
- Muni Metro line and stop
- F-Market Streetcar
- C 41 J F — Transit line beginning/end

D0068435

San Francisco For Dummies, 5th Edition

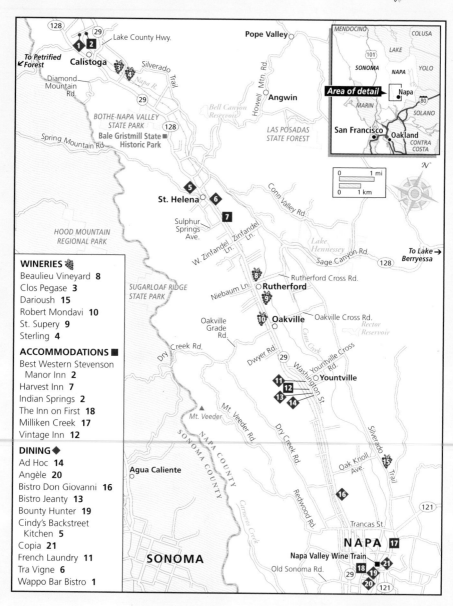

128
29
Lake County Hwy.
Pope Valley

To Petrified Forest
Calistoga
Silverado Trail
Napa R.

Diamond Mountain Rd.
29

Howell Mtn. Rd.
Angwin

BOTHE-NAPA VALLEY STATE PARK
128
Bale Gristmill State Historic Park

Bell Canyon Reservoir

Spring Mountain Rd.

LAS POSADAS STATE FOREST

HOOD MOUNTAIN REGIONAL PARK

St. Helena
5 6
7

Sulphur Springs Ave.

Conn Valley Rd.

W. Zinfandel Ln. Zinfandel Ln.

Lake Hennessey

Sage Canyon Rd.
128

To Lake Berryessa

WINERIES
Beaulieu Vineyard **8**
Clos Pegase **3**
Darioush **15**
Robert Mondavi **10**
St. Supery **9**
Sterling **4**

ACCOMMODATIONS
Best Western Stevenson Manor Inn **2**
Harvest Inn **7**
Indian Springs **2**
The Inn on First **18**
Milliken Creek **17**
Vintage Inn **12**

DINING
Ad Hoc **14**
Angèle **20**
Bistro Don Giovanni **16**
Bistro Jeanty **13**
Bounty Hunter **19**
Cindy's Backstreet Kitchen **5**
Copia **21**
French Laundry **11**
Tra Vigne **6**
Wappo Bar Bistro **1**

SUGARLOAF RIDGE STATE PARK

Niebaum Ln.
8 Rutherford Cross Rd.
Rutherford
9

Oakville Grade Rd.
10 **Oakville** Oakville Cross Rd.
Rector Reservoir

Conn Creek

Dry Creek Rd.
Dwyer Rd.
29
Yountville Cross Rd.
Washington St.
11 12 **Yountville**
13 14

Mt. Veeder
Mt. Veeder Rd.

SONOMA COUNTY
NAPA COUNTY

Dry Creek Rd.

Silverado Trail

Oak Knoll Ave.
15

Agua Caliente

Carneros Creek

16
121

Redwood Rd.

Trancas St.

NAPA 17

SONOMA

Napa Valley Wine Train
Old Sonoma Rd.
29 18 19 21
20
121

Area of detail (inset)
MENDOCINO COLUSA
LAKE
101
SONOMA NAPA YOLO
Area of detail Napa
MARIN 80 SOLANO
San Francisco **Oakland**
CONTRA COSTA

0   1 mi
0   1 km

N

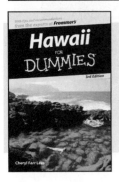
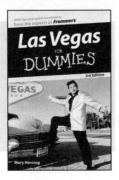
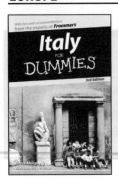

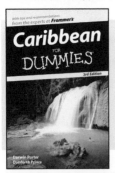
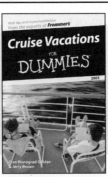

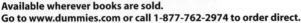

San Francisco

FOR

DUMMIES®

5TH EDITION

by Paula Tevis

WILEY

Wiley Publishing, Inc.

San Francisco For Dummies®, 5th Editon

Published by
Wiley Publishing, Inc.
111 River St.
Hoboken, NJ 07030-5774
www.wiley.com

Copyright © 2009 by Wiley Publishing, Inc., Indianapolis, Indiana

Published simultaneously in Canada

No part of this publication may be reproduced, stored in a retrieval system, or transmitted in any form or by any means, electronic, mechanical, photocopying, recording, scanning, or otherwise, except as permitted under Sections 107 or 108 of the 1976 United States Copyright Act, without either the prior written permission of the Publisher, or authorization through payment of the appropriate per-copy fee to the Copyright Clearance Center, 222 Rosewood Drive, Danvers, MA 01923, 978-750-8400, fax 978-646-8600. Requests to the Publisher for permission should be addressed to the Permissions Department, John Wiley & Sons, Inc, 111 River Street, Hoboken, NJ 07030, 201-748-6011, fax 201-748-6008, or online at http://www.wiley.com/go/permissions.

Trademarks: Wiley, the Wiley Publishing logo, For Dummies, the Dummies Man logo, A Reference for the Rest of Us!, The Dummies Way, Dummies Daily, The Fun and Easy Way, Dummies.com and related trade dress are trademarks or registered trademarks of John Wiley & Sons, Inc., and/or its affiliates in the United States and other countries, and may not be used without written permission. Frommer's is a trademark or registered trademark of Arthur Frommer. Used under license. All other trademarks are the property of their respective owners. Wiley Publishing, Inc., is not associated with any product or vendor mentioned in this book.

For general information on our other products and services, please contact our Customer Care Department within the U.S. at 800-762-2974, outside the U.S. at 317-572-3993, or fax 317-572-4002.

For technical support, please visit www.wiley.com/techsupport.

Wiley also publishes its books in a variety of electronic formats. Some content that appears in print may not be available in electronic books.

ISBN: 978-0-470-38523-4

Manufactured in the United States of America

10 9 8 7 6 5 4 3 2 1

WILEY

About the Author

A California native, **Paula Tevis** made many treks to San Francisco as a young girl before moving to her favorite city in 1983. After an eclectic but blessedly brief career that included stints in the computer and nonprofit sectors, she and her husband produced a couple of children in quick succession, and Paula happily relinquished the 9-to-5 world for the 24/7 one that parenting brings. Upon regaining consciousness, Paula recalled a childhood ambition and declared herself a writer. From her humble beginnings word-processing cookbook manuscripts for a local publisher, Paula metamorphosed into a freelance copy editor and soon received her first break as a professional writer with *Parenting* magazine, crafting a column on kids who cook. Over the years, she has contributed articles and essays to *Family Fun* magazine, the *San Francisco Chronicle,* Citysearch.com, *Frommer's Las Vegas, Frommer's New Orleans,* and *Variety.* She is the co-author of *California For Dummies* and author of the original *Frommer's San Francisco with Kids.*

Author's Acknowledgments

Thanks to my dear cousins Irene Levin Dietz and Ina Levin Gyemant, who have added so much to my life in San Francisco for over 30 years. Eating in the city wouldn't be the same without Bev Chin or the guidance of Patricia Unterman; revisiting my favorite neighborhoods is an even greater pleasure with my cadre of friends, including Marjie Graham, Vicki Pate, Cynde Ahart Wood, Helene and Charles Wright, Andrea and Jeff Tobias, and Sarah Wilcox. Thanks also to Donna Joyner for her Wine Country insights. Living, no matter where, is pretty terrific and lots of fun with my husband, Mark Katz, and our very wonderful daughters, Madeleine and Lili.

Publisher's Acknowledgments

We're proud of this book; please send us your comments through our Dummies online registration form located at www.dummies.com/register/.

Some of the people who helped bring this book to market include the following:

Editorial

Editors: Alexia Travaglini and Marie Morris, Development Editors; Suzanna R. Thompson and M. Faunette Johnston Production Editors

Copy Editor: Cara Buitron

Cartographer: Liz Puhl

Editorial Assistant: Jessica Langan-Peck

Senior Photo Editor: Richard Fox

Cover Photos:
Front: © Pegaz/Alamy
Back: © Brett Shoaf/Artistic Visuals

Cartoons: Rich Tennant (www.the5thwave.com)

Composition Services

Project Coordinator: Kristie Rees

Layout and Graphics: Melissa K. Jester, Julie Trippetti, Christine Williams

Proofreaders: Melissa Bronnenberg, Debbye Butler

Indexer: Claudia Bourbeau

Publishing and Editorial for Consumer Dummies

Diane Graves Steele, Vice President and Publisher, Consumer Dummies

Kristin Ferguson-Wagstaffe, Product Development Director, Consumer Dummies

Kelly Regan, Editorial Director, Travel

Publishing for Technology Dummies

Andy Cummings, Vice President and Publisher, Dummies Technology/General User

Composition Services

Gerry Fahey, Vice President of Production Services

Debbie Stailey, Director of Composition Services

Contents at a Glance

Maps at a Glance

Table of Contents

Introduction

*M*any years ago, long before mandatory seat-belt laws, my mother would occasionally squeeze my sister Patience and me into her little red sports car and zoom up Highway 101 for a weekend in San Francisco. We lived 350 miles south, in Santa Barbara, but thanks to my mom's lead foot, we'd be cruising along the bay in no time, past a hill filled with rows of boxy pastel-colored houses, then onto the boulevard that led to our cousin Mildred's beautiful home. My desire to live in a big city (and drive really fast) no doubt developed during these trips, and many subsequent ones in my teens, but my ties to San Francisco actually extend back further. My grandmother Sarah and her sister, Lottie, grew up here. At 18 and 20 years of age, they camped in Golden Gate Park after the 1906 earthquake, and in later years they lived in a series of houses in the Richmond District.

When I had the chance to move to San Francisco in 1982, I didn't think twice. My future husband and I lived near Haight Street, then moved to a neighborhood near the Mission District and Bernal Heights. Eventually, I found myself working at one time or another around the Richmond District, Civic Center, Potrero Hill, and South of Market. I loved getting acquainted with different areas of the city, and in hindsight I realize my early, admittedly dilettantish, professional life helped prepare me for the greatest (and perhaps longest-lasting) job I've ever held — writing about San Francisco.

The San Francisco of my grandmother's day was elegant enough to attract the most famous people of its time yet still wild enough to garner an exciting reputation. The multicultural, expansive, and liberal city of today continues in that tradition, and even improves upon it. After more than 25 years of familiarity, I continue to marvel at everything San Francisco has to offer, and I'll bet that after a day or two spent here, you'll do the same.

About This Book

San Francisco For Dummies, 5th Edition, is foremost a reference guide for people who intend to vacation in San Francisco and need basic, clear-cut information on how to plan and execute the best possible trip. If you like, you can begin reading from Chapter 1 and head straight through to the appendix. But if you turn directly to the restaurant chapter or to the pages on Wine Country because that's the piece that interests you at the moment, the book works just as well. I haven't included absolutely everything San Francisco has to offer in the way of attractions, hotels, restaurants, or diversions — a book that size would be too heavy to pack and probably too bothersome to read. What I've done is picked and chosen what I believe to be worth your time and your money while still offering enough variety to please a range of tastes, budgets, and family configurations.

Let me underscore that travel information is subject to change at any time — and in San Francisco this is especially true of restaurants as well as prices. Therefore, I suggest that you write or call ahead for confirmation when making your travel plans. The authors, editors, and publisher cannot be held responsible for the experiences of readers while traveling. Your safety is important to us, however, so we encourage you to stay alert and be aware of your surroundings. Keep a close eye on cameras, purses, and wallets, all favorite targets of thieves and pickpockets.

Conventions Used in This Book

So, San Francisco, here you come! You've picked a stunner of a destination, with a wide variety of wonderful sites to see, fabulous foods to sample, and interesting places to visit. But don't be overwhelmed. You've made a smart decision in buying *San Francisco For Dummies,* 5th Edition. This book walks you through all the nitty-gritty details to make sure that planning your trip goes smoothly and that the trip itself is memorable.

In this book, I include lists of hotels, restaurants, and attractions. As I describe each, I often include abbreviations for commonly accepted credit cards. Take a look at the following list for an explanation of each:

AE: American Express

CB: Carte Blanche

DC: Diners Club

DISC: Discover

JCB: Japan Credit Bank

MC: MasterCard

V: Visa

I've divided the hotels into two categories: my personal favorites and those that don't quite make my preferred list but still get my hearty seal of approval. Don't hesitate to consider these "runner-up" hotels if you're unable to get a room at one of my favorites or if your preferences differ from mine — the amenities that the runners-up offer and the services that each provides make all these accommodations good choices to consider as you determine where to rest your head at night.

I also include some general pricing information to help you as you decide where to unpack your bags or dine on the local cuisine. I use a system of dollar signs to show a range of costs for one night in a hotel or a meal at a restaurant (including appetizer, main course, dessert, one drink, tax, and tip). Check out the following table to decipher the dollar signs, and note that Wine Country hotels (see Chapter 14) have a slightly different price scale:

Cost	SF Hotels	SF and Wine Country Restaurants
$	$125 or less	$30 or less
$$	$126–$175	$31–$60
$$$	$176–$300	$61–$100
$$$$	$301 or more	$101 or more

Foolish Assumptions

As I wrote this book, I made some assumptions about you and what your needs may be as a traveler:

✔ You may be an inexperienced traveler looking for guidance on whether to take a trip to San Francisco and how to plan for it.

✔ You may be an experienced traveler who doesn't have a lot of time to devote to trip planning or doesn't have a lot of time to spend in San Francisco. You want expert advice on how to maximize your time and enjoy a hassle-free trip.

✔ You're not looking for a book that discusses the history and architecture of the city, provides all the data available about San Francisco, or lists every hotel, restaurant, or attraction. Instead, you're looking for a book that focuses on the places that will give you the best or uniquely San Francisco experience.

If you fit any of these criteria, then *San Francisco For Dummies,* 5th Edition, provides the information you're looking for!

How This Book Is Organized

Like all *For Dummies* guides, this book is organized in parts that contain anywhere from two to four chapters of related information. You don't need to start at the very beginning (though it's a very good place to start); feel free to turn directly to the chapter that intrigues you the most.

Part 1: Introducing San Francisco

This part gives you an overview of San Francisco, with particular attention to the lodging, dining, and touring highlights. Chapter 2 offers an overview of the city's history and suggests some background material that will get you counting the days until your vacation begins. The calendar of events in Chapter 3 may influence your decision about when to arrive, and the text on San Francisco seasons may convince you to land when the rest of the tourists have gone home.

Part II: Planning Your Trip to San Francisco

Because you're reading this, you probably aren't the type to just show up without an appointment — you intend to do a good bit of planning. That's a good idea, and this part covers what you need to know about travel costs, with tips on how to budget and directions for getting to San Francisco, particularly if you plan to fly. Because this book is intended for a varied audience, I include specific advice for family travelers, travelers with disabilities, seniors, and gay and lesbian visitors. Then I help you decide whether to rent a car, why travel insurance may be a good idea, and how to stay in touch while you're away from home.

Part III: Settling into San Francisco

In an unfamiliar city, figuring out where you are can take days, but Part III saves you time by explaining how to get to town from the airport and how to get around the most important neighborhoods. A thorough discussion on local transportation options follows, including everything I know about parking — although luck and patience usually play a more important role than mere words. When it comes to figuring out where to sleep, I include a rundown of the major neighborhoods where visitors stay, offering tips on getting the most room for your money and brief but informative descriptions of my favorite hotels. A lengthy and tasty chapter on dining will have you discussing the intricacies of the local food scene as if you spend all your weekends dining in these parts. And if you prefer to eat and run, you'll get a head start with a section on food to go — and you won't mistake it for fast food.

Part IV: Exploring San Francisco

You likely have an idea of what you want to see, and this part provides the information you need to conquer the most popular sites. Along with the big stuff, I've categorized other fun and intriguing options under lots of different interests and suggested some amusing guided tours. Many people come to the city specifically to exercise their charge cards, and my chapter on shopping will keep even the most avid consumer on his or her toes. My three- and five-day itineraries in Chapter 13 will help you focus and plan your days with all the precision you care to muster up. Got a case of wanderlust? Don't stay away long, but have a wonderful time investigating a few of the beautiful areas an hour or less from the city.

At the end of this part, I help you plan a day trip to Berkeley, an overnighter to Half Moon Bay, and a getaway to Wine Country, including winery tours and a mud bath.

Part V: Living It Up after Dark: San Francisco Nightlife

As my husband says during his annual pilgrimage to JazzFest in New Orleans, "You can sleep when you're dead." But first, you need to figure out where to go after dinner, and that's what you'll discover in Part V. From opera to swing dancing to barhopping to cinema, you can always find something stimulating to do or see around town.

Part VI: The Part of Tens

This is where I get to lurch from the sublime (the best views) to the practical (what to do if it's raining; glorious San Francisco souvenirs for under $10) and on to the ridiculous (how not to look like a tourist). But plenty of useful information is yours in Part VI.

I also include an appendix — your Quick Concierge — containing lots of handy information you may need when traveling in San Francisco, such as phone numbers and addresses, numbers to call for emergency personnel and area hospitals and pharmacies, contact information for babysitters, lists of local newspapers and magazines, protocol for finding taxis, and more. Check out this appendix when searching for answers to lots of little questions that may come up as you travel.

Icons Used in This Book

Keep an eye out for the Bargain Alert icon as you seek out money-saving tips and/or great deals.

Best of the Best highlights the best San Francisco has to offer in all categories — hotels, restaurants, attractions, activities, shopping, and nightlife.

Watch for the Heads Up icon to identify annoying or potentially dangerous situations such as tourist traps, unsafe neighborhoods, budgetary rip-offs, and other things to beware.

Find useful advice on things to do and ways to schedule your time when you see the Tip icon.

Look to the Kid Friendly icon for attractions, hotels, restaurants, and activities that are particularly hospitable to children or people traveling with kids.

Part of the fun of traveling to a city other than your own is seeing all the things that you won't find anywhere else — especially when so much of the landscape is dotted with the same old same old. This icon highlights sights and activities that really help you get a feel for San Francisco and its uniqueness.

Where to Go from Here

Grab some sticky notes to mark the pages that you may want to refer to later, clear your calendar, check the condition of your suitcase, and get ready to hit the road.

Part I
Introducing San Francisco

The 5th Wave   By Rich Tennant

In this part . . .

1 give you a taste of the best of San Francisco, with a spotlight on the top restaurants, hotels, attractions, sights, and sounds that make up this unique city. I do my best to guide you to what is hot and new, as well as to the old standards. I tell you where to find the best San Francisco has to offer. I also steer you to places both on and off the beaten path.

In the pages that follow, I give you a brief history of San Francisco, as well as overviews of the architecture and cuisine, and finish up with a list of books and films you may enjoy as you get ready to leave your heart. . . .

Chapter 1

Discovering the Best of San Francisco

* *

* *

*W*ith a wink and a wave to the past, San Francisco continues to reinvent herself like a determined matron plotting the next round of cosmetic surgery. In her starring role as the heartbeat of the Internet economy, this gracious city sashayed toward the 21st century with an energy and style that caused even the old guard to gasp in admiration. Then, before there was time to dump all the stock options, the bubble burst, the old-timers scrambled to diversify their portfolios, and young commercial real-estate brokers and Web designers seriously considered dental school. Fortunately, some things remain the same: The beautiful scenery continues to dazzle, the top-flight dining continues to garner raves, and the entertainment possibilities continue to grow in sophistication and imagination.

No matter how the economy fares, San Francisco consistently rates as one of the top tourist destinations in the world, and the reason is no secret. The city's treasured cable cars provide both thrills and great views as they whiz down and around our hills; a majestic golden bridge suspends travelers over the deep blue of the bay; hidden staircases lead to lovely gardens and eye-catching homes. And where else can you savor freshly made miniature chocolate truffles, meander down the most crooked street in the world, and escape from Alcatraz — all in one action-packed day?

Summarizing San Francisco is not easy. When it comes to culture, the city delivers everything from grand opera to leather-clad, fire-dancing performance artists. As for dining, we can down a burrito for lunch and polish off a multicourse designer meal for dinner — and critique both with equal passion. Our neighborhoods are more like *villages,* each with its own retail corridor, park, and distinct personality. For in the face of rampant cultural homogeneity — the malling of America, so to speak — San Francisco holds tight to its individualism and enthusiastically applauds, or quietly salutes, those who do the same. What is consistent about the city, from the top of Telegraph Hill to sunny China Basin, is constant surprise. As you round a bend in the road, a lovely vista unexpectedly pops into your line of sight. As you savor a glass of chardonnay, a Chinese funeral cortege may suddenly glide past your cafe table, the band playing a pop classic. Or the smell of roasting coffee beans may waft down the street and completely erase thoughts of anything but where to find an espresso. Give your senses free rein to guide you through your days here, and you'll have a vacation like no other.

Because I consider the following to be the best San Francisco experiences, I've marked them with a Best of the Best icon when they appear elsewhere in the book.

Best San Francisco Travel Experiences

Strolling along the Embarcadero to Aquatic Park: This walk is a quintessential San Francisco activity, ideally experienced on a sunny day. I prefer to start across from the baseball stadium on Third Street, although exiting Muni at the **Embarcadero** (see Chapter 8) and beginning there is more convenient. With the water on one side and city landmarks on the other, a leisurely walk past the piers, through **Fisherman's Wharf** (see Chapter 8), leads to **Aquatic Park** and the **Municipal Pier.** Be sure to hike all the way to the end of the pier, stopping to see what, if anything, the anglers have caught. Your reward will be million-dollar bay vistas.

Shopping at the Ferry Plaza Farmers Market: Saturday morning finds home cooks and food lovers of all ages crowding the stalls in front of and behind the **Ferry Building.** You can sample stellar organic fruits, homemade conserves, and goat cheeses, or you can chow down on the freshest morning pastries, bread, and heartier dishes from some of the city's well-known restaurants. This is a ritual for lots of local chefs who chat up their favorite vendors and bag the choicest morsels. See Chapter 10.

Rooting for the Giants at AT&T Park: You don't have to be a baseball fan to enjoy an afternoon or evening at this diamond of a ballpark with the ever-changing corporate name. Bleacher seats go on sale on game days, but if you prefer something with more cachet, you can usually buy seats online from season-ticket holders. You'll find the best food, including amazing hot dogs, at the concession stands — load up on the sauerkraut and mustard, and then maybe scramble for a fly ball. See Chapter 11.

Biking in Golden Gate Park: Rentals are easy to arrange along Stanyon Street and around Stow Lake. John F. Kennedy Drive, which closes to automobile traffic on Sunday, holidays, and summer Saturdays, will take

The Bay Area

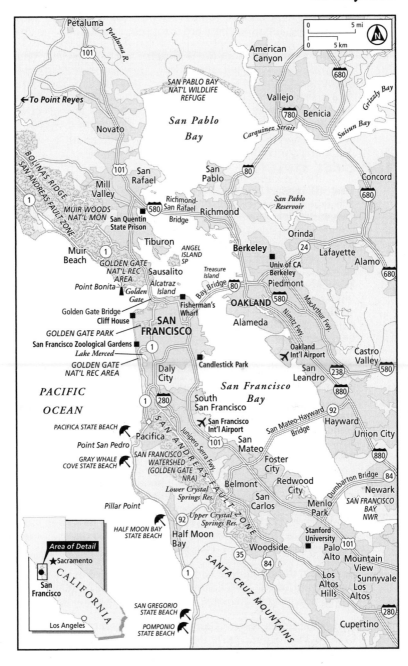

you on a meandering route through this lovely slice of green. At the end of the road you'll be near the newly restored **Murphy's Windmill.** From there, head north toward Fulton Street to see the **Dutch Windmill.** In early spring, the tulips here are in full, glorious bloom. See Chapter 11.

Sipping a cappuccino in North Beach: On a weekday morning when everyone else is at work, sitting with a newspaper and an espresso defines contentment — but it's a great idea anytime. You'll have your pick of cafes in North Beach, and I'm happy to recommend bright, roomy **Caffe Roma** (see Chapter 10), which has a fine selection of high-carb goodies. Plus, the staff roasts the coffee beans on-site.

The Best Hotels

Best All-Around Family Hotels: The playful and warm **Serrano Hotel,** 405 Taylor St. (☎ **866-289-6561** or 415-885-2500), can provide young families with complimentary cribs, strollers, and even booster seats; older children will be delighted to find games scattered around the public areas and extras that include mini Etch-a-Sketches in the minibar. The moderately priced **Hotel Del Sol,** 3100 Webster St. (☎ **877-433-5765** or 415-921-5520), has goodies for the kids plus a fab outdoor pool. The **Hotel Monaco,** 501 Geary St. (☎ **866-622-5284** or 415-292-0100), combines style with all the practicalities you want in an upscale hotel, such as an excellent restaurant, top-quality staff, and a spa. Although I'd never suggest that you abandon the children (for too long), you could have a massage downstairs while they hang out in the room watching a movie and enjoying room service.

Best Hotels for a Romantic Weekend: The outdoor soaking tubs at the **Hotel Vitale,** 8 Mission St. (☎ **888-890-8688** or 415-278-3700), seem to me a good place to start the fun. Then, reserve a deluxe waterfront room and hang out the DO NOT DISTURB sign. If you're out to impress, the spacious Bolero penthouse suite in the **Hotel Adagio,** 550 Geary St. (☎ **800-228-8830** or 415-775-5000), boasts a lovely outdoor terrace, and the hotel itself is lively.

Best View: You can be assured of a breathtaking view from the bay rooms at the cozy **Harbor Court Hotel,** 165 Steuart St. (☎ **866-792-6283** or 415-882-1300). Cityscapes from the windows of the **W San Francisco,** 181 Third St. ☎ (**877-946-8357** or 415-777-5300) look even more magnificent from the hotel's newly redesigned rooms. Request a "spectacular" bay view room above the 14th floor.

Best Hotel Pool: Children under 16 aren't allowed in the pool at the **Huntington Hotel,** 1075 California St. (☎ **800-227-4683** or 415-474-5400), so you'll be the one to blame for the splashing and noise.

Best Hotel If You Have a Car: For stays around Union Square, the **Galleria Park Hotel,** 191 Sutter St. (☎ **800-792-9639** or 415-781-3060), sits over a parking garage, so the valet shouldn't take too long to retrieve your car. All the downtown hotels charge at least $30 per day (plus tax); if you really can't live without the car, be sure to inquire about parking packages when you book your room. Parking is free at the **Cow Hollow Motor Inn & Suites,** 2190 Lombard St. (☎ **415-921-5800**), and Lombard Street takes you to the Golden Gate Bridge. Japantown's **Hotel Kabuki,** 1625 Post St. (☎ **800-553-4567** or 415-922-3200), gets my commendation for having soothingly attractive rooms and relatively reasonable parking fees ($25/day).

The Best Restaurants

Best for a Romantic Meal: I like **Absinthe,** 398 Hayes St. (☎ **415-551-1590**), for the food and décor, and **Quince,** 1701 Octavia St. (☎ **415-775-8500**), which is so personable and delicious that eating there will make you quite fond of whomever you're with.

Best with Kids: You can't go wrong with **Chow,** 215 Church St. (☎ **415-552-2469**), or **Park Chow,** 1240 Ninth Ave. (☎ **415-665-9912**), which have identical menus. The price is right; the food is nonthreatening, recognizable, and tasty; and the casual atmosphere is relaxing.

Best for a Splurge: This category is not an easy one, because there are lots of amazing kitchens to choose from, but I have no qualms about directing you to **Restaurant Gary Danko,** 800 North Point St. (☎ **415-749-2060**). This place is inviting yet sophisticated, completely professional on every level, and the food is superb. For splurging in a more formal atmosphere, the Michelin-starred **Dining Room** at the Ritz-Carlton, 600 Stockton St. (☎ **415-773-6168**), illustrates the meaning of "to die for."

Best Neighborhood Spots: In the Mission District, **Range,** 842 Valencia St. (☎ **415-282-8283**), is all the rage — and deservedly so — while the **Blue Plate,** 3218 Mission St. (☎ **415-282-6777**), feels like one of those secret finds that you want to visit again and again. Around Cow Hollow (or anywhere in the city, really), **Isa,** 3324 Steiner St. (☎ **415-567-9588**), is plainly a winner, with absolutely delicious food and delightful service.

Best Views: Forget about the overpriced tourist traps around PIER 39 — you can't see much at night, anyway. For the best views at bargain prices, have lunch at the **San Francisco Art Institute cafe,** 800 Chestnut St. (☎ **415-771-7020**). For a gourmet vegetarian dinner and great scenery, **Greens Restaurant,** Fort Mason, Building A, off Marina Boulevard at Buchanan Street (☎ **415-771-6222**), sets the standard.

The Best Shopping

Best for Generalists: Kids, men, brides, your mother — there's something for everyone who has excellent taste at **Dandelion,** 55 Potrero Ave. (☎ **415-436-9500**).

Best for Books: This is more than a bookstore: **City Lights,** 261 Columbus Ave. (☎ 415-362-8193), is representative of an era and a movement. Owner-poet Lawrence Ferlinghetti was one of the founders of the Beat movement. That it's also a terrific place to browse and buy is not completely incidental.

Best for People Who Consider Themselves Cool: Naturally, if you fall into this category, you wouldn't advertise it (that wouldn't be cool, now would it?), but of course even cool people have to shop. You'll find clothing, gifts, and skateboards on **Haight Street** (best if you are shopping with your kids), and clothing, gifts, and oddities on even hipper **Valencia Street.**

Best for People Who Love Brand Names: Union Square. The labels you want are all within a 2- or 3-block radius.

The Best Bars and Clubs

Best for *American Idol* Fans: You won't find better entertainment for the price of a cocktail than at the **Mint Karaoke Lounge,** 1942 Market St. (☎ 415-626-4726), and the patrons are pretty friendly. Given that it's in the Castro, you may want to take extra care with your appearance, especially if you plan to take the stage!

Best for *Lost* Fans: The exotic décor at trendy **Bambuddha Lounge,** at the Phoenix Hotel, 601 Eddy St. (☎ 415-885-5088), complements the sultry, sulky clientele stirring apple martinis while awaiting small plates of Southeast Asian goodies. Word is the service is uppity, but no one will ask you to discuss your past.

Best for *How To Look Good Naked* Fans: It's really tacky, but if you want to see what plastic surgeons can accomplish these days, reserve seats at the bar at **AsiaSF,** 201 Ninth St. (☎ 415-255-2742; see Chapter 10), where "gender illusionists" strut their implants for 10 minutes each hour.

Best for *Dancing with the Stars* Fans: Friday and Saturday nights at the **Top of the Mark** in the InterContinental Mark Hopkins hotel, 1 Nob Hill (☎ 415-616-6916), the Black Market Jazz Orchestra performs for your dancing pleasure. Dress up and practice your dipping technique.

Best for Dr. John Fans: Yoshi's Jazz Club, 1330 Fillmore St. (☎ 415-665-5600), is a spin-off of the famous East Bay music venue. The swanky restaurant and club, in a revitalized section of the Fillmore, has become an exciting destination for jazz enthusiasts. Plan ahead if you want tickets, because shows sell out.

Chapter 2

Digging Deeper into San Francisco

In This Chapter
- ▶ Revisiting San Francisco history
- ▶ Getting acquainted with the local cuisine
- ▶ Reading about and viewing San Francisco in books and films

*U*nlike American cities that evolved in a less interesting fashion, San Francisco has been molded politically, socially, and physically by a variety of (literally) earth-shaking events. In this chapter, I give you a quick rundown on the history of the City by the Bay, along with some other useful background on local views and customs that give visitors insight into the city and its inhabitants.

History 101: The Main Events

As late (relatively speaking) as 1846, San Francisco was a sparsely populated town, described by the writer and California historian Robert Ernest Cowan as "the squalid little village." A mere two years later, the sleepy collection of shacks and saloons multiplied almost overnight into a thriving, lawless, still squalid but much larger burg, and nothing — not rampant corruption, numerous fires, or hordes of unsuccessful miners — could keep endless waves of people from arriving here by ship or other means to seek their fortunes.

But first, a little background: Portuguese sailors navigated the coastline of the Bay Area as early as 1542, and although the area was an object of speculation among European explorers, it remained the unmolested province of the Ohlone Indian tribes until the late 18th century. Europeans didn't discover San Francisco Bay itself until 1769, when Sergeant Jose Francisco de Ortega, on a scouting mission for Gaspar de Portola, found the mouth of the port. Seven years later, a contingent of Spanish Catholics arrived, establishing a fort on the site of today's Presidio and one of many Franciscan missions, Nuestra Señora de Dolores, a mile away in what is now the Mission District. The first service took place five days before the signing of the Declaration of Independence in 1776. (Mission Dolores, the oldest building in the city and one of the few to survive earthquakes and fire, is Registered Landmark Number 1 of the city and county of San Francisco.) After this flurry of excitement, there wasn't much to report until Mexico severed ties with Spain in 1821 and became sovereign over California. American ships from Boston then began a vigorous trade with the settlement for otter and beaver skins, and later for goods such as tallow (rendered animal fat used for soap and candles). A slow migration into the area by hunters and trappers from the Eastern Seaboard, and occasionally by AWOL sailors from merchant ships, helped increase the local population to around 250 by 1833. In January 1847, now officially under American rule, Yerba Buena (Spanish for "good herb") was renamed San Francisco.

San Francisco timeline, 1776–2008

1776 The first colonizing party, headed by Captain Juan Bautista de Anza of Spain, arrives and establishes the Presidio of San Francisco and Mission Dolores, effectively founding San Francisco.

1835 The settlement of Yerba Buena develops around the port, now under the rule of Mexico.

1847 The United States annexes Yerba Buena and renames it San Francisco in honor of St. Francis of Assisi.

1847 James Marshall discovers gold at Sutter's Mill, near Sacramento; by the following year, San Francisco's population booms from around 800 to 26,000.

1849 Isadore Boudin, an experienced French baker, introduces the ordinary sourdough yeast used by miners to a French-style loaf of bread and creates San Francisco sourdough bread.

1850 On September 9, California becomes the 31st state in the Union.

1868 The *Daily Morning Chronicle,* later the *San Francisco Chronicle,* begins publishing.

1869 The transcontinental railroad reaches San Francisco.

1873 Andrew Hallidie, inspired by an accident he witnesses when a team of horses slips on a rainy San Francisco hill, invents the cable car.

1887 George Hearst purchases a small daily newspaper, the *San Francisco Examiner,* to promote his race for the U.S. Senate. His son, William Randolph Hearst, turns it into a very successful tabloid.

1906 On April 18 at 5:13 a.m., a major earthquake rocks San Francisco and starts more than 50 fires, which burn uncontrollably for four days. Two-thirds of the city is destroyed, 250,000 people are left homeless, and more than 3,000 are killed or missing.

1915 The Panama-Pacific International Exposition celebrates the city's restoration and the completion of the Panama Canal.

1933 Alcatraz becomes a federal prison.

1936 The San Francisco–Oakland Bay Bridge opens on November 12. It remains one of the largest bridges in the world and carries more than 270,000 vehicles each day — more traffic than any other toll bridge.

1937 The Golden Gate Bridge opens to pedestrian traffic on May 26 and to automobile traffic on May 27.

1945 The United Nations Charter is drafted in the War Memorial Veterans Building in San Francisco's Civic Center and signed by representatives of 50 countries at the Opera House.

1950 The Beat generation moves into the bars and cafes of North Beach.

1965 Jefferson Airplane opens at the Matrix on Fillmore.

1978 Supervisor Harvey Milk, America's first openly gay politician, and Mayor George Moscone are assassinated in City Hall by former supervisor Dan White.

1978 PIER 39 opens. One of San Francisco's most popular attractions, it draws an estimated 10.5 million people each year.

1989 On October 17 at 5:04 p.m., right before the start of Game 3 of the World Series between the Oakland A's and the San Francisco Giants, a 7.1-magnitude earthquake hits the Bay Area. Sixty-three people die, including one person at Candlestick Park who suffers a heart attack.

1995 The new San Francisco Museum of Modern Art opens.

1996 Former Assembly Speaker Willie Brown is elected mayor of San Francisco for the first of two terms.

2000 Pacific Bell Park (now AT&T Park), the new home of the San Francisco Giants, opens.

2002 The San Francisco Giants make it to the World Series but lose to the Anaheim Angels in Game 7.

2004 Thirty-six-year-old supervisor Gavin Newsom becomes the city's 42nd mayor and quickly makes headlines by authorizing marriage licenses for same-sex couples. Six months later, the state supreme court invalidates the 3,955 gay marriages that have taken place.

2005 The new, seismically correct $202-million de Young Museum opens in Golden Gate Park.

2006 San Francisco's Japantown neighborhood celebrates its 100th anniversary.

2008 The California Academy of Sciences returns to Golden Gate Park, housed in a glorious "green" Renzo Piano–designed building featuring a 2.5-acre living roof.

The discovery of gold in the American River near Sutter's Mill at the end of 1847 was the mighty force that propelled San Francisco into the big leagues. When word got out late in 1848, San Francisco's population of 812 quickly contracted as every able-bodied man and boy took off for the Sierra Nevada. By 1849, immigrants were arriving in San Francisco at the rate of 1,000 per week. The smart money stayed in the city and started businesses to take advantage of the newly rich and those hoping to join them — drinking establishments, gambling dens, and houses of prostitution most prominent among the enterprises. Naturally, crime and corruption were rife. By 1851, vigilante groups formed to do what police and politicians were bribed not to, and after a few well-placed hangings, things slowly began to calm down.

By 1870, barely 23 years old, San Francisco was already the tenth-largest city in the United States. In that time, it had survived a remarkable migration, a half-dozen fires, inflation, vice, graft, torrential rains, and an earthquake (in 1865). The transcontinental railroad linked the East and West coasts, and the thousands of Chinese laborers who had laid the rail became objects of vilification for underemployed whites, who appeared to forget that they were immigrants, too.

Still, San Francisco thrived — not even Mother Nature, it seems, could stop the momentum. Certainly, the great earthquake of April 18, 1906, was a momentous catastrophe; fires raged for four days and more than 3,000 people (of a population of 400,000) died in collapsed and burning buildings or from related ills. Two-thirds of the city was destroyed, and thousands of homeless people went to live in Golden Gate Park until housing could be constructed. But rebuilding began immediately, and in 1915, San Francisco reintroduced herself to the world by hosting the Panama-Pacific International Exposition.

The Gold Rush was responsible for the first mass influx of people into San Francisco, and World War II precipitated the second, as workers from the South flocked to the city's shipyards. Postwar prosperity combined with an anything-goes reputation attracted nonconformists, artists, writers, and free thinkers, paving the way for the Beats, and later the hippie movement, to influence an entire nation. The second half of the 20th century found San Francisco grappling with the murders of its mayor, George Moscone, and the country's first openly gay politician, Supervisor Harvey Milk, in 1978. Dan White, a homophobic former city supervisor, was convicted of manslaughter in the killings. California Senator Dianne Feinstein, at that time the president of San Francisco's Board of Supervisors, became mayor.

San Francisco's most recent big earthquake, an attention-getting 7.1 on the Richter scale, hit in the afternoon on October 17, 1989, as the Giants were preparing to play Game 3 of the World Series. In those days before cellphones and wireless Internet, the city came to a halt. With buses and streetcars unable to operate, sections of the Bay Bridge damaged, and fires and collapsed buildings in the Marina neighborhood, the city felt strangely vulnerable. Miraculously, only 63 people died.

The 1990s will be remembered for the dot.com boom-and-bust years. San Francisco may not have been as obviously wild as it was during the aftermath of the Gold Rush, but it isn't a stretch to draw a few comparisons. Millionaires were created overnight in the frenzy to take rather specious companies public, while investors threw money at young entrepreneurs who turned out to have less-than-feasible business plans. Real-estate prices went mad, and even sensible people went looking for a technology start-up to join.

And then, it was over. The 21st century had barely introduced itself before the terrorist attacks of September 11, 2001, devastated the country. With the stock market on a downward spiral and the economy reeling, a town that relies on tourism and business travel took a hit. Yet, nearing the end of this decade, San Francisco is in the midst of a thriving building boom. The phoenix, the mythical bird that arose whole from the ashes and graces San Francisco's official flag, is an apt symbol for this vibrant, beautiful, and unquestionably desirable city.

Taste of San Francisco: Local Cuisine

San Francisco's reputation as a food-lover's paradise is well deserved and tested on a daily basis. You can find thousands of restaurants around town, from dives to divas, all with loyal followings and all under constant scrutiny by critics and self-proclaimed gourmands. Between the competition and the narrowed eyes of the food patrol, a restaurateur has to stay sharp, or at least hire a crackerjack public-relations firm, to survive the first year in business. The constant buzz and change in the food scene can be a little nerve-racking to track, but it serves to make dining an event for locals and tourists alike. In the end, fortunately, it all comes down to ingredients. And where else but in San Francisco do you find the freshest, most beautiful, and even most politically correct fruits, veggies, fish, and organically raised meats? Well, Berkeley, maybe, but certainly nowhere else.

Background Check: Recommended Books and Movies

Getting acquainted with San Francisco through the work of authors and filmmakers will provide an extra dimension to your trip and perhaps some added excitement when you happen upon a location you recognize from a favorite cinematic moment or literary passage. San Francisco's own Chronicle Books publishes a great variety of material on the city, for children, cooks, art and architecture students, and readers of memoir and fiction. One of Chronicle's best books to stimulate your interest and curiosity is *San Francisco Stories: Great Writers on the City,* edited by John Miller. This collection of short pieces covers the personal and the political as recalled by acclaimed authors including Mark Twain, Jack

Kerouac, Tom Wolfe, and Amy Tan. To find out about a smaller, more intimate city, check out Chronicle's *Good Life in Hard Times: San Francisco in the '20s and '30s,* by former journalist and San Francisco native Jerry Flamm.

One of the more famous and beloved pieces of modern fiction based in San Francisco is Armistead Maupin's *Tales of the City* (published by Perennial). If you've seen the miniseries, and especially if you haven't, this is a "must read" for a leisurely afternoon — or the inbound plane ride. Maupin's 1970s soap opera covers the residents of 28 Barbary Lane (Macondry Lane on Russian Hill was the inspiration), melding sex, drugs, and growing self-awareness with enormous warmth and humor.

A work of fiction featuring San Francisco during the Gold Rush is *Daughter of Fortune,* by acclaimed novelist and Marin County resident Isabel Allende (published by HarperTorch). Allende's vivid depiction of life in California during the mid–19th century is one of the novel's strengths.

As one of the loveliest spots on the planet, San Francisco has been a favorite of location scouts since the beginning of the film industry. Hundreds of movies and television shows have been shot or set in San Francisco, making the hills and bridges among the most recognized of backgrounds. It may be difficult to locate at your local video store, but the 1936 Clark Gable–Jeanette MacDonald romance *San Francisco* is lauded for its dramatic reenactment of the 1906 earthquake and for MacDonald's rendition of the song of the same name. *The Maltese Falcon* (1941), Dashiell Hammett's classic detective story, with Humphrey Bogart starring as Sam Spade, includes shots of the Bay Bridge, the Ferry Building, and Burrit Alley (above the Stockton Tunnel). **John's Grill,** mentioned in the novel, continues to flog its association with Hammett's hero from its location at 63 Ellis St. (between Stockton and Powell streets).

Alfred Hitchcock's *Vertigo* (1958), starring James Stewart and Kim Novak, is admittedly an obvious choice on the list of great San Francisco films, but it's always worth viewing. Stewart plays a former detective hired to tail the wife of an old college friend, but the woman's identity is less than clear. In the meantime, Stewart becomes obsessed with his prey as they make their way around the **Palace of the Legion of Honor, Fort Point, Mission Dolores,** and the detective's apartment at **900 Lombard St.** The city also fared well in the 1968 thriller *Bullitt,* starring Steve McQueen. Along with the hair-raising car chase over many hills, you'll see the Bay Bridge from a recognizable point on the **Embarcadero, Mason Street** heading north next to the **Fairmont Hotel,** the front of the **Mark Hopkins Hotel, Grace Cathedral,** and the fairly unchanged **Enrico's Sidewalk Café.**

For a change of pace and no tragic law-enforcement characters, screen the romantic comedy *What's Up Doc?* (1972), with Barbra Streisand and Ryan O'Neal. Along with being a very funny film, it has another car chase scene that includes **Lombard Street** and **Chinatown** and ends at **Alta Plaza Park** in **Pacific Heights.** If you have kids to rev up, the 1993 comedy *Mrs. Doubtfire,* starring Sally Field and the city's favorite son, Robin Williams, shows San Francisco under blue skies and cable cars with plenty of room. The house where the character's estranged wife and children live is at **2640 Steiner St.** (at Broadway), in case you care to gawk.

24 Hours on Craigslist (see Chapter 11) is a documentary that covers a day in the life of the Internet community bulletin-board phenom. The filmmaker posted an ad on Craigslist, followed up with a handful of volunteers — an Ethel Merman impersonator seeking a Led Zeppelin cover band; a couple looking for others to join a support group for diabetic cats; a single, older woman in search of a sperm donor — and sent film crews to cover their stories. Unlike other films that show the physical splendors of San Francisco, *24 Hours on Craigslist* will give you a sense of the city's psyche, or at least offer an explanation of why non–San Franciscans think the place is populated with . . . uh . . . unusual types.

Finally, as I type this, Gus Van Sant is directing Sean Penn in *Milk,* a biopic of the late supervisor Harvey Milk (see San Francisco Timeline) scheduled for release in 2009. The film crew has been in and around City Hall, and set designers have redecorated Castro Street to resemble the '70s—not that it's changed that much.

Chapter 3

Deciding When to Go

. . . .

In This Chapter

▶ Choosing the best season to visit
▶ Finding events that will get you going

. . . .

*Y*ou may not have much choice when it comes to scheduling your trip, especially if you have to plan around school vacations and holidays. But in case you do have some leeway, in this chapter I outline what's going on in San Francisco at different times of the year in terms of weather, crowds, and special events. The weather we locals long for is days of balmy temperatures and clear skies. I can only hope you find the same, but in case you don't, bring a warm jacket and maybe a hat, no matter when you're visiting. And remember, a little fog never hurt anybody.

Revealing the Secret of the Seasons

Because of its temperate Northern California address, San Francisco beckons to tourists and business travelers year-round. It's most crowded between June and October. If you visit during this time of the year, I'd recommend that you make hotel and car reservations *at least* six weeks in advance, reserve a table at the better-known restaurants three to four weeks in advance, and purchase your tickets to Alcatraz (see Chapter 11) shortly after you commit to the trip. Don't arrive in the city with just a suitcase, a camera around your neck, and a smile. You don't want to waste your time and energy searching for accommodations or squabbling with your traveling companion because the Slanted Door (see Chapter 10) couldn't seat you.

Something to remember about the San Francisco "summer" is that it may not be the season you're expecting. Temperatures rarely top 70 degrees Fahrenheit and are often quite cool before lunchtime. Bring a sweater and be prepared for morning fog — at any time of year.

The city is at its warmest and most glorious in September and October. In an average year, these months are also the busiest. Fisherman's Wharf is packed to the gills, every cable car overflows with bodies, and there's not an available hotel room in sight. Unless something unusual is keeping the tourists home, don't even think about trying to get a discount on accommodations during this time.

School vacation schedules will probably dictate your travel dates if you're bringing the kids. Normally, July and August days start out with heavy fog and eventually clear enough for you to lose the jacket or sweatshirt. Prepare for crowds, especially at the most popular tourist destinations. Fortunately, a little imaginative planning can help you entertain your children while avoiding some (though not all) of the masses. (See Chapter 11 for some offbeat sightseeing ideas.)

During the winter, the visitors do thin out considerably. (Those seeking a tan at this time of year should try Florida or maybe Singapore.) November through March, when the weather can be damp and chilly, is downtime for tourists in San Francisco. But if you don't mind sightseeing while carrying an umbrella, or bundled up in a sweater and a hat, you can get a terrific deal at a nice hotel. You may even find yourself pleasantly surprised by blue skies and temperatures in the low 60s (and no fog!) in the middle of February. In general, room rates are lower between November and mid-April, unless a big convention is in town (check with the **San Francisco Convention & Visitors Bureau** at ☎ **415-391-2000;** www.onlyinsanfrancisco.com). A few attractions even reduce their entrance fees at this time of year.

Winter can be a great time to see San Francisco, in spite of the weather, which will still be an improvement over much of the United States. A good number of the larger hotels offer packages, and some have special events for kids. You can admire the Christmas windows decorating Union Square, skate around the Embarcadero Center's outdoor ice rink, and take in one of many *Nutcracker* ballet and music performances.

In the following sections, I fill you in on the pros and cons of each season. For information on average temperatures and rainfall, take a look at Table 3-1.

Table 3-1 San Francisco's Average Temperatures and Rainfall

	Jan	Feb	Mar	Apr	May	June	July	Aug	Sept	Oct	Nov	Dec
High (°F/°C)	56/ 13	59/ 15	60/ 16	61/ 16	63/ 17	64/ 18	64/ 18	65/ 18	69/ 21	68/ 20	63/ 17	57/ 14
Low (°F/°C)	46/ 8	48/ 9	49/ 9	49/ 9	51/ 11	53/ 12	53/ 12	54/ 12	56/ 13	55/ 13	52/ 11	47/ 8
Rain (in./cm)	4.5/ 11.5	2.8/ 7	2.6/ 6.5	1.5/ 4	0.4/ 1	0.2/ 0.5	0.1/ 0.3	0.1/ 0.3	0.2/ 0.5	1.1/ 3	2.5/ 6.5	3.5/ 9

Winter

You're unlikely to see snow unless you drive to Tahoe, but the weather won't exactly be balmy, either. Still, a winter visit to San Francisco has its advantages, including the following:

- ✔ Hotel prices are lower, especially on weekends.
- ✔ Cable cars aren't jam-packed.
- ✔ Store windows are decorated for the holidays.
- ✔ The January sales linger into February.
- ✔ Restaurants won't be as busy as during the rest of the year.

But keep in mind the following wintertime minus:

- ✔ The skies may be gray and/or rainy.

Spring

Spring is a popular time for travel, but in San Francisco, it's also a popular time for conventions. Here are some of the advantages to expect if you're considering a springtime visit:

- ✔ Flowers are in bloom in the parks.
- ✔ The weather can be glorious.
- ✔ The major sites will be less crowded than in summer.

But keep in mind the following springtime drawback:

- ✔ Convention season starts, bringing hotel costs up and making it even harder than usual to get reservations at the most popular eateries.

Summer

Many travelers are surprised at how cool and foggy San Francisco summers are. Here are some of the advantages to visiting in the summer months:

- ✔ Mimes are out in full force.
- ✔ Longer days make evening tours of Alcatraz more attractive.
- ✔ The city sponsors free weekend concerts at Golden Gate Park and Stern Grove.
- ✔ The fruit and vegetable bounty available at the Ferry Plaza Farmers Market is mouthwateringly spectacular.

But here are some negatives about visiting in the summertime:

- ✔ Mimes are out in full force.
- ✔ PIER 39 and Fisherman's Wharf are madhouses.
- ✔ Hotels are packed.
- ✔ Foggy mornings are downers.

Fall

If reliably warm, sunny days are a top priority for you, fall is the best time to visit. Here are some other advantages to planning your trip for the autumn months:

- ✔ It's the finest weather of the year, on average.
- ✔ The cultural season begins.

But keep in mind the following drawbacks:

- ✔ Napa Valley is solidly booked on the weekends.
- ✔ The heavy events calendar lures additional crowds.

Marking Your Calendar

I list San Francisco's most popular or unusual special events and festivals in the following sections. However, I don't have room to mention the tons of other street fairs, film festivals, and happenings. For more events, check out the *San Francisco Bay Guardian* Web site (www.sfbg.com), the *San Francisco Chronicle* Web site (www.sfgate.com), or the Citysearch Web site (www.sanfrancisco.citysearch.com), or order the free Convention and Visitors Bureau Visitors Kit, which includes a Festivals and Special Events calendar (see the appendix). Call the phone numbers listed for each event for exact dates, locations, and ticket prices (if any).

You pay no entry charge for street fairs and holiday festivals, but bring along some cash for the crafts booths and food.

How do you keep a festival festive? Don't drive. Parking is always impossible, and you'll just get frustrated driving around in circles. Walk, take public transportation, or, if all else fails, grab a cab — it's well worth the expense.

January/February

An important, well-attended, two-week event in San Francisco's Chinatown is **Chinese New Year** (☎ 415-982-3071; www.chineseparade.com). Included in the event are lots of free entertainment, an exciting parade, and colorful sights. Dates vary.

March

A fair number of Irish expats live in San Francisco, making St. Patrick's Day a big excuse for a party. The **St. Patrick's Day Parade** (☎ 415-675-9885; www.sfstpatricksdayparade.com), along Market Street from Second Street to Civic Center, features marching bands from around the bay. Sunday closest to March 17.

Indie music fans and the bands who love them converge for **Noise Pop** (☎ 415-375-3370; www.noisepop.com), a week of concerts held at all the coolest clubs around the end of the month. Past bookings have included the White Stripes and Flaming Lips; the festival has grown to include film, alternative comedy, and even workshops on how to get your band noticed. For exact dates and ticket info, monitor the Web site.

April

The 15-day **San Francisco International Film Festival** (☎ 925-866-9559; www.sffs.org) is one of the oldest in the United States. It features more than 200 films and videos from over 50 countries, shown at the Castro Theatre on Castro Street, the Palace of Fine Arts in the Marina, and the Sundance Kabuki Cinemas at Fillmore and Post streets. Call for a schedule. April through early May.

Celebrate Japanese culture at the **Cherry Blossom Festival** (☎ 415-563-2313; www.nccbf.org) in Japantown. In this event, spanning two weekends, you'll find flower arranging, sumo wrestling, traditional drumming, and a parade that begins at Civic Center and ends in Japantown. Mid- to late April.

Men wear chaps outside the Castro for several reasons, including the steer-wrestling, bull-riding, and bareback-riding competitions at the **Grand National Rodeo, Horse, and Stock Show** (☎ 415-404-4111; www.grandnationalrodeo.com) at the Cow Palace. The ten-day event also features horse shows and country-music concerts. Check the Web site for exact dates.

For an opportunity to tour a grand Pacific Heights mansion and view the latest in home décor, don't miss the **San Francisco Decorator Showcase** (☎ 415-447-5830; www.decoratorshowcase.org). A fundraiser for University High's financial aid program, it executes an extreme makeover of one lucky house, with jaw-dropping results. Tickets ($30) are for sale at the door. Check the Web site for this year's address. Four weeks beginning the last weekend in April.

May

Whether you're commemorating Mexico's victory over the French in 1862 at the Battle of Puebla or just looking for some good food and music, you can find it at the **Cinco de Mayo Celebration** (☎ 415-647-1533; www.sfcincodemayo.com) at Dolores Park, 18th and Dolores streets. Festivities include Mexican and Central American music, crafts, and food. First Sunday in May.

If you like crowds and scantily dressed samba dancers, **Carnaval San Francisco** (☎ 415-920-0122; www.carnavalsf.com) in the Mission District (on Harrison between 16th and 23rd streets) is a must-see. More than a half-million revelers turn out for this two-day celebration culminating in a Sunday morning parade. Memorial Day weekend.

June

The **Lesbian/Gay/Bisexual/Transgender Pride Celebration Parade** (☎ 415-864-FREE; www.sfpride.org), which runs from the Embarcadero to the two large plazas of the city's Civic Center, is a major happening. Held on Sunday morning, the parade is entertaining and often quite moving. Last weekend in June.

World dance and music performances make for exciting theater at the **Ethnic Dance Festival** (☎ 415-474-3914; www.worldartswest.org), held at the Palace of Fine Arts Theater, next to the Exploratorium. Weekends all month.

Music, entertainment, food, drink, eco-friendly arts and crafts, and a "green" focus — the **Union Street Eco-Urban Festival** (☎ 800-310-6563; www.unionstreetfestival.com), on Union from Gough to Steiner streets, is as *au courant* as street fairs get. First weekend in June.

Head to the **North Beach Festival** (☎ 415-989-2220; www.sfnorth beach.org), on Washington Square Park, Grant Avenue in North Beach, for the music, the arts and crafts, and the people-watching. Organizers claim that this festival is the oldest urban street fair in the country. Around the third weekend in June.

On summer Sundays at 2pm, the **Stern Grove Festival** (☎ 415-252-6252; www.sterngrove.org) produces free professional music and dance performances in the park's beautiful tree-lined amphitheater. Arrive early (the M and K Muni lines stop 1 block west of the park, at 19th Avenue and West Portal) if you hope to snare a seat. Middle of June through the middle of August.

July

The **Fourth of July Waterfront Festival,** Fisherman's Wharf (☎ 415-705-5500; www.pier39.com), begins at 1pm at PIER 39. It features live music and lots of activities, culminating in fireworks. July 4.

It sounds like just another street fair, but the **Fillmore Street Jazz Festival** (☎ 800-310-6563; www.fillmorejazzfestival.com), between Jackson and Eddy streets, has three stages with live music as well as everything you need to eat, drink, or display on your credenza. Independence Day weekend.

August

The **American Craft Show** (☎ **800-836-3470** or 212-274-0630; www.craft council.org/sf), at Fort Mason Center, is an exhibition and sale featuring juried crafts by some of the most gifted artists in the country. It's a treat for fans and a revelation to everyone else. Middle of August.

September

The **Autumn Moon Festival** (☎ **415-982-6306;** www.moonfestival. org), on Grant Street between California and Pacific streets in Chinatown, features moon cakes (round, egg-studded pastries), children's activities, and traditional dances. Dates vary.

Both national and local musicians perform on the Great Meadow at Fort Mason during the **San Francisco Blues Festival** (☎ **415-979-5588;** www. sfblues.com), the biggest outdoor blues event on the West Coast. Bring a blanket. Late September.

The **San Francisco Fringe Festival** (☎ **415-673-3847;** www.sffringe. org) is a marathon of experimental theater and performance art held at the Exit Theater and various venues downtown. Twelve days starting the first weekend in September.

October

Hardly Strictly Bluegrass, Golden Gate Park (☎ **415-788-5111;** www. hardlystrictlybluegrass.com), provides two full days of great roots music by top talent — and it's free! The crowds arrive early to mark territory for an 11 a.m. start. First weekend in October.

Hundreds of local artists invite the public into their studios every weekend throughout this month, as part of **Artspan/San Francisco Open Studios** (☎ **415-861-9838;** www.artspan.org). Call for information, including how to obtain a studio map. Every weekend.

Community organizations and local merchants entertain a few hundred thousand people at the **Castro Street Fair** (☎ **415-841-1824;** www. castrostreetfair.org), from Market to 19th streets, between Noe and Collingwood streets, in the Castro District. First Sunday in October.

Held in venues around the city, the world-renowned five-week **San Francisco Jazz Festival** (☎ **866-920-5299** or 415-788-7353; www.sf jazz.org) sells out fast. Mid-October to mid-November.

November

San Francisco International Automobile Show, Moscone Center (☎ 415-331-4406; www.sfautoshow.com), has cars, and lots of 'em, with all the newest models and special exhibits from American and international automakers. Admission is $8 for adults. Last week of November.

December

The annual **Teddy Bear Tea** (☎ 415-773-6198; www.ritzcarlton.com) at the Ritz-Carlton is a popular parent-child bonding experience. Reservations open in August and are necessary, especially for weekends. Thanksgiving through Christmas.

Part II

Planning Your Trip to San Francisco

In this part . . .

This part of the book covers the basics of trip planning. If you're an experienced traveler, you may opt to skim the next four chapters for any pearls of brilliance that apply to you. If you're a travel novice, here you discover various options, including which airport to use. I thoroughly cover money — how much you need and what you're likely to spend it on. Then I move on to specific tips for families, seniors, travelers with disabilities, and gay and lesbian visitors to San Francisco. If you think you may need a car while you're in San Francisco, be sure to weigh the pros and cons of driving around the city noted in Chapter 7.

Chapter 4

Managing Your Money

In This Chapter

▶ Figuring out the cost of things
▶ Knowing where to go for money
▶ Cutting your expenses down to size

*V*acationing in San Francisco can be costly. Convention and Visitors Bureau statistics show that the average daily per capita spending for all visitors, not including those who stay with relatives or friends, was a substantial $244.33 in 2005, and it has only increased since then. The major expenditure is lodging. Food takes the next-largest bite out of your pocketbook.

Money may or may not make the world go 'round, but nothing spoils a vacation faster than stressing over a higher-than-expected dinner tab or running out of dough altogether. This chapter covers everything from figuring the cost of your trip to the nitty-gritty of how to get your cash while you're in town.

Planning Your Budget

Creating a travel budget is easy, but sticking to it can be difficult, especially in a city that provides so many enticements to open your wallet. The Bay Area is not a cheap date. You'll likely spend the largest proportion of your funds on airfare (if you're flying) and lodging. You can spend as lavishly as you like on food, but you can also eat well inexpensively. I don't recommend that you rent a car (see Chapter 7 for my reasons), and that will save a bundle on parking alone. Other expenses to consider include transportation around the city, snacks and beverages, attraction admission fees, shopping, entertainment, and incidentals such as telephone calls. After you figure your expenses, follow my general rule and add 15 percent. (Unless you're unusually disciplined, you won't come in under budget.)

Transportation

Most people arriving in San Francisco do so by plane or car. If you're driving, be aware that gas prices in Northern California are among the highest in the country.

The cost of things to come

Knowing what to expect is always comforting, especially when it comes to counting the cost. Here are some average prices for goods and services in San Francisco:

- ✔ Small lemonade at PIER 39: $2.25

- ✔ Latte in North Beach: $3

- ✔ Anchor Steam draft beer at Johnny Foley's: $5

- ✔ Lunch for one at the Cliff House Bistro (moderate): $16–$27

- ✔ Lunch for one at Cafe Asia (inexpensive): $10

- ✔ Three-course dinner for one (excluding tax and tip) at the Blue Plate (moderate): $40

- ✔ Three-course dinner for one at Home (inexpensive): $23

- ✔ Super Shuttle from airport to hotel (excluding tip): $16

- ✔ Taxi from airport to city center (excluding tip): $35–$45

- ✔ One-way Muni/bus fare to any destination within the city (adult): $1.50

- ✔ One-way Muni/bus fare anywhere within the city (senior or child 5–17): 50¢

- ✔ Movie ticket at the Sundance Kabuki for an adult: $12.50

- ✔ Ticket to *Beach Blanket Babylon:* $25–$78

Airline ticket prices depend on so many variables that I would be foolish to suggest what you'll pay to fly. See Chapter 5 for tips on how to get the best deal. Always contact low-cost carriers, such as **Southwest Airlines** or **JetBlue,** which don't show up on most travel Web sites. As of this writing, a round-trip flight in July from New York's JFK to Oakland on JetBlue was $460. Checking on Expedia.com, American had round-trip flights from JFK to San Francisco starting at $386. Of course, the more convenient flight times cost considerably more, and fuel surcharges may add to the cost.

Lodging

Chapter 9 discusses everything you need to know about hotels, but to summarize, prices depend on occupancy rates, and occupancy rates depend on variables such as the economy and the time of year. I've included a range of rooms to suit pocketbooks large and small, but keep in mind that bargains are relative. I've seen $79 rooms that would ruin some vacations. Remember: You get what you pay for.

Dining

Dining out is a big deal in the Bay Area. If your hometown is bereft of decent restaurants, budget for at least one splurge meal in San Francisco. Study Chapter 10 for ideas on where to eat well on the cheap.

Sightseeing

Many of San Francisco's enduring attractions are free — like the Golden Gate Bridge, the parks, the hidden staircases, and neighborhood walks. Others, such as the cable cars, are inexpensive. Part IV includes lots of ways to see the city without bruising your bank account.

Shopping

Souvenirs both annoy and inspire me. I fondly recall a small replica of the Eiffel Tower an older brother left on a bookcase in my childhood home, but still I cluck disparagingly over the useless trinkets my family brings home from trips (and vice versa). My best suggestion is to give any kids in your party a sum of money to spend and gentle reminders that when it's gone, it's gone. Adults should pat themselves on the back for contributing to the local economy, which is much appreciated, I'm sure.

On the other hand, if you consider giving your credit card a workout a necessary part of vacation, you've come to the right place. You'll see plenty of upscale chains and boutiques in San Francisco that you may not find back home. Chapter 12 discusses where to shop, no matter what your budget, and gives a few suggestions for finding low-cost gifts.

Nightlife

You can live large with seats for the ballet or nurse a beer in a Mission District music club for under ten bucks — it just depends on your predilections (and your budget). Chapters 15 and 16 cover some of the entertainment options and tell you where to find all the local listings.

Taxing your wallet

Along with the more obvious expenses, such as souvenir bridges and *Escape from Alcatraz* T-shirts, you have those little extras called taxes. In our fair city, add sales tax of 8.5 percent to the price of just about everything but snacks and take-out food. Additionally, a hotel tax of 14 percent is added to the cost of your room, and an additional 14 percent hikes up hotel valet parking fees. The good news is that most of the money goes to fund local arts organizations, which makes it a bit more palatable, I hope. Separate from the 15 percent to 20 percent tip servers expect, many restaurants add a small surcharge to the bill to help cover legally mandated employee health benefits.

Cutting Costs — but Not the Fun

San Francisco can be expensive, but you can save money by following some of these tips:

- ✔ **Go in the off season.** If you can travel at nonpeak times (Nov–Mar, for example), you'll find hotel prices almost half the rates you see during peak months.

- ✔ **Travel midweek.** If you can travel on a Tuesday, Wednesday, or Thursday, you may find cheaper flights. When you ask about airfares, see if you can get a cheaper rate by flying on a different day. For more tips on getting a good fare, see Chapter 5.

- ✔ **Try a package tour.** For many destinations, you can book airfare, hotel, ground transportation, and even some sightseeing just by making one call to a travel agent or packager, for a price much less than if you put the trip together yourself. (See Chapter 5 for more on package tours.)

- ✔ **Reserve a room with a refrigerator and coffeemaker.** You don't have to slave over a hot stove to cut a few costs; several motels have minifridges and coffeemakers. Buying supplies for breakfast will save you money — and probably calories.

- ✔ **Always ask for discount rates.** Membership in AAA, frequent-flier plans, trade unions, AARP, or other groups may qualify you for savings on car rentals, plane tickets, hotel rooms, and even meals. Ask about everything; you may be pleasantly surprised.

- ✔ **Ask if your kids can stay in the room with you.** A room with two double beds usually doesn't cost any more than one with a queen-size bed. And many hotels won't charge you the additional person rate if the additional person is pint-size and related to you. Even if you have to pay $10 or $15 extra for a rollaway bed, you'll save hundreds by not taking two rooms.

- ✔ **Try expensive restaurants at lunch instead of dinner.** Lunch tabs are usually a fraction of what dinner would cost at a top restaurant, and the menu often boasts many of the same specialties.

- ✔ **Get out of town.** In many places, big savings are just a short drive or taxi ride away. Less conveniently located hotels can be great bargains. Outlying motels often have free parking, with lower rates than downtown hotels offering amenities that you may never use. Sure, at a motel you'll be carrying your own bags, but the rooms are often just as comfortable and a whole lot cheaper. See Chapter 9 for more on hotels.

- ✔ **Don't rent a gas guzzler.** Renting a smaller car is cheaper, and you save on gas to boot. Unless you're traveling with kids and need lots of space, don't go beyond the economy size. For more on car rentals, see Chapter 7.

✔ **Don't rent a car.** The city is easily navigable on foot or by public transit. You save as much as $50 a day on hotel parking by not having a car, too.

✔ **Ride public transportation, such as Muni or BART.** Purchase a Muni Passport and use it often (see Chapter 8).

✔ **Walk a lot.** A good pair of walking shoes can save lots of money on taxis and other local transportation. As a bonus, you'll get to know your destination more intimately, as you explore at a slower pace.

✔ **Skip the souvenirs.** Your photographs and your memories could be the best mementos of your trip. If you're concerned about money, you can do without the T-shirts, key chains, salt-and-pepper shakers, and other trinkets.

Handling Money

You're the best judge of how much cash you feel comfortable carrying and which alternative form of currency is your favorite. That's not going to change much on your vacation. True, you'll probably be moving around more and incurring more expenses than you generally do (unless you happen to eat every meal out when you're at home), and you may let your mind slip into vacation gear and not be as vigilant about your safety as when you're in work mode. But, those factors aside, the only type of payment that won't be quite as available to you away from home is your personal checkbook.

Using ATMs and carrying cash

The easiest and best way to get cash away from home is from an ATM (automated teller machine), sometimes referred to as a "cash machine" or "cashpoint." The **Cirrus** (☎ **800-424-7787;** www.mastercard.com) and **PLUS** (☎ **800-843-7587;** www.visa.com) networks span the globe; look at the back of your bank card to see which network you're on, then call or check online for ATM locations at your destination. Be sure you know your personal identification number (PIN) before you leave home, and be sure to find out your daily withdrawal limit before you depart. Also keep in mind that many banks impose a fee every time you use your card at a different bank's ATM. On top of this, the bank from which you withdraw cash may charge its own fee. To compare banks' ATM fees within the U.S., use www.bankrate.com.

Charging ahead with credit cards

Credit cards are safe and provide a convenient record of all your expenses. You can also withdraw cash advances from your credit cards at banks or ATMs, provided you know your PIN. If you've forgotten yours, or didn't even know you had one, call the number on the back of your credit card and ask the bank to send it to you. It usually takes five to seven business days, though some banks will provide the number over the phone if you tell them your mother's maiden name or some other personal information.

Toting traveler's checks

These days, traveler's checks are less necessary because most cities (including San Francisco) have 24-hour ATMs that allow you to withdraw small amounts of cash as needed. However, keep in mind that you will likely be charged an ATM withdrawal fee if the bank is not your own, so if you're withdrawing money every day, you might be better off with traveler's checks.

You can buy traveler's checks at most banks. They are offered in denominations of $20, $50, $100, $500, and sometimes $1,000. Generally, you'll pay a service charge ranging from 1 percent to 4 percent. The most popular traveler's checks are offered by **American Express** (☎ **800-807-6233,** or 800-221-7282 for cardholders — this number accepts collect calls, offers service in several foreign languages, and exempts gold and platinum cardholders from the 1 percent fee); **Visa** (☎ **800-732-1322**); and **MasterCard** (☎ **800-223-9920**).

If you choose to carry traveler's checks, be sure to keep a record of their serial numbers separate from your checks in the event that they are stolen or lost. You'll get a refund faster if you know the numbers.

Dealing with a lost or stolen wallet

Be sure to tell all of your credit card companies the minute you discover your wallet has been lost or stolen, and file a report at the nearest police precinct. Your credit card company or insurer may require a police report number or record of the loss. Most credit card companies have an emergency toll-free number to call if your card is lost or stolen; they may be able to wire you a cash advance immediately or deliver an emergency credit card in a day or two. Visa's U.S. emergency number is ☎ **800-847-2911** or 410-581-9994. American Express cardholders and traveler's check holders should call ☎ **800-221-7282**. MasterCard holders should call ☎ **800-307-7309** or 636-722-7111. For other credit cards, call the toll-free number directory at ☎ **800-555-1212**.

If you need emergency cash over the weekend, when banks and American Express offices are closed, you can have money wired to you through **Western Union** (☎ **800-325-6000**; www.westernunion.com).

Identity theft and fraud are potential complications of losing your wallet, especially if you've lost your driver's license along with your cash and credit cards. Notify the major credit-reporting bureaus immediately; placing a fraud alert on your records may protect you against liability for criminal activity. The three major U.S. credit-reporting agencies are **Equifax** (☎ **800-766-0008**; www.equifax.com), **Experian** (☎ **888-397-3742**; www.experian.com), and **TransUnion** (☎ **800-680-7289**; www.transunion.com). Finally, if you've lost all forms of photo ID, call your

Unearthing those hidden expenses

My credit-card bill never ceases to amaze me. I often wonder where half those charges came from, and then reminisce fondly about the recent past as I dig through the statement. You may not want to be reminded of your vacation in such a potentially harsh manner — better to stick with photographs — but that means paying attention to expenses that are less obvious than shelter and sustenance. For example, remember that the cost of your hotel is more than the stated room rate. The total includes the 14 percent hotel tax, plus any minibar, telephone, bar, or room-service charges. Parking in San Francisco can bankrupt you. Remember, too, minor items such as bridge tolls; San Francisco sweatshirts times the number of people in your family who forgot to pack a jacket; and tips for the bell staff, servers, and tour bus drivers (they add up quickly). Do you have to kennel your dog? May as well include that, too.

airline and explain the situation; you may be able to board your flight home if you have a copy of your passport or birth certificate and a copy of the police report you've filed.

Chapter 5

Getting to San Francisco

● ●

In This Chapter

▶ Flying to San Francisco
▶ Exploring other ways to get there
▶ Choosing an escorted or package tour

● ●

*T*he Internet has made it possible for anyone to play travel agent. You want to compare flight schedules and ticket prices? You want to take a virtual tour of a hotel or restaurant? You want to purchase theater tickets online? It's getting easier by the day. Or would you rather let your local travel agent make the calls? If you do use a travel agent, make sure the agent has in-depth knowledge of the destination and isn't just reserving the hotel that promises the largest commission. In-laws of mine (who shall remain nameless) let their travel agent recommend the hotel on their last trip to San Francisco, and it turned out to be a dump because the agent hadn't done her homework. The pitiful looks on their faces made me want to hit them over their heads — with *San Francisco For Dummies,* of course.

Flying to San Francisco

The most convenient airports to San Francisco are **San Francisco International** (SFO), which is 14 miles south of downtown, and **Oakland International Airport** (OAK), which is across the Bay Bridge, off Interstate 880. SFO is closer, and more airlines fly into this major hub. Oakland is smaller and easier to get in and out of, but you'll pay about 10 percent more for cab fares and 50 percent more for shuttles.

You can sometimes get a lower fare or a more convenient flight into Oakland, so always compare prices and travel times for each airport. Oakland also generally enjoys better weather than San Francisco. Foggy conditions frequently delay flights into SFO, a fact worth remembering as you mull over just how much reading material to bring with you on the plane.

International travelers flying directly to the Bay Area don't have a choice of airports — it's SFO or nothing. But the spacious International Terminal has lots of good dining and shopping choices, plus convenient connections to BART and car-rental desks.

Finding out which airlines fly to San Francisco

Airlines that fly into SFO include:

- ✔ **Air Canada** (☎ 888-247-2262; www.aircanada.ca)

- ✔ **Alaska Airlines** (☎ 800-252-7522; www.alaskaair.com)

- ✔ **American Airlines** (☎ 800-443-7300; www.aa.com)

- ✔ **British Airways** (☎ 800-247-9297; www.british-airways.com)

- ✔ **Continental Airlines** (☎ 800-523-3273; www.continental.com)

- ✔ **Delta Air Lines** (☎ 800-221-1212 or 404-765-5000; www.delta.com)

- ✔ **Northwest Airlines** (☎ 800-225-2525; www.nwa.com)

- ✔ **United Air Lines** (☎ 800-864-8331; www.united.com)

- ✔ **US Airways** (☎ 800-288-2118; www.usairways.com)

- ✔ **Virgin America** (☎ 877-359-8474; www.virginamerica.com)

- ✔ **Virgin Atlantic Airways** (☎ 800-821-5438; www.virgin-atlantic.com)

Airlines that fly into Oakland International Airport include many of the same carriers that serve SFO, plus **JetBlue** (☎ 800-538-2583; www.jetblue.com) and **Southwest Airlines** (☎ 800-435-9792; www.southwest.com).

Getting the Best Deal on Your Airfare

Competition among the major U.S. airlines is unlike that in any other industry. Every airline offers virtually the same product (basically, a coach seat is a coach seat is a . . .), yet prices can vary by hundreds of dollars.

Business travelers who need the flexibility to buy their tickets at the last minute and change their itineraries at a moment's notice — and who want to get home before the weekend — pay (or at least their companies pay) the premium rate, known as the *full fare*. But if you can book your ticket far in advance, stay over Saturday night, and travel midweek (Tues–Thurs), you can qualify for the least expensive price — usually a fraction of the full fare. Obviously, planning ahead pays.

Search the Internet for cheap fares. The most popular online travel agencies are **Travelocity.com** (www.travelocity.co.uk); **Expedia.com** (www.expedia.co.uk and www.expedia.ca); and **Orbitz.com.** In the U.K., go to **Travelsupermarket** (☎ 0845-345-5708; www.travelsupermarket.com), a flight search engine that offers comparisons for the budget airlines whose seats often end up in bucket-shop sales. Other Web sites for booking airline tickets online include **Cheapflights.com,**

SmarterTravel.com, Priceline.com, and **Opodo** (www.opodo.co.uk).
Meta search sites (which find and then direct you to airline and hotel
Web sites for booking) include **Sidestep.com** and **Kayak.com** — the
latter includes fares for budget carriers like JetBlue as well as the major
airlines. **Lastminute.com** is a great source for last-minute flights and getaways. In addition, most **airlines** offer online-only fares that even their
phone agents know nothing about.

Watch local newspapers for **promotional specials** or **fare wars,** when
airlines lower prices on their most popular routes. Also keep an eye on
price fluctuations and deals at Web sites such as **Airfarewatchdog.com**
and **Farecast.com.**

Frequent-flier membership doesn't cost a cent, but membership may
entitle you to better seats, faster response to phone inquiries, and
prompter service if your luggage is stolen or your flight is canceled or
delayed, or if you want to change your seat (especially after you've
racked up some miles). And you don't have to fly to earn points; **frequent-
flier credit cards** can earn you thousands of miles for doing your every-
day shopping. With more than 70 mileage awards programs on the
market, consumers have never had more options. Investigate the program details of your favorite airlines before you sink points into any one.
Consider which airlines have hubs in the airport nearest you, and, of
those carriers, which have the most advantageous alliances, given your
most common routes. To play the frequent-flier game to your best
advantage, consult the community bulletin boards on **FlyerTalk** (www.
flyertalk.com) or go to Randy Petersen's **Inside Flyer** (www.inside
flyer.com). Petersen and friends review all the programs in detail and
post regular updates on changes in policies and trends.

Driving to San Francisco

You can get to San Francisco by driving along three major highways.
Interstate 5 runs through the center of the state. This route intersects
with **Interstate 80,** which goes over the Bay Bridge into the city. Getting
to San Francisco from Los Angeles along Interstate 5 takes about six
hours. The other major route you can take is **Highway 101,** which heads
from Los Angeles through San Francisco (about seven hours) to Marin
County, Napa, Sonoma, and other points north. **Highway 1** is the more
scenic coastal route, which takes you closer to Monterey and Santa
Cruz. It's lovely, but the trip from Los Angeles takes a lot longer —
approximately eight to ten hours.

Arriving by Other Means

Amtrak (☎ **800-872-7245** or 800-USA-RAIL; www.amtrak.com) doesn't
stop in San Francisco proper, but it does stop in Emeryville, a small town
just south of Berkeley. Passengers then ride an Amtrak bus (which

departs shortly after each train arrives) from Emeryville to the Ferry Building or the Caltrain station in downtown San Francisco.

Traveling by train may seem romantic, but don't assume it's cheaper than flying. At this writing, the lowest round-trip train fare from Los Angeles to San Francisco is $100, which is more expensive than a 14-day advance-purchase ticket on one of the airlines serving the Los Angeles–San Francisco corridor. The trip from Chicago takes two days and costs at least $145 one way. But consider taking the train for the experience of chugging across the country, if you have the time, or if you're like my mother-in-law, who flunked a workshop on getting over one's fear of flying. (She skipped the graduation flight.)

Joining an Escorted Tour

You may be one of the many people who love escorted tours. The tour company takes care of all the details and tells you what to expect on each leg of your journey. You know your costs upfront and, in the case of the tame ones, you don't get many surprises. Escorted tours can take you to the maximum number of sights in the minimum amount of time with the least amount of hassle.

If you decide to go with an escorted tour, I strongly recommend purchasing travel insurance, especially if the tour operator asks to you pay upfront. But don't buy insurance from the tour operator! If the tour operator doesn't fulfill its obligation to provide you with the vacation you paid for, there's no reason to think it will fulfill its insurance obligations, either. Get travel insurance through an independent agency. (I tell you more about the ins and outs of travel insurance in Chapter 7.)

Depending on your budget, I recommend one of the following tour companies: **Globus** (☎ 866-755-8581; www.globusjourneys.com), or **Tauck** (☎ 800-788-7885; www.tauck.com), both of which offer week-long tours to San Francisco and Wine Country. Tauck is the more upscale choice. Escorted tours almost always encompass more than one city and, in the case of these operators, can take in California highlights.

For more information on escorted general-interest tours, including questions to ask before booking your trip, see www.frommers.com/planning.

Choosing a Package Tour

For lots of destinations, package tours can be a smart way to go. In many cases, a package tour that includes airfare, hotel, and transportation to and from the airport costs less than the hotel alone on a tour you book yourself. That's because tour operators buy packages in bulk and resell them to the public. It's kind of like buying your vacation at a warehouse store — except the tour operator is the one who buys the 1,000-count box of garbage bags and resells them ten at a time at a cost that undercuts the local supermarket.

Package tours can vary widely. Some offer a better class of hotels than others; others provide the same hotels for lower prices. Some book flights on scheduled airlines; others sell charters. In some packages, your choice of accommodations and travel days may be limited. Some let you choose between escorted vacations and independent vacations; others allow you to add a few excursions or escorted day trips (also at discounted prices) without booking an entirely escorted tour.

To find package tours, check out the travel section of your local Sunday newspaper or the ads in the back of national travel magazines such as *Travel + Leisure, National Geographic Traveler,* and *Condé Nast Traveler.* **Liberty Travel** (call ☎ 888-271-1584 to find the store nearest you; www.libertytravel.com) is one of the biggest packagers in the Northeast, and usually boasts a full-page ad in Sunday papers.

Another good source of package deals is the airlines themselves. Most major airlines — including **American Airlines Vacations** (☎ 800-321-2121; www.aavacations.com), **Delta Vacations** (☎ 800-654-6559; www.deltavacations.com), **Continental Airlines Vacations** (☎ 800-301-3800; www.covacations.com), and **United Vacations** (☎ 888-854-3899; www.unitedvacations.com) — offer air/land packages. American Airlines tends to have particularly good packages to San Francisco, because it's one of the airline's hubs.

Several big **online travel agencies** — Expedia, Travelocity, Orbitz, and Lastminute.com — also do a brisk business in packages. If you're unsure about the pedigree of a smaller packager, check with the Better Business Bureau in the city where the company is based, or visit www.bbb.org. If a packager won't tell you where it's based, don't fly with that packager.

British travelers should check **Travel Bag** (☎ 0800-804-8911; www.travelbag.co.uk).

For more information on package tours and for tips on booking your trip, see www.frommers.com/planning.

Chapter 6

Catering to Special Travel Needs or Interests

A h, don't you long for the good old days when you could grab a backpack, throw in a pair of jeans, and venture out into the world? Now there's the family to consider, with Junior needing to run around and drain his batteries every few hours, your teenage daughter determined to track down the perfect pair of jeans, and your spouse needing a break and maybe a beer. Or perhaps you have a physical limitation that makes traveling a challenge. Or maybe you want to take advantage of your status as an elder statesperson. Read on, friend! I like nothing better than dispensing advice.

San Francisco, already celebrated as a haven for gay and lesbian visitors, pretty much holds hajjlike status under the leadership of Mayor Gavin Newsom. If you're gay or lesbian, the resources I list in this chapter will help you find areas of the city and entertainment venues that will be of special interest to you.

Focusing on the Family

Babes in backpacks and strollers are a common sight on the streets of San Francisco, so you can be assured that munchkins are welcome here. But taking a vacation with your kids can sometimes mean *you're* not exactly on vacation, at least in my experience. Here are some tried-and-true ways to make your trip as relaxed and enjoyable as possible.

Looking at the trip from a kid's point of view

Before you board the plane or pack up the car, sit down with your family and this book and go over the sights and activities listed in Chapter 11. Let your kids choose three to six things to see and do (based on the number of days you plan to stay in San Francisco), and then have them rate their choices in order of preference. You do the same for the places you want to visit. Next, fill a calendar with the days or times you plan to do a kid activity and the times you plan to do something more adult-oriented, such as enjoying the Museum of Modern Art or joining a walking tour (see Chapter 11). Remember to block out time for eating, snacking, resting, and dropping by neighborhood parks.

Family trips are supposed to be fun, but kids turn cranky when exhaustion sets in (doesn't everybody?), so don't pull them in a hundred different directions. Neither you nor they need to see everything in one day. A long afternoon in Golden Gate Park watching the squirrels may be more memorable than dashing from Coit Tower to Alcatraz. Bring along books, paper, crayons and pencils, perhaps an inexpensive camera, an iPod, or any other unobtrusive, portable toys and games your children can easily carry in their backpacks. Give kids their own copy of the itinerary that your family worked out together to remind them that their time will come.

Finding kid-friendly sleeps, eats, and entertainment

Most hotels are more than happy to accommodate your entire clan. Chapter 9 offers tips for figuring out what kind of accommodations are right for you and yours.

Chapter 11 describes various places to go and things to do with young kids as well as teenagers. If you'd like more direction, consider the itinerary in Chapter 13 or look for the Frommer's guide *San Francisco with Kids* (published by Wiley Publishing). And don't forget to look out for the Kid Friendly icon to point you toward hotels, restaurants, and attractions that may especially appeal to the children. You'll have no trouble planning the perfect trip for tots, teens, and in-betweens.

Locating a baby sitter

You and your spouse or a friend may want to go out on the town without the little, or not-so-little, ones in tow. Many hotels (particularly the pricey ones) recommend baby-sitting services for their guests, although, for liability reasons, you'll have to make the arrangements. Rates vary, as do add-ons, such as transportation and agency fees, but you can expect to pay from $15 to $25 per hour with a four-hour minimum. Many downtown hotels use **Bay Area Child Care Agency** (☎ 415-309-5662; www.bayarea-childcare.com) and **Bay Area 2nd Mom** (☎ 888-926-3666; www.2ndmom.com). Call at least a day or two in advance.

You can find good family-oriented vacation advice on Web sites like the **Family Travel Forum** (www.familytravelforum.com), a comprehensive resource that offers customized trip planning; **Family Travel Network** (www.familytravelnetwork.com), an award-winning site that offers travel features, deals, and tips; **Traveling Internationally with Your Kids** (www.travelwithyourkids.com), a comprehensive site that

offers customized trip planning; and **Family Travel Files** (www.the
familytravelfiles.com), which offers an online magazine and a directory of off-the-beaten-path tours and tour operators for families.

Making Age Work for You: Advice for Seniors

Mention the fact that you're a senior citizen when you make your travel
reservations. Although the major U.S. airlines have cancelled their senior
discount programs, many hotels still give seniors a break. In most cities,
people over 62 qualify for reduced admission to theaters, museums, and
other attractions, as well as discounted fares on public transportation.

Members of **AARP** (formerly known as the American Association of
Retired Persons), 601 E St. NW, Washington, DC 20049 (☎ **888-687-2277**
or 202-434-2277; www.aarp.org), get discounts on hotels, airfares, and
car rentals. AARP offers members a wide range of benefits, including
AARP The Magazine and a monthly newsletter. Anyone over 50 can join.

Another reason to celebrate reaching, or passing, 55 years is **Elderhostel**
(☎ **877-426-8056;** www.elderhostel.org). This organization provides
amazing travel/learning opportunities all over the world that may
encompass a weekend of art lectures and museum viewings or multiple
weeks on safari with the grandkids. Prices are reasonable and include
hotels, excursions, and most meals. San Francisco–based programs
include a six-day wine and food extravaganza with day trips to Napa
Valley. **ElderTreks** (☎ **800-741-7956;** www.eldertreks.com) offers
small-group tours to off-the-beaten-path or adventure-travel locations,
restricted to travelers 50 and older.

Recommended publications offering travel resources and discounts
for seniors include: the quarterly magazine *Travel 50 & Beyond* (www.
travel50andbeyond.com); *Travel Unlimited: Uncommon Adventures
for the Mature Traveler* (Avalon); and *101 Tips for Mature Travelers,*
available from Grand Circle Travel (☎ **800-221-2610** or 617-350-7500).

Seniors 65 and older get automatic discounts on public transportation
fares in San Francisco. Just present identification showing your age for
reduced admission at movies, museums, and many other attractions.
Many tour companies also offer a discount for those over 62.

For more information and resources on travel for seniors, see
www.frommers.com/planning.

Accessing San Francisco: Advice for Travelers with Disabilities

Most disabilities shouldn't stop anyone from traveling. There are more
options and resources out there than ever before. Thanks to provisions

in the Americans with Disabilities Act, most public places are required to comply with disability-friendly regulations. Almost all public establishments (including hotels, restaurants, and museums, but not certain National Historic Landmarks), and at least some modes of public transportation provide accessible entrances and other facilities for patrons with disabilities.

Many travel agencies offer customized tours and itineraries for travelers with disabilities. **Flying Wheels Travel** (☎ 507-451-5005; www.flying wheelstravel.com) offers escorted tours and cruises that emphasize sports and private tours in minivans with lifts. **Access-Able Travel Source** (☎ 303-232-2979; www.access-able.com) offers extensive access information and advice for traveling around the world with disabilities. **Accessible Journeys** (☎ 800-846-4537 or 610-521-0339; www.accessiblejourneys.com) is an organization that provides travel planning resources and information for wheelchair travelers and their families and friends.

Avis Rent A Car has an "Avis Access" program that offers such services as a dedicated 24-hour toll-free number (☎ 888-879-4273) for customers with special travel needs; car features such as swivel seats, spinner knobs, and hand controls; and accessible bus service.

Organizations that offer assistance to travelers with disabilities include **MossRehab** (www.mossresourcenet.org), which provides a library of accessible-travel resources online; **Society for Accessible Travel and Hospitality** (SATH; ☎ 212-447-7284; www.sath.org; annual membership fees: $45 adults, $30 seniors and students), which offers a wealth of travel resources for all types of disabilities and informed recommendations on destinations, access guides, travel agents, tour operators, vehicle rentals, and companion services; and the **American Foundation for the Blind** (AFB; ☎ 800-232-5463; www.afb.org), a referral resource for the blind or visually impaired that includes information on traveling with Seeing Eye dogs.

For more information, check out the quarterly magazine *Emerging Horizons* ($14.95 per year, $19.95 outside the United States; www.emerginghorizons.com) and *Open World* magazine, published online by SATH.

The Bay Area–based **Center for Independent Living** publishes a 25-page booklet, *San Francisco Access,* covering hotels, transportation options, and other information helpful to travelers with disabilities. Request a free copy from the San Francisco Convention & Visitors Bureau (☎ 415-391-2000; www.onlyinsanfrancisco.com). The organization also has a fine Web site, www.accessnca.com, with detailed information on traveling all around Northern California.

Touring on wheels

If you're a wheelchair user, you'll find San Francisco's public areas quite accessible. All sidewalks have curb cuts, and ramps permit easy on/off access throughout the municipal railway system (Muni). You can find some buses equipped with wheelchair lifts as well. For information on public transportation accessibility, request a free copy of the **Muni Access Guide** from Muni's Accessible Services Program by phoning ☎ **415-923-6142** or writing the program at 949 Presidio Ave., San Francisco, CA 94115. If you need a ramped taxi, phone **Yellow Cab** at ☎ **415-626-2345** — there's no extra charge.

Many of the major car-rental companies now offer hand-controlled cars for drivers with disabilities. Avis can provide such a vehicle at any of its locations in the United States with 48-hour advance notice; Hertz requires notice between 24 and 72 hours in advance at most of its locations. **Wheelchair Getaways** (☎ **800-642-2042;** www.wheelchair getaways.com) rents specialized vans with wheelchair lifts and other features for travelers with disabilities in more than 100 cities across the United States.

Staying accessible

The Americans with Disabilities Act requires hotels to be much more accessible than in the past. However, lodgings in old buildings may have entry stairs, tiny elevators, narrow hallways, and minuscule bathrooms, making them unsuitable for anyone having to maneuver in a wheelchair.

The **Tuscan Inn** near Fisherman's Wharf and the **Orchard Hotel** near Union Square (see Chapter 9) are somewhat newer properties that are fully accessible. Also, look for the chain hotels, such as the **Embarcadero Hyatt Regency** or **Westin Market Street** (see Chapter 9), that are equipped to provide certain services such as TTY phones.

When making reservations, advise the reservation clerk at your hotel of your needs — be it TTY phones or grip bars — to make your stay more comfortable.

All newly built or restored restaurants are also up to date when it comes to meeting requirements for accessible bathrooms and entrances. If you have any doubts about access, ask when you call for a table.

Getting to the sights

You won't have any problem accessing the main attractions in San Francisco. **Golden Gate Park** is completely accommodating, as are the museums, the **Exploratorium,** and many other sites. Some areas are not very accessible, though (for example, places that have a series of stairs, such as the **Filbert Street Steps**). **Fort Point** has a wheelchair ramp, and its first floor is easily maneuverable; a walk or roll above **Fort Funston** is also accessible for travelers with disabilities.

Anyone who would prefer to admire the hills without actually trekking over them will appreciate the easy, flat walks that omit both stairs and vertical climbs detailed by **On the Level San Francisco Excursions.** The company publishes 20-page color booklets of self-guided walking tours in various neighborhoods and parks, with historical highlights and helpful hints on parking and obstacles. Each booklet is $3.95 and for sale online at www.onthelevelsf.com. Guided walks are also available for $20 per person. Call ☎ **415-921-1382** or check the Web site for information on locations and schedules.

For more on organizations that offer resources to travelers with disabilities, go to www.frommers.com/planning.

Following the Rainbow: Advice for Gay and Lesbian Travelers

San Francisco is an important and historic destination for gay travelers. You'll find the majority of gay bars and inns in the **Castro District,** the heart of San Francisco's gay community. The lesbian community resides mostly in portions of **Noe Valley** and the **Mission District** (with Valencia Street as the main drag).

Check out these great Web sites for your trip planning: **Gay.com** (www.gay.com) and **Citysearch** (www.sanfrancisco.citysearch.com), which has a complete section devoted to gay and lesbian nightlife and an interesting history of the Castro. Also take a look at the handy print guide *GayPocket San Francisco* (www.gaypocketusa.com). You can obtain a free copy of this quarterly pint-sized must-have throughout the Castro, or order one by mail: Send a $5 check to Gay Pocket Guides, 2215-R Market St., PMB 500, San Francisco, CA 94114. When you get to the city, pick up a copy of the *Bay Area Reporter* for comprehensive entertainment listings. It's free and available at coffeehouses, in bookstores, and around the Castro.

For information on specific hotels that cater to gay visitors, check out *Frommer's San Francisco* (Wiley Publishing). But there aren't any compelling reasons to plunk yourself down in such a hotel unless you don't intend to leave the Castro. And if that's the case, you'll be missing out on the alternative gay scene **South of Market** (see Chapter 16).

The International Gay and Lesbian Travel Association (IGLTA; ☎ 800-448-8550 or 954-776-2626; www.iglta.org) is the trade association for the gay and lesbian travel industry and offers an online directory of gay- and lesbian-friendly travel businesses; go to its Web site and click on "Members."

Many agencies offer tours and travel itineraries specifically for gay and lesbian travelers. **Above and Beyond Tours** (☎ **800-397-2681** or 760-325-0702; www.abovebeyondtours.com) is the exclusive gay and lesbian tour operator for United Airlines. **Now, Voyager** (☎ **800-255-6951** or

415-626-1169; www.nowvoyager.com) is a well-known San Francisco–based gay-owned and -operated travel service.

The following travel guides are available at many newsstands, most travel bookstores, and gay and lesbian bookstores: *Out and About* (☎ **415-834-6500;** www.outandabout.com), which offers guidebooks and a newsletter ($20 per year; ten issues) packed with solid information on the global gay and lesbian scene; *Spartacus International Gay Guide* (Bruno Gmünder Verlag; www.spartacusworld.com/gayguide) and *Odysseus,* both good, annual English-language guidebooks focused on gay men; the *Damron* guides (☎ **800-462-6654** or 415-255-0404; www.damron.com), with separate, annual books for gay men and lesbians; and *Gay Travel A to Z: The World of Gay & Lesbian Travel Options at Your Fingertips* by Marianne Ferrari (Ferrari International; Box 35575, Phoenix, AZ 85069), a very good gay and lesbian guidebook series.

For more gay and lesbian travel resources, visit www.frommers.com/planning.

Chapter 7

Taking Care of the Remaining Details

. . . .

In This Chapter

▶ Buying travel insurance — or not
▶ Dealing with illness away from home
▶ Deciding whether to drive

. . . .

*I*n case you need something to worry about, this chapter covers 21st-century issues such as whether or not you need travel insurance, what to do if you fall ill, and how to deal with all those people staring at your shoes in the airport security lines. I also flog my opinion about driving in San Francisco; whether you decide to get behind the wheel or eschew driving in the city, you don't want to miss my parking tips.

Renting a Car (or Six Reasons You Shouldn't!)

If lots of traffic, steep hills, no parking spaces, one-way streets, crazy bike messengers, and the occasional threat of a tow are your idea of fun, then get yourself a car. If you'd rather not deal with those sorts of hassles (and did I mention overly enthusiastic parking enforcement agents?), plenty of taxis are available to cart you all over the city.

San Francisco doesn't have an enviable public-transportation system like those in other cities; a bus can take you just about anywhere, slowly, but the municipal railway system (Muni Metro) is fairly limited. The Muni streetcars can get you close to where you want to go, but often you'll still need to catch a bus, grab a cab, or walk to many places. However, because San Francisco neighborhoods are small and distinct, and because you'll find beautiful or bizarre happenings around every corner, walking around is delightful.

Day-tripping: The one reason you should rent a car

If you plan on any out-of-city excursions, like wine tasting (if you don't like escorted tours, that is), you may want to rent a car. To avoid parking fees, wait until the day of your trip to pick up your auto. Most companies, including **Enterprise Rent-A-Car** (☎ 800-261-7331; www.enterprise.com) can pick you up and drop you off at your hotel.

If you must rent: Getting the best rate

Car rental rates vary even more than airline fares. The price depends on the size of the car, the length of time you keep it, where and when you pick it up and drop it off, where you take it, and a host of other factors. Asking a few key questions may save you hundreds of dollars.

- ✔ Weekend rates may be lower than weekday rates. If you're keeping the car five or more days, a weekly rate may be cheaper than the daily rate. Ask if the rate is the same for pickup Friday morning as it is Thursday night.

- ✔ Some companies may assess a drop-off charge if you don't return the car to the same rental location; others, notably National, don't.

- ✔ Check whether the rate is cheaper if you pick up the car at a location in town rather than at the airport

- ✔ Find out whether age is an issue. Many companies add a fee for drivers under 25, and some don't rent to them at all.

- ✔ If you see an advertised price in your local newspaper, be sure to ask for that specific rate; otherwise you may pay the standard (higher) rate. Don't forget to mention membership in AAA, AARP, and trade unions. These memberships usually entitle you to discounts ranging from 5 percent to 30 percent.

- ✔ Check your frequent-flier accounts. Not only are your favorite (or at least most-used) airlines likely to have sent you discount coupons, but most car rentals add at least 500 miles to your account.

- ✔ As with other aspects of planning your trip, using the Internet can make comparison shopping for a rental car much easier. You can check rates at most of the major agencies' Web sites. Plus, all the major travel sites — **Travelocity** (www.travelocity.com), **Expedia** (www.expedia.com), **Orbitz** (www.orbitz.com), and **Smarter Living** (www.smarterliving.com), for example — have search engines that can dig up discounted car-rental rates. Just enter the car size you want, the pickup and return dates, and location, and the server returns a price. You can even make the reservation through any of these sites.

In addition to the standard rental prices, optional charges apply to most car rentals (as do some not-so-optional charges, such as taxes). Many credit card companies cover the *Collision Damage Waiver* (CDW), which requires you to pay for damage to the car in a collision. Check with your credit card company before you go so you can avoid paying this hefty fee (as much as $20 a day).

The car rental companies also offer additional *liability insurance* (if you harm others in an accident), *personal accident insurance* (if you harm yourself or your passengers), and *personal effects insurance* (if your luggage is stolen from your car). Your insurance policy on your car at home probably covers most of these unlikely occurrences. However, if your own insurance doesn't cover you for rentals or if you don't have auto insurance, definitely consider the additional coverage (ask your car rental agent for more information). Unless you're toting around the Hope diamond — and you don't want to leave that in your car trunk anyway — you can probably skip the personal effects insurance, but driving around without liability or personal accident coverage is never a good idea. Even if you're a good driver, other people may not be, and liability claims can be complicated.

Some companies also offer *refueling packages:* You pay for your initial full tank of gas upfront and can return the car with an empty tank. The prices can be competitive with local gas prices, but you don't get credit for any gas remaining in the tank. If you reject this option, you pay only for the gas you use, but you have to return the car with a full tank or face high charges for any shortfall. If you usually run late and a fueling stop may make you miss your plane, you're a perfect candidate for the fuel-purchase option.

Playing It Safe with Travel and Medical Insurance

The types of insurance that travelers are most likely to need are trip-cancellation insurance and medical insurance. The cost of travel insurance varies widely, depending on the cost and length of your trip, your age and health, and the type of trip you're taking. You can get estimates from various providers through **InsureMyTrip.com.** Enter your trip cost and dates, your age, and other information, for prices from more than a dozen companies.

U.K. citizens and their families who make more than one trip abroad per year may find an annual travel insurance policy cheaper than paying to insure individual trips. Check www.moneysupermarket.com, which compares prices across a wide range of providers for single- and multitrip policies.

Most big travel agencies offer their own insurance and will probably try to sell you a package when you book a holiday. Think before you sign. **Britain's Consumers' Association** recommends that you insist on seeing the policy and reading the fine print before buying travel insurance. The **Association of British Insurers** (☎ 020-7600-3333; www.abi.org.uk) gives advice by phone and publishes *Holiday Insurance,* a free guide to policy provisions and prices. You might also shop around for better deals: Try **Columbus Direct** (☎ 0870-033-9988; www.columbusdirect.net).

Here is my advice on trip-cancellation and medical insurance.

✔ **Trip-cancellation insurance** will help retrieve your money if you have to back out of a trip or depart early, or if your travel supplier goes bankrupt. Trip cancellation traditionally covers such events as sickness, natural disasters, and State Department advisories. The latest news in trip-cancellation insurance is the availability of **expanded hurricane coverage** and of **"any-reason"** cancellation coverage — which costs more but covers cancellations made for any reason. You won't get back 100 percent of your prepaid trip cost, but you'll be refunded a substantial portion. **TravelSafe** (☎ **888-885-7233;** www.travelsafe.com) offers both types of coverage. Expedia also offers any-reason cancellation coverage for its air-hotel packages. For details, contact one of the following recommended insurers: **Access America** (☎ **866-807-3982;** www.access america.com); **Travel Guard International** (☎ **800-826-4919;** www.travelguard.com); **Travel Insured International** (☎ **800-243-3174;** www.travelinsured.com); and **Travelex Insurance Services** (☎ **888-457-4602;** www.travelex-insurance.com).

✔ For domestic travel, buying **medical insurance** for your trip doesn't make sense for most travelers. Most existing health policies cover you if you get sick away from home — but check before you go, particularly if you're insured by an HMO.

✔ International visitors to the U.S. should note that unlike many European countries, the United States does not usually offer free or low-cost medical care to its citizens or visitors. Doctors and hospitals are expensive, and in most cases they require advance payment or proof of coverage before they render their services. Good policies will cover the costs of an accident, repatriation, or death. European automobile clubs and travel agencies sell packages such as **Europ Assistance's "Worldwide Healthcare Plan"** at attractive rates. **Worldwide Assistance Services, Inc.** (☎ **800-777-8710;** www.worldwideassistance.com) is the agent for Europ Assistance in the United States. Though lack of health insurance may prevent you from being admitted to a hospital in nonemergencies, don't worry about being left on a street corner to die: The American way is to fix you now and bill the daylights out of you later.

✔ If you're ever hospitalized more than 150 miles from home, **Medjet-Assist** (☎ **800-527-7478;** www.medjetassistance.com) will pick you up and fly you to the hospital of your choice in a medically equipped and staffed aircraft 24 hours day, seven days a week. Annual memberships are $225 individual, $350 family; you can also purchase short-term memberships.

✔ **Canadians** should check with their provincial health plan offices or call **Health Canada** (☎ **866-225-0709;** www.hc-sc.gc.ca) to find out the extent of their coverage and what documentation and receipts they must take home in case they are treated in the United States.

✔ Travelers from the **U.K.** should carry their European Health Insurance Card (EHIC), which replaced the E111 form as proof of entitlement to free or reduced-cost medical treatment abroad (☎ **0845-606-2030;** www.ehic.org.uk). Note, however, that the EHIC only covers "necessary medical treatment." For repatriation costs, lost money, baggage, or cancellation, look into travel insurance from a reputable company (www.travelinsuranceweb.com).

Lost-luggage insurance

Lost-luggage insurance is not necessary for most travelers. On domestic flights, checked baggage is covered up to $2,500 per ticketed passenger. If you plan to check items more valuable than the standard liability, see if your homeowner's policy covers your valuables, get baggage insurance as part of your travel-insurance package, or buy Travel Guard's "BagTrak" product. Don't buy insurance at the airport — it's usually overpriced. Be sure to take any valuables or irreplaceable items with you in your carry-on luggage, because airline policies don't cover many valuables (including books, money, and electronics).

If your luggage is lost, immediately file a lost-luggage claim at the airport, detailing the luggage contents. For most airlines, you must report delayed, damaged, or lost baggage within four hours of arrival. The airlines are required to deliver luggage, once found, directly to your house or destination free of charge.

Staying Healthy When You Travel

Getting sick will ruin your vacation, so I *strongly* advise against it (of course, last time I checked, the bugs weren't listening to me any more than they probably listen to you).

Avoiding "economy-class syndrome"

Deep vein thrombosis, or, as it's known in the world of flying, "economy-class syndrome," is a blood clot that develops in a deep vein. The potentially deadly condition can be caused by sitting in cramped conditions, such as an airplane cabin, for too long. During a flight (especially a long-haul flight), get up, walk around, and stretch your legs every 60 to 90 minutes. Other preventive measures include frequent flexing of the legs while sitting, drinking lots of water, and avoiding alcohol and sleeping pills. If you have a history of deep vein thrombosis, heart disease, or another condition that puts you at high risk, some experts recommend wearing compression stockings or taking anticoagulants when you fly; always ask your physician about the best course for you. Symptoms of deep vein thrombosis include leg pain or swelling, or even shortness of breath.

For information on purchasing additional medical insurance for your trip, see the previous section.

Talk to your doctor before leaving on a trip if you have a serious or chronic illness. For conditions such as epilepsy, diabetes, or heart problems, wear a **MedicAlert identification tag** (☎ **888-633-4298;** www. medicalert.org), which immediately alerts doctors to your condition and gives them access to your records through MedicAlert's 24-hour hotline. Contact the **International Association for Medical Assistance to Travelers** (☎ **716-754-4883** or, in Canada, 416-652-0137; www.iamat. org) for tips on travel and health concerns.

Staying Connected by Cellphone or E-mail

Using a Cellphone

If you're not from the U.S., you'll be appalled at the poor reach of the **GSM (Global System for Mobile Communications) wireless network,** which is used by much of the rest of the world. Your phone will probably work in most major U.S. cities; it definitely won't work in many rural areas. To see where GSM phones work in the U.S., check out www. t-mobile.com/coverage. And you may or may not be able to send SMS (text messaging) home.

Voice over Internet Protocol (VoIP)

If you have Web access while traveling, consider a broadband-based telephone service (in technical terms, **Voice over Internet protocol,** or **VoIP**) such as Skype (www.skype.com) or Vonage (www.vonage.com), which allow you to make free international calls from your laptop or in a cybercafe. Neither service requires the people you're calling to have that service (though there are fees if they do not). Check the Web sites for details.

Accessing the Internet Away From Home

Travelers have any number of ways to check their e-mail and access the Internet on the road. Of course, using your own laptop, PDA (personal digital assistant), or electronic organizer gives you the most flexibility. But even if you don't have a computer, you can still find ways to access your e-mail and even your office computer.

Without Your Own Computer

I have seldom walked past our local **Apple Stores** (on Stockton and Chestnut sts.) without seeing many, many "customers" checking their e-mail on the various laptops on display. **Public libraries** also offer free computer access, although you'll be competing for a terminal with the local homeless population. Besides the Main Library in Civic Center, pop into the Chinatown branch, at 445 Grant St., or the North Beach branch, at 2000 Mason St. Should you want to spend quality time online, you'll be better off paying for access and comfort. **Quetzal Internet Cafe,** 1234 Polk St., at Bush Street (☎ **415-673-4181**) is open from 6 a.m. to 11 p.m. weekdays and 7 a.m. to 10 p.m. weekends. It has a full menu and serves fair-trade coffee.

With Your Own Computer

City Hall is working with a company called Meraki to provide free Wi-Fi throughout San Francisco. You can check its progress if you get the urge to log on in the Mission District, North Beach, and parts of SoMa. Look for **Free the Net** on your computer's list of available wireless networks and give it a try. Almost all the hotels in town offer free Internet connection to their customers, with the exception of Starwood properties, which continue to charge rather high fees. Lots of cafes advertise Internet access, either free or for a small fee. One comfortable spots I like is Caffe Roma, 526 Columbus Ave., in North Beach (☎ **415-296-7942;** www.cafferoma.com). Most Tully's Coffee shops are wireless hotspots. They're all over the Financial District, including inside the Crocker Galleria, 50 Post St. (☎ **415-956-8680;** www.tullys.com/freewifi).

Keeping Up with Airline Security

With the federalization of airport security, security procedures at U.S. airports are more stable and consistent than ever. Generally, you'll be fine if you arrive at the airport **one hour** before a domestic flight and **two hours** before an international flight; if you show up late, tell an airline employee and he or she will probably whisk you to the front of the line.

Bring a **current, government-issued photo ID** such as a driver's license or passport. Keep your ID at the ready to show at check-in, the security checkpoint, and sometimes even the gate. (Children under 18 do not need government-issued photo IDs for domestic flights, but they do for international flights to most countries.)

In 2003, the Transportation Security Administration (TSA) phased out **gate check-in** at all U.S. airports. And **E-tickets** have made paper tickets nearly obsolete. Passengers with E-tickets can beat ticket-counter lines by using airport **electronic kiosks** or even **online check-in.** Online check-in involves logging on to your airline's Web site, accessing your reservation, and printing out your boarding pass — and the airline may even offer you bonus miles to do so! If you're using a kiosk at the airport, bring the credit card you used to book the ticket or your frequent-flier card. Print out your boarding pass from the kiosk and simply proceed to the security checkpoint with your pass and a photo ID. **Curbside check-in** is also a good way to avoid lines, although a few airlines still ban it; call before you go.

Speed up security by **not wearing metal objects** such as big belt buck-les. If you have metallic body parts, a note from your doctor can prevent a long chat with the security screeners. Keep in mind that only **ticketed passengers** are allowed past security, except for folks escorting passen-gers with disabilities or children, or meeting returning armed-forces service members.

Federalization has stabilized **what you can carry on** and **what you can't.** Travelers in the U.S. are allowed one carry-on bag, plus a "per-sonal item" such as a purse, briefcase, or laptop bag. Carry-on hoarders can stuff all sorts of things into a laptop bag; as long as it has a laptop in it, it's still considered a personal item. The TSA has issued a list of restricted items; check its Web site (www.tssa.dhs.gov) for details.

Airport screeners may need to hand-search your checked luggage. Some luggage locks allow screeners to open and relock a checked bag if hand-searching is necessary. Look for Travel Sentry certified locks at luggage or travel shops and Brookstone stores (you can buy them online at www.brookstone.com). For more information on the locks, visit www.travelsentry.org.

Part III
Settling into San Francisco

By Rich Tennant

SAN FRANCISCO'S AMAZING CABLE CARS

Travelers can ride from Market Street to the Financial District, through the Rocky Mountains and on to Denver, all for the price of one Muni Passport.

In this part . . .

*B*ack in his student days, my husband was the kind of traveler who would blithely arrive in some distant destination without any notion of where he would eat or sleep, expecting that those things would somehow manage themselves. I, however, have always preferred the security of knowing a pillow, an airplane seat, or a theater ticket has my name on it. Go ahead and guess which one of us does the travel planning.

The hard truth, especially for people like my spouse who prefer, shall we say, to see the big picture, is that you have a better trip when you solidify your plans prior to setting foot on the airplane or the gas pedal. (Spontaneity is also a virtue, but usually after your suitcase is unpacked and you have a vague idea of where you are.) This part takes you from the airport to the city, introduces you to the neighborhoods, and explains how to use San Francisco's public-transportation system. If you're driving, you can flip directly to the tips for upping your parking karma — you need it around San Francisco! I also prod you to think about what you require in the way of accommodations, so you can make a good match with a hotel or motel. This part is also where you can get some recommendations on where to go for a great meal at any time of the day.

Chapter 8

Arriving and Getting Oriented

In This Chapter
- Figuring out how to get where you want to go
- Exploring the neighborhoods
- Gathering information

*Y*ou can't really glean much about a place from its airports and high-ways. But as you head toward San Francisco, the industrial sites and parking lots you pass gradually become the neighborhoods and landmarks you may have seen in films and photographs or heard about from fellow travelers. Even those of us who know the city as well as we know our best friends can't help but let out a sigh of delight when the Golden Gate Bridge or the downtown skyline comes into view. Welcome to San Francisco!

The Ins, but Especially the Outs, of Bay Area Airports

San Francisco International Airport (SFO) consists of four main termi-nals: North (Terminal 3), South (Terminal 1), Central (Terminal 2), and International. The baggage level of each terminal also houses informa-tion booths. Bank of America operates a branch on the mezzanine level of the North terminal, and you can find ATMs on the upper level of all terminals. International visitors will find Travelex currency exchange offices throughout the International terminal.

You can call the airport (☎ **800-435-9736** or 650-821-8211) for recorded information, or ☎ **650-817-1717** for transit information. The information desk in each of the terminals can also give you information on how to reach your destination. Or go to the SFO Web site, www.flysfo.com, for more about the airport and ground transportation.

To reach your destination by taxi or shuttle, here are the specifics:

- ✔ **Taxis** line up for passengers at the center island outside the lower level of the airport. The 14-mile trip to Union Square takes 20 to 30 minutes or so, depending on traffic, and should cost around $35 to $45 plus tip.

- ✔ If you're patient enough to wait 10 to 20 minutes for the one heading to your neighborhood, shuttle vans offer door-to-door service from the airport. However, the shuttle may make up to three stops before it's your turn to exit. You can find the shuttles by leaving the airport from the upper level and heading to the center island outside the ticket counter nearest you. A guide will direct you. Look for exact shuttle fares posted throughout the terminals; most charge around $17 per passenger. **Super Shuttle** (☎ 415-558-8500; www.supershuttle.com) is my personal favorite. You don't need to make reservations, but you will save a little money by doing so.

- ✔ **Bay Area Rapid Transit,** known as BART, connects travelers from the airport to San Francisco, the East Bay, and the Millbrae Caltrain Station, a few miles south of the airport. The BART fare into San Francisco is $5.35. At Millbrae, you can board Caltrain and ride to the depot at Fourth and King streets in San Francisco. The fare is a bargain at $4 for adults and $2 for children and seniors, and the ride takes under 30 minutes. For the train schedule, go to www.caltrain.com or call ☎ 510-817-1717. BART airport stations are on level 3 of the International terminal, or you can take the automated AirTrain to the Garage G/BART Station stop from the domestic terminals.

- ✔ If you're **renting a car,** the free AirTrain will transport you to the building that holds all the counters and cars. Catch the AirTrain on level 5 in any of the domestic terminal garages.

To drive yourself into town, follow the airport signs to Highway 101 North and Highway 280. Stay toward the left, so you don't end up on 280. If you want to go to Union Square, exit 101 North at Fourth Street. Traffic is manageable until rush hour, from 3 to 7 p.m.

At **Oakland International** (OAK; ☎ 510-563-3300; www.flyoakland.com), all ground transportation is on one level. A shuttle service called **Bayporter Express** (☎ 415-467-1800; www.bayporter.com) picks up passengers from Terminal 1 at the center island and from Terminal 2 around the corner from baggage claim. The fare to San Francisco is $29 for one person, $44 for two people in the same party, and $10 for kids under 12. You'll have an easier time if you make reservations for the 45- to 60-minute ride. To take a **cab** downtown, expect to pay around $45; the trip takes 30 to 40 minutes, depending on traffic. If you need cash, you can find ATMs in the airport.

BART (☎ 510-465-2278; www.bart.gov) also runs from Oakland into the city. You can catch the **AirBART** shuttle (☎ 510-430-9440), which runs every 20 minutes, in front of Terminal 1 or 2. The fare (exact change or prepaid ticket only) is $3 for adults, $1 for children and seniors for the 15-to-30-minute ride to the Oakland Coliseum BART station. From there, transfer to a BART train into San Francisco; the fare is $3.55. Purchase your ticket from a kiosk inside the airport or at the BART station. If you're staying around Union Square, exit BART on Powell Street; the trip takes about 25 minutes.

All the major rental-car counters are inside the terminals. If you're driving into San Francisco, exit the airport on Hegenberger Road. Follow it north to Highway 880 toward San Francisco. From there, follow the signs to Highway 80 to San Francisco. When you reach the Bay Bridge, you'll have to pay $4 at the tollbooth. On the other side, exit on Fifth Street to reach Union Square.

Arriving by Train or Car

Taking the train to San Francisco can be fun and romantic (as long as you're not in a hurry), and although I hope you'll pay attention to my advice not to drive in San Francisco, there's no reason you shouldn't drive there and put the car away when you arrive.

By train

Amtrak trains arrive in Emeryville, just south of Berkeley. From there, an Amtrak bus will take you to downtown San Francisco. The buses stop at the Caltrain station, where there's a Muni streetcar line to the Embarcadero (and thus, into downtown), and at the Ferry Building. The Ferry Building is more convenient to the hotels around the Embarcadero and Fisherman's Wharf. From the Caltrain station or the Ferry Building, you can take a taxi or streetcar to Union Square or wherever.

By automobile

Drivers arriving from east of town will cross the Bay Bridge into downtown — have $4 ready for the toll collector. Cars coming from the south on Highway 101 will pass Candlestick Park en route to downtown. Anyone making the journey along Highway 101 from the north will enter San Francisco on the Golden Gate Bridge. After you pass the tollbooth (it's $5 coming into the city), exit along the bay to Van Ness Avenue.

Figuring Out the Neighborhoods

San Francisco is at the end of a 32-mile-long peninsula between the Pacific Ocean and San Francisco Bay. The city covers just 7 square miles. Streets are laid out in a grid pattern, except for two major diagonal arteries, **Market Street** and **Columbus Avenue.** Market cuts through town from the Embarcadero up toward Twin Peaks. Columbus runs at an angle through North Beach, beginning near the Transamerica Pyramid in the

San Francisco Neighborhoods

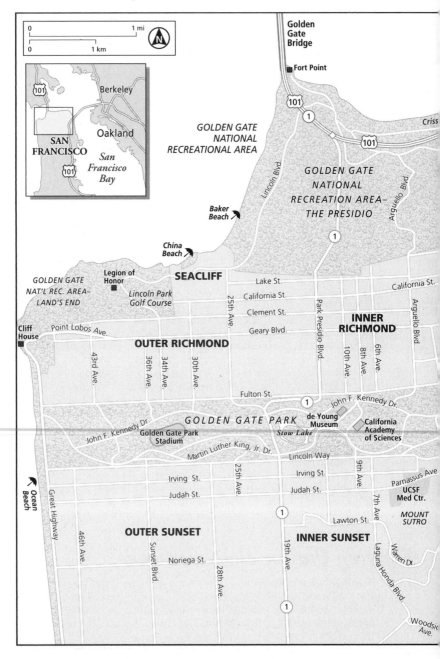

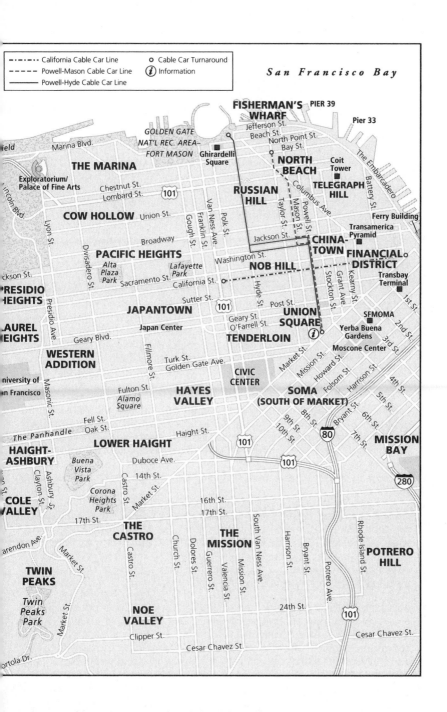

- – - – - California Cable Car Line
- – – – Powell-Mason Cable Car Line
—— Powell-Hyde Cable Car Line

o Cable Car Turnaround
(i) Information

San Francisco Bay

FISHERMAN'S WHARF — PIER 39

Jefferson St.
Beach St.
North Point St.
Bay St.

Pier 33

GOLDEN GATE NAT'L REC. AREA– FORT MASON

Ghirardelli Square

NORTH BEACH

Coit Tower

THE MARINA

Marina Blvd.

ield

Exploratorium/ Palace of Fine Arts

Chestnut St.
Lombard St.

101

RUSSIAN HILL

TELEGRAPH HILL

Columbus Ave.

Battery St.

The Embarcadero

COW HOLLOW

Union St.

Van Ness Ave.
Franklin St.
Gough St.
Polk St.

Taylor St.
Mason St.
Powell St.

Ferry Building

Lincoln Blvd.

Lyon St.

Broadway

Jackson St.

CHINA-TOWN

Transamerica Pyramid

PACIFIC HEIGHTS

Divisadero St.

Alta Plaza Park

Lafayette Park

Washington St.

Sacramento St.

California St.

NOB HILL

FINANCIAL DISTRICT o

ckson St.

PRESIDIO HEIGHTS

Presidio Ave.

Sutter St.

JAPANTOWN

101

Hyde St.

Post St.

Grant Ave.
Stockton St.
Kearny St.

Transbay Terminal

1st St.

LAUREL HEIGHTS

Masonic Ave.

Geary Blvd.

Japan Center

Geary St.
O'Farrell St.

UNION SQUARE

(i)

SFMOMA

Yerba Buena Gardens

2nd St.
3rd St.

WESTERN ADDITION

Fillmore St.

Turk St.
Golden Gate Ave.

TENDERLOIN

CIVIC CENTER

Moscone Center

4th St.

niversity of an Francisco

Masonic St.

Fulton St.

Alamo Square

Market St.
Mission St.
Howard St.
Folsom St.
Harrison St.

HAYES VALLEY

SoMA (SOUTH OF MARKET)

Bryant St.

5th St.
6th St.

The Panhandle

Fell St.
Oak St.

Haight St.

9th St.
10th St.

8th St.

80

7th St.

MISSION BAY

HAIGHT-ASHBURY

Buena Vista Park

Duboce Ave.

101

101

COLE VALLEY

Ashbury St.
Clayton St.

14th St.

Castro St.

Corona Heights Park

Market St.

16th St.
17th St.

280

TWIN PEAKS

arendon Ave.

Clarendon Ave.

Market St.

17th St.

THE CASTRO

Church St.
Dolores St.
Guerrero St.
Valencia St.
Mission St.

THE MISSION

South Van Ness Ave.
Harrison St.
Bryant St.
Potrero Ave.

Rhode Island St.

POTRERO HILL

Twin Peaks Park

Castro St.

Market St.

NOE VALLEY

Clipper St.

24th St.

101

ortola Dr.

Cesar Chavez St.

Cesar Chavez St.

Financial District and ending near the Hyde Street Pier. You'll find numbered *streets* downtown, and numbered *avenues* in the Richmond and
Sunset districts southwest of downtown.

San Francisco neighborhoods are a diverse and interesting group.
Of course, you'll have no trouble distinguishing Union Square from
Chinatown, but even if you amble through largely residential neighborhoods, you'll notice distinct differences in the makeup of the residents
and the commercial establishments. The best way to immerse yourself
in the local culture is to pick a neighborhood and take a stroll.

This section gives you a general outline of the six most popular neighborhoods to tour and lodge in, and the advantages and disadvantages
of staying in each. I follow that with brief descriptions of other worthy
neighborhoods to explore. See the "San Francisco Neighborhoods" map
to orient yourself, and Chapter 11 for more on the major attractions in
these areas.

Union Square

The center of tourist activity, Union Square is tucked inside Sutter,
Grant, Market, and Mason streets. Big department stores, expensive boutiques, theaters, restaurants, and the greatest concentration of hotels in
the city surround the square itself, which underwent a $25-million face-
lift in 2002. It lies on top of the very first underground garage in the
United States and features a central plaza outlined in palm trees, a good
cafe, outdoor tables, the TIX Bay Area outlet for half-price tickets, a See's
Candy outlet, and a shop selling San Francisco–related necessities such
as sweatshirts, posters, and gifts.

Union Square is about as convenient as it gets. Chinatown, SoMa (South
of Market Street), and the Financial District are within easy walking distance, and public transportation can take you just about anywhere from
here. Buses, Muni, BART, and the Powell Street cable cars all run through
the area. You can even hail a cab on street corners in Union Square,
whereas in other parts of town you usually need to call for one. Urbanites
will love it.

On the downside, be prepared for heavy traffic and noise. Hotel rooms
are generally quiet, but you can often hear sirens piercing through the
walls or garbage trucks on their early-morning rounds. Most of the
hotels are in older buildings, which can be charming; however, this
means that the rooms and bathrooms often are somewhat small. Valet
parking in the area runs $30 to $50 a day.

Although Union Square sits next to the Tenderloin, a low-income neighborhood of immigrant families, druggies, and the down-and-out, the area
is basically safe, as are most neighborhoods in San Francisco (see the
appendix for more information on safety). Because of the many locals
and tourists out and about, you do see plenty of street people and
vagrants aggressively seeking handouts. Pickpockets can be a problem,

and women shouldn't walk around unescorted at night. Certain sections of the Tenderloin should be avoided at any time.

The benefits of staying in Union Square include the following:

- ✔ Chinatown is around the corner.
- ✔ You have dining, shopping, and nightlife all in one place.
- ✔ Public transportation is excellent.

But here are the drawbacks:

- ✔ You're right near the Tenderloin.
- ✔ The traffic is relentless during the day.
- ✔ The panhandling can get on your nerves.

Nob Hill

Just above Union Square is Nob Hill, one of the oldest and most fashionable addresses in town. Enveloping California Street from Leavenworth to Stockton and overlooking the Financial District, the area boasts beautiful, upper-crust residential apartments and the majestic Grace Cathedral. You can find the swanky Pacific Heights neighborhood (home to the Gettys and author Danielle Steel) to the west. A small selection of plush hotels cascades down the hill toward the Financial District, along with the California Street cable-car line.

Nob Hill accommodations are pricey, with good reason. They offer a quiet, sophisticated, residential atmosphere that contrasts with the hustle and bustle of Union Square and Fisherman's Wharf. Here you see well-dressed business travelers and tourists going about their business, in contrast to the panhandlers and down-and-outers hanging around Market Street. Nob Hill is also quite safe, even at night. Although you will be walking up and down very steep grades, Nob Hill is really just a short stroll from Union Square. Muni buses and the California Street cable car provide public transportation connections. And access to some of the city's finest bars and restaurants is often just an elevator ride away. Nob Hill streets also offer breathtaking views of downtown.

The benefits of staying in Nob Hill include the following:

- ✔ The area is very safe.
- ✔ It's more peaceful and residential than Union Square.

But here are the drawbacks:

- ✔ You need to be in good condition to walk up and down the hills.
- ✔ It's expensive.
- ✔ Fewer shops and restaurants are nearby.

SoMa

South of Market Street (or SoMa for short) between Tenth, King, and Steuart streets has exploded in the past two decades, particularly along Mission Street between Second and Fifth. The George Moscone Convention Center, on Howard Street between Third and Fourth, pioneered the renaissance of this section of downtown. The **San Francisco Museum of Modern Art**, the **Cartoon Art Museum, Yerba Buena Gardens** (see Chapter 11), and, most recently, high-rise condos followed. Clubs have multiplied around Harrison Street; restaurants and bars are thick from Howard Street down to the tiny South Park enclave.

Still, vestiges of the old neighborhood remain. On nearby Sixth Street you'll find seedy residential hotels and corner stores specializing in cheap wine. Market Street itself is depressing west of Sixth Street — a combination of low-rent tourist shops, peep shows, and check-cashing counters, with a few legitimate theaters. And you're competing for space in hotels with thousands of guys wearing plastic name tags and rushing to Moscone for that panel discussion on skeletal malocclusions.

The benefits of staying in SoMa include the following:

- ✔ It's center stage for cutting-edge art and performance.
- ✔ Many museums cluster around Yerba Buena Center.
- ✔ Some great restaurants and clubs are in the area.

But here are the drawbacks:

- ✔ It still has a fringe element about it.
- ✔ The hotel choices are more limited than around Union Square.
- ✔ You get lots of convention traffic.

The Embarcadero

Liberated from the pylons and cement of the Embarcadero Freeway, which was damaged by the 1989 Loma Prieta earthquake and subsequently torn down, the Embarcadero now glows in the light reflected off the waters of the bay. Paralleling the eastern edge of Fisherman's Wharf to the beginning of China Basin, the lovely stretch of road wraps around the northeast side of the city. The views it offers are some of the most sigh-inducing in town — the Bay Bridge soars above you, Alcatraz seems a mere stone's throw away, and on sunny weekends, sailboats blissfully glide around the bay. The newly remodeled Ferry Building, a fitting centerpiece at the end of Market Street, contains the best of the best food purveyors.

This is a very safe area and is generally quiet in the evenings, except during rush hour, when it's a major thoroughfare for bridge traffic. The most popular activities at the Embarcadero consist of promenading slowly down Herb Caen Way (a stretch of sidewalk near the Ferry

Building named for the *San Francisco Chronicle*'s legendary columnist), jogging, biking, skateboarding, and shopping. With the Ferry Building drawing the locals, sections of the Embarcadero are as lively as Union Square. Some of the hottest kitchens are here, too, and you can find music and nightlife in unexpected venues.

Financial District workers swarm the Embarcadero Center, a collection of five multiuse office and retail buildings connected by bridges and walkways. Independent and foreign film lovers should check out Landmark's five-screen theaters in Embarcadero Center 1. You can catch BART and Muni streetcars from the Embarcadero underground station to just about anywhere. A Muni extension from the Embarcadero to the Caltrain station rolls southeast past the magnificent downtown ballpark, and charming old streetcars breeze down Market Street, turn northwest toward Fisherman's Wharf, and run back. As for accommodations, the hotels are expensive. The neighborhood's popularity is apparent in the amount of building and remodeling completed around the waterfront.

The benefits of staying in the Embarcadero include the following:

- ✔ Well-placed hotel rooms enjoy beautiful bay views.
- ✔ The location is great for strollers and joggers.
- ✔ Public transportation options are excellent.
- ✔ Shopping and dining are convenient.

 But here are the drawbacks:

- ✔ Rush-hour traffic is heavy.
- ✔ Hotel choices are limited (and expensive).
- ✔ Walks to other neighborhoods are relatively long.

North Beach/Fisherman's Wharf

Although just a few blocks separate North Beach from Fisherman's Wharf, the neighborhoods are as different as focaccia and sourdough. North Beach isn't an actual beach — it's the old Italian neighborhood next to Chinatown. Head here to sit in cafes, to browse in City Lights bookstore, and to sample the selections at the various delis and pastry shops. Columbus Avenue is the main street, but you can find family-style restaurants and crowded bars from Washington to Grant. XXX-rated clubs stick together on Broadway; Telegraph Hill is to the east, behind Coit Tower and the Filbert steps.

North Beach is the most European of any neighborhood in town, and the one in which I'd most like to wake up. Ducking into a cafe for a cappuccino, choosing a pastry from any number of Italian bakeries, watching Chinese senior citizens practicing tai chi in Washington Square Park — what a heavenly way to pass the morning. Stores sell goods you haven't already seen a thousand times over, and the food is divine and diverse.

And then there's Fisherman's Wharf. I suppose 15.7 million tourists can't all be wrong, but just between you and me, I don't get it. Located on Bay Street between Powell and Polk streets, the piers were once the center of the city's harbor and fishing industries. Now, waterfront life is limited to a few sport-fishing boats for tourist attractions, and the sounds of cash registers have usurped the old-timers.

A group of chain hotels huddles around North Point Street, about two blocks from the Hyde Street cable-car turnaround. A walk west along the waterfront, through the most tourist-oriented section, ends at the delightful Aquatic Park, but along the way, you pass a gauntlet of T-shirt emporiums, fast-food eateries, knick-knack shops, and beggars, one of whom camouflages himself with branches and jumps out at unsuspecting pedestrians — I kid you not.

 As you may guess, prices are slightly lower off-season in North Beach and Fisherman's Wharf, but so is the safety factor. Watch your wallet, particularly around PIER 39. Auto break-ins are also a problem. Depending on the weather, North Beach can be raucous during the evening, and blocks of Broadway pulsate with bars and girlie clubs. Parking in either district is impossible unless you head for the nearest garage, which can get expensive.

The benefits of staying in Fisherman's Wharf/North Beach include the following:

✔ You can navigate your way through either location on foot.

✔ You can find plenty of great meals in North Beach.

✔ You have access to convenient public transportation.

 But here are the drawbacks:

✔ You're surrounded by tourists on Fisherman's Wharf.

✔ The parking is a nightmare.

✔ Hotel choices are limited.

The Marina/Cow Hollow

Between Van Ness Avenue, Broadway Street, Lyon Street, and Marina Boulevard is the Marina/Cow Hollow neighborhood, a residential utopia for singles of all ages. In these parts, you'll find famous Union Street and, 4 blocks farther north, Chestnut Street, both popular for their trendy shops, restaurants, and young urban professionals. Architecture and history fans can get a close look at the **Octagon House** (circa 1861) at 2645 Gough St. (at Union).

If you're driving to San Francisco or renting a car while you're here, this neighborhood has its advantages. Outdoorsy types love the location, which is close to the Presidio and Crissy Field. Most, but not all, of the accommodations here include free parking. You can walk to several great sights from the Marina/Cow Hollow area, including the **Exploratorium,** the **Palace of Fine Arts, Fort Mason,** and the **Golden Gate Bridge.** This is a good neighborhood for families, because the prices are more reasonable than in more tourist-oriented areas.

The downside of staying here is also the location. The majority of lodgings in the area are motels along Lombard Street, a four- to six-lane conduit to the Golden Gate Bridge and Van Ness Avenue and the busiest street in the city. Most visitors find the traffic horrendous. A few hotels lie off the main drag (I review some in Chapter 9), but great places to stay are somewhat hard to find.

The benefits of sleeping in the Marina/Cow Hollow area include the following:

- ✔ It's near Chestnut Street and Union Street shopping.
- ✔ Hotel and motel parking is usually free.
- ✔ It's within walking distance of the Marina and the Golden Gate Bridge.

But here are the drawbacks:

- ✔ Accommodations choices are almost exclusively motels and B&Bs.
- ✔ Traffic is heavy on Lombard Street.
- ✔ The immediate surroundings are less scenic.

Other 'hoods to discover

If you really want to get to the heart of San Francisco, make your way to the districts discussed below.

The Castro

A historic and active gay community is the Castro's claim to fame. Visitors can admire the beautifully restored Victorian homes, visit the **Castro Theatre,** and try out a new image in the superb men's clothing stores. For shopping and people-watching, head to Castro Street, between Market and 18th streets.

China Basin/Mission Bay

This neighborhood is old, but before the **Giants** relocated here, visitors had no reason to explore the area. Boy, have things changed: The area teems with new offices and live/work developments. King Street from Third Street to the Embarcadero is the main drag; that's where you can find restaurants, bars, and the boys of summer. West of Third Street along the water is the new Mission Bay development, featuring UCSF's latest campus for research and teaching, condos galore, and an entirely new neighborhood to serve them.

Chinatown

The borders of Chinatown are always in a state of flux, but this densely packed area lies roughly between Broadway, Taylor, Bush, and Montgomery streets. It is every bit as vivid and fascinating as advertised. The **Dragon Gate** entrance on Grant Avenue leads to touristy shops, but you'll swear you're in another country after you wander up Stockton and down the abundant alleyways.

Civic Center and Hayes Valley

If you're seeking the **New Main Library;** the **Asian Art Museum;** the **Ballet, Symphony,** and **Opera** buildings; or **City Hall,** then Civic Center, bordered by Van Ness and Golden Gate avenues, and Franklin, Hyde, and Market streets, is where you want to be.

This neighborhood has a large homeless population and is dicey after dark. If you have plans in the area at night, I recommend taking a cab.

Hayes Valley, west of Civic Center, is bounded by Franklin Street to the east, Webster Street to the west, Grove Street to the north, and Page Street to the south. Here you'll find trendsetting places to shop and many quality restaurants.

Financial District

The Financial District encompasses prime bay real estate roughly between Montgomery Street and the Embarcadero, on either side of Market Street. The **Transamerica Pyramid,** at Montgomery and Clay streets, is a skyline landmark. Seek out **Belden Place,** an alley between Kearny, Bush, and Pine streets, for outdoor dining opportunities. Antiques hounds will like the hunting grounds around Jackson Square.

Haight-Ashbury

The Haight, or Haight-Ashbury, is surrounded by Stanyan Street to the east, Divisadero Street to the west, Fulton Street to the north, and Waller Street to the south. The area still hasn't fully recovered from what must have been a bummer to some of its residents — the demise of the '60s. You can find most of the action on Haight Street, which retains its magical appeal to scruffy groups of youngsters campaigning for handouts. Used-clothing stores compete for space with all kinds of commercial endeavors, most of which are perfectly legit.

Japantown

Off Geary, between Webster and Laguna streets, is Japantown, which at first glance appears to consist of ugly indoor shopping centers. Look closer and you'll find some good, inexpensive noodle restaurants and interesting shops in these buildings. A revitalized section of Fillmore Street lies within walking distance. Check out the **Sundance Kabuki movie theaters** here, or soak at the **Kabuki Hot Springs.** Across Sutter

Street (between Fillmore and Webster), look for Cottage Row, the last morsel left of the old Japantown. Bus service to Union Square is efficient and easy.

The Mission District

Located from Cesar Chavez Street to Market Street, between Dolores and Potrero streets, the Mission District is a busy, largely Hispanic community home to a growing number of artsy types seeking cheap (well, relatively cheap) rentals. Check out Mission Dolores, Dolores Park, and 24th Street, along with a plethora of affordable restaurants and eye-catching outdoor murals. A growing multitude of restaurants operates on Valencia and Guerrero streets between 16th and 23rd streets, and on 16th Street between Mission and Guerrero.

Pacific Heights

Pacific Heights, which is bordered by Broadway, Pine, Divisadero, and Franklin streets, is where the wealthy lounge around their extravagant but tasteful homes. You can visit the **Haas-Lilienthal House,** an 1886 Queen Anne Victorian at 2007 Franklin St., at Washington, and stare at *Mrs. Doubtfire*'s fictional digs at Broadway and Steiner. The closest shopping blocks are Fillmore Street between Jackson and Pine streets.

The Presidio

These 1,500 acres on the westernmost point of the city are part of the **Golden Gate National Recreation Area.** If you love to hike, go to the visitor center for maps and suggestions — the views and landscape are sensational. If you'd rather play tenpins, a great little bowling alley is also here. A patch of Presidio land along the bay, a park named **Crissy Fields,** features wetlands, picnic areas, bay views, and a drop-in center with weekend activities. That collection of buildings facing the bay belongs to George *(Star Wars)* Lucas and is the Letterman Digital Arts Center campus.

The Richmond District

Stretching from **Golden Gate Park** at one edge to the Pacific Ocean at the other, this large neighborhood is home to **Lincoln Park, Land's End,** the **California Palace of the Legion of Honor museum,** and the recently remodeled **Cliff House.** Clement Street is akin to Chinatown, without the fun architecture or alleyways, and you can find authentic Russian food on Geary.

Russian Hill

Polk Street from Broadway up to around Greenwich Street has become *très* chic. This is a delightful area for shopping and snacking, with some terrific little restaurants, bakeries, antiques shops, and boutiques. Just to the northwest, you'll find the wiggly part of Lombard Street and Macondry Lane, immortalized in Armistead Maupin's *Tales of the City.*

The Tenderloin

The blocks bounded by Sutter and Mason streets and Van Ness and Golden Gate avenues are a section of town currently home to immigrant families — largely from Southeast Asia — attempting to live their lives alongside flophouses, bars, massage parlors, and people subsisting on the fringes of society. A slim rectangle of real estate from roughly O'Farrell to Market streets between Larkin and Polk is dangerous at night and rough during the day. The only place worth visiting here is **Glide Memorial Church** for Sunday services, although the city is promoting the growing presence of Vietnamese restaurants.

The Western Addition

I mention this old neighborhood between Geary, Haight, Gough, and Divisadero streets because people studying their maps often believe it's an easy walk from Civic Center to Golden Gate Park by way of Oak or Fell streets. That's not entirely accurate. First, it's hilly. Second, it's not the safest section of town. And third, it's much farther than it appears.

Finding Information After You Arrive

If you need more information about the city, ask your concierge or desk clerk; stop by the **Convention and Visitors Bureau Information Center** on the lower level of Hallidie Plaza, 900 Market St. (at Powell); or call ☎ **800-220-5747** or 415-391-2000. The office is open Monday through Friday from 9 a.m. to 5 p.m., Saturday and Sunday from 9 a.m. to 3 p.m. during the summer. It's closed New Year's Day, Easter Sunday, Thanksgiving, Christmas, and Sundays from November to April.

Look for a free *Bay Guardian* or *SF Weekly* at sidewalk kiosks and coffeehouses for listings of city events and entertainment. The Convention and Visitors Bureau also operates a 24-hour events line at ☎ **415-391-2001.**

Getting Around San Francisco

Having a car in the city isn't advised and isn't necessary most of the time. San Francisco really caters to walkers, with benches appearing just when you need one and cafes at hand for a shot of caffeine when energy flags. Getting around on a bus or Muni metro streetcar is cheap if not perfect. In the rare instance that you do need a car, renting one downtown is easy and convenient.

This section contains everything you need to know about cruising around the city *sans* auto. It even includes some inside tips on parking should you decide to throw caution to the wind and join the legendary drivers — and I don't mean that in a good way — gracing our city's roads and highways.

The one-stop-shopping number for traffic or public transit information is ☎ **415-817-1717.** This number connects you to whatever you need, whether BART and Muni routes or traffic conditions.

Heading Out on Foot

Walking is the best way to travel if you aren't in a rush, and it's the only way to really see and enjoy the neighborhoods. I recommend some walking tours in Chapter 11, and I can't urge you enough to take one or more. Walking is the only means of seeing the city properly, and if you get a good tour guide, you'll discover some interesting tidbits as well.

 Use caution when walking, because San Francisco is no stranger to vehicle-pedestrian accidents. Be alert at all times. Watch for drivers running red lights (a common occurrence) or turning right on a red light; make absolutely sure bus drivers see you entering the crosswalk.

 Among the best neighborhoods for walkers are **Chinatown, North Beach, Russian Hill,** and the **Embarcadero.** If you're in good shape and don't mind a little wind, a walk across the **Golden Gate Bridge** is much more satisfying than a drive, especially if you're the one who has to keep your eyes on the road.

Traveling by Streetcar

Walking probably won't take you everywhere you want to go. But getting around by public transportation is a breeze when you know a few basics. The **San Francisco Municipal Railway,** known as Muni (☎ **415-673-6864;** www.sfmta.com), is much maligned by locals for inefficiency, but tens of thousands of daily commuters rely on its buses and electric streetcars for a lift to the office. The fare is $1.50 for an adult and 50¢ for seniors 65 and older and children 5 to 17 to ride a bus or streetcar anywhere in the system; exact change is required. Muni Passports, accepted on buses, streetcars, and even cable cars, are a bargain for visitors planning to take public transportation extensively. A one-day pass is $11, a three-day pass is $18, and a seven-day pass is $24. You can purchase them at the Tix Bay Area booth in Union Square, at the cable-car ticket booth on Market and Powell streets, at the Beach and Hyde streets cable-car ticket booth, and even the Walgreens at 825 Market St. (at Fourth St.). You may also purchase single-day passes onboard the cable cars.

 A **Citypass** (☎ **888-330-5008;** www.citypass.net) is a booklet of discounted tickets for six major attractions (the **Museum of Modern Art, Palace of the Legion of Honor/de Young** museums, **California Academy of Sciences & Steinhart Aquarium** or the **Asian Art Museum,** the **Exploratorium, Aquarium of the Bay,** and a **Blue & Gold Bay Cruise**). The pass includes a seven-day Muni Passport, making it quite a bargain for those ambitious enough to use all the coupons — they're good for nine days from the date of purchase. The price is $54 for adults, $44 for kids, and you can buy a pass online or at the participating attractions.

At the underground Muni stops from Civic Center to the Embarcadero, the fare boxes (which are at the entry point prior to reaching the escalators) accept only coins or tokens, an important point to remember if you're in a hurry and have only dollar bills in hand. Change machines are on the walls next to the BART ticket dispensers.

Muni streetcars run underground downtown and aboveground in the outlying neighborhoods from from 6 a.m. until 1 a.m. The five Muni metro streetcar lines — the J, K, L, M, and N — make the same stops as BART (see the discussion later) along Market Street, including Embarcadero Station, Montgomery and Powell streets (both near Union Square), Civic Center, and Van Ness Avenue. Past Van Ness Avenue, the routes go off in different directions. The N-Judah line serves Haight-Ashbury and parallels Golden Gate Park on its way down Judah Street to the ocean. The J-Church line passes close to Mission Dolores and the Castro. The L-Taraval line travels through the Sunset District within walking distance of the San Francisco Zoo. The new T-Third streetcar operates as an extension to the K line, connecting all the Third Street neighborhoods.

A collection of vintage streetcars from the United States and Europe operates on the most picturesque line, the **F-Market.** It runs along Market Street to the Castro Street station. The rejuvenated cars continue from Market Street over to Mission Street and down the Embarcadero to Fisherman's Wharf. Muni cars marked MISSION BAY end their journey at the Caltrain Station on King Street, just past the AT&T baseball park. These streetcars have their own fan club, the nonprofit Market Street Railway, which operates a tiny new **museum** at 77 Steuart St. (☎ **415-974-1948;** open: Wed–Sun 10 a.m.–6 p.m.), where the line stops. Trainspotters will find it moving.

Spend the $3 for the Official San Francisco Street and Transit Muni Map. It is invaluable for public transportation users. It shows all bus, streetcar, cable-car, and BART routes and stations. You can buy the maps at the Convention and Visitors Bureau Information Center and cable-car ticket booths. You can also call ☎ **415-673-MUNI** for route information.

Trekking by Bus

Muni buses are clearly numbered on the front and run through the city from 6 a.m. to midnight. I don't recommend taking them late at night, however. Street-corner signs and painted yellow bands on utility poles and on curbs mark bus stops. Buses come by every 5 to 20 minutes, depending on where you want to go and the time of day. Rapid transit — in the truest sense of the adjective — they are not, but with 80 routes, they are the most complete. Muni metro streetcars are faster, but the buses cover a wider area. Expect most buses to be extremely crowded during rush hours (from 7–9 a.m. and 4–6 p.m.).

Exact change is required on the buses, as it is on the streetcars (for information on fares, see the section "Traveling by Streetcar," earlier in this chapter). Ask the driver for a transfer, which is good for a second ride within 90 minutes. If you plan to ride another bus or streetcar within the time limit, you'll be happy to have that slip of paper.

Befriending BART

BART (☎ **415-989-2278;** www.bart.gov), which stands for Bay Area Rapid Transit, is not Muni. Tourists often get the two systems mixed up because they share the same underground stations downtown. You won't get into too much trouble if you get the systems confused within the city limits, but BART runs all over the Bay Area, and if you're inattentive, you may end up in a place far different from where you expected to go. More than one unsuspecting traveler has ended up in Fremont when he intended to exit at the Embarcadero. If BART is what you want, check the signs in the stations and pay attention to the cars themselves. The silver-and-blue BART trains do not resemble Muni's orange-trimmed electric streetcars in the least. You purchase tickets for BART from machines at the station. The fare to or from any point in the city is $1.55 each way; outside the city, fares vary depending on how far down the line you go. You can't use Muni transfers, tokens, or passes on BART.

Getting Around by Cable Car

There's no city statute that says you have to ride the cable cars, but what self-respecting tourist would leave San Francisco without climbing aboard? Three lines cross the downtown area. If you're in the mood for some scenery, take the **Powell-Hyde line,** which begins at Powell Street and ends at the turnaround across from Ghirardelli Square. The **Powell-Mason line** goes through North Beach and ends near Fisherman's Wharf. The **California Street line,** the least scenic, crests at Nob Hill and then makes its way to Van Ness Avenue. (The lines of people waiting to board the California Street cable cars are usually much shorter than the others because the route isn't as twisty.) Rides are $5 one-way, so buy a Muni Passport and take all three as often as you like. The pass is worth every penny. You may board cable cars only at specific, clearly marked stops.

Cable cars operate from 6:30 a.m. to 12:30 a.m., but I suggest taking one early or late in the day if you want to have a little elbow room. Plus, the fare is only $1 before 7 a.m. and after 9 p.m.

Catching a Taxi

You can easily get a taxi downtown, especially in front of hotels, but you have to call a cab to retrieve you almost anywhere else. Unfortunately,

Cable Car Routes

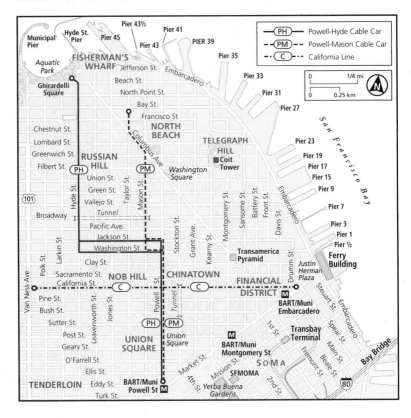

reaching the taxi companies by phone can take a while. Keep these numbers handy:

- ✓ **Desoto Cab:** ☎ 415-970-1300
- ✓ **Luxor Cabs:** ☎ 415-282-4141
- ✓ **Veteran's Cab:** ☎ 415-648-1313
- ✓ **Yellow Cab:** ☎ 415-626-2345

Rates are about $3.10 for the first ⅕ mile and 45¢ for each additional ⅕ mile or fraction thereof.

Motoring Around on Your Own

Drivers unfamiliar with the area often have a difficult time navigating the heavy downtown traffic and multitude of one-way streets. Add to these problems the lack of parking and heavy-handed meter maids, and leaving your car outside the city limits makes sense. However, if you plan to go over the Golden Gate or Bay bridges, or south to Monterey and Santa Cruz, a car will be essential.

Dealing with rush hour

During the week, traffic backs up on bridge approaches throughout the Financial District and downtown from 3 until about 7 p.m. North Beach is usually busy from the late afternoon into the evening, and because the streets bump into Columbus Avenue, navigating the area can be confusing. On the weekends, Lombard Street and Van Ness Avenue take the brunt of the cars inching toward the Golden Gate Bridge. Getting through Chinatown's narrow, crowded streets by car is basically impossible during waking hours. If you must cross town, I suggest taking California Street past the Financial District.

For sanity's sake, avoid traveling outbound on the Golden Gate and Bay bridges between 3 and 7 p.m. weekdays. If you plan to drive to Wine Country (see Chapter 14), do *not* leave on a Friday after 2 p.m., if at all possible. Traffic across the Golden Gate Bridge is awful on weekends, especially if the weather is nice. Go before noon on Friday, and avoid returning on Sunday afternoon.

Driving by the rules

California law requires that both drivers and passengers wear seat belts. You may turn right at a red light (unless otherwise indicated) after yielding to traffic and pedestrians and after making a complete stop. Cable cars and streetcars always have the right of way, as do pedestrians, especially if they use intersections and crosswalks. On Market Street, one lane is exclusively for buses unless you're making a right turn. Heed the signs.

Being cautious with red lights

San Francisco drivers have a tendency to run red lights, so pause to check oncoming traffic before entering an intersection just after the light turns green.

Parking the car

I'm not going to take up space discussing the many parking laws. Just take my advice: Park in a garage. They are expensive but could save you some money, because parking tickets start at $40.

Legal street parking spaces are next to unpainted curbs. Yellow-, white-, green-, and red-painted curbs are all off-limits in general — the only exception being commercial zones (yellow curbs), which are okay to park in after delivery hours. Pay attention to the signs posted on the streets. Be aware of tow-away zones. You can't park on most streets downtown between 4 and 6 p.m. without running the risk of having your car towed. If it is, you'll find your rental at the **AutoReturn Lot,** 450 Seventh St., at Harrison Street (☎ **415-865-8200**), faster than you can say "Where'd I park the car?" If your wheels aren't where you thought you left them, call ☎ **415-553-1239** to find out whether your vehicle has been towed or merely stolen. If your car has been towed, you'll need to go to AutoReturn in person to pay the ticket and the storage charges (which vary depending on how long the car has been there). This misadventure will cost you at least $185, cash or credit card only.

Legal parking spots are hard to come by. If you're driving, park in a public garage or use the services of a valet. And if you do happen to find a legal space within walking distance of your destination, *grab it.*

Improving your parking karma

So, you want a parking space, huh? You'll have to be one step ahead of the crowd. Try these suggestions for a little edge:

- ✔ **Carry quarters.** Most parking meters accept nothing else; 25¢ buys six minutes in most parts of town.

- ✔ **Watch the clock.** Many crosstown downtown streets do not allow parking during rush hour, from 4 to 6 p.m. Get to the Financial District, Union Square, SoMa, or Nob Hill a few minutes before 6 p.m. to grab the great street parking space of your choice.

- ✔ **Spring for valet parking.** The extra money now may be worth avoiding the headache of finding a parking spot later.

- ✔ **Check out public parking garages.** Public parking garages are cheaper than private ones. In North Beach, park in the garage on Vallejo Street (between Kearny and Green). In Chinatown, park at the Portsmouth Square garage on Kearny Street.

- ✔ **Make note of street-sweeping times.** If you find street parking galore in some outlying neighborhood, check signs for sweeping hours and days. That's generally the real reason for your good luck. Don't park without checking the signs, unless you want to give the Department of Traffic a $35 donation. If your timing is right, however, you'll pull up after the sweeper trucks have made their rounds, when it's perfectly okay to park.

- ✔ **Stop "runaway" car syndrome.** To keep your car from rolling away while you're parked on a hill, put the car in gear, apply the hand brake, and *curb your wheels* — turn your wheels toward the curb when facing downhill and away from the curb when facing uphill. It's the law! (This tip won't contribute to your finding a parking place, but it will help you keep the one you found.)

Chapter 9

Checking In at San Francisco's Best Hotels

In This Chapter

▶ Choosing your chain or independent hotel
▶ Getting the best rates
▶ Using the Internet to uncover hotel deals
▶ Knowing the questions to ask to get the room you want
▶ Getting a room if you don't have reservations
▶ Discovering the perfect San Francisco hotel

So, you're ready to make San Francisco your home — for a short time, at least. You probably have an idea of how much you're willing to spend (if not, check out Chapter 4), and you may have an idea of what neighborhood suits your fancy (see Chapter 8 for descriptions). Other features and amenities will be important to you, too. If you don't stay in hotels very often, you may not know what level of service or quality of room you need to enjoy your stay. Consider, among other variables, whether you really care if your room resembles something out of *Condé Nast Traveler,* has an unobstructed view of the bay, is vulnerable to street noise, or has a bathtub large enough for you and a close friend. Will you feel despondent if the hotel can't supply a cup of herbal tea at 10 p.m.? Will you behave badly all day if you can't hit the treadmill first thing in the morning? If you're traveling with your laptop, is Wi-Fi a necessity? If you're traveling with your lap dog, is the hotel Fido friendly? Avoid disappointment and surprises by discussing your requirements with the reservations staff.

The hotel selections in this chapter are, in my opinion, among the best in the city, balancing comfort, location, character, and price. With few exceptions, each has a distinct, only-in-San-Francisco style I believe you'll find memorable and pleasing. For those traveling on frequent-flier miles (which you can sometimes redeem for rooms), you won't find many of the big chain hotels listed here, but there are plenty: Turn to the appendix for toll-free numbers and Web sites. I also leave out the majority of hotels on less desirable blocks, many of the priciest palaces, as well as those that are a bit too far from the action.

San Francisco Hotels

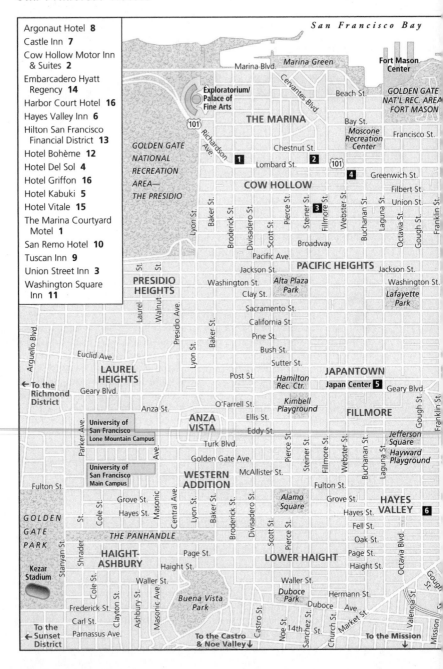

Argonaut Hotel **8**

Castle Inn **7**

Cow Hollow Motor Inn & Suites **2**

Embarcadero Hyatt Regency **14**

Harbor Court Hotel **16**

Hayes Valley Inn **6**

Hilton San Francisco Financial District **13**

Hotel Bohème **12**

Hotel Del Sol **4**

Hotel Griffon **16**

Hotel Kabuki **5**

Hotel Vitale **15**

The Marina Courtyard Motel **1**

San Remo Hotel **10**

Tuscan Inn **9**

Union Street Inn **3**

Washington Square Inn **11**

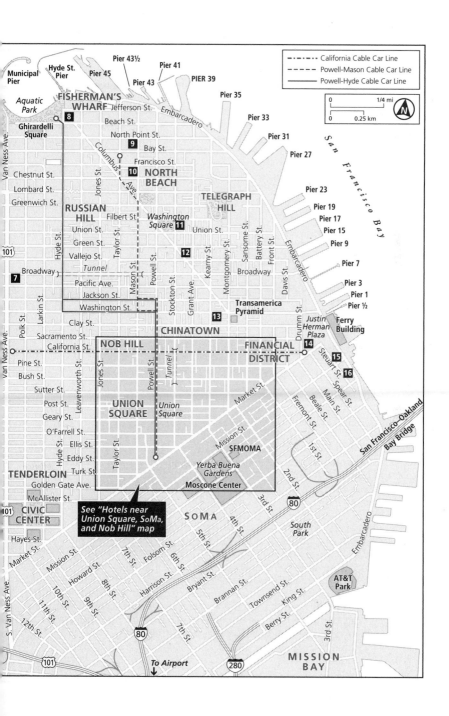

See the indexes at the end of this chapter for lists of recommended hotels, organized by neighborhood and price.

No matter where you stay in San Francisco, you're no more than 20 minutes by cab from the major sites, shopping areas, and restaurants. The majority of the city's hotels are in a few of the central neighborhoods.

With guidance from Chapter 8, pick the neighborhood you want to stay in based on your interests and needs — for example, are you hoping to shop the major stores? Are you an enthusiastic museum-goer? Do you hope to find peace and quiet? Or do you want to be close to the bay?

Refer to *Frommer's San Francisco* (Wiley Publishing) for accommodations in neighborhoods outside the central part of the city that aren't covered here, or go to **Citysearch** (www.sanfrancisco.citysearch. com), where you can search for hotels by area and price.

Getting to Know Your Options

Hotels come in many shapes, sizes, and price ranges. You'll find chain hotels and motels, independent hotels, and hotels that serve business travelers rather than vacationers. So what are the differences between these various accommodations?

Choosing between chain hotels and independent hotels

Hotels affiliated with huge chains, such as Holiday Inn, Hilton, Sheraton, Marriott, and Hyatt, are often monolithic or merely architecturally homely structures that are a bit on the boring side and look pretty much the same wherever you travel. Even the rooms will have similar, if not identical, décor. But there's comfort in that, and for travelers who like the assurance of a brand name, chains are a fine choice. In San Francisco, businesspeople and conventioneers often make up the clientele at these hotels. The appendix at the back of this book lists toll-free telephone numbers for the major chains.

Independent hotels (sometimes also called *boutique hotels*) are smaller in scope than the big-name properties. They target travelers who want a unique, individualized atmosphere with a local slant. Some appeal to older couples seeking quiet and cozy budget lodgings, while other independents seek to attract the sophisticated traveler with hip furnishings and wild color schemes. San Francisco is a leader in the boutique hotel scene, with a great assortment. If you want more interesting surroundings, where your fellow guests may be movie fans, literati, musicians, or shopaholics, you may enjoy a stay in a boutique hotel.

Make sure you know what you're getting into, though — boutique hotels are not for everyone. Lower-end independent hotels may not meet a business traveler's needs, and staff members are not always immediately available to answer questions or provide services. Room service is also iffy unless a restaurant is connected to the property. However, San Francisco's boutique properties tend to provide good to amazing service and amenities.

Do 1 really get breakfast in bed? Unpacking in a B&B

B&Bs, or bed-and-breakfast inns, can come in the form of an extra bedroom or two in a private home or a house renovated for the purpose of providing accommodations to visitors. Some B&Bs are lavishly decorated, with an owner who prides himself on serving gourmet breakfasts and afternoon sherry. Other owners put less effort into the business, keeping some food in the fridge and engaging in casual conversation with guests about the local sites, rather than providing any official tour guidance. Accommodations at a B&B usually come with a continental or full breakfast. You may have to share the bathroom with fellow guests. Rooms at B&Bs are usually more economical than hotel accommodations, but a few luxury B&Bs have equally high-end prices.

Some small hotels advertise as B&Bs. In general, these properties have a dozen or so guest rooms, include continental breakfast (usually coffee and pastries) in the room rate, and often offer wine in the afternoon.

I recommend a few stellar B&Bs in this book, but plenty more are in the city. For more information on bed-and-breakfasts and lists of properties, the following resources can help:

- ✔ **Bed & Breakfast San Francisco** (☎ 415-899-0060; www.bbsf.com). This organization has information on small B&Bs.

- ✔ **California Association of Bed and Breakfast Inns,** 414 Twenty-Ninth Street, Sacramento, CA 95816 (☎ 800-373-9251; www.cabbi.com). The Web site has links to member inns.

- ✔ **Bed and Breakfast Inns of Napa Valley** (☎ 707-944-4444; www.napavalley.com/lodging). This organization is a great resource if you plan to take a side trip to Wine Country.

Family ties: Choosing a kid-friendly hotel

The younger generation loves San Francisco for its beauty, wealth of activities, great food, and those cable cars. Hotels are waking up to the fact that families appreciate attention paid to children, but by and large, that means different things to different marketing departments. The Ritz-Carlton, for example, will send a bellhop to baby-proof your quarters and provide the nanny with some aspirin, while the desk clerk at the Hotel Del Sol will dig out a beach ball for the kids. Few hotels have swimming pools, by the way. (For more on accommodations for families, take a look at *Frommer's San Francisco with Kids,* published by Wiley

Publishing.) If you're taking your darlings along on this trip, you have three choices for sleeping arrangements: Share a room with them, rent two rooms, or reserve a suite.

Sharing a room with your family means reserving a *double/double, queen/queen,* or *king/king* — one room with two double, queen, or king beds. Double/doubles are the least expensive option and work best for a family of four with kids too young to have a room of their own. If you come to terms with the fact that you won't be staying up late, you won't be sleeping in, and this trip will revolve around the kids' needs, you can have a calm holiday.

Renting two rooms connected by an interior door or across the hall from each other is a great option if you have a large family or are traveling with older, more independent kids. Although you end up spending twice the money, renting two rooms ensures that you can get some R&R, if only for a few blissful hours.

Reserving a suite may seem like an extravagant way to give yourself a little space while keeping a close eye on the children, but it's really a clever way to enjoy a high-quality hotel experience. Look at it this way: $300 buys you two rooms at the Golden Gate Hotel near Union Square, but at the Grosvenor, $269 sets the nuclear family up in a two-bedroom suite complete with a compact kitchenette and continental breakfast in the tony environs of Nob Hill. King suites at the Tuscan Inn near Fisherman's Wharf won't be more than $369, and the hotel offers all sorts of discounted rates.

Unlike in resort destinations, few hotels in San Francisco offer special kids' programs or amenities. The hotels that I designate as Kid Friendly are the ones that suit families because of room size, location, or their willingness, in my opinion, to accommodate a family's needs and make them feel welcome.

Finding the Best Room Rate

The **rack rate** is the maximum rate a hotel charges for a room. It's the rate you get if you walk in off the street and ask for a room for the night. You sometimes see these rates printed on the fire/emergency exit diagrams posted on the back of your door.

Hotels are happy to charge you the rack rate, but you can almost always do better. Perhaps the best way to avoid paying the rack rate is surprisingly simple: Just ask for a cheaper or discounted rate. You may be pleasantly surprised.

In all but the smallest accommodations, the rate you pay for a room depends on many factors — chief among them being how you make your reservation. A travel agent may be able to negotiate a better price with certain hotels than you can get by yourself. (That's because the hotel often gives the agent a discount in exchange for steering his or her business toward that hotel.)

Reserving a room through the hotel's toll-free number may also result in a lower rate than calling the hotel directly. On the other hand, the central reservations number may not know about discount rates at specific locations. For example, local franchises may offer a special group rate for a wedding or family reunion, but they may neglect to tell the central booking line. Your best bet is to call both the local number and the toll-free number and see which one gives you a better deal.

Room rates (even rack rates) change with the season, as occupancy rates rise and fall. (See Chapter 3 for advice on the best months to get deals on hotels.) Even within a given season, room prices are subject to change without notice, so the rates quoted in this book may be different from the rate you receive when you make your reservation. Be sure to mention membership in AAA, AARP, frequent-flier programs, and any other corporate rewards programs you can think of — or your Uncle Joe's Elks lodge in which you're an honorary inductee, for that matter — when you call to book. You never know when the affiliation may be worth a few dollars off your room rate.

The rack rates I give in the hotel listings do not include the 14 percent hotel tax. And those outrageous valet garage prices — also taxed at 14 percent — are *per day*. You will pay extra to park an oversized vehicle. Many of these hotels offer weekend discounts and parking or breakfast packages. Before you book, always ask if any specials, packages, or promotions are going on that may get you a better deal.

If you're driving, don't feel obliged to use the hotel's valet to park. The cost just keeps increasing. If you're planning to keep the car garaged, drop your luggage at the hotel and head to the nearest public parking structure. Around Union Square, you'll find the **Ellis-O'Farrell Garage,** 123 O'Farrell St. ($34/day; ☎ **415-986-4800;** www.eofgarage.com); the **Sutter-Stockton Garage,** 444 Stockton St. ($34/day; ☎ **415-982-7275**); and the **Union Square Garage,** 333 Post St. ($31/day; ☎ **415-397-0631**). SoMa has the city's largest facility, the **Fifth and Mission Garage,** 833 Mission St. ($30/day; ☎ **415-982-8522;** www.fifthandmission.com). Of course, you don't get in-and-out privileges, nor will anyone fetch the car for you, but one of the biggest complaints hotel guests have is how slow the valets are to bring the cars around. Save yourself time and money and self-park.

Getting the Best Room at the Best Rate

Obviously, you can get all the service and style you want if price is no object. But when it is, as is so often the case, here's a little advice for chatting up the reservations-desk staff: Charm is useful; being completely clear about your expectations is just as important.

Finding the best rate

Make sure you cover all the bases when researching hotels. Besides checking with the hotel's reservations staff and toll-free number (see "Finding the Best Room Rate," above), surf the Web. Most hotels are likely to meet any price you can get on an Internet hotel reservation service. That way they still get your business without paying a commission to the service.

 If you reserve over the Internet, print out your booking transaction (including your confirmation number) and bring it with you. Hotels have been known to make mistakes on the final bill, such as charging for parking or breakfast when a package or promotion included it, and proof in hand will smooth negotiations.

 When budgeting for hotel rates, watch out for hidden fees and extra costs. Knowing things up front is better than getting stuck later. Traveling with man's best friend? Be sure to ask if there's a cleaning charge for pets on top of the room rate.

 Consider joining the hotel's loyalty program prior to making your reservation. Sure, it's a marketing tool, but in exchange for your e-mail address and some benign personal information, you may receive upgrades and slightly more attentive service, especially if you become a return customer. In San Francisco, Joie de Vivre, Personality Hotels, and Kimpton all offer perks for membership.

Figuring in taxes and extra expenses

A hotel room that costs $99 a night actually will end up closer to $114 because of the hotel tax. It's steep, and it's unavoidable. Room-service charges can also inflate your final room tab. Local phone calls, treats that cram the minibar in your room, enticing baskets of goodies on an end table — none of these are gratis (unless they're marked "complimentary").

 If you like to snack in bed, buy your favorite goodies at a nearby market or convenience store, and bring them up to your room.

Don't forget that most hotels tack on a fee for merely dialing out on the phone in your room. The charge starts at 75¢ and increases depending on what the market will bear. This is, of course, in addition to long-distance charges. Triple-check that you have your cellphone and charger. For dinner reservations or event tickets, let your hotel concierge do the talking.

Bargain hunting in season

Officially, the low season in San Francisco is from November to March, but one highly experienced downtown concierge joked that the low season was the weekends (when business travelers leave town). Although more tourists do visit between spring and early fall, your actual concerns should center on convention and business travelers.

The San Francisco Convention and Visitors Bureau (see the appendix) keeps a calendar of major conventions, and I recommend checking it before you finalize your plans. Union Square and SoMa hotels and restaurants are always packed when Moscone Center is booked.

Generally, you'll get your best rate in the winter, on weekends when the suits go home, and around holidays when you're supposed to be at Cousin Seymour's and not gallivanting around San Francisco. Don't let that discourage you from arriving whenever it's convenient for you, of course. Just make your reservations far in advance.

As room rates fluctuate with the season (and the economy), occupancy rates also rise and fall. A hotel is less likely to extend discount rates if it is close to full, but most (the Ritz-Carlton being an exception) will negotiate if they're close to empty. Tourist-oriented hotels usually offer discounted rates for midweek stays because they're typically most crowded on weekends. The reverse is true for business hotels downtown. Wine Country hotels tend to charge the most in the fall, around harvest time, and on weekends during the summer. Rates listed in this book are probably different from the rate you'll be quoted when you make your reservation, because room prices are subject to change without notice. In addition, discounts for membership in AAA, AARP, frequent-flier programs, and other programs can change room rates significantly, regardless of the season. The word on the street is that hotel room prices are on the increase, as are occupancy rates.

Surfing the Web for Hotel Deals

Shopping online for hotels is generally done one of two ways: by booking through the hotel's own Web site or through an independent booking agency (or a fare-service agency like Priceline). These Internet hotel agencies have multiplied in mind-boggling numbers of late, competing for the business of millions of consumers surfing for accommodations around the world. This competition can be a boon to consumers who have the patience and time to shop and compare the online sites for good deals — but shop they must, for prices can vary considerably from site to site. And keep in mind that hotels at the top of a site's listing may be there for no other reason than that they paid money for the placement.

In addition to the online travel booking sites **Travelocity, Expedia, Orbitz, Priceline,** and **Hotwire,** you can book hotels through **Hotels.com, Quikbook** (www.quikbook.com), and **Travelaxe** (www.travelaxe.net).

HotelChatter.com is a daily webzine offering smart coverage and critiques of hotels worldwide. Go to **TripAdvisor.com** or **HotelShark.com** for helpful independent consumer reviews of hotels and resort properties.

It's a good idea to **get a confirmation number** and **make a printout** of any online booking transaction.

Don't assume that the hotels offered on the sites are all in handy, safe neighborhoods or offer the amenities you want. These sites merely list the properties; they don't judge them.

In the opaque Web site category, **Priceline** (www.priceline.com) and **Hotwire** (www.hotwire.com) are even better for hotels than for airfares; with both, you're allowed to pick the neighborhood and quality level of your hotel before offering up your money. On the downside, many hotels stick Priceline guests in their least desirable rooms. Be sure to go to the **BiddingForTravel** Web site (www.biddingfortravel.com) before bidding on a hotel room on Priceline; it features a fairly up-to-date list of hotels that Priceline uses in major cities. For both Priceline and Hotwire, you pay upfront, and the fee is nonrefundable. Note: Some hotels don't provide loyalty-program credits or other frequent-guest amenities when you book a room through opaque online services.

The Web can be a good resource for hotel deals, but in my humble opinion, you usually get the most accurate information by calling the hotel directly. No matter what assurances you receive from online agencies, travel agency Web sites *cannot* guarantee specific rooms (unless, perhaps, you requested the bridal or presidential suite), and they know very little about the hotel they're selling. In many cases, the "reviews" you read online are provided and paid for by the hotels and, therefore, are likely to be promotional rather than critical.

Another problem recently brought to my attention is the difficulty in getting a refund from some of these reservation services if you have to cancel your stay. The service, not the hotel, has your money until it settles with the hotel after you've checked out. Finally, there may be a difference between the amount of dough you pay the agency for your room and the amount the agency pays the hotel (that's the profit motive for you). If you don't like the place, again, you're stuck negotiating for a refund from the online agency rather than the hotel itself.

Reserving the best room

After you make your reservation, asking one or two pointed questions can go a long way toward making sure you get the best room in the house. Always ask for a corner room. They're usually larger, quieter, and have more windows and light than standard rooms, and they don't always cost more. Also ask if the hotel is renovating; if it is, request a room away from the renovation work. Inquire, too, about the location of restaurants, bars, and discos in the hotel — all sources of annoying noise. And if you aren't happy with your room when you arrive, talk to the staff members at the front desk. If they have another room, they should be happy to accommodate you, within reason.

You can smoke outside in San Francisco to your heart's content, but be aware that the city has stringent antismoking laws inside public buildings, restaurants, and even bars. A sizable number of hotels, especially the smaller ones, are smoke-free. Other hotels have smoking rooms only on designated floors. Common courtesy in San Francisco is to ask before lighting up; you'd be surprised at the number of people who are allergic to smoke. If a smoking (or nonsmoking) room is important to you, let the reservations desk know when you call.

Arriving Without Reservations

I am amazed at how many people come to San Francisco without hotel reservations, believing that a fabulous $30-a-night room is awaiting them in a fancy hotel. They usually end up sleeping in a "No-Tell Motel" in a dicey neighborhood because that's all that was available. Or they spend the better part of a day looking for accommodations, wasting valuable vacation time searching for a bargain or, finally, just a room, when there are none to be had. Don't be one of those people. Reserve your vacation lodgings ahead of time.

However, if you're reading this book in the airport while waiting to board your flight to our fair city, you can try the following suggestions if you don't have a place to stay already:

✔ Call a free reservation service such as **San Francisco Reservations** (☎ **800-677-1570** or 510-628-4450; www.hotelres.com) or **California Reservations** (☎ **415-252-1107**).

✔ Make your way to a boutique hotel and hope the desk clerk takes pity on you. Most of the boutique properties in town are part of small, independent companies, and a good-hearted staff person may be willing to make some calls to sister hotels to help you secure a room.

✔ Find a friendly concierge you can leave your luggage with so you can look for a room in the neighborhood unencumbered. If the town appears to be booked solid (ask the desk clerk's opinion), don't be picky or cheap. You can always move the next day if something better opens up.

Getting the Most for Your Money

Every accommodation that I recommend in this book is marked with one to four dollar signs. Here's a quick breakdown of the price categories, and what amenities and services you should expect in each range. All rates are for a standard double-occupancy room, excluding taxes.

✔ **$ ($125 or less):** Accommodations in this category are often in older buildings that may show their age. Room service, laundry or dry cleaning, valet parking, and porters do not come with the package, but the rooms are carefully tended, and the properties themselves exhibit some charm. The least expensive rooms may not have their own bathrooms.

The rooms I recommend in this price category tend to be on the "cozy" side and are typically furnished with inexpensive bedspreads, towels, and curtains. You won't find irons, swank toiletries in the bathrooms, or robes in the closet. Air-conditioning is also considered a luxury, although you rarely need it in San Francisco. A concierge won't be at the ready to cater to your every whim, but most desk clerks are delighted to help you arrange tours, tickets for shows, and dinner reservations. Many of the budget hotels recommended here include continental breakfast in the room rate, making them especially good deals.

✔ **$$ ($126–$225):** In this price category, I recommend some wonderful, charming places with stylish (but still small) rooms, handsome lobbies, and good to great service. Antique armoires and marble-tiled bathrooms are standard issue in a few picks, but in general, these properties are for leisure travelers with minimal demands beyond comfort and appealing décor. A separate concierge desk is not always available, but the front desk staff is usually willing to make reservations and book tours. Parking is sometimes valet, but more often it's self-parking at lots up to 3 blocks away. Room service is usually nonexistent, although you will probably find a cafe or restaurant attached to the property. Make sure to inquire about extras such as bathrobes and Wi-Fi if those things are important to you. Often the more expensive suites are well equipped, but the low-end rooms won't have that all-important hair dryer unless you ask for it.

✔ **$$$ ($226–$350):** At this price, expect attentive service — usually including valet parking and porters — and larger rooms with finer fabrics and décor, including the de rigueur iPod docks and flat-panel TVs. Many properties in this range also have on-site StairMasters, and at least one has a pool. Although at the low end of this scale you may not find hand-milled soaps in the bathroom, at the high end, you'll feel pretty pampered.

When you're willing to pay this kind of money for a hotel, you probably have certain expectations. Make them known when you make your reservation. Don't wait until check-in to ask if you can receive faxes or if valet parking actually means a bellhop is going to fetch your car for you at 6 a.m.

✔ **$$$$ ($351 or more):** Your big bucks buy views, personal service, a chauffeured car to the Financial District, and high-thread-count linens. Be prepared for the well-trained staff to kowtow to you. Large rooms usually feature fancy products and thick terry robes in the mirrored bathroom, an iron in the closet, art on the walls, and, in some cases, umbrellas and flowers. Honor bars and baskets of overpriced goodies are also standard. For this much money, it would be a shame if you didn't spend some quality time in the hotel, fingering the drapes and calling down to the concierge desk for a weather report. Again, room rates are tied to location, with Nob Hill and Embarcadero properties charging whatever the market will bear.

San Francisco's Best Hotels

The Andrews Hotel
$–$$ **Union Square**

The services and location make this 48-room 1905 Victorian hotel a deal for singles or couples on a budget, although the rooms and bathrooms are pretty small, even by local standards. You do get a continental breakfast buffet provided on each floor, evening wine *gratis* at Café Fino, next door, and attractive, homey, wood-trimmed décor. Amiable receptionists serve double duty as concierge staff. You won't have air-conditioning or a tub in which to soak (most rooms have showers only), but you can open the windows. Amenities include fresh flowers and in-room VCRs; complimentary videos are available from the reception desk. Seriously consider spending the extra $20 per night on a sunny Bay King room like no. 403. Avoid the dark, tiny rooms ending in 08. If street noise keeps you awake, request a room in the rear of the building.

See map p. 96. 624 Post St., between Taylor and Jones streets, 2 blocks west of Union Square. ☎ *800-926-3739 or 415-563-6877. Fax: 415-928-6919.* www.andrews hotel.com. *Parking: $28. Rack rates: $109–$149. Ask about AARP and extended-stay discounts. AE, MC, V.*

Argonaut Hotel
$$$—$$$$ **North Beach/Fisherman's Wharf**

In an enviable position on the western side of the Cannery, this perky boutique hotel makes the innumerable chains around Fisherman's Wharf blush in comparison. Many of the heavily nautical-themed rooms have a view of either Alcatraz or the Golden Gate Bridge, while the less expensive interior rooms are touted as being quieter. Designers kept the 1907 brick walls and wooden beams in place, where possible, adding plantation shutters and using a palette of primary colors, which makes the place fun and attractive to families and visitors who want quality lodgings in this admittedly touristy area. Guest rooms are fairly spacious, but I was surprised at the ordinary-looking bathrooms with shallow tubs. Amenities are generous, including Aveda products, flat-panel TVs, DVD players, robes, well-stocked minibars, and coffeemakers. The hotel's restaurant, **Blue Mermaid,** serves all day and is better than average for wharf food.

See map p. 84. 495 Jefferson St., at Hyde Street. ☎ *866-415-0704 or 415-563-0800. Fax: 415-563-2800.* www.argonauthotel.com. *Parking: $39. Rack rates: $289–$389. Check Web site for special rates. AE, DC, DISC, MC, V.*

Castle Inn
$–$$$ **Russian Hill**

The Castle Inn is a good choice, away from Union Square and the worst traffic on Van Ness Avenue. Units at this convenient, friendly motel have maple furniture, in-room VCRs, microwave ovens, and small refrigerators. Rates include continental breakfast and Wi-Fi. Guests are within walking

Hotels near Union Square, SoMa, and Nob Hill

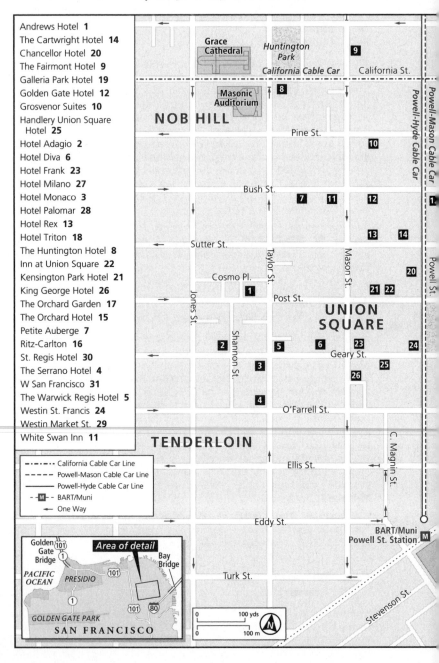

Andrews Hotel **1**
The Cartwright Hotel **14**
Chancellor Hotel **20**
The Fairmont Hotel **9**
Galleria Park Hotel **19**
Golden Gate Hotel **12**
Grosvenor Suites **10**
Handlery Union Square Hotel **25**
Hotel Adagio **2**
Hotel Diva **6**
Hotel Frank **23**
Hotel Milano **27**
Hotel Monaco **3**
Hotel Palomar **28**
Hotel Rex **13**
Hotel Triton **18**
The Huntington Hotel **8**
Inn at Union Square **22**
Kensington Park Hotel **21**
King George Hotel **26**
The Orchard Garden **17**
The Orchard Hotel **15**
Petite Auberge **7**
Ritz-Carlton **16**
St. Regis Hotel **30**
The Serrano Hotel **4**
W San Francisco **31**
The Warwick Regis Hotel **5**
Westin St. Francis **24**
Westin Market St. **29**
White Swan Inn **11**

- - - - - California Cable Car Line
- - - - Powell-Mason Cable Car Line
——— Powell-Hyde Cable Car Line
- M - - BART/Muni
← One Way

Grace Cathedral
Huntington Park
California Cable Car
California St.

Masonic Auditorium

NOB HILL

Pine St.

Bush St.

Sutter St.

Cosmo Pl.

Post St.

Taylor St.

Mason St.

Jones St.

Shannon St.

UNION SQUARE

Geary St.

O'Farrell St.

TENDERLOIN

Ellis St.

C. Magnin St.

Eddy St.

BART/Muni
Powell St. Station

Powell-Hyde Cable Car
Powell-Mason Cable Car
Powell St.

Golden Gate Bridge
Area of detail
Bay Bridge
PACIFIC OCEAN
PRESIDIO
GOLDEN GATE PARK
SAN FRANCISCO

Turk St.

0   100 yds
0   100 m

N

Stevenson St.

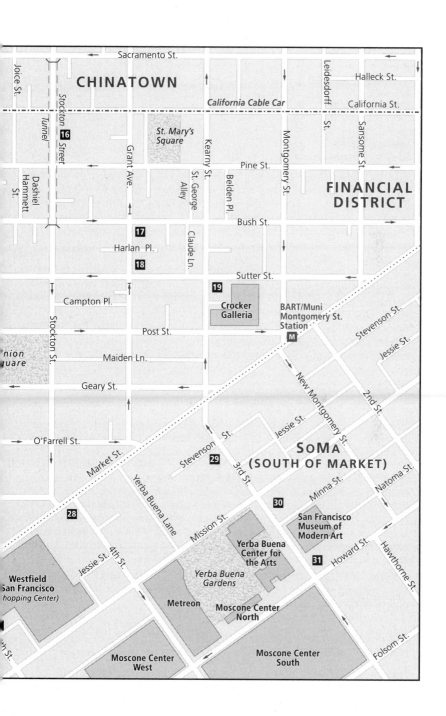

distance of Polk Street's bars and restaurants and Fisherman's Wharf. If you have a car to park and want to avoid the exorbitant garage fees in Union Square and around Fisherman's Wharf, the Castle Inn is a smart pick; but it's not so great if you want to be closer to shops and theater.

See map p. 84. 1565 Broadway, at Van Ness Avenue. ☎ *800-822-7853 or 415-441-1155. Fax: 415-775-2237.* www.castleinnsf.com. *Free parking. Rack rates: $85–$259. AE, CB, DC, DISC, MC, V.*

Chancellor Hotel
$$–$$$ Union Square

The 137-room Chancellor has been owned and managed by the same family since 1917 and offers a level of intimacy and value you just won't find in many other comparable inns. It's right on the Powell Street cable-car line, a handbag's throw from Saks Fifth Avenue. The little bathrooms are well stocked; the petite guest rooms are brightly decorated and comfortably furnished; and you get a choice of pillows. For views, request front rooms ending in 00 to 05, but aim for the higher floors — the garbage trucks start their rounds at 5 a.m., and you don't want to be near the street. Amenities include ceiling fans (instead of air-conditioning), and coffee and cookies at the front desk. The hotel restaurant serves breakfast and lunch and provides room service. Smoking is prohibited.

See map p. 96. 433 Powell St., between Post and Sutter streets. ☎ *800-428-4748 or 415-362-2004. Fax: 415-362-1403.* www.chancellorhotel.com. *Parking: $35. Rack rates: $178–$250. AAA, AARP discounts available. AE, DC, DISC, MC, V.*

Cow Hollow Motor Inn & Suites
$–$$$ The Marina/Cow Hollow

These serviceable, nonsmoking motel rooms, unfortunately reached by elevators inside the parking garage, are clean and quiet, thanks to a diligent staff and double-paned windows, respectively. The early Sears Roebuck furnishings may not yet have made a style comeback, but you'll appreciate the in-room coffeemakers, hair dryers, and relatively spacious bathrooms. What makes the Cow Hollow Motor Inn of particular interest, besides free parking, free Wi-Fi, and low rates, is that it's around the corner from the best blocks of Chestnut Street, where the shopping and dining set a high standard. Families can settle into one of six suites with kitchens and a separate entrance right on Chestnut Street. Try to avoid rooms ending in 28, which are next to noisy ice machines.

See map p. 84. 2190 Lombard St., at Steiner Street. ☎ *415-921-5800. Fax: 415-922-8515.* www.cowhollowmotorinn.com. *Free parking. Rack rates: $79–$145 double; $235–$285 suite. AE, MC, V.*

The Fairmont Hotel
$$$–$$$$ Nob Hill

I've always had a soft spot for the regal Fairmont because it's the first hotel I remember staying in when I was a child. I'm still bowled over when I stroll into the pillared, golden-colored lobby, which is usually humming with businesspeople and older leisure travelers. Depending on the time of year, you can get relatively decent rates (around $250), albeit in one of the "cozy" queens in the main building. These are the same size as similar rooms in the Tower building but don't have views and are priced accordingly. Tower rooms also have gorgeous marble tubs with separate showers; all guest rooms are filled with amenities. Make sure to have a drink in the kitschy **Tonga Room** and marvel at the regularly scheduled storms. If you have kids along, take advantage of the 5 to 7 p.m. happy hour, featuring a $9.50 all-you-can-eat Asian-inspired buffet — lots of young locals do. Should you be interested in a real San Francisco treat, you'll find it at the Fairmont, but if it's five-star treatment you're after, head for the Ritz or the St. Regis.

See map p. 96. 950 Mason St., at California Street. ☎ ***800-441-1414*** *or 415-772-5000.* www.fairmont.com. *Parking: $57. Rates: $259–$750 double. AE, CB, DC, DISC, MC, V.*

Golden Gate Hotel
$–$$ Union Square

If you're flexible (or broke) enough to share a bathroom, this cheerful, charming, 23-room Edwardian hotel with the feel of a B&B is a fabulous deal, in a great location for cable-car lovers and walkers. Traveling with older children? Take two of the small, pretty rooms, and buy yourself some privacy. Rates include continental breakfast and afternoon tea, which adds to the feeling that the Golden Gate is run for love rather than money. The property has a cat and a dog, so if you're allergic, this unfortunately isn't the spot for you. The hotel has no air-conditioning.

See map p. 96. 775 Bush St., between Powell and Mason streets, 2 blocks from the Chinatown gate. ☎ ***800-835-1118*** *or 415-392-3702. Fax: 415-392-6202.* www.golden gatehotel.com. *Self-parking: A relative bargain at $20. Rates: $95 (shared bathroom) or $150 (private bathroom) double. DC, MC, V.*

Grosvenor Suites
$–$$$ Nob Hill

Visitors who require the conveniences of home — laundry facilities, ample closets, and the ability to reheat leftovers — will be very pleased with these roomy nonsmoking studio and one-bedroom suites. The furnishings are, shall we say, a bit tired, but given the location, the tidy kitchenettes (in every room), the complimentary continental breakfast, and the views (sixth floor and up), it's a great value. The sole two-bedroom suite, complete with two bathrooms, is an especially terrific deal for families. An online cash rebate from the hotel's Web site reduces the tariff to bargain rates. Amenities are spare; bring your own iPod dock if necessary.

See map p. 96. 899 Pine St., between Mason and Powell streets. ☎ ***415-421-1899.*** *Fax: 415-982-1946.* www.grosvenorsuites.com. *Self-parking: $35. Rack rates: $119–$269. Ask about Internet specials. AE, CB, DC, JCB, MC, V.*

Handlery Union Square Hotel
$$–$$$ Union Square

This favorite with tour packagers happens to be one of the better family hotels near Union Square: It features a small, heated outdoor pool — a rarity in San Francisco — as well as Nintendo, if you consider that a positive. (And kids under 15 stay free!) The regular doubles with smallish bathrooms have been renovated, as has the lobby, but splash out on one of the larger Club Rooms in an adjacent building. They feature a dressing area, cozy robes, the morning paper, and extra space. The hotel's two-bedroom suites are also a good value, and refrigerators are provided on request. Rooms by the pool are quietest.

See map p. 96. 351 Geary St., between Powell and Mason streets, ½ block from Union Square. ☎ *800-843-4343 or 415-781-7800. Fax: 415-781-0269.* www.handlery.com. *Parking: $43. Rack rates: $139–$259. Ask about AAA discount; corporate, federal government, and senior citizen rates; and Internet specials. AE, CB, DC, JCB, MC, V.*

Harbor Court Hotel
$$$–$$$$ The Embarcadero

Located just steps from the bay, this Kimpton hotel is an especially romantic and sophisticated property, lower key than the Hotel Vitale but equally stylish. Rooms were remodeled in 2005, and although they are pretty small, they're so warmly decorated and comfy I can imagine moving in for a long weekend, stirring only to watch the yoga channel on the flat-screen TV. Reserve or upgrade to a queen or king bay room, which features dramatic views of the water and Bay Bridge. Guests have free access to the state-of-the-art Embarcadero YMCA pool and health club right next door. A complimentary wine reception takes place each evening, and afterward you can step into trendy **Ozumo,** which is accessible from the lobby.

See map p. 84. 165 Steuart St., between Mission and Howard streets. ☎ *866-792-6283 or 415-882-1300. Fax: 415-882-1313.* www.harborcourthotel.com. *Parking: $40. Rack rates: $209–$359. AE, CB, DC, DISC, MC, V.*

Hayes Valley Inn
$ Civic Center/Hayes Valley

In the not-so-distant past, I'd never have recommended spending the night in this neighborhood, but the upscale shopping and dining opportunities have developed to such an extent that they override any other concerns (such as panhandlers). Hotel choices are limited, but for budget travelers — or anyone who prefers to spend his or her dough on good meals or local designers — this 28-room Edwardian B&B is a find. Yes, you'll have to share the very clean toilets and showers, but you can brush your teeth at the sink/vanity in your sweetly decorated room. Expect to meet European tourists over cereal, bagels, orange juice, and coffee (included in the rates). Street-side rooms are larger but noisier. The Van Ness Muni station and F-Market streetcars are a few minutes' walk east. The Asian Art Museum, opera, ballet, and symphony are a few minutes north.

See map p. 84. 417 Gough St., near Hayes Street. ☎ ***800-930-7999*** *or 415-431-9131. Fax: 415-431-2585.* www.hayesvalleyinn.com. *Parking: Self-park in nearby lots. Rack rates: $76–$112 double. MC, V.*

Hilton San Francisco Financial District
$$–$$$$ **Financial District/Chinatown**

Given that I'm no booster of huge corporate hotels, you might wonder what a Hilton is doing in this chapter. Well, $45 million worth of remodeling plus brilliant views plus a solid gold location where Chinatown meets the Financial District meets North Beach turned my head. Ignore the façade and call in your frequent-guest chits for a bay view room (12th floor and higher). Yes, the décor is uninspiring and the bathrooms very small, but the beds are comfy, and wireless Internet access is free, unlike at Starwood's properties. The Tru Spa off the lobby is another selling point, as is easy parking. But dock your auto yourself in the Portsmouth Square Garage, across the street. You'll save enough on valet fees to pay for a massage. Look for deals here on Priceline.

See map p. 84. 750 Kearny St., at Washington Street. ☎ ***800-HILTONS*** *or 415-433-6600. Fax: 415-765-7891.* www.sanfranciscohiltonhotel.com. *Parking: $45. Rack rates: $189–$459 double. Ask about AAA discount; corporate, federal government, and senior citizen rates; and Internet specials. AE, CB, DC, DISC, MC, V.*

Hotel Adagio
$$–$$$ **Union Square**

In a previous incarnation, this 1929 Colonial Revival building housed the tired Shannon Court Hotel, but a total face-lift in 2003 turned Joan Crawford into Cindy Crawford. The Adagio's modern guest rooms and clean, masculine lines won't appeal to frill-seekers, but the hotel is closer in spirit to the W and the Clift (which is just down the block) — albeit more competitively priced. Sleek young things already jostle for space in the bar and a table in the *mucho caldo* **Cortez** restaurant (see Chapter 10). Because this is an older building, air-conditioning consists of ceiling fans and windows that open. A nicely fitted fitness center, complimentary high-speed and wireless Internet access, high-end bath products, complimentary coffee and tea, and executive-level guest rooms that come with views and continental breakfast bring the hotel squarely into the here and now.

See map p. 96. 550 Geary St., between Taylor and Jones streets. ☎ ***800-228-8830*** *or 415-775-5000. Fax: 415-775-9388.* www.jdvhotels.com/hotels/adagio. *Parking: $40. Rack rates: $189–$299. AE, CB, DC, DISC, MC, V.*

Hotel Bohème
$$ **North Beach/Fisherman's Wharf**

Set in the heart of North Beach, this charming, intimate hotel echoes the area's old bohemian feel. Fifteen small but romantic, beautiful rooms are vividly painted and have iron beds and generous in-room amenities, including free wireless. Teensy bathrooms have showers only, no tubs. The accommodating staff is happy to assist with tours, rental cars, and restaurant reservations; you'll have to schlep your own luggage up the narrow stairs, though. The hotel has no air-conditioning, but the windows open. You're likely to find a younger, less conservative crowd staying here than at the Washington Square Inn, another small hotel in this neighborhood and price range.

See map p. 84. 444 Columbus Ave., between Vallejo and Green streets. ☎ *415-433-9111. Fax: 415-362-6292.* www.hotelboheme.com. *Self-parking: $31 in a garage 1½ blocks away. Rack rates: $174–$194. AE, CB, DC, DISC, JCB, MC, V.*

Hotel Del Sol
$$–$$$ The Marina/Cow Hollow

Paint, mosaic tiles, and imagination can do a lot to reinvent a motel, and there's no better example than the Del Sol. You'll think you're in Southern California (after the fog lifts), except that you can walk around this neighborhood without getting startled looks from drivers. The heated pool and a hammock suspended between palm trees complete the hallucination. Multicolored, fun, reasonably sized guest rooms and suites could have stepped out of a '90s Habitat catalog, and one is configured especially for families, with games and bunk beds. The best parts: Parking is free, and you're not on busy Lombard Street.

See map p. 84. 3100 Webster St., at Filbert Street. ☎ *877-433-5765 or 415-921-5520. Fax: 415-931-4137.* www.thehoteldelsol.com. *Free parking. Rack rates: $139–$239. AE, DC, DISC, MC, V.*

Hotel Frank
$$–$$$$ Union Square

Formerly the Maxwell, this 100-year-old hotel was under renovation at press time, and new owner Personality Hotels was relaunching it as Hotel Frank. The guest rooms, which are either spacious and light or small and dark, depending on your pocketbook or the kindness of the desk clerk, no longer show signs of the old Art Deco décor. All feature flat-panel TVs suspended on brass poles, bold black-and-white carpeting, and a hanging light fixture that reminds me of a family of pygmy spaceships hovering above the landing site. I quite like it. The location, which isn't subject to updating, remains prime for shopping and nightlife. **Max's on the Square** provides room service. Be sure to check prices on the junior suites, especially off season.

See map p. 96. 386 Geary St., at Mason Street. ☎ *800-553-1900 or 415-986-2000. Fax: 415-397-2447.* www.hotelfranksf.com. *Parking: $28 valet, $26 at a nearby garage. Rack rates: $169–$469. Ask about packages and corporate discounts. AE, DC, DISC, MC, V.*

Hotel Griffon
$$$–$$$$ The Embarcadero

Once the homely sister among the boutique hotels in this area, the Griffon jazzed up its rooms in 2007, with tangerine-colored paint, new furniture, pillow-top mattresses, flat-panel TVs, and iPod docks. The original brick remains, as well as sink/vanity combos in some of the small guest rooms, but that's part of this hotel's boho charm. For those who require natural light, six end rooms plus two suites offer unsurpassed bay views; three city-side suites have decks. It's now a toss-up between the Griffon and the neighboring Harbor Court, but both have more personality than the Embarcadero Hyatt, and I like the location — very close to the water. A well-equipped YMCA (free for guests) is next door, and a good restaurant is off the lobby. Rates include continental breakfast and Wi-Fi. This is a nonsmoking hotel.

See map p. 84. 155 Steuart St., between Mission and Howard streets. ☎ *800-321-2201 or 415-495-2100. Fax: 415-495-3522.* www.hotelgriffon.com. *Parking: $40. Rack rates: $339–$699. AE, DC, DISC, MC, V.*

Hotel Kabuki
$$–$$$ Japantown

The beautifully calm Hotel Kabuki, redesigned and rechristened in 2007, has helped raise this little neighborhood outside the tourist fray to true destination status. An easy 10-minute bus ride from Union Square, the hotel is steps away from Fillmore Street's excellent boutiques, restaurants, and music clubs. If you love to take baths, this is the place for you: It features Japanese soaking tubs in many of the Eastern-themed rooms. And, if you take umbrage with panhandlers, most are down around Union Square. Corner rooms are nicest; suites are truly spacious. This is a nonsmoking property, and as at all Joie de Vivre hotels, Wi-Fi is free.

See map p. 84. 1625 Post St., between Laguna and Buchanan streets. ☎ *800-533-4567 or 415-922-3200. Fax: 415-614-5498.* www.hotelkabuki.com. *Self-parking: $25. Rack rates: $149–$300. AE, DC, DISC, MC, V.*

Hotel Milano
$–$$$ SoMa

This well-designed and -maintained Italian-themed boutique hotel isn't flashy or hip, but if you can get a rate under $150, you won't find a better value in SoMa. Amenities include a spacious on-site fitness room, a bar, and more floor space in your room than you'll find in other hotels in this price range. The multistory San Francisco Shopping Centre and new Westfield Centre are a few feet away, and Yerba Buena Gardens is just around the corner, covering your retail, restaurant, and cultural needs. Personally, I prefer the intimacy of this hotel to the atmosphere at the much larger Westin Market Street (2 blocks away), but if you're looking for a SoMa room with a view or a hotel with more services, the Westin is a better bet.

See map p. 96. 55 Fifth St., between Market and Mission streets. ☎ *800-398-7555 or 415-543-8555. Fax: 415-543-5885.* www.hotelmilanosf.com. *Parking: $35. Rack rates: $109–$209. AE, DC, DISC, MC, V.*

Hotel Monaco
$$$–$$$$ Union Square

You'll wish you'd brought your foxtail-trimmed scarf and vintage Vuitton steamer trunk when you sashay into the Art Deco–inspired Monaco. The medium-size rooms are lushly decorated with patterned wallpaper, floral prints, and canopied beds. All the amenities — like room service and a spa and fitness center — are available, plus it's a pet-friendly hotel. The aptly named **Grand Cafe** restaurant is next door. If you're feeling lonely, the hotel will deliver a bowl of goldfish to your room. If you're carting along the children, tell the desk staff — they provide milk and cookies for munchkins.

See map p. 84. 501 Geary St., at Taylor Street. ☎ **866-622-5284** *or 415-292-0100. Fax: 415-292-0111.* www.monaco-sf.com. *Parking: $49. Rack rates: $199–$579. AE, CB, DC, DISC, MC, V.*

Hotel Palomar
$$$–$$$$ SoMa

This extremely grown-up hotel sits above a busy corner close to Union Square and the attractions south of Market. The hotel was designed for sophisticated business and leisure travelers; you can expect a high-quality experience (at high-quality prices) in luxuriously sedate surroundings. The ample guest rooms are fitted for work and play, with multiline phones, fax machines, DVD players, free Wi-Fi, spa tubs, and L'Occitane products. There's room service, a tiny fitness center, and the **Fifth Floor,** one of the more glamorous restaurants in town. Hotel Palomar compares in price to its neighbor, the W. So what's the difference? The Palomar is what the W will be when it's all grown up. But the W is convinced it's having more fun.

See map p. 96. 12 Fourth St., at Market Street. ☎ **866-373-4941** *or 415-348-1111. Fax: 415-348-0302.* www.hotelpalomar-sf.com. *Parking: $42. Rack rates: $259–$429. Rates include morning paper and shoeshine. AE, DC, DISC, MC, V.*

Hotel Rex
$$–$$$ Union Square

Dorothy Parker fans will appreciate this 94-room delight, which, despite its artsy leanings, is warm and unpretentious. Listen to the cable cars clank by or peruse a book from the lobby library while drinking complimentary wine. The rooms are all smartly designed and decorated; they vary in size from smallish doubles to more ample executive kings. Amenities include CD players, free Wi-Fi, and **Café Andrée,** which serves room service, three squares, and Sunday brunch. The hotel hosts live jazz music on Friday night.

See map p. 96. 562 Sutter St., between Powell and Mason streets. ☎ **800-433-4434** *or 415-433-4434. Fax: 415-433-3695.* www.thehotelrex.com. *Parking: $35. Rack rates: $189–$249. Rates include evening wine. AE, DC, DISC, MC, V.*

Hotel Triton
$$–$$$ Union Square

The music of the Grateful Dead and/or their close personal friends blares from lobby speakers in this hip 'n happening ode to rock 'n' roll. Doubles are bite-size, but oh, baby, are they funky. This wacky (and smoke-free) place is heavy on playful style but also provides plenty of amenities, including Nintendo, gratis Wi-Fi, and happy hour with free wine and beer. To pay homage to the gods of abs, there's a small on-site fitness room. The fabulous location, across from Chinatown's Dragon Gate, makes standing outside on the sidewalk an exotic experience. Rooms ending in 07 are especially compact, so you probably want to avoid them.

See map p. 96. 342 Grant Ave., at Sutter Street, across from the Dragon Gate. ☎ *888-364-2622 or 415-394-0500. Fax: 415-394-0555.* www.hoteltriton.com. *Parking: $43. Rack rates: $199–$349. AE, CB, DC, DISC, MC, V. Well-behaved dogs welcome.*

Hotel Vitale
$$$–$$$$ The Embarcadero

If you consider yourself urbane yet earthy, practical yet appreciative of the better things in life, the Hotel Vitale has a room with your name on it. Expensive but not over-the-top extravagant, this contemporary property occupies the most coveted patch of earth in town — right across the boulevard from the Ferry Building. Spoiled by delicious views, guests can catch an F-Market streetcar right behind the building, which lies within walking distance of well-regarded restaurants and BART. Inside, it is a delight as well. You'll notice first how good the place smells (small vials with dried lavender grace the hallways), and attention to detail continues inside the guest rooms. Deluxe waterfront sanctuaries feature sexy walk-in showers rather than the skimpy tub/shower combos in the viewless (yet spacious) interior rooms. A spa with two outdoor soaking tubs and a daily yoga class provide centering.

See map p. 84. 8 Mission St., at Steuart Street. ☎ *888-890-8688 or 415-278-3700. Fax: 415-278-3750.* www.hotelvitale.com. *Parking: $45. Rack rates: $319–$775. AE, CB, DC, DISC, MC, V. Dog friendly and nonsmoking.*

The Huntington Hotel
$$$$ Nob Hill

The Boston Brahmin in you will adore this refined, quiet, nonsmoking oasis, with its subtle elegance, impeccable service, and a gorgeous spa. The 1924 building originally housed apartments, so guest rooms and bathrooms are larger than average; most are labeled suites. Rooms above the eighth floor have views; the ones below are extra spacious and have iPod docks and wireless Internet. Children are welcome in the hotel (but not in the pool or spa), and manicured Huntington Park, complete with a playground, is across the street. The staff, concierge included, will anticipate your every need. If you can afford to lay down the cash for a room here, you could also choose to stay at the Fairmont or Ritz-Carlton, the Huntington's Nob Hill neighbors, but I love the old-fashioned San Franciscan feel of the Huntington. If you want the total San Francisco experience, this is it. You'll certainly be pampered here, but if you're looking for something more glamorous and less old world, go with the Ritz.

See map p. 96. 1075 California St., at Taylor Street. ☎ *800-227-4683 or 415-474-5400. Fax: 415-474-6227.* www.huntingtonhotel.com. *Parking: $39. Rack rates: $325–$525 double; $625–$925 suites. AE, DC, DISC, MC, V.*

Hyatt Regency San Francisco
$$–$$$$ The Embarcadero

This enormous (you're likely to get lost looking for your room) corporate hotel at the foot of Market Street gets the thumbs up for its location close to the Ferry Building and the Embarcadero Center shops. For the money, however, I'd stay at the Harbor Court or Vitale. Rooms are well equipped and spacious, and some have beautiful views. The atrium lobby holds a restaurant, bar, and a few shops, and the hotel has a fitness center. This is probably your best bet for a hotel in the Embarcadero area if you're traveling with kids, who will love the glass elevators. Around the winter holidays, an outdoor ice skating rink is minutes from the lobby. If you won't need the car, self-park it in an Embarcadero Center lot for $30 per day.

See map p. 84. 5 Embarcadero Center, at Market Street. ☎ *800-233-1234 or 415-788-1234. Fax: 415-398-2567.* www.sanfrancisco.regency.hyatt.com. *Parking: $49. Rack rates: $195–$369. Corporate discounts available. AE, CB, DC, DISC, MC, V; personal checks from U.S. banks. Dogs welcome.*

Inn at Union Square
$$$–$$$$ Union Square

This small, very discreet hotel is just the ticket if you desire a bit of luxury but don't care to make a scene. You get those little extras — continental breakfast, newspapers, bathrobes, wine and cheese in the early evening, nice linens, 24-hour concierge, health-club access, complimentary Wi-Fi — combined with very reasonable rates that make it a pleasure to part with some, but not too much, of your money. Tasteful rooms range from small queens to two-room suites, and all have benefited from a recent tidying with new furniture, fabrics, and wallpaper. The hotel has no air-conditioning and bans smoking.

See map p. 96. 440 Post St., near Powell Street. ☎ *800-288-4346 or 415-397-3510. Fax: 415-989-0529.* www.unionsquare.com. *Parking: $36. Rack rates: $229–$389. AE, CB, DC, DISC, MC, V.*

Kensington Park Hotel
$$–$$$$ Union Square

This charming 92-room property, in the same 1925 Moorish-style building that houses the Post Street Theatre and the Elks Club, offers old–San

Francisco–style ambience and a convenient heart-of-the-city location for less cash than the St. Francis. The larger-than-average nonsmoking (and pet-friendly) rooms were renovated in the last two years. The marble bathrooms are already among the handsomest in the neighborhood. Request a Royal Court room for more space and better views. Workout facilities are available off-site, complimentary sherry and tea are served in the afternoon, Wi-Fi is free, and the staff is delightful. The hotel has no air-conditioning; rooms are equipped with ceiling fans.

See map p. 96. 450 Post St., between Mason and Powell streets. ☎ *800-553-1900 or 415-788-6400. Fax: 415-399-9484.* www.kensingtonparkhotel.com. *Parking: $35. Rack rates: $159–$389. AE, CB, DC, DISC, JCB, MC, V.*

The Marina Motel
$–$$ The Marina/Cow Hollow

Originally an apartment building, this funky, flower-bedecked, courtyard-style budget motel features 15 units (out of 38) with fully equipped kitchens. A granddaughter of the original owner redecorated the medium-sized studios with Italian bathroom tiles, Mission-style furniture, and pretty quilts, making this one of the few places on Lombard Street with even a hint of charm. Families can reserve two connecting rooms with a shared bathroom. Surprisingly, considering the location, rooms off the street are remarkably quiet. The front desk clerk will arrange tours or rental cars at your request. It is the definition of cheap and cheerful.

See map p. 84. 2576 Lombard St., near Divisadero Street. ☎ *800-346-6118 or 415-921-9406. Fax: 415-921-0364.* www.marinamotel.com. *Free parking in little garages on the premises. Rack rates: $75–$145; family room $89–$145; suites $89–$169. AE, MC, V. Dogs welcome.*

The Orchard Garden Hotel
$$–$$$ Union Square

California's first sustainable, energy-efficient hotel, designed and built to receive U.S. Green Building Council LEED certification, makes it easier being green. Some initiatives — such as in-room recycling and key cards that switch on the room lights — are more apparent than others (chemical-free cleaning products). The small, Wi-Fi-enabled, well-appointed rooms have larger-than-average bathrooms stocked with upscale organic Aveda products. Like its sister property, the Orchard Hotel, the nonsmoking Orchard Garden Hotel feels calm and low-key. It doesn't have much of a lobby, but there are a small bar and a restaurant with good food. If you want a livelier, more youthful atmosphere, the Hotel Triton (also near Chinatown's Dragon Gate) may suit you better; if you want an oasis after a hard day of sightseeing or even work, this is a feel-good pick.

See map p. 96. 466 Bush St., next to Chinatown's Dragon Gate. ☎ *888-717-2881 or 415-399-9807. Fax: 415-399-9817.* www.theorchardgardenhotel.com. *Parking: $38. Rack rates: $169–$299. AE, DC, MC, V.*

The Orchard Hotel
$$–$$$ Union Square

Opened in 2001, the sedate 105-room Orchard was built from scratch and boasts some of the largest guest rooms and most luxurious bathrooms in the neighborhood. It may have less va-va-voom than older, true boutique hotels such as Hotel Rex or the Serrano (yet oceans more than your Hiltons or Sheratons), but for sheer comfort, this is probably your best bet in this price range around Union Square. The conservatively decorated guest rooms will gratify business as well as vacation travelers. They have CD/DVD players, free high-speed Internet access, and top amenities, including room service, provided by the well-mannered and charming staff. Cable cars stop just around the corner.

See map p. 96. 665 Bush St., between Stockton and Powell streets. ☎ *888-717-2881 or 415-362-8878. Fax: 415-362-8088.* www.theorchardhotel.com. *Parking: $34. Rack rates: $229–$299. Rates include continental breakfast. AE, DC, MC, V.*

Petite Auberge
$$–$$$ Union Square

Romantics will find happiness here among the florals and French country effects. The high-end rooms are enormous, the less expensive rooms are cozy and have showers only, and all are comfortable. Along with a full breakfast served downstairs in the homey dining room, the hotel offers complimentary tea, wine, and hors d'oeuvres in the afternoon. Petite Auberge is well known and exceedingly popular, so if you want to experience the charms of a Provençal inn in the city, book well in advance.

See map p. 96. 863 Bush St., between Mason and Taylor streets. ☎ *800-365-3004 or 415-928-6000. Fax: 415-673-7214.* www.jdvhotels.com/hotels/petite_auberge. *Parking: $32. Rack rates: $149–$269. AE, DC, MC, V.*

The Ritz-Carlton
$$$$ Nob Hill

Okay, big spenders, here's your hotel. The Ritz takes posh to the extreme, and those who want to be treated like landed gentry will feel their money was well spent. After you settle into your beautiful, spacious nest (with Wi-Fi, flat-panel TVs, fancy showerheads, and 400-thread-count sheets, in case you were counting), you can swim in the indoor pool, exercise in the first-class fitness center, shop for antiques, and eat in a nationally renowned restaurant, all without ever leaving the cushy confines. There's no reason to skimp on anything less than a club lounge room; the lounge is the stage for a lavish buffet breakfast plus drinks and snacks throughout the day.

See map p. 96. 600 Stockton St., between Pine and California streets. ☎ *800-241-3333 or 415-296-7465. Fax: 415-291-0288.* www.ritzcarlton.com. *Parking: $59. Rack rates: Well, if you have to ask . . . $729–$8,500. Special-occasion packages available. AE, DC, DISC, MC, V.*

The St. Regis San Francisco
$$$$ SoMa

With the 40-story, purpose-built St. Regis on San Francisco's five-star scene, you can rest assured that pampering has reached, well, new heights. A distinctive presence on the skyline, the hotel (floors 22–40 are residences) is awash in understated, unquestionable great taste and comfort, from the handsome lobby bar to the lose-yourself-in-luxe guest rooms with deep soaking tubs, huge plasma TVs, and digitized remote control so one needn't rustle the high-thread-count sheets to close the window coverings or signal the butler. The fitness center and spa are among the best in town. I also like the fact that each floor holds just 18 rooms. Views begin on the eighth floor. The hotel's fine-dining room, **Ame** (see Chapter 10), is a destination in itself. All in all, the St. Regis is swell.

See map p. 96. 125 Third St., between Market and Mission streets. ☎ **415-284-4000.** *Fax: 415-284-4100.* www.starwoodhotels.com/stregis. *Parking: $52. Rack rates: $407–$749 double. AE, CB, DC, DISC, MC, V.*

The San Remo Hotel
$ North Beach/Fisherman's Wharf

Staying in this 1906 building is something like bunking at a pal's home, because you're going to have to share the bathrooms. Rooms are small but adorable (they look like something your grandmother may have done up — a long time ago), and guests are relaxed and friendly, thrilled to have found such a bargain close to the bay. The penthouse, with a private bathroom, is prized for its views. However, ambience from the low-income housing project on the next block may not be the sort you crave. Laundry facilities are available, and the **Fior d'Italia** (the country's oldest Italian restaurant) is downstairs. The rooms have no air-conditioning, televisions, or phones.

See map p. 84. 2237 Mason St., near Chestnut Street, 2 blocks from the Cannery. ☎ **800-352-7366** *or 415-776-8688. Fax: 415-776-2811.* www.sanremohotel.com. *Parking: $16–$17 at one of the two garages within 2 blocks. Rack rates: $70–$90. Penthouse $175–$185. AE, DC, JCB, MC, V.*

Serrano Hotel
$$–$$$ Union Square

A stellar example of what a boutique hotel should be, the Serrano is beautiful, relaxed, friendly, and well appointed. It's a terrific hotel for tourists as well as business travelers who don't mind sacrificing square footage for great value. The small rooms are full of color and amenities, and double-paned windows effectively reduce street noise. Guest rooms on upper floors even have city views. The Spanish Revival lobby is a gem — seating groups are arranged beneath the handsome beamed ceiling, and it's a convivial place in the early evening when complimentary wine is served and a tarot-card reader drops by to entertain. The pet-friendly hotel's only drawback, and it's minor, is the proximity to Ellis Street, which can seem dicey at times. In fact, it's just a 3-block walk to Union Square and 2 blocks to the Powell Street cable-car turnaround. **Ponzu,** the hotel's excellent restaurant, is a popular pretheater spot.

See map p. 96. 405 Taylor St., at O'Farrell Street. ☎ *866-289-6561 or 415-885-2500. Fax: 415-474-4879.* www.serranohotel.com. *Parking: $40. Rates: $179–$289. Check the Web site for packages. AE, DC, DISC, MC, V.*

Tuscan Inn
$$–$$$ North Beach/Fisherman's Wharf

The pet-friendly Best Western Tuscan is a welcome change from the rest of the chain hotels on Fisherman's Wharf. Personality doesn't abound, but the rooms are fairly large by local standards, and kids like the location. The concierge is enthusiastic and friendly, and all the amenities you expect, including free Wi-Fi, are available. At the early-evening wine reception, you can meet your neighbors. In warm weather, the hotel restaurant offers alfresco dining. The Argonaut Hotel, the Tuscan's only rival on the wharf in this comfort zone, outdoes this property in style, but I'll bet the rates here will be better.

See map p. 84. 425 North Point St., between Mason and Taylor streets. ☎ *800-648-4626 or 415-561-1100. Fax: 415-561-1199.* www.tuscaninn.com. *Parking: $38. Rack rates: $189–$279. Ask about AAA, corporate, and senior discounts. AE, CB, DC, DISC, MC, V.*

The Union Street Inn
$$–$$$ The Marina/Cow Hollow

This elegant B&B has five richly appointed rooms, a carriage house in the garden that affords extra privacy, and a choice location on a prime shopping street. If you want a bit less urban color, this is a fantastic and romantic retreat. The charming managers serve as concierge and cook a full breakfast as part of the package. Guest rooms are large, but beware of the steep stairs to the front door, which make this an impractical choice for anyone who has difficulty walking.

See map p. 84. 2229 Union St., between Fillmore and Steiner streets. ☎ *415-346-0424. Fax: 415-922-8046.* www.unionstreetinn.com. *Parking: $15 at a lot 1½ blocks away. Rack rates: $189–$329. AE, DISC, MC, V.*

W San Francisco
$$$–$$$$ SoMa

The recent redecoration of the lobby, bar, and guest rooms added a pleasing mellowness to the W, which still attracts hip, young business travelers. They generally head for the airport on Friday, leaving the playful Eastern-themed, moderate-sized rooms available to the rest of us. Marvel at the deluxe amenities, the iPod docking station, and the views (from the 15th floor) in the "spectacular" and corner "fabulous" rooms. A lap pool, fitness room, Bliss spa, restaurant, cafe, bar, room service, and well-trained staff add heft to an already solid package. Find free Wi-Fi on the second floor in the "library" corner.

See map p. 96. 181 Third St., at Howard Street. ☎ **877-946-8357** *or 415-777-5300. Fax: 415-817-7860.* www.whotels.com. *Parking: $49. Rack rates: $259–$2,500. AE, DC, DISC, JCB, MC, V. Dogs welcome.*

Washington Square Inn
$$–$$$ North Beach/Fisherman's Wharf

The European atmosphere in North Beach makes this little hotel a wonderful choice; and if you plan to walk the neighborhoods, you won't find a better location. Less expensive rooms are small, but amenities such as fresh flowers, continental breakfast, afternoon tea, and evening wine and hors d'oeuvres in the antiques-filled lobby make them a terrific deal. Recent upgrades include flat-screen televisions and free Wi-Fi. The staff will help you with your bags and assist with tour and dinner reservations. The hotel is nonsmoking and has a two-night minimum on weekends.

See map p. 84. 1660 Stockton St., at Filbert Street, across from Washington Square Park. ☎ **800-388-0220** *or 415-981-4220. Fax: 415-397-7242.* www.wsisf.com. *Parking: $20–$25. Rack rates: $169–$309. AE, DC, DISC, JCB, MC, V.*

The Westin St. Francis
$$$$ Union Square

It's all about location. A prime corner across from Union Square and a glittering, bustling lobby are what give the historic St. Francis its air of excitement and glamour. But underneath it all is a really big, impersonal hotel — albeit one with 24-hour room service, concierges, shops, dining opportunities (including ultraglam Michael Mina), and Westin's Heavenly beds. In any case, if you are here for the ambience, stick to the original (main) building. Its moderate-sized standard doubles, with their romantic antique chandeliers, have finally been updated. Bathrooms are on the small side, though. Ask for a view or a corner room to get some natural light, and avoid rooms by the ever-busy elevators. Deluxe and Grandview rooms are the best in the house, while the standard queens are just large enough for a single traveler. My suggestion is to stay at the Orchard Hotel and drop by the Westin St. Francis to ride in the glass elevator or spend $15 and enjoy the new unwind hour from 5 to 7 p.m. It offers local cheeses paired with local wines, and the people-watching is unparalleled.

See map p. 96. 335 Powell St., across from Union Square. ☎ **800-937-8461** *or 415-397-7000. Fax: 415-774-0124.* www.westinstfrancis.com. *Parking: $49. Rack rates: $389–$489. AE, DC, DISC, JCB, MC, V.*

White Swan Inn
$$–$$$ Union Square

The 26 spacious guest rooms in this English-style B&B are designed to be lingered in. You'll want to take advantage of the four-poster beds and fireplaces. Rates include continental breakfast buffet, afternoon tea, and evening wine and hors d'oeuvres served downstairs in the parlor. You'll think you're visiting a well-to-do British aunt. Back rooms are sunnier; the queen rooms have showers only. As at the neighboring Petite Auberge, advance reservations are imperative here, and smoking is not allowed.

See map p. 96. 845 Bush St., between Mason and Taylor streets. ☎ *800-999-9570 or 415-775-1755. Fax: 415-775-5717.* www.jdvhotels.com/hotels/white_swan_inn. *Parking: $32. Rack rates: $179–$289. AE, DC, MC, V.*

Runner-up hotels

Having trouble finding a bed? If the hotels listed earlier in this chapter are full, try booking one of the following accommodations. They may have saved you some room.

Galleria Park Hotel

$$–$$$$ **Union Square**   This is a pleasant, small hotel in a convenient location close to Chinatown, the Financial District, and Union Square. Unlike most downtown properties, it has on-site parking, which is handy for travelers who need quick access to their vehicles. An update completed in 2007 added free Wi-Fi, luxury linens, and a restful, modern teal-and-brown color scheme. Interior rooms are a bit dark, but quieter than streetside doubles. *See map p. 96. 191 Sutter St., at Kearny Street.* ☎ *800-792-9639 or 415-781-3060. Fax: 415-433-4409.* www.galleriapark.com. *Parking: $35. Rack rates: $169–$509. AE, CB, DC, DISC, MC, V.*

Hotel Diva

$$–$$$$ **Union Square**   Traveling with small children? This hotel's 2-room "Little Divas Suite," complete with bunk beds, dress-up clothes, and a pint-size sink, may ruin them for ordinary digs. Grown-up rooms are a bit edgy for me, but the signature rolled-steel headboard and black leather couches may seduce you. It has a good location, room service, complimentary Wi-Fi, helpful staff, and a Salon Floor with upgraded amenities, including continental breakfast. *See map p. 96. 440 Geary St., near Mason and Taylor streets.* ☎ *800-553-1900 or 415-202-8700. Fax: 415-885-3268.* www.hotel diva.com. *Parking: $35. Rack rates: $159–$439. Check Web site for deals. AE, DC, DISC, JCB, MC, V.*

King George Hotel

$$ **Union Square**   The King George's guest rooms are minuscule, as are the bathrooms, but the entire hotel was nicely remodeled in 2002, and the guest rooms recently received new soft goods and a paint job. They even have free Wi-Fi. The bar is exceedingly low-key and pleasant — the proper English tea, served on weekends, is popular enough to require reservations. The staff is terrific. Guest rooms for smokers are available. Check the Web site for deals that drop the room rate as low as $109. *See map p. 96. 334 Mason St., at Geary Street.* ☎ *415-781-5050. Fax: 415-391-6976.* www.kinggeorge.com. *Self-parking: $28–$32. Rack rates: $149–$189. AE, CB, DC, DISC, JCB, MC, V.*

Larkspur Hotel Union Square

$$–$$$$ **Union Square** This pleasant hotel, formerly the Cartwright, just emerged from renovations, but some aspects, such as room size, can't be modified. Standard guest rooms are on the small side (reserve a deluxe king if you're claustrophobic); the two-bedroom suites will suit a family. Along with high-end in-room amenities, there's free Wi-Fi and an afternoon wine reception. European in feel, the well-managed, pet-friendly hotel is convenient to Union Square and Chinatown and has a friendly, helpful staff. *See map p. 96. 524 Sutter St., near Powell Street.* ☎ *800-919-9779 or 415-421-2865. Fax: 415-398-6345.* www.larkspurhotelunionsquare.com. *Parking: $27–$44. Rack rates: $169–$349 double. Check Web site for discounts. AE, DC, DISC, MC, V.*

Warwick San Francisco Hotel

$–$$$$ **Union Square** Formerly the Warwick Regis, this is the closest you can get to a French chateau downtown. If circa–Louis XVI armoires, brocade fabrics, crown-canopied beds, and marble-tiled bathrooms get your heart racing, you're going to adore this hotel. Twice-daily house-keeping, fresh flowers, great amenities, a restaurant/bar, and 24-hour room service complement the intimate atmosphere. Smoking rooms are available. *See map p. 96. 490 Geary St., at Taylor Street.* ☎ *800-827-3447 or 415-928-7900. Fax: 415-441-8788.* http://warwicksf.com. *Parking: $35. Rack rates: $119–$359. AE, DC, DISC, JCB, MC, V.*

The Westin Market Street

$$–$$$ **SoMa** Formerly the Argent, this Westin is a sizable convention hotel. All of the larger-than-average rooms have been updated with signature Heavenly beds and new furniture. What earns it a place in this chapter, besides a stellar location near Yerba Buena Gardens and the Museum of Modern Art, are the nearly floor-to-ceiling windows providing great views from rooms and suites above the 14th floor. A restaurant, fitness center, sauna, and pretty garden also help. *See map p. 96. 50 Third St., near Market Street.* ☎ *888-627-8561 or 415-974-6400. Fax: 415-543-8268.* www.westinsf.com. *Parking: $46. Rack rates: $179–$349. Check Web site for deals. AE, DC, DISC, JCB, MC, V.*

Index of Accommodations by Neighborhood

The Marina Motel ($–$$)
The Union Street Inn ($$–$$$)

Nob Hill
The Fairmont Hotel ($$$–$$$$)
Grosvenor Suites ($–$$$)
The Huntington Hotel & Nob Hill Spa
($$$$)
The Ritz-Carlton ($$$$)

North Beach/Fisherman's Wharf
Argonaut Hotel ($$$–$$$$)
Hotel Bohème ($$)
The San Remo Hotel ($)
Tuscan Inn ($$–$$$)
Washington Square Inn ($$–$$$)

Russian Hill
Castle Inn ($–$$$)

SoMa
Hotel Milano ($–$$$)
Hotel Palomar ($$$–$$$$)
St. Regis San Francisco ($$$$)
W San Francisco ($$$–$$$$)

The Westin Market Street ($$–$$$)

Union Square
Andrews Hotel ($–$$)
Chancellor Hotel ($$–$$$)
Galleria Park Hotel ($$–$$$$)
Golden Gate Hotel ($–$$)
Handlery Union Square Hotel ($$–$$$)
Hotel Adagio ($$–$$$)
Hotel Diva ($$–$$$$)
Hotel Frank ($$–$$$$)
Hotel Monaco ($$$–$$$$)
Hotel Rex ($$–$$$)
Hotel Triton ($$–$$$)
Inn at Union Square ($$$–$$$$)
Kensington Park Hotel ($$–$$$$)
King George Hotel ($$)
Larkspur Hotel Union Square
($$–$$$$)
The Orchard Garden Hotel ($$–$$$)
The Orchard Hotel ($$–$$$)
Petite Auberge ($$–$$$)
Serrano Hotel ($$–$$$)
Warwick San Francisco Hotel ($–$$$$)
The Westin St. Francis ($$$$)
White Swan Inn ($$–$$$)

Index of Accommodations by Price

$
Andrews Hotel (Union Square)
Castle Inn (Russian Hill)
Cow Hollow Motor Inn & Suites (The
Marina/Cow Hollow)
Golden Gate Hotel (Union Square)
Grosvenor Suites (Nob Hill)
Hayes Valley Inn (Civic Center/Hayes
Valley)
Hotel Milano (SoMa)
The Marina Motel (The Marina/Cow
Hollow)
The San Remo Hotel (North
Beach/Fisherman's Wharf)
Warwick San Francisco Hotel (Union
Square)

$$
Andrews Hotel (Union Square)
Castle Inn (Russian Hill)
Chancellor Hotel (Union Square)
Cow Hollow Motor Inn & Suites (The
Marina/Cow Hollow)
Galleria Park Hotel (Union Square)
Golden Gate Hotel (Union Square)
Grosvenor Suites (Nob Hill)
Handlery Union Square Hotel (Union
Square)
Hilton San Francisco Financial District
(Financial District/Chinatown)
Hotel Adagio (Union Square)
Hotel Bohème (North
Beach/Fisherman's Wharf)

Hotel Del Sol (The Marina/Cow Hollow)
Hotel Diva (Union Square)
Hotel Frank (Union Square)
Hotel Kabuki (Japantown)
Hotel Milano (SoMa)
Hotel Rex (Union Square)
Hotel Triton (Union Square)
Hyatt Regency San Francisco (The Embarcadero)
Kensington Park Hotel (Union Square)
King George Hotel (Union Square)
Larkspur Hotel Union Square (Union Square)
The Marina Motel (The Marina/Cow Hollow)
The Orchard Garden Hotel (Union Square)
The Orchard Hotel (Union Square)
Petite Auberge (Union Square)
Serrano Hotel (Union Square)
Tuscan Inn (North Beach/Fisherman's Wharf)
The Union Street Inn (The Marina/Cow Hollow)
Warwick San Francisco Hotel (Union Square)
Washington Square Inn (North Beach/Fisherman's Wharf)
The Westin Market Street (SoMa)
White Swan Inn (Union Square)

$$$

Argonaut Hotel (North Beach/Fisherman's Wharf)
Castle Inn (Russian Hill)
Chancellor Hotel (Union Square)
Cow Hollow Motor Inn & Suites (The Marina/Cow Hollow)
The Fairmont Hotel (Nob Hill)
Galleria Park Hotel (Union Square)
Grosvenor Suites (Nob Hill)
Handlery Union Square Hotel (Union Square)
Harbor Court Hotel (The Embarcadero)
Hilton San Francisco Financial District (Financial District/Chinatown)

Hotel Adagio (Union Square)
Hotel Del Sol (The Marina/Cow Hollow)
Hotel Diva (Union Square)
Hotel Frank (Union Square)
Hotel Griffon (The Embarcadero)
Hotel Kabuki (Japantown)
Hotel Milano (SoMa)
Hotel Monaco (Union Square)
Hotel Palomar (SoMa)
Hotel Rex (Union Square)
Hotel Triton (Union Square)
Hotel Vitale (The Embarcadero)
Hyatt Regency San Francisco (The Embarcadero)
Inn at Union Square (Union Square)
Kensington Park Hotel (Union Square)
Larkspur Hotel Union Square (Union Square)
The Orchard Garden Hotel (Union Square)
The Orchard Hotel (Union Square)
Petite Auberge (Union Square)
Serrano Hotel (Union Square)
Tuscan Inn (North Beach/Fisherman's Wharf)
The Union Street Inn (The Marina/Cow Hollow)
W San Francisco (SoMa)
Warwick San Francisco Hotel (Union Square)
Washington Square Inn (North Beach/Fisherman's Wharf)
The Westin Market Street (SoMa)
White Swan Inn (Union Square)

$$$$

Argonaut Hotel (North Beach/Fisherman's Wharf)
The Fairmont Hotel (Nob Hill)
Galleria Park Hotel (Union Square)
Harbor Court Hotel (The Embarcadero)
Hilton San Francisco Financial District (Financial District/Chinatown)
Hotel Diva (Union Square)
Hotel Frank (Union Square)
Hotel Griffon (The Embarcadero)

Hotel Monaco (Union Square)
Hotel Palomar (SoMa)
Hotel Vitale (The Embarcadero)
The Huntington Hotel (Nob Hill)
Hyatt Regency San Francisco (The Embarcadero)
Inn at Union Square (Union Square)
Kensington Park Hotel (Union Square)
Larkspur Hotel Union Square (Union Square)

St. Regis San Francisco (SoMa)
The Ritz-Carlton (Nob Hill)
W San Francisco (SoMa)
Warwick San Francisco Hotel (Union Square)
The Westin St. Francis (Union Square)

Chapter 10

Dining and Snacking in San Francisco

*W*hether you're a genuine gourmet or a fledgling foodie, San Francisco has more culinary options than you can shake a nice bunch of organic basil leaves at. But no matter where you rank yourself on the scale of serious eating, there's no excuse to waste a meal in this city. Fast-food counters, chain restaurants, marketing enterprises masquerading as dining establishments — you'll find them here, but do yourself a favor and pass 'em by. Instead, take advantage of the fresh, local ingredients and skilled chefs that keep San Francisco in the culinary spotlight, and I guarantee you'll dine to your heart's content.

Getting the Dish on the Local Scene

Restaurants debut in this town with great hoopla, but what's hot today may be out of business by the time you turn this page. At the moment, the newest trend is sharing. I don't mean spilling your life story — I mean sharing plates of food with your tablemates. Although this isn't news in your average Chinese restaurant, it is in other eateries, so if you sup at Restaurant Lulu, for example, be advised that those hefty portions really are meant for the entire party. On the other end of the spectrum, small plates, an offshoot of the Spanish penchant for tapas, are still the rage, and they, too, are meant to be shared. This can get nasty if three plump scallops arrive and you're part of a party of four, so try to dine with at least one vegetarian or be prepared to cover the tabletop with a lot of little dishes. And, speaking of tables, communal ones crop up in lots of new dining rooms. I don't know if this is supposed to promote fellowship or save space, but for lone diners, large parties, or couples who are looking for fresh conversationalists, your table is ready.

San Francisco Dining

A-16 **3**
Absinthe **40**
Ame **23**
B-44 **22**
Bechelli's **2**
Bistro Aix **4**
Blue Bottle Café **25**
Bodega Bistro **29**
Boulevard **17**
Brenda's French Soul Food **30**
Butterfly **8**
Cafe du Nord **37**
Canteen **28**
Chow **35**
Citizen Cake **41**
City View **20**
Colibri Mexican Bistro **26**
Cortez **27**
Dino's Pizzeria **46**
Ducca **24**
Gold Mountain **12**
Greens **5**
Hayes Street Grill **39**
Hog Island Oyster Company **15**
Home **36**
Isa **4**
Jardinière **42**
Kokkari Estiatoria **14**
Le Charm **31**
Lichee Garden **11**
L'Osteria del Forno **10**
Lulu **32**
Mamacita **1**
Miller's East Coast Delicatessen **6**
Quince **44**
R&G Lounge **21**
Restaurant Gary Danko **7**
The Slanted Door **15**
SPQR **45**
supperclub **33**
Tadich Grill **19**
Teatro Zin Zanni **9**
1300 **43**

Tommaso's **13**
Town's End **34**
Town Hall **18**
Yank Sing **16**
Yoshi's **43**
Zuni Café **38**

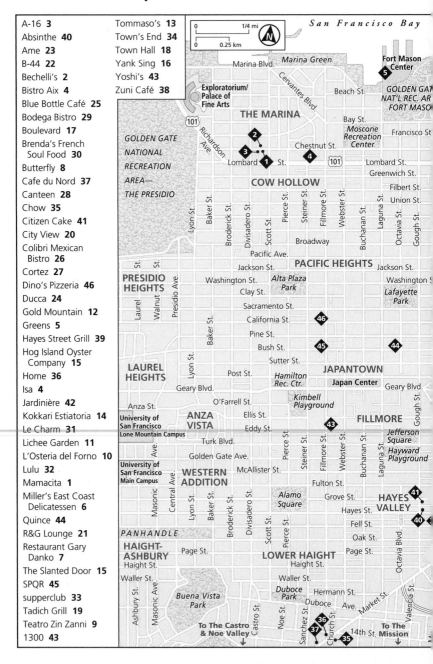

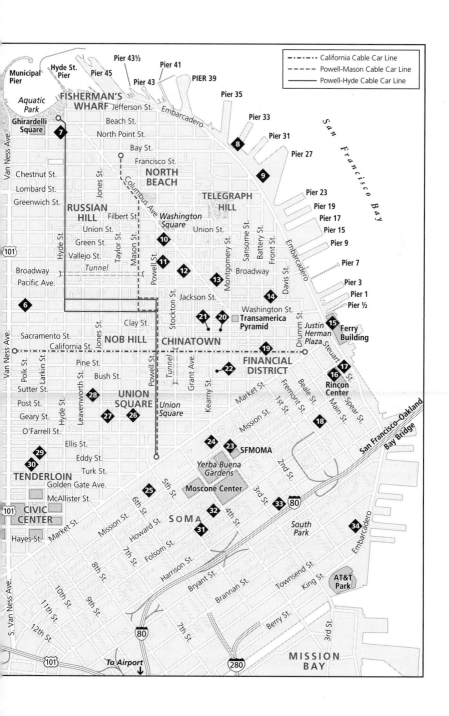

Municipal Pier

Hyde St. Pier

Pier 45

Pier 43½

Pier 43

Pier 41

PIER 39

Pier 35

Pier 33

Pier 31

Pier 27

Aquatic Park

FISHERMAN'S WHARF

Jefferson St.

Embarcadero

Beach St.

North Point St.

Bay St.

Ghirardelli Square

7

Van Ness Ave.

Chestnut St.

Lombard St.

Greenwich St.

Francisco St.

NORTH BEACH

8

9

101

RUSSIAN HILL

Filbert St.

Washington Square

TELEGRAPH HILL

Union St.

Jones St.

Columbus Ave.

Union St.

Green St.

Vallejo St.

Hyde St.

Taylor St.

Mason St.

Powell St.

Sansome St.

Battery St.

Front St.

Davis St.

Embarcadero

San Francisco Bay

Pier 23

Pier 19

Pier 17

Pier 15

Pier 9

Pier 7

Pier 3

Pier 1

Pier ½

10

Broadway

Pacific Ave.

Tunnel

11

12

13

Broadway

14

6

Jackson St.

Clay St.

Sacramento St.

California St.

NOB HILL

CHINATOWN

Washington St.

Transamerica Pyramid

21

20

Justin Herman Plaza

15

Ferry Building

19

Van Ness Ave.

Polk St.

Larkin St.

Jones St.

Pine St.

Bush St.

Stockton St.

Tunnel

Grant Ave.

Powell St.

FINANCIAL DISTRICT

22

Drumm St.

Steuart St.

17

16

Rincon Center

Sutter St.

Post St.

Geary St.

O'Farrell St.

Leavenworth St.

Hyde St.

28

UNION SQUARE

Union Square

Kearny St.

Market St.

Mission St.

1st St.

Fremont St.

Beale St.

Main St.

Spear St.

18

27

26

Ellis St.

Eddy St.

Turk St.

29

30

TENDERLOIN

Golden Gate Ave.

24

23

SFMOMA

Yerba Buena Gardens

2nd St.

San Francisco–Oakland Bay Bridge

McAllister St.

101

CIVIC CENTER

Hayes St.

Market St.

25

5th St.

6th St.

Moscone Center

SOMA

Howard St.

Mission St.

7th St.

Folsom St.

4th St.

3rd St.

32

31

33

80

South Park

34

Harrison St.

8th St.

9th St.

Bryant St.

Brannan St.

Townsend St.

King St.

AT&T Park

S. Van Ness Ave.

10th St.

11th St.

12th St.

80

7th St.

Berry St.

3rd St.

MISSION BAY

101

To Airport

280

----- California Cable Car Line

- - - - Powell-Mason Cable Car Line

———— Powell-Hyde Cable Car Line

Finding the trendiest tables

San Francisco has no lack of sizzling white-tablecloth restaurants. Getting last-minute reservations at **Restaurant Gary Danko** (☎ 415-749-2060), **Ame** (☎ 415-284-4040), or **Quince Restaurant** (☎ 415-775-8500;** see listings later in this chapter) is tough. Call ahead — way, way ahead — if you have your heart set on supping at these bastions of chic. Equally challenging is wrangling a table at the always-sublime **Dining Room at the Ritz-Carlton** (☎ 415-773-6168), where Ron Siegel (the kitchen god who bested the Japanese television phenom "Iron Chef") is at the helm. And despite the increase to 200 seats with the move to the Ferry Building, the wait for dinner at the **Slanted Door** (☎ 415-861-8032; see listing later in this chapter) is three weeks. You might try for lunch at the bar instead. For anyone traveling to Yountville to eat at the **French Laundry** (☎ 707-944-2380), one of the most coveted reservations in the country, bookings are accepted two months to the day in advance. OpenTable.com (see "Making reservations," later in this chapter) has exactly two tables available online, with a separate page devoted to the reasons you're going to get frustrated getting your hands on one. Determined eaters who can't wait to spend $240 on a prix fixe (okay, it's an amazing experience) should mark their calendars and exercise their dialing fingers, while giving OpenTable.com a try as well. Or forget about it and eat at Keller's **Ad Hoc** (☎ 707-944-2487; see Chapter 14).

Cooking up San Francisco cuisine

International influences are the inspiration for most Bay City menus. This is not odd considering the ethnic makeup of the city's population, but it may throw you for a loop when your menu runs the gamut from East to West with a little Southern comfort thrown in for good measure. Restaurants serving tapas are the keenest to take advantage of various culinary styles, and it's a clever way for a young chef to show his or her stuff. These small plates are also a pleasing way to order a meal. You don't have to choose between dishes that sound equally appealing, because the prices are low enough, and the portions modest enough, to sample them all.

With its emphasis on local, organic, and sustainable ingredients, California cuisine will always have a presence here, although it's being usurped by Modern American or New American cuisine. California cuisine features fresh, seasonal ingredients prepared in simple and light ways. New American cuisine also uses seasonal ingredients, but whatever foreign cuisines interest the chef also influence the preparations. Although the subtleties may be lost on you if you don't deconstruct your meals, I mention this because many new restaurants describe their cooking in these terms.

Another welcome dining trend has to do with accommodating the organizationally challenged. Many excellent restaurants in town, including **Boulevard** and **Restaurant Gary Danko** (see listings later in this chapter), accommodate walk-ins with counter seats or service in their bar

Dining near North Beach and Chinatown

Cafe Zoetrope **11**
Capp's Corner **5**
City View **12**
Gold Mountain **8**
Il Pollaio **3**

Lichee Garden **7**
Liguria Bakery **1**
L'Osteria del Forno **4**
Mario's Bohemian
  Cigar Store **2**

Molinari Delicatessen **9**
R&G Lounge **13**
Tommaso's **10**
Victoria Pastry Co. **6**

Dining near Union Square, SoMa, and Nob Hill

Ame **19**
B-44 **14**
Café de la Presse **10**
Café Mason **9**
Canteen **4**
Colibri Mexican Bistro **8**
Cortez **5**
Dottie's True Blue Cafe **7**
Ducca **18**
Grand Cafe **7**
Harry Denton's
  Starlight Room **3**
Kokkari Estiatorio **11**
Mixt Greens **15**
Palio Paninoteca **12**
Plouf **14**
Shalimar **6**
Specialty's Café
  & Bakery **17**
Tadich Grill **13**
Top of the Mark **1**
Town Hall **16**
Uncle Vito's Pizzadelli **2**

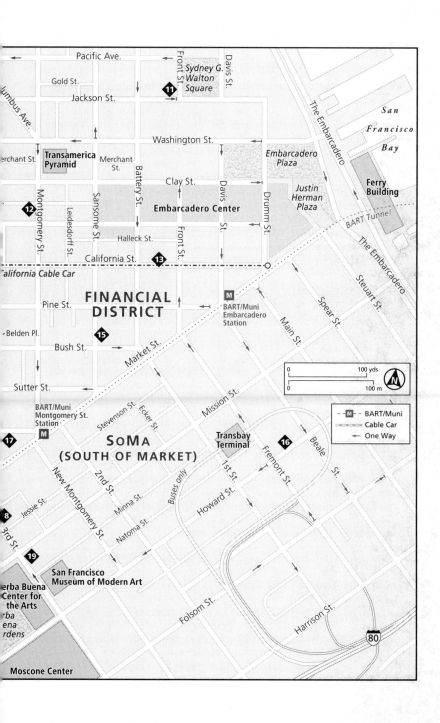

areas. This is your best chance to eat at these top spots if you don't have reservations.

Making reservations

If you really want to experience some high-profile restaurants while you're in town, make sure you book a table before you get here. It's not that the hostess takes pleasure in turning you away on a Friday at 8 p.m. — but did you notice all the other people drinking in the bar who also thought they could amble in and get seated?

Besides picking up the phone, you can contact a vast number of restaurants through the **OpenTable** Web site (www.opentable.com). I've used this free Internet site many times, always with excellent results. You may also put your hotel concierge to work by requesting that he assist you with dinner reservations. If you're really desperate, you can show a little chutzpah like my old friend Josephine, who has been known to march up to the host, look him in the eye, and announce she has reservations, even when that's not entirely accurate. The caveat is to make sure your dining partners don't buckle under pressure.

Exploring the dining zones

Cafes and restaurants often congregate on certain blocks, making it easy to stroll down the street until an enticing odor or empty table calls out to you. One of my absolute favorite dining destinations is pedestrian-only **Belden Place** in the Financial District, a 1-block alley off Bush and Pine streets between Kearny and Montgomery. Weekdays, in good weather, the outdoor tables are coveted lunch spots. Two standouts on multicultural Belden are **Plouf** (☎ 415-986-6491), a delightful French restaurant specializing in fish and shellfish, and **B-44** (☎ 415-986-6287; see listing later in this chapter), a Spanish charmer specializing in paella and Catalan dishes. **North Beach** is awash in Italian cafes, Italian restaurants of all persuasions, and some inexpensive little eateries. The family-style **Capp's Corner,** 1600 Powell St., at Green Street (☎ 415-989-2589), is almost the last of the breed, where complete meals are no understatement. You order a bottle of Chianti and watch as your table fills with bread and a tureen of minestrone, a salad featuring iceberg lettuce, followed by a huge serving of penne, and then a main course if you've ordered one. Spumoni's for dessert, natch.

The **Mission District** gourmet ghetto continues to explode, especially around Valencia and 16th streets, where you'll find the popular creperie **Ti Couz,** 3108 16th St. (☎ 415-252-7373), and **Bar Tartine,** 561 Valencia St. (☎ 415-487-1600), the Cal-Med brasserie opened by the brilliant team from **Tartine Bakery** at 18th and Guerrero streets (☎ 415-487-2600). Mexican-food lovers should try **Pancho Villa,** 3071 16th St., at Valencia Street (☎ 415-864-8840), which draws a crowd with its fresh, inexpensive burritos, tacos, and specialty platters, or **Taqueria Cancun,** 2288 Mission St., between 18th and 19th streets (☎ 415-252-9560), which stays open until 2 a.m. on weekends. The mood in this neighborhood is

The Mission District

BARS & CLUBS
Blondie's Bar & No Grill **3**
Doc's Clock **27**
El Rio **31**
Elbo Room **6**
Latin American Club **23**
Make-Out Room **29**
Revolution Café **24**
Roccapulco **30**
12 Galaxies **26**

DINING
Bar Tartine **4**
The Blue Plate **32**
Burger Joint **12**
Delfina **10**
Dosa **18**
Farina **8**
Foreign Cinema **25**
Luna Park **7**
Pancho Villa **2**
Pizzeria Delfina **10**
Range **15**
Ritual Coffee Roasters **19**
Taqueria Cancun **11**
Tartine Bakery **9**
Ti Couz **1**

PERFORMING ARTS
The Marsh **21**
Theatre Artaud **5**

SHOPPING
City Art **14**
Dema **20**
Encantada Gallery of Fine Arts **17**
Laku **22**
Little Otsu **16**
Paxton Gate **13**
Skechers USA **28**

casual and urban; it's home to students, artists, a large Hispanic community, and a fair number of street people. Parking requires patience and luck, but there's a BART stop at 16th and Mission — a rather dicey station, so you may want to take a cab home.

You can take the N-Judah streetcar to Irving Street and Ninth Avenue, near Golden Gate Park, to find another great couple of blocks of moderately priced, high-quality restaurants. **Chow,** 215 Church St. (☎ 415-552-2469; see listing later in this chapter), has a location here, and the good Japanese and Thai restaurants nearby include **Ebisu,** 1283 Ninth Ave. (☎ 415-566-1770).

Discovering off-the-beaten-track restaurants

Restaurants are mining new territory, as evidenced by the dozens of places opening in neighborhoods most visitors would have shunned once upon a time. The blocks around **Dolores, Valencia,** and **Guerrero streets** in the **Mission District** from 16th to 23rd streets are just one example. Storefronts and former corner markets have become the domain of chefs hoping to create the next big thing. **Delfina,** 3621 18th St., at Guerrero Street (☎ 415-552-4055; see listing later in this chapter), is one of the area's pioneers. If you can't wrangle a table there, line up at **Dosa** (☎ 415-642-3672; see listing later in this chapter) for South Indian cuisine, or **Farina,** 3560 18th St., at Guerrero Street (☎ 415-565-0360). The handkerchiefs of house-made pasta are the stuff of dreams.

Glen Park, a little neighborhood not far from the outer Mission, is most definitely off the tourist track. It's so easy to reach, however, that if you're staying anywhere near a BART station, you're practically there already. Simply head south from the Embarcadero and exit at the Glen Park stop. You are now 1 to 2 blocks from some excellent eating. Join the line waiting for a table at **Gialina,** 2842 Diamond St. (☎ 415-239-8500). Chef Sharon Ardiana's wild nettle pizza with pancetta is easily the best pie I have ever eaten (and I am not exaggerating). Share a locally farmed arugula salad to start, sip some wine, and you'll return to your hotel feeling like a savvy local. Otherwise, pick up your cellphone and make reservations at either **Chenery Park,** 683 Chenery St. (☎ 415-337-8537), or **Le P'tit Laurent,** 699 Chenery St., at Diamond Street (☎ 415-334-3235). The former is a bastion of solid American cuisine, while the latter offers authentic French, including a tarte Tatin that would make Carla Bruni blush with pleasure. Laurent offers a $20 three-course menu until 7 p.m. Monday through Thursday — the bargain of the year.

Sampling San Francisco's ethnic eats

As in other big cities, certain neighborhoods in San Francisco are hubs for particular regional cuisines. You can find several ethnic enclaves, with **Chinatown** the most obvious example. Head to **North Beach,** thick with trattorie and bakeries, for authentic Italian. Not to be outdone, the **Mission District** abounds with terrific, inexpensive *taquerias,* and you can see Central American cafes alongside new gourmet restaurants. The tasty, authentic fare is worth the trip.

Over in the **Richmond District** (see Chapter 8), you'll notice a clutch of Russian bakeries, delicatessens, and restaurants, most notably **Katia's, A Russian Tea Room,** 600 Fifth Ave., at Balboa Street (☎ 415-668-9292), open Wednesday through Friday for lunch and Wednesday through Sunday for dinner. You can also find many more Asian and Chinese eateries in the Richmond District. Another local Asian favorite is **Ton Kiang,** 5821 Geary Blvd., near 23rd Avenue (☎ 415-386-8530), open daily for excellent dim sum, lunch, and dinner. Call for evening reservations.

Japantown is bargaintown when it comes to dining. Inside the **Japan Center** on Post Street (at Webster Street) are a number of noodle houses and sushi bars, with more across the way. **Mifune,** 1737 Post St., Ste. 375 (☎ 415-922-0337), upstairs in the Japan Center, is a perennial favorite for big bowls of udon noodles in broth with slices of beef or chicken and vegetables. It's open until 9:30 p.m. Sunday to Thursday, until 10 p.m. Friday to Saturday. **Isuzu,** 1581 Webster St. (☎ 415-922-2290), is a great spot for sushi or tempura.

Trimming the Fat from Your Budget

Do not head to the nearest fast-food counter, even if your travel budget doesn't allow for a $100 dinner for two every night. You can limit the stress on your credit card, and save your waistline, if you share an appetizer and dessert, or order beer instead of wine, or bring a favorite bottle of *vino* (you'll have to pay a corkage charge), or skip the alcohol entirely. (The markup on wine is usually outrageous!) If you're dying to try a certain restaurant that's way too expensive, have lunch there instead of dinner, if it's open; you'll get the same quality of food for less money. Or you can eat brunch or have an inexpensive picnic lunch and direct your savings toward a really nice dinner.

The best choice for inexpensive, flavorful dishes is one of the city's many ethnic restaurants. Taxi to the **Tenderloin** for Vietnamese, Indian, and Pakistani; to the **Mission District** for cheap Mexican, Salvadoran, and Cambodian food; to Geary and Clement streets in the **Richmond District** for Vietnamese, Chinese, and Thai; and to **Japantown** for tempura and noodles. Your wallet will thank you, and your taste buds will still be satisfied.

San Francisco's water, supplied from Hetch-Hetchy up in Yosemite, is possibly the best in the nation. It's so good that most restaurants are happy to eschew the Evian and deliver a pitcher of the local H_2O to your table. Save your money for a bottle of California wine.

So, what are you in the mood for? Chinese? California-Mediterranean? Catalan tapas? *Pho?* There's no reason to go hungry seeking the right restaurant. Due to space considerations, the recommendations in this chapter only scratch the surface of my favorite places. What you have here is a representative cross-section of the best the city has to offer, in a variety of price ranges and neighborhoods. And unless the kitchen is having an off night, there's not a lemon in the bunch.

Restaurants that I've designated with the Kid Friendly icon have items on the menu that most kids like, and they'll treat your children with respect. If things like crayons at the tables and booster seats are important to your little ones, call the restaurants directly for more information.

Experiencing dinner as theater

Foreign Cinema in the Mission District (☎ 415-648-7600; see listing later in this chapter) screens films on a wall in the patio, which is handy if you don't have much to say to your date. For live entertainment to accompany your meal, stay tuned.

San Francisco has always had its fair share of fair maidens, many of whom shave twice daily, and there is no better or safer place to gawk at "gender illusionists" than **AsiaSF,** 201 Ninth St., at Howard (☎ 415-255-2742). This SoMa nightclub/restaurant serves small plates of fusion dishes (such as duck quesadillas) at the bar and on small tables. Once an hour, the "ladies" lip-synch to pop hits while strutting down the vinyl bar in very high heels and tight jeans. It could not be tackier, but the food is okay and the wait staff is very sweet.

Down at **Pier 29** on the Embarcadero, look for a stylized 1926 *Spiegelent* (a circular, tented pavilion), the home of **Teatro ZinZanni** (☎ 415-438-2668; www.teatrozin zanni.org). Tickets are $116 to $140, and shows run Wednesday through Sunday. This is an immensely hilarious dinner show with a twist: The audience is part of the proceedings. Don't worry — you won't be asked to get up and recite. Along with an acceptable, if not stellar, five-course meal (it reminds me of hotel wedding suppers), diners are entertained by a talented group of performers, who combine cabaret, opera, acrobatics, comedy, and improv in most unusual ways. The cast changes periodically; strangely enough, Joan Baez has appeared occasionally, so it's worth investigating who's in the lineup when you come to town. This isn't a cheap date, but it's something to consider if you're celebrating or looking for an evening out of the ordinary.

And for something completely different, slip into **supperclub,** 657 Harrison St. between Second and Third streets (☎ 415-348-0900; www.supperclub.com), an offshoot of the Amsterdam original. Be prepared to spend your entire evening here, lounging barefoot against the pillows that surround your bed/seating area, drinking, eating, watching, listening, participating, and giving yourself over to whatever the experience offers. Every night it changes somewhat. Expect performance art, wandering masseuses, costumes, drag queens, DJs, and who knows what else. A set five-course meal of varying consistency costs $60 on Sunday, Tuesday, Wednesday, and Thursday, and $70 on Friday and Saturday. Secure reservations at least one month in advance.

Dining and dancing

The **Top of the Mark** in the InterContinental Mark Hopkins hotel, 1 Nob Hill, at Mason and California streets (☎ 415-616-6916), has it all — views, music, dancing, and a convivial crowd of suits. The hotel serves a $59 prix-fixe dinner on Friday and Saturday nights; with 7:30 p.m. reservations (the band starts at 9 p.m.), a night on the town is a done deal. **Harry Denton's Starlight Room,** in the Sir Francis Drake Hotel on Union Square, 450 Powell St. (☎ 415-395-8595), attracts tons of hotel guests and locals who appreciate the Starlight Orchestra, the drop-dead views, and the adult prom-night atmosphere. It's a glorious room for drinking expensive glasses of whatever, dancing, and having a little bite. Reservations on the weekend are advised. A younger, hip group congregates at **Cafe du Nord,** below the Swedish American Hall, 2170 Market St., at Sanchez Street (☎ 415-861-5016; www.cafedunord.com). The basement-level club serves a reasonably priced dinner (sandwiches, salad, chicken, and steak), but the draw is the live music. Check the Web site to see which shows are "all ages" (usually offered upstairs) if you have teens along. Cafe du Nord is open seven days a week, although it doesn't always schedule live music Sunday and Monday.

The dollar signs attached to the restaurant recommendations in this chapter give you an idea of how much you'll have to shell out for dinner for one person, including appetizer, main course, dessert, one non-alcoholic drink, tax, and tip. A city-mandated health-care initiative has driven some restaurants to add a surcharge to the bill, while others have increased prices to help pay for employee health insurance.

If a place is marked with $, a meal there will run $30 or less. At $$ places, expect to spend between $31 and $60. Restaurants with $$$ will cost from $61 to $100. Feel like going for broke? You'll sup on fine china in sedate surroundings and then fork over lots more than $100 at $$$$ places. To locate a restaurant based on its cost, location, or cuisine, see the indexes at the end of this chapter.

San Francisco's Best Restaurants

A-16
$$ The Marina/Cow Hollow   ITALIAN

A-16 refers to the highway through the Campania region of Italy (Naples is the major city), and the menu at this stylishly spare restaurant not only reflects the cuisine of southern Italy but also uses ingredients from the area. Favorite dishes include *burrata,* a delicious mozzarella with a soft, creamy center; various house-cured *salumi;* and, among a handful of excellent main courses, halibut with Meyer lemons and almonds. You'll also find a choice lineup of authentic Neapolitan pizzas and pasta dishes. I love the varied seating options here — an outdoor patio, butcher-paper-covered tables, banquettes, and stools at the bar where you can watch the chefs in action.

See map p. 118. 2355 Chestnut St., between Scott and Divisadero streets. ☎ *415-771-2216.* www.a16sf.com. *Reservations accepted. 22-Fillmore, 28–19th Ave., 30-Stockton, or 43-Masonic bus. Main courses: $16–$23. AE, MC, V. Open: Wed–Fri 11:30 a.m.–2:30 p.m., Sun–Thurs 5–10 p.m., Fri–Sat until 11 p.m.*

Absinthe Brasserie & Bar
$$$ Civic Center/Hayes Valley   FRENCH

I recommend this warm-hearted restaurant a short cab ride from Union Square for a cozy dinner with your beloved (or a really good friend). You can't miss with a selection from the oyster bar or a classic frisée salad to start. Depending on the day, the chef may be cooking like a *grandmère*, preparing French onion soup or confit of pork. Absinthe is a hot spot for preconcert dining, so you may want to book a table after the curtain and savor the romantic room and seasonal menu. Weekend brunch is busy (arrive just before 11a.m.), but you can walk in for lunch if you're shopping in the neighborhood.

See map p. 118. 398 Hayes St., at Gough Street. ☎ *415-551-1590.* www.absinthe.com. *Reservations recommended, especially on weekends. Muni to Van Ness Ave. and walk north 2 blocks to Hayes Street. Turn left. Main courses: $24–$29. AE, DC, MC, V. Open: Tues–Fri 11:30 a.m. to midnight, Sat 11 a.m. to midnight, Sun 11 a.m.–10 p.m.*

Ame
$$$$ SoMa   NEW AMERICAN

Husband and wife Hiro Sone and Lissa Doumani, of the brilliant Terra in St. Helena, created this restaurant at the stunning St. Regis Hotel. The pairing is another perfect match. There's no need to speed to the Napa Valley for Sone's signature sake-marinated, broiled black cod and shrimp dumplings in shiso broth — a blessing considering the price of gasoline. If the sashimi bar doesn't waylay you, start with the delicious burrata cheese bruschetta and spring vegetable "bagna cauda," if only to admire the beauty of the composition. The quietly luxe room feels deceptively casual; the service meets the high standards of the globally inspired menu.

See map p. 118. 689 Mission St., at Third Street, in the St. Regis Hotel. ☎ *415-284-4040.* www.amerestaurant.com. *Reservations recommended. Muni to Montgomery St., or 15-Third, 30-Stockton, or 45-Union/Stockton bus. Main courses: $28–$38. AE, DC, DISC, MC, V. Open: Daily 11:30 a.m.–2 p.m. and 6–10 p.m.*

B-44
$$ Financial District   SPANISH

You won't find authentic, homey Spanish food like this outside of Barcelona — the cod cheeks are a treat, a variety of paellas abound with treasures, and you can make a happy meal of tapas, starting with my favorite, *morcilla,* sausage and white beans. This modern spot isn't within

Where to eat when you don't have reservations

Not every restaurant accepts reservations, and among those that do, some keep tables for walk-ins. Others accommodate free spirits in the bar. If it's getting late and you forgot or didn't get around to deciding where to eat, try any of the following:

Restaurants that don't take reservations: Brenda's, Chow, Park Chow, Gialina, L'Osteria del Forno, Pizzeria Delfina, SPQR, Tadich Grill, Tommaso's Restaurant

Restaurants that serve in the bar or at a counter: Absinthe Brasserie & Bar, A-16, Bistro Aix, Boulevard, Brenda's French Soul Food, Dosa, Foreign Cinema, Hayes Street Grill, Home, Jardinère, Kokkari Estiatorio, Le P'tit Laurent, Restaurant Gary Danko, the Slanted Door, SPQR, Tadich Grill, Town Hall

a mile of a lace fan or flamenco guitarist, so don't come expecting a Spanish-themed evening. But if you want to feel that you're eating something out of the ordinary, you'll be well rewarded.

See maps p. 118 and p. 122. 44 Belden Place, off Bush Street. ☎ *415-986-6287.* www. b44sf.com. *Reservations recommended. Follow Stockton Street north from Union Square to Bush Street and walk east for 2 blocks. Main courses: $15–$21. AE, MC, V. Open: Mon–Fri 11:30 a.m.–10:30 p.m., Sat 5–10:30 p.m., Sun 4–9 p.m.*

Bistro Aix
$–$$ The Marina/Cow Hollow   FRENCH

This casual French-style bistro caters to lucky neighborhood residents who don't have to look for parking. Dining alfresco on the heated, covered back patio is a delight in any season. It's the perfect setting to enjoy a bottle of wine and plates of crispy-skinned chicken, fresh pasta, grilled sirloin, and perfectly dressed salads. The $20 prix-fixe menu, served from 6 to 8 p.m. Sunday through Thursday, would be a bargain even if the food were only half as good.

See map p. 118. 3340 Steiner St., between Chestnut and Lombard streets. ☎ *415-202-0100.* www.bistroaix.com. *Reservations recommended. 22-Fillmore, 28-19th Ave., 30-Stockton, or 43-Masonic bus. Main courses: $12–$20; prix-fixe menu $20. AE, DC, MC, V. Open: Mon–Thurs 6–10 p.m., Fri–Sat 6–11 p.m., Sun 5:30–9:30 p.m.*

The Blue Plate
$$ Mission District   CALIFORNIA

Eat here and then go home and regale your less adventurous friends with tales of the fabulous little restaurant you discovered in an out-of-the-way neighborhood in San Francisco. Worth the ride from wherever you are, the Blue Plate exemplifies the best of intimate, staff-driven local places with fresh, usually organic ingredients and a quirkiness in design that even dour people can appreciate. My friend Vicki, who is a regular, always orders the Sonoma duck confit (or tries to — the menu changes daily), but plenty of other diners can't pass on the smoked bacon and cornmeal fried oysters over greens to start, or the meatloaf with mashed potatoes. Vicki's boys (husband included) consistently order a few sides of macaroni covered in Spanish goat's cheese, whether they need it or not. Sit in the back room by the patio, or on the patio itself, weather permitting.

See map p. 125. 3218 Mission St., north of 29th Street by the Bank of America parking lot. ☎ *415-282-6777.* www.blueplatesf.com. *Reservations recommended. J-Church Muni to 30th and Dolores, turn left on Mission Street; or take a cab. Main courses: $14–$28. AE, DISC, MC, V. Open: Mon–Thurs 6–10 p.m., Fri–Sat 6–10:30 p.m.*

Boulevard
$$$$ The Embarcadero AMERICAN

Housed in an elegant turn-of-the-20th-century building with views of the Bay Bridge (from tables in the very back only), this favorite of both visitors and locals serves excellent, generous plates of seasonal comfort food. Noisy but comfortable, the place caters to an upscale, older crowd. Start with the pan-seared foie gras, before the food police run it off the menu. Main courses might include tender lamb chops or lamb *osso buco* accompanied by local asparagus in season. Counter and bar seating is available for those without reservations; call three or four weeks in advance for a prime-time table.

See map p. 118. 1 Mission St., at Steuart Street. ☎ *415-543-6084.* www.boulevard restaurant.com. *Reservations advised three weeks in advance. Any Muni streetcar to Embarcadero; walk 1 block east to Mission Street. Main courses: $29–$40. AE, CB, DC, MC, V. Open: Mon–Fri 11:30 a.m.–2 p.m., Thurs–Sat 5:30–10:30 p.m., Sun–Wed 5:30–10 p.m.*

Brenda's French Soul Food
$ Civic Center BREAKFAST/CREOLE

Open only for breakfast and lunch, this tiny storefront on a bleak block not far from City Hall is proof that a great biscuit is the culinary equal of a better mousetrap. Everyone interested in good food is beating a path to Brenda Buenviaje's door, loving the grits that accompany her *maque choux* (veggie) omelet or ordering a flight of beignets (there are four kinds, including a savory crawfish) as a starter. Her fried oyster po' boy is second to none, including any you'd find in New Orleans, which happens to be Brenda's hometown. There's likely to be a line waiting for a table (put your name on the list), but if there's a stool at the counter and you are impatient, grab it.

See map p. 118. 652 Polk St., at Eddy Street. ☎ *415-346-6506.* www.frenchsoul food.com. *Reservations not accepted. 38-Geary bus. Main courses: $6.75–$9.75. AE, DISC, MC, V. Open: Wed–Mon 8 a.m.–3 p.m.*

Butterfly
$$$ The Embarcadero   PAN-ASIAN

This is a beautiful restaurant on the water, a comfortable place to take in the bay, with drinks and maybe some oysters before the sun sets. Butterfly started in the Mission (where the original is now a bar/lounge), and its roaring success led chef-owner Robert Lam to salvage this room with a view after the previous owners couldn't weather the last economic downturn. Lam's use of local ingredients in recipes that pick and choose from various Asian cuisines makes for unusual eating. If you're in the mood for something different, try crispy, fried whole fish with kimchi, black bean sauce, and Chinese sausage. You won't know what to admire more — the shimmering water or your dinner plate.

See map p. 118. Pier 33 on the Embarcadero at Bay Street. ☎ *415-864-8999.* www. butterflysf.com. *Reservations recommended. F-Market streetcar. Main courses: $18–$39. AE, MC, V. Open: Mon–Fri 11:30 a.m.–3 p.m., Sun–Wed 5–10 p.m., Thurs–Sat 5–11 p.m., happy hour Mon–Fri 3–5 p.m., brunch Sat–Sun 11 a.m.–3 p.m.*

Canteen
$$ Union Square   CALIFORNIA

Minuscule Canteen is the domain of the much-admired chef Dennis Leary, whose bona fides include four years at Rubicon prior to opening this 20-seat upscale diner. The fact that you'll need a reservation even to eat at the counter (the place has but four tiny booths), should clue you in that this is an unusual venture. Leary does the shopping as well as all the cooking, and his menu changes weekly to reflect what he finds appealing. If you're staying around Union Square, breakfast is stellar, especially the smoked salmon omelet or stuffed pancake. Work the phones to land a dinner seat, or come for lunch and see what all the fuss is about.

See maps p. 118 and p. 122. 817 Sutter St., next to the Commodore Hotel. ☎ *415-928-8870.* www.sfcanteen.com. *Reservations accepted (and needed) for dinner only. Main courses: $20–$25. AE, DC, MC, V. Open: Mon–Fri 7–11 a.m., Wed–Fri 11:30 a.m.–2 p.m. and 6–10 p.m., weekend brunch 8 a.m.–2 p.m.*

Chow
$ The Castro   AMERICAN

If there weren't so many people eagerly waiting at this noisy, casual, friendly joint, it might qualify as a quick-bite place. But after you score a table, it's more fun to sit awhile and savor the straightforward pasta dishes, brick-oven-roasted chicken, beef short ribs, thin-crusted pizzas, and yummy desserts (love that ginger cake). A great price performer, too. The second location, **Park Chow,** 1240 Ninth Ave., near Golden Gate Park (☎ **415-665-9912**), is just as terrific and just as busy.

See map p. 118. 215 Church St., at Market Street. ☎ *415-552-2469. Reservations not accepted. J-Church or F-Market streetcar to Church Street. Main courses: $7.50–$15. MC, V. Open: Sun–Thurs 11 a.m.–11 p.m., Fri–Sat 11 a.m. to midnight.*

Colibrí Mexican Bistro
$$ Union Square MEXICAN

Colibrí's menu features a different region of Mexico each month, and each is worth exploring from the comfortable confines of this warmly decorated bistro. Don't look for $5 oversized burritos (you'll find those in the Mission District); instead, expect more interesting dishes, such as prawns in tamarind mole or marinated lamb shank steamed in banana leaves. Mexican beer goes well with any of the small plates featuring chewy hand-made corn tortillas. Gourmet Mexican makes a welcome change if you mostly associate south-of-the-border food with *taquerías*.

See maps p. 118 and p. 122. 438 Geary St., next to the Hotel Diva. ☎ **415-440-2737.** www.colibrimexicanbistro.com. *Reservations advised. Main courses: $14–$18. AE, MC, V. Open: Mon 11:30 a.m.–10 p.m., Tues–Thurs 11:30 a.m.–11 p.m., Fri 11:30 a.m. to midnight, Sat 10 a.m. to midnight, Sun 10 a.m.–10 p.m.*

Cortez
$$$ Union Square MEDITERRANEAN

Hotel restaurants aren't the formal, grown-up, boring affairs they once were, and — at least around Union Square — they've become *the* places to be. Among them is this destination for couture tapas in the Hotel Adagio. The buzz is palpable from the bar and the Mondrian-meets-Miro dining room. The surprise (if you're mistrusting of glitz) is that the small plates — such as prawns a la plancha or a salad of frisée, roasted beets, and Point Reyes blue cheese — are beautifully presented and totally delicious.

See maps p. 118 and p. 122. 550 Geary St., in the Hotel Adagio. ☎ **415-292-6360.** www.cortezrestaurant.com. *Reservations advised. Main courses: $6–$17. AE, MC, V. Open: Daily 5:30–10:30 p.m.*

Delfina
$$ Mission District ITALIAN

This wonderfully friendly restaurant defines what's incredible about the city's neighborhood eats. Dishes such as Niman Ranch flatiron steak, pristine salmon with warm lentil salad, and bitter greens combined simply with walnuts and pancetta are full of flavor and feature the freshest ingredients, a smattering of herbs, and thoughtful preparation. Under the same ownership, the more casual **Pizzeria Delfina** (☎ 415-437-6800) is next door. Open from 11 a.m. Tuesday through Sunday (dinner only on Mon), it's the happening place for Neopolitan-style pizza and yummy antipasti. It doesn't take reservations — look for the line on the sidewalk.

See map p. 125. 3621 18th St., between Dolores and Guerrero streets. ☎ **415-552-4055.** www.delfinasf.com. *Reservations advised three weeks in advance. J-Church Muni line to 18th Street, then walk east 2 blocks. Main courses: $11–$26. MC, V. Open: Sun–Thurs 5:30–10 p.m., Fri–Sat 5:30–11 p.m.*

Dosa
$ Mission District   INDIAN

Dosas are thin, lacy, gargantuan crepes, often filled with spicy combinations of potatoes and vegetables, used to scoop up a variety of chutneys. The restaurant, a colorful, lively spot near some interesting shops, works if you need a fast, delicious brunch at the bar (weekends only) or intend to take a leisurely tour of the dinner menu. Join the Mission District hipsters who fill the modern, urbane dining room and try sambars (lentil dumplings) and delectable Tamil lamb curry along with the dosas.

See map p. 125. 995 Valencia St., near 21st St. ☎ *415-642-3672.* www.dosasf.com. *Reservations recommended. BART to 24th St. Main courses: $9.50–$14. AE, MC, V. Open Sun–Thurs 5:30–10 p.m., Fri–Sat 5:30–11 p.m.; weekend brunch 11:30 a.m.–3:30 p.m.*

Ducca
$$$ SoMa   ITALIAN

This handsome restaurant in the newly remodeled Westin Market Street seduced me in part with its interesting Venetian-inspired menu and in part with its enticing outdoor dining possibilities. You might want to stop by for a drink just to soak up the ambience, although the clubby atmosphere makes a meal here feel a bit special. Pasta dishes are available in half portions — go for the lamb ragu rather than the bucatini with fresh sardines. The grass-fed burgers and polenta fries ratchet lunch up a notch.

See map p. 118. 50 Third St., at Market Street. ☎ *415-977-0271.* www.duccasf.com. *Reservations recommended. Main courses: $22–$32. AE, DC, DISC, MC, V. Open: Daily 6:30 a.m.–10:30 p.m. (lounge open until 1 a.m.).*

Foreign Cinema
$$$ Mission District   NEW AMERICAN/FRENCH

Mission District regulars nearly lost their *empanadas* when the shiny, chic Foreign Cinema opened in 1999. The expansive dining room — plus outdoor patio where the restaurant screens foreign films on a concrete wall — would throw anyone at first, but some oysters from the raw bar followed by an elegant plate of endive and smoked trout helped lower resistance to the inevitable changes in the neighborhood. Ten years later, the restaurant continues to be a must stop for hip gourmands.

See map p. 125. 2534 Mission St., between 21st and 22nd streets. ☎ *415-648-7600.* www.foreigncinema.com. *Reservations highly recommended. BART to 24th Street. Main courses: $16–$27. AE, DISC, MC, V. Open: Mon–Thurs 6–10 p.m., Fri–Sat 6–11 p.m., weekend brunch 11 a.m.–3 p.m.*

Greens Restaurant
$$–$$$ The Marina/Cow Hollow   VEGETARIAN

If you haven't eaten in a gourmet vegetarian restaurant, or if your vegetarian dining has been limited to alfalfa sprouts and tofu, you're in for a marvelous culinary experience. The Saturday-evening four-course prix-fixe menu is a deal, especially when you factor in the gorgeous views that come with the meal. This attractive, bright room is a particularly brilliant destination for lunch if you're exploring the Marina.

See map p. 118. Fort Mason, Building A, off Marina Boulevard at Buchanan Street. ☎ *415-771-6222.* http://greensrestaurant.com. *Reservations highly recommended at least two weeks in advance. Take the 30-Stockton bus to Laguna and transfer to the 28–19th Avenue into Fort Mason. Main courses: $18–$25; prix-fixe menu (Sat only) $49. AE, DISC, MC, V. Open: Tues–Sat noon to 2:30 p.m., Sun 10:30 a.m.–2 p.m., daily 5:30–9 p.m.*

Hayes Street Grill
$$ Civic Center/Hayes Valley   SEAFOOD

This respected 30-plus-year veteran is one of the premier fish restaurants in the city. The kitchen prepares whatever's been caught that morning simply, carefully, and with integrity. The nonfish selections, such as a Niman Ranch pork chop, are equally delicious. The restaurant quiets down considerably around 8 p.m. when the opera/symphony/ballet-goers dash off to the show. Walk-ins can always eat at the bar.

See map p. 118. 320 Hayes St., between Gough and Franklin streets. ☎ *415-863-5545.* www.hayesstreetgrill.com. *Reservations recommended. Take any Muni Metro to the Civic Center Station and walk north on Gough. Main courses: $19–$25; $29 prix fixe after 7:30 p.m. Sun–Thurs. AE, DISC, MC, V. Open: Mon–Fri 11:30 a.m.– 2 p.m., Mon–Thurs 5–9:30 p.m., Fri–Sat 5:30–10:30 p.m., Sun 5–8:30 p.m.*

Home
$–$$ The Castro   AMERICAN

When Union Square hotel restaurants start giving your wallet an inferiority complex, catch the F-Market streetcar to the corner of Market and Church streets and you'll be at Home. Start on the patio with a cocktail, and then head to the slightly moody dining room for better-than-home cooking such as mac and cheese or pot roast that'll make you cry, or at least ask for the recipe. Saturday and Sunday brunch features a do-it-yourself Bloody Mary bar, and the daily early-bird special is a 3-course prix fixe for $11!

See map p. 118. 2100 Market St., at Church Street. ☎ *415-503-0333.* www.home-sf. com. *J-Church or F-Market streetcar. Main courses: $10–$17. AE, DISC, MC, V. Open: Daily 5 to midnight, weekend brunch 10 a.m.–2 p.m.*

Isa
$$ The Marina/Cow Hollow   FRENCH

I had a running argument with my cousin Irene over who made the wisest picks at this stellar chef-owned-and-operated find. My crab salad was full of freshly cracked crabmeat, but Irene's baked goat's cheese, surrounded by pesto and perfectly ripe tomato, elicited a bit of a fork fight. We reached an impasse over the grilled flatiron steak and the potato-wrapped sea bass, but we agreed that based on price, atmosphere, service, and taste, this was among the best meals we've shared in San Francisco. Luke Sung, the genius behind the stove, was recognized as a Rising Star Chef of the Year by the James Beard Foundation twice, and I can't argue with that.

See map p. 118. 3324 Steiner St., at Chestnut Street. ☎ *415-567-9588.* www.isa restaurant.com. *30-Stockton bus. Main courses: $12–$18. MC, V. Open: Mon–Thurs 5:30–10 p.m., Fri–Sat until 10:30 p.m.*

Jardinière
$$$$ Civic Center/Hayes Valley CALIFORNIA/FRENCH

This is where the upscale crowd sups before the opera, ballet, or symphony. Expect sophisticated surroundings, a lively bar, and highly touted, high-priced food. Signature dishes include a bread salad I wish were in front of me right this minute and duck confit that will change your mood for the better. The wine-braised short rib is lovely. Let the highly personable and well-trained waitstaff choose your wine.

See map p. 118. 300 Grove St., at Franklin Street. ☎ *415-861-5555.* www. jardiniere.com. *Reservations required. Muni Metro to Civic Center; walk 4 blocks north on Franklin. Main courses: $25–$46. AE, DC, MC, V. Open: Sun–Wed 5–10:30 p.m., Thurs–Sat 5–11:30 p.m.*

Kokkari Estiatorio
$$$ Financial District GREEK

Your average Mediterranean shipping tycoon would feel perfectly comfortable underneath the beamed ceilings of this richly appointed taverna. The California-meets-Greek menu does feature some familiar dishes, such as moussaka, but it takes them to Mount Olympus–style heights. Order *yiaourti graniti* (yogurt sorbet with tangerine ice) for dessert, even if you're full.

See maps p. 118 and p. 122. 200 Jackson St., at Front Street. ☎ *415-981-0983.* www.kokkari.com. *Reservations required. 2, 3, or 4 bus; transfer to 42-Downtown loop; exit at Sansome and Jackson streets and walk 2 blocks west to Front. Main courses: $19–$39. AE, DISC, MC, V. Open: Mon–Fri 11:30 a.m.–2:30 p.m., Mon 5:30–10 p.m., Fri–Sat 5:30–11 p.m.*

La Terrasse
$$ The Marina/Cow Hollow FRENCH

There are currently three good restaurants in the Presidio, but the bus drops you off at the doorstep of this little cafe, which makes life simple, *n'est-ce pas?* A glass of wine and some duck confit are all some of us need for complete happiness; others may find mussels and fries or salade Niçoise their ticket to Paris. The produce is organic, the meats are hormone free, and the very French management uses local producers where possible. Light-filled La Terrasse is a good choice on your way back from viewing the Golden Gate Bridge or walking around Crissy Field.

215 Lincoln Blvd., the Presidio. ☎ **415-922-3463**. www.laterrassepresidio. com. *Reservations accepted. 28–19th Ave., 29-Sunset, 43-Masonic bus. Main courses: $12–$29. MC, V. Open: Mon–Fri 7 a.m.–10 p.m., Sat 11 a.m.–10 p.m., Sun 10 a.m.–4 p.m.*

Le Charm French Bistro
$$ SoMa   FRENCH BISTRO

Bargain-hunter alert! The Parisian-inspired three-course prix-fixe dinner for $30 is the real deal at this popular little sponge-painted bistro. Diners choose from a menu that may include roasted quail served on salad greens, gnocchi with wild mushrooms, and, in season, a dessert soup of fresh apricots and cherries. Le Charm is also a winner for lunch, especially if the weather is decent and you can get a table outside in the garden.

See map p. 118. 315 Fifth St., between Folsom and Howard streets (near Yerba Buena Center). ☎ **415-546-6128.** http://lecharm.com. *Reservations accepted. Powell Street Muni; 27-Bryant or 30-Stockton bus. Main courses: $19–$24. AE, MC, V. Open: Mon–Fri 11:30 a.m.–2 p.m., Tues–Fri 6–9:30 p.m., Sat 5:30–10 p.m., Sun 5–8:30 p.m.*

Lichee Garden
$ Chinatown   CHINESE/DIM SUM

A particularly reliable family-style Cantonese restaurant, popular with locals, Lichee Garden has a huge menu filled with familiar dishes (like egg foo young), lots of seafood, and every Chinese dish you remember from childhood — unless you were raised in China. It also serves a good dim sum lunch. Prices are inexpensive (Peking duck being the biggest extravagance), service is fine, and the room is bright and lively.

See maps p. 118 and p. 121. 1416 Powell St., near Broadway. ☎ **415-397-2290.** licheegarden.ypguides.net. *Reservations accepted. Powell-Mason cable car. Main courses: $6.50–$25. MC, V. Open: Daily 7 a.m.–9:15 p.m.*

L'Osteria del Forno
$ North Beach   ITALIAN

A tiny storefront with an equally tiny kitchen, L'Osteria manages to dish up fine thin-crusted pizzas, pasta dishes that change daily, and a tender roast pork loin cooked in milk. It's equally satisfying to make a meal of antipasti. Don't pass up *insalata rustica,* a tuna and white bean salad you'll want to duplicate at home. This is one North Beach restaurant that feels and tastes authentic.

See maps p. 118 and p. 121. 519 Columbus Ave., between Green and Union streets. ☎ **415-982-1124.** www.losteriadelforno.com. *Reservations not accepted. Powell-Mason cable-car line; 30-Stockton bus. Main courses: $10–$15. No credit cards. Open: Sun–Mon and Wed–Thurs 11:30 a.m.–10 p.m., Fri–Sat 11:30 a.m.–11 p.m.*

Luna Park
$$ **Mission District   NEW AMERICAN**

The funky abstract art, rustic red walls, and gold velvet drapes announce that décor is in the eye of the decorator, but it's all part of the fun. Luna Park's exceedingly well-priced menu attracts people from all parts of the city, making weekend nights especially loud, but that does make it comfortable for families. Start with the tuna "poke" appetizer or one of the five beautiful green salads, and then consider the "jerk" chicken with roasted yams, flatiron steak, or oven-roasted sea bass. Attention, campers: Make-your-own s'mores light up the dessert list!

See map p. 125. 694 Valencia St., at 18th Street. ☎ **415-553-8584**. www.lunapark sf.com. *Reservations advised for dinner. BART to 16th Street; walk west to Valencia and south 2 blocks. Main courses: $13–$29. MC, V. Open: Mon–Fri 11:30 a.m. –2:30 p.m., Sat–Sun 11:30 a.m.–3 p.m., Mon–Thurs 5:30–10:30 p.m., Fri–Sat 5:30–11:30 p.m., Sun 5:30–10 p.m.*

Mamacita
$$ **The Marina/Cow Hollow   MEXICAN**

Mamacita serves south-of-the-border treats that surpass expectation. Don't miss the carnitas tacos, an irresistible heap of slow-cooked pork, roasted hominy, avocado, and cream, so delectable-looking that it's a toss-up whether to admire them or finish 'em off in a bite or two. Larger plates, such as seared ahi, are equally good, but you'll run the risk of not having room for dessert — and who wants to miss out on cinnamon churros? This place gets crowded and noisy as the evening wears on. Arrive early if you don't have reservations; half the tables are saved for walk-ins.

See map p. 118. 2317 Chestnut St., between Scott and Divisadero streets. ☎ **415-346-8494**. www.mamacitasf.com. *Reservations advised. 30-Stockton bus. Main courses: $10–$17. AE, MC, V. Open: Daily 5:30–10:30 p.m. Bar open until midnight.*

Quince Restaurant
$$$ **Pacific Heights   ITALIAN**

Not long after opening in 2003, Quince became, and remains, one of the more sought-after reservations in town. Chef-owner Michael Tusk, an alumnus of Chez Panisse and Oliveto, and his wife, Lindsey, have created a refined retreat where every dish feels nurtured. The menu changes daily; if a crudo appears under the first-course selections, don't be shy, even if you think you don't like raw fish. The house-made pasta in any form will be equally inspired. Unlike so many restaurants that equate noise with buzz, Quince offers a grown-up dining experience in calm surroundings.

See map p. 118. 1701 Octavia St., at Bush Street. ☎ **415-775-8500**. www.quince restaurant.com. *Reservations necessary. Take a cab. Valet parking available. Main courses: $18–$34; six-course tasting menu $105. AE, MC, V. Open: Mon–Thurs 5:30–10 p.m., Fri–Sat 5–10 p.m.*

R&G Lounge
$ Chinatown   CHINESE

Downstairs, you get excellent Hong Kong Chinese dishes in a setting that reminds me of an airport lounge, with lackluster service. The small dining room upstairs is more attractive, so talk your way to a table up there. In either case, you'll have a chance to order live spot shrimp from the downstairs tank and fresh, crisp vegetables such as Chinese broccoli and *yin choy* (a leafy green vegetable with a red root, often boiled and then braised with garlic).

See maps p. 118 and p. 121. 631 Kearny St., between Sacramento and Clay streets. ☎ **415-982-7877.** www.rnglounge.com. *Reservations accepted. 15-Third bus. Main courses: $7.25–$9.50. AE, MC, V. Open: Daily 11 a.m.–9:30 p.m.*

Range
$$ Mission District   CALIFORNIA

Range is a prime example of the modern San Francisco neighborhood restaurant. Opened by a kitchen-savvy husband and wife team (Cameron and Phil West), it offers a small, seasonal menu that features flavor over flash, backed by charming service. Coffee-rubbed pork shoulder is a favorite, and Range's delicate take on meat and potatoes — pan-roasted, thinly sliced bavette steak (cut from the short loin) with narrow fingerlings — satisfies on a more primal level. Two simple yet warm dining rooms, fronted by an attractive bar, allow for conversation, a nice touch given how often restaurants seem designed to make that impossible.

See map p. 125. 842 Valencia St., between 19th and 20th streets. ☎ **415-282-8283.** www.rangesf.com. *Reservations recommended. 14-Mission bus or taxi. Main courses: $18–$24. MC, V. Open: Sun–Thurs 5:30–10 p.m., Fri–Sat 5:30–11 p.m.*

Restaurant Gary Danko
$$$$ Russian Hill   FRENCH/NEW AMERICAN

The ovens were barely lit at this fine-dining center before the food and wine cognoscenti were all over Danko's like hollandaise, proclaiming it among the best restaurants not only in town but in the country. They were right. Choose your own three-course (or more if you like) meal from the menu — perhaps a composed lobster salad followed by day-boat scallops, ending with a Meyer lemon soufflé or selections from the cheese cart — then let the kitchen make magic. If you don't mind eating at the bar, you can walk in without reservations.

See map p. 118. 800 North Point St., at Hyde Street. ☎ **415-749-2060.** www.gary danko.com. *Reservations advised four weeks in advance. Powell-Hyde cable-car line. Prix-fixe menu: $65–$96. DC, DISC, MC, V. Open: Daily 5:30–10 p.m.*

Restaurant Lulu
$$ SoMa MEDITERRANEAN

With the buoyant feel of a lively Provençal brasserie, the mouthwatering scent of the oak-fired rotisserie, and a lengthy menu of appealing dishes, Lulu seduces on many levels. If you're anywhere near Yerba Buena Center, don't think twice about having lunch or dinner at this local institution. Most dishes are meant to be shared, such as the daily rotisserie specials, the wonderful rosemary-scented chicken, and an antipasti plate of your own design. Dinnertime can be pretty noisy, but you'll be surrounded by a buzz of happiness from the throng at the bar, emanating throughout the cavernous room.

See map p. 118. 816 Folsom St., at Fourth Street. ☎ *415-495-5775.* www.restaurant lulu.com. *Reservations advised. 45-Union/Stockton or 30-Stockton bus. Main courses: $16–$30. AE, DC, DISC, MC, V. Open: Daily 11:30 a.m.–3 p.m., Mon–Thurs 5:30–10 p.m., Fri–Sat 5–11 p.m., Sun 5–10 p.m.*

The Slanted Door
$$ The Embarcadero VIETNAMESE

The city's premier Vietnamese eatery occupies the city's premier location — the glorious Ferry Building. Savvy travelers and locals pour in for the buttery steamed sea bass, caramelized chicken, and plates of "shaking" beef. Even if dinner reservations seem impossible to come by, call at 5:30 p.m. the evening you want to dine and see whether there is a cancellation. You may get lucky. You even need a reservation for lunch, especially since the James Beard Foundation named chef Charles Phan Best Chef in California in 2004 and made the Slanted Door a finalist in the 2008 Outstanding Restaurant competition.

See map p. 118. 1 Ferry Building, Embarcadero and Market Street. ☎ *415-861-8032.* http://slanteddoor.com. *Reservations a must. BART or Muni to the Embarcadero Station. Main courses: $16–$33. AE, MC, V. Open: Daily 11:30 a.m.– 2:30 p.m., Sun–Thurs 5:30–10 p.m., Fri–Sat 5:30–10:30 p.m.*

SPQR
$$ Pacific Heights ITALIAN

Tables at this wildly popular little place are so close together that if you don't make new acquaintances while waiting in line, you'll certainly do so once you sit down and eye what the guy next to you is eating. Everyone starts with a combination of at least three hot, cold, or fried antipasti. You can't go wrong with any of them, but the fried Brussels sprouts are deservedly a big favorite. Continue with house-made pasta, or just cut to the chase and order dessert. The rice pudding is lovely.

See map p. 118. 1911 Fillmore St. at Bush Street. ☎ *415-771-7779.* www.spqrsf. com. *Reservations not accepted. 4-Sutter or 22-Fillmore bus. Main courses: $12–$20. AE, MC, V. Open: Mon–Fri 11:30 a.m.–2:30 p.m., dinner nightly 5:30–11 p.m., Sat and Sun brunch 10:30 a.m.–2:30 p.m.*

Tadich Grill
$$ Financial District   SEAFOOD

If you're making the rounds of old San Francisco, lunch here or at Sam's Grill, 374 Bush St. (☎ 415-421-0594), is mandatory. This turn-of-the-last-century watering hole, with waiters to match, features a daily printed menu advertising dishes so old-fashioned (had Lobster Newburg lately?) that they're probably the next big thing (like liberals, or walking). Order defensively: Stick with whatever fresh fish is available and the delicious creamed spinach.

See maps p. 118 and p. 122. 240 California St., between Front and Battery streets. ☎ *415-391-1849. Reservations not accepted. Take any Muni streetcar to the Embarcadero Station. Main courses: $12–$18. MC, V. Open: Mon–Fri 11 a.m.– 9:30 p.m., Sat 11:30 a.m.–9:30 p.m.*

1300 Fillmore
$$$ Japantown/Western Addition   AMERICAN/SOUTHERN

Anchoring the new Fillmore Jazz Heritage blocks, within walking distance of Japantown, upmarket 1300 is a fine place to spend an evening. Start in the attractive bar, where you can listen to the jazz trio while sipping a cocktail from the expansive drinks menu. When your table is ready, linger over shrimp hush puppies before tucking into some organic fried chicken or a grilled pork chop. Try not to fill up on the excellent cornbread, or you won't be able to eat dessert; the banana cream pie is worth the sacrifice. Although it's kind of expensive, 1300 is more fun than similarly priced North Beach or Union Square restos.

See map p. 118. 1300 Fillmore St., at Eddy Street. ☎ *415-771-7100.* www.1300 fillmore.com. *Reservations advised. 38-Geary or 22-Fillmore bus. Main courses: $18–$29. AE, DISC, MC, V. Open: Sun–Wed 5–11 p.m., Thurs–Sat 5 p.m.–1 a.m., Sun brunch 10:30 a.m.–2:30 p.m.*

Tommaso's Restaurant
$$ North Beach   ITALIAN

The specialty at this old-time basement restaurant is pizza; the wood-fired brick oven dates from 1935 and is credited with inspiring Wolfgang Puck to build one a lot like it. Bring a big appetite or plan to share — portions are generous. Spinach salad, full of slivered almonds and dressed with a reduced balsamic, is a good way to start and will easily feed two. Lasagna is a point of pride in the kitchen, and all the old-school recipes are available, including eggplant Parmigiana and chicken marsala. Tommaso's is a local favorite, so plan to wait for a table.

See map p. 118. 1042 Kearny St. near Broadway. ☎ *415-398-9696.* http:// tommasosnorthbeach.com. *Reservations not accepted. 30-Stockton bus. Main courses: $12–$19. AE, DISC, MC, V. Open: Tues–Sat 5–10:45 p.m., Sun 4–9:45 p.m.*

Town Hall
$$$ SoMa   NEW AMERICAN

The latest destination spot to wow the city that knows how to eat (I saw Robin Williams there), Town Hall oozes confidence like Tom Cruise at the end of a rope. Heavy hitters from the local cuisine scene, most prominently the Rosenthal brothers of Postrio fame, automatically raised the restaurant's profile, and their cooking will keep it in the big leagues. If you like New Orleans–style dishes — multiflavored, multitextured, ample portions — you'll love the cornmeal-fried oysters with baby spinach, covered in a jazzy bacon dressing, and scallops with andouille sausage jambalaya. There's nothing shy about this food, and you don't have to share unless you really want to.

See maps p. 118 and p. 122. 342 Howard St., at Beale Street. ☎ **415-908-3900.** www. townhallsf.com. *Reservations advised. 1-California, 12-Folsom, or 14-Mission bus. Main courses: $19–$26. AE, MC, V. Open: Mon–Fri 11:30 a.m.–2:30 p.m., Sun–Thurs 5:30–10 p.m., Fri–Sat 5:30–11 p.m.*

Yoshi's
$$$ Japantown/Western Addition   JAPANESE/SUSHI

Connected to the popular jazz club of the same name (see Chapter 16), the airy, high-ceilinged restaurant at Yoshi's empties a bit after the show starts. You may find it easier to get a table then. Sushi and sashimi are pristine and gorgeously arranged on white ceramic plates; the variety and presentation will please even sushi snobs. Tempura of seasonal organic vegetables is as politically correct (and tasty) as anything deep-fried is allowed to be. The upstairs lounge has a view of the kitchen, providing a show in itself, and you can order from the bar menu.

See map p. 118. 1330 Fillmore St., near Eddy Street. ☎ **415-655-5600.** http://sf. yoshis.com/sf/restaurant. *Reservations advised. 22-Fillmore or 38-Geary bus. Main courses: $14–$20. AE, MC, V. Open: Mon–Wed 5:30–10:30 p.m., Thurs–Sat 5:30–11 p.m., Sun 5–10 p.m.*

Zuni Café
$$ Civic Center/Hayes Valley   CALIFORNIA

There's always a palpable buzz from the smartly dressed crowd hanging about Zuni's copper bar drinking vodka, snarfing oysters, and waiting for a table. Everything from the centrally located brick oven is terrific, but the signature roast chicken with bread salad for two is downright divine. Don't opt for an outside table; the view on this section of Market Street isn't all that pleasant.

See map p. 118. 1658 Market St., between Franklin and Gough streets. ☎ **415-552-2522.** www.zunicafe.com. *Reservations recommended. Muni Metro F-Market to Van Ness, walk 2 blocks southwest. Main courses: $13–$29. AE, MC, V. Open: Tues–Sat 11:30 a.m. to midnight, Sun 11 a.m.–11 p.m.*

Dim sum 101

I wasn't sure what to expect the first time I tried dim sum, way back when. I'll admit — and only because you were kind enough to buy this book — that I was a little hesitant. The idea of eating these Chinese dumplings, filled with ingredients I couldn't identify at first, was a bit scary. But I'm delighted to report that I quickly overcame my initial wariness and now adore dim sum. If you haven't tried it, I urge you to do so.

In many Chinese restaurants, dim sum is served from late morning until around 2 p.m., but not later. In fact, if you arrive past 1 p.m., you run the risk of the kitchen's losing interest in providing much of anything to eat. It's best to arrive around 11 a.m. Dim sum generally enters on carts wheeled about the room by waitresses. (Otherwise, you order from a menu.) Ask for a table near the kitchen in order to get first crack at whatever's on its way around the room. The ladies with their carts will stop by your table and show you what they have. If it looks appealing to you, nod or say, "yes"; if not, just say, "no, thanks." It's okay to order slowly — finishing one plate, sipping tea, and then ordering something else. By the way, if you run out of tea, open the teapot lid.

Here's a rundown of dim sum that first-timers will definitely enjoy:

✔ **Har gau:** Shrimp dumplings encased in a translucent wrapper and steamed

✔ **Siu mai:** Rectangles of pork and shrimp in a sheer noodle wrapper

✔ **Gau choi gau:** Dumplings filled with chives, alone or with shrimp or scallop

✔ **Jun jui kau:** Rice pearl balls with seasoned ground pork and rice

✔ **Law mai gai:** Sticky rice with bits of meat and mushrooms wrapped in a lotus leaf

✔ **Char siu bau:** Steamed pork buns — bits of barbecued meat in a doughy roll

✔ **Guk char siu ban:** Baked pork buns — bits of barbecued meat in a glazed roll

✔ **Chun guen:** Spring rolls — smaller, less crowded version egg rolls

✔ **Gau ji:** Potstickers —thick, crescent-shaped dough filled with ground pork

Where to go

Those in the know consider **Yank Sing** one of the premier dim sum houses in town. It's also the most expensive, although you get a lot in terms of quality and surroundings. On the Embarcadero at Rincon Center, 101 Spear St. (☎ **415-957-9300;** www.yank sing.com), and at 49 Stevenson St., near First Street (☎ **415-541-4949;** lunch only).

In Chinatown, **Gold Mountain** is typical of the cavernous dim sum parlors that serve hundreds of families on the weekends. 644 Broadway, near Stockton Street (☎ **415-296-7733**).

Attractively decorated **City View** is a very good spot for dim sum, particularly popular with Financial District workers and comfortable enough for a business lunch. The ladies who walk about with the trays and carts of dim sum all speak English, which is comforting if you really want to know what they're serving. 662 Commercial St., between Kearny and Montgomery streets. (☎ **415-398-2838;** lunch only).

Dining and Snacking on the Go

With the exception of Fisherman's Wharf, where people attempt to walk while balancing bread bowls filled with questionable clam chowder, street food is practically nonexistent in San Francisco. (Although, in a very weak moment, and for research purposes only, I once bought a hot dog from a cart on PIER 39.) But that doesn't mean you should seek out the closest fast-food chain for a meal on the go. Instead, head to one of the many sandwich counters, Asian bakeries, Italian delis, coffeehouses, and pastry shops that provide a grand variety of delicious foodstuffs quickly and for reasonable to downright cheap prices.

Whether you're feeling a bit peckish or positively peaked, you'll find something tempting to tide yourself over until the next big meal.

Have food, will travel

Just 2 long blocks west of the Ferry Building on the Embarcadero, next to Pier 5, is a bench-lined, refurbished wooden wharf with fine views that practically begs for an impromptu picnic lunch. Plenty of other spots around the city beckon you to unpack a brown bag, too.

You can generously fill your lunch pail at **Molinari Delicatessen,** a second-generation, family-run Italian place with a fantastic assortment of cheeses, inexpensive Italian wines, and friendly people who make excellent sandwiches to go. It's at 373 Columbus Ave. in North Beach (☎ 415-421-2337) and is open Monday through Friday 8 a.m. to 6 p.m. and Saturday 7:30 a.m. to 5:30 p.m.

Also in North Beach, on the corner of Columbus Avenue and Kearny Street, is a Parisian-inspired Italian cafe owned by the director Francis Ford Coppola. Surprisingly, **Cafe Zoetrope** (☎ 415-291-1700; www.cafe zoetrope.com) — part wine bar, part kitchen store — serves the most delicious muffuletta (olive salad, mortadella, ham, salami, and provolone) outside of New Orleans. This sandwich once made my husband so ecstatic he squirreled away half to eat the following day. The cafe is open from 11 a.m. until 10 p.m. Tuesday through Friday and opens at noon on weekends, closing at 10 p.m. Saturday and 9 p.m. Sunday. It's closed Monday.

In the Financial District at **Palio Paninoteca,** 505 Montgomery St., near California Street (☎ 415-362-6900; www.paliopaninoteca.com), $7.75 gets you a panini large enough for two. Fillings range from grilled vegetables or meat to smoked prosciutto with Gorgonzola, mascarpone, and arugula. It's closed weekends. Weekdays, it's open from 6:30 a.m. to 4 p.m. Prefer a salad? **Mixt Greens,** 120 Sansome St., at Bush Street (☎ 415-433-6498), provides a lovely range of made-to-order, organic gourmet salads (and a selection of sandwiches) that you can eat on premises or take away. The SoMa location, at 560 Mission St., between First and Second streets, is convenient to the Embarcadero. Both shops are open weekdays 10:30 a.m. to 3 p.m.

Closer to Union Square, with two other locations in the Financial District, is **Specialty's Cafe & Bakery,** 1 Post St., at Market Street (☎ 415-896-2253 or 877-502-2837; www.specialtysdirect.com). This spot is popular for a vast array of fresh sandwiches served on made-from-scratch breads. It's closed on weekends. Weekdays, it's open from 6 a.m. to 7 p.m.

The Ferry wonderful Building

If you only had a few hours to spend in San Francisco, I'd send you to the splendidly remodeled Ferry Building on the Embarcadero at the foot of Market Street. A landmark completed in 1898, the building gradually fell into disuse after the Bay Bridge opened in 1936, allowing commuters from the East Bay to drive, rather than take a ferry, into the city. The revitalization of the Embarcadero seems complete now that the clock tower shines beaconlike in the evening, and the Ferry Building marketplace is a hub once more, drawing people from around the Bay Area. Open every day (a few shops close on Sun), the light-filled space houses the best local purveyors of food and food-related items. To grab a quick bite, food to go, a picnic, or a complete meal, you can find something satisfying just by making a tour of the open-front shops. Some highlights: **Hog Island Oyster Company** oyster bar, with gorgeous bay views from the counter; **Mastrelli's Delicatessen,** the sister store to Molinari Delicatessen in North Beach, where you can order freshly made sandwiches to go; and **Golden Gate Meat Company,** a small counter that sells lunch meats as well as organic meats— my pastrami sandwich emitted such a delicious odor and looked so luscious, I actually had people stopping me to ask where I'd bought it. You'll also find a Japanese deli, a French rotisserie, chocolate, gelato, cookbooks, and gifts.

Down on the farm — farmers market, that is

Twice a week, the **Ferry Plaza Farmers Market** operates in front of and behind the Ferry Building. Basket- and canvas-sack-wielding shoppers pick over the heirloom tomatoes and grab the last of the wild strawberries while juggling coffee and cellphones. The simple beauty of the organic vegetables and flowers makes a walk around the market an enormous pleasure, despite the crowds. The **Hayes Street Grill** and **Rose Pistola** restaurants cook gourmet breakfasts at outdoor booths on Saturdays, and other vendors sell items such as bottles of olive oil, jars of local honey, and exotic orchid plants. This is also a great place to gather picnic food — fresh bread, artisan cheeses, and fruit — for later in the day. The F-Market streetcar drops you almost at the door. The market operates Tuesday (open: 10 a.m.–2 p.m.), but the day to visit is Saturday, when the selection of vendors is wider and the hours are longer (open: 8 a.m.–2 p.m.).

Snacking at the wharf

Let's be frank. **PIER 39/Fisherman's Wharf** is the most touristy part of town. The restaurants that crowd Jefferson Street exist for the people who are here today and gone tomorrow. I've learned to accept this, if not to embrace it, and I'm not going to sneer at anybody who spends part of a day here on the way to Alcatraz or just to see what all the fuss is about.

But let's say that this person is hungry. Let's say that this person has heard about all the crab vendors and the sourdough bread and thinks to himself, "That sounds like lunch to me." This is what I'd suggest: Buy a bottle of beer, buy a little round of sourdough bread, and ask one of the guys at a crab stand (try **Fisherman's Grotto No. 9**) to cook, clean, and crack a live crab for you. Then take these goodies and lots of napkins through the doors marked "Passageway to the Boats," walk down this relatively quiet area, sit on the dock, and have a good time. Remember: The local Dungeness crab season is from November through May. In the summer, the crabs are flown in from Alaska or parts east.

Unless you purchase a freshly cracked crab, rest assured that the $5.25 crab cocktail you ordered is made of canned crab — or even imitation crab.

Boudin Bakery (the sourdough bread people) operates a nifty demonstration bakery/cafe/museum on Fisherman's Wharf, 160 Jefferson St., at Taylor Street (☎ 415-928-1849). You can watch bread being prepared from a glass-walled catwalk suspended above the action, take a tour, sample the wares, and tuck into your soup at indoor and outdoor tables. Boudin created San Francisco's distinctive sourdough loaves in 1849, and for an icon, they taste pretty darn good.

Flour power

You can have a swell time hunting and gathering among the bakeries in North Beach. For starters, drop by **Liguria Bakery,** on the corner of Stockton and Filbert streets (☎ 415-421-3786), for a sheet of plain focaccia, or maybe one topped with green onions or tomato. They're all delicious and wrapped for portability. Liguria is open every day by 8 a.m. and closes when the last piece of focaccia is sold, usually by 2 p.m. I also love **Victoria Pastry Co.,** 1362 Stockton St., at Vallejo Street (☎ 415-781-2015), which sells a large selection of Italian sweets (the chewy almond cookies are good enough to give as a gift) and slices of its justly popular cakes.

Citizen Cake, 399 Grove St., in Hayes Valley (☎ 415-861-2228), creates homemade cookies, cakes, and desserts that ignite a love/hate relationship between your taste buds and your hips. The spacious cafe also serves lunch and dinner Tuesday through Friday (8 a.m.–10 p.m.) and brunch and dinner on weekends (Sat 10 a.m.–10 p.m.; Sun 10 a.m.–5 p.m.) It's near the stylish Hayes Street shopping blocks, which makes eating and spending so efficient.

A small chain of **Boulangerie Bay Bread** bakery/cafes has popped up in the Haight-Ashbury, Cow Hollow, Fillmore, and Russian Hill neighborhoods. My favorite is **Boulange de Polk,** 2310 Polk St., at Green Street (☎ 415-345-1107). Along with lovely French pastries (the *cannelés de*

Bordeaux are swoon-worthy), you can order savory tarts, sandwiches, and salads to go or to eat at one of the coveted outdoor tables.

Chinese bakeries

Chinese bakeries, which sell savory as well as sweet items, abound in **Chinatown,** in the **Sunset District** on Irving Street, and in the **Richmond District** on Clement Street. For snacking on the premises or on the go, delicious baked or steamed pork buns (baked buns are golden brown, and steamed buns are white) are ideal. They're also a big hit with kids. If you want something on the sweet side, custard tarts and sesame-seed-covered balls of rice surrounding a bit of sweet bean paste are standard issue. Look also for *bo lo bow,* slightly puffy and sweet bread with a crust that resembles the outside of a pineapple, or *chung yow bow,* green-onion bread. You may have to point to whatever looks appetizing, because the folks behind the counter don't necessarily speak English.

Coffee and tea, if you please

Places to sit and sip are as prevalent as pigeons in this caffeine-crazed piece of paradise. Coffeehouses — and I'm not even including the mega-chains — nestle in every neighborhood, seemingly on every block. I don't think drinking coffee as a lifestyle was invented in North Beach, but based on sheer numbers, it could have been. Regulars have their favorite blends and favorite tables, but no one will argue against hanging out at **Mario's Bohemian Cigar Store** on the corner of Columbus Avenue and Union Street (☎ 415-362-0536). Along with excellent coffee (Graffeo), you can graze on a mouth-watering chicken parmigiana on focaccia. **Caffe Trieste,** Vallejo and Grant streets (☎ 415-982-2605; www.caffetrieste.com), is a mob scene on Saturday afternoon, when the owners and friends take turns singing at the microphone. Coffee is served daily with or without opera. The roasting apparatus at **Caffe Roma,** 526 Columbus Ave. (☎ 415-296-7942), sits up front near the door. If you ask, and the staff members aren't busy making the perfect cappuccino, you could learn about the life cycle of the coffee bean.

Although that Seattle-based coffee Goliath continues to snap up real estate in a quest to make everyone drink frappuccinos, we have our own local chain to kick around. Actually, caffeine aficionados worship **Peet's Coffee & Tea.** If you love really strong coffee, it's worth dropping by one of the many stores. The one closest to Union Square is in the Financial District at 22 Battery St., at Bush Street (☎ 415-981-4550; www.peets.com). You can also try the shop on Chestnut Street between Steiner and Pierce streets in the Marina (☎ 415-931-8302) or the one in the Ferry Building (☎ 415-593-3831). They're all open daily. In Hayes Valley, the community kaffeeklatsch takes place on the pavement in front of a custom furniture workshop at 30 Linden St., an alley off Gough Street. Look for the seemingly makeshift bar of the **Blue Bottle Coffee Co.,** progenitor of the Blue Bottle Cafe (see the next section). You can eavesdrop or make new friends while waiting in line for a good strong cup.

Self-described coffee snobs have little choice but to drop by **Ritual Coffee Roasters,** 1026 Valencia St. in the Mission (☎ **415-641-1024**). The beans come from Portland, Oregon's Stumptown Coffee. The roomy storefront has a glass case filled with treats, free wireless, and long hours (open: until 11 p.m. Mon–Sat, until 9 p.m. Sun).

The peaceful **Imperial Tea Court,** in the Ferry Building on the Embarcadero (☎ 415-544-9830), is a must stop in which to rest your feet and take stock of your life — or maybe just the last half-hour — over a pot of exotic leaves and blossoms that would make Celestial Seasonings think twice. This is the place to sample the highest-quality teas as they were meant to be brewed, and the staff is happy to show you how it's done. Open weekdays 10 a.m. to 6 p.m., Saturday 9 a.m. to 6:30 p.m., Sunday 10:30 a.m. to 6 p.m.

Breakfast of champions

Touring is hard work; you need a good breakfast. Around Union Square, you can find lots of restaurants serving in the morning, including the **Grand Cafe** (☎ 415-292-0101) on Geary next to the Hotel Monaco, open daily; and **Dottie's True Blue Café,** 522 Jones St., between Geary Boulevard and O'Farrell Street (☎ 415-885-2767). Dottie's is my favorite after Brenda's (see listing this chapter). Open Wednesday through Monday only, it's a tiny diner that offers daily specials as well as the basics — eggs, pancakes, sausage — all prepared with great flair. The baked goods are so delicious you may want to purchase some to go. Expect to wait in line on the weekends. When the lines at Dottie's and Brenda's appear too daunting, just walk over to **Café Mason,** 320 Mason St. between Geary and O'Farrell streets (☎ 415-544-0320), for all kinds of fruit-enhanced pancakes, eggs any way, or maybe yogurt and fresh fruit. Prices are reasonable for Union Square, and the food's fine. Across from the Chinatown gate is **Café de la Presse,** 352 Grant Ave. (☎ 415-398-2680), very European in feel, with excellent lattes, croissants, newspapers, and lots of windows. Lines here move faster than you might think.

Bechelli's, in the Marina/Cow Hollow neighborhood at 2346 Chestnut St., between Divisadero and Scott streets (☎ 415-346-1801), serves a substantial breakfast until 3 p.m. during the week, and until 4 p.m. Saturday and Sunday. To my mind, the booths, scruffy leatherette chairs, and beat-up, horseshoe-shaped wooden counter add to the charm of this neighborhood institution, but more important, the breakfast menu is nearly as huge as the portions. Buttermilk pancakes, French toast, homemade corned beef hash, and lots of omelets could potentially hold you for a good part of the day. Kids often enjoy bellying up to the counter, and the place has a very relaxed, family-friendly atmosphere. No reservations; credit cards are accepted.

Hidden on an alleyway very near the Westfield Centre on Market and Fifth is the hippest spot in town for coffee and a bite, as evidenced by the crowd there on an otherwise deserted Sunday morning. **Blue Bottle Cafe,** on the corner of Mint and Jessie streets, between Market and

Mission streets (☎ 415-495-3394), siphons its coffee into glass containers and serves it with a selection of dishes, including beautifully browned Belgian waffles. Open weekdays 7 a.m. to 7 p.m., Saturday 8 a.m. to 8 p.m., and Sunday 8 a.m. to 4 p.m., it's a tight squeeze and a welcome change to this part of the neighborhood.

Around the Embarcadero at 2 Townsend St. is the aptly named **Town's End** (☎ 415-512-0749), one of the great places for a traditional brunch. The selection of dishes is comprehensive (from blintzes to huevos rancheros), the quality is high, and the prices are fair. But if you are just as content to have a couple of fried eggs, bacon, and hash browns with a view of the bay, cross the street and walk toward the ballpark. Look for a little shack with a few outdoor tables next to the South Beach harbor at Pier 40. This is the **Java House** (☎ 415-495-7260; www.javahousesf. com), an institution since 1912. Cash only, and you'll have to bus your dishes yourself.

Finally, if you have a soft spot for diners — and I mean the real thing, not *Happy Days* replicas — make your way to the end of Geary Boulevard (the name changes to Point Lobos Avenue) where it meets the Great Highway. The little joint overlooking the old Sutro Baths is **Louis,** 902 Point Lobos Ave. (☎ 415-387-6330), which opened in 1937 and has an endless view of the Pacific Ocean. Louis serves breakfast and lunch daily from 6:30 a.m. It's nothing to write home about, but there's something comfortable and familiar about the décor (linoleum, worn booths) and a big plate of eggs over easy, country ham, and hash browns. This is a fine place to eat before hiking along the Coastal Trail, golfing at Lincoln Park, or heading to Golden Gate Park. Cash and traveler's checks only.

Pizza and other cheap eats

Although I'm known to criticize fast food, I consider pizza an exception. Good pizza can make a perfectly satisfying, easygoing, low-rent meal. And although San Francisco doesn't have the reputation of New York or Chicago, you won't have any difficulty finding a ready slice in any neighborhood.

Uncle Vito's Pizzadelli, on the corner of Bush and Powell streets (☎ 415-391-5008), serves credible pies with a big selection of toppings, good salads, and enough pasta dishes to carbo-load for the next day's adventures. Uncle Vito's is inexpensive and convenient to Nob Hill and Union Square, so you'll see lots of foreign tourists here, attempting to put together just the right combination of pizza and beer. When shopping on Fillmore Street, stop by **Dino's Pizzeria** (☎ 415-922-4700) to check up on sports scores and dig into one of Dino's thick-crusted, cheesy creations. It's on the corner of Fillmore and California streets, where you'll often find Dino at the door eyeing passersby and chatting up the regulars.

If too much exposure to coddled food makes you long for a touch of grease, you can find a couple of places to deal with your craving for hamburgers, fries, and a shake. **Mo's Grill,** which makes many kinds of burgers, is South of Market at Folsom and Fourth streets, on the south-west side of Yerba Buena Gardens (☎ 415-957-3779). You can also find a branch in North Beach on Grant Street, between Vallejo and Green streets (☎ 415-788-3779). Because I have a soft spot for '50s-patterned Formica and bright colors, my favorite place to chew the fat is **Burger Joint,** 807 Valencia St., in the Mission (☎ 415-824-3494). And, despite my protestations against fast food, **Taylor's Refreshers** at the Ferry Building makes a great burger and a greater milkshake. Anyway, they aren't *that* fast.

North Beach also shelters at least two eateries specializing in roasted chicken, the older being **Il Pollaio,** 555 Columbus Ave., between Union and Green streets (☎ 415-362-7727). A very casual place to sit down for savory chicken and other meats and salads, this is where you go when the kids start rolling their eyes if you mention dim sum or sea bass. It's also a good choice when you're tired of spending too much money on dinner.

Adventure eaters in the mood for Indian food will barely feel a strain on their pocketbooks at **Shalimar,** 532 Jones St., between Geary and O'Farrell streets (☎ 415-928-0333), another Formica-tabled hole-in-the-wall in the Tenderloin/Union Square area. Order at the counter, sit at your table, watch for your food to come up, and then enjoy delicious curries, savory naan bread, and tandoori. It's open daily for lunch and dinner; cash only. Another highly recommended restaurant in the Tenderloin, and attractive enough for a date, is the **Bodega Bistro,** 607 Larkin St. at Eddy Street (☎ 415-921-1218). The *pho ga,* Vietnamese chicken noodle soup, is simply wonderful, due in part to brilliant chicken stock. Another can't-miss dish is papaya salad, but in fact, the dishes here are some of the best in the category. If you are uncomfortable in the neighborhood, come for lunch. Cash only.

The real dill

Oh, happy day. A genuine delicatessen, with bagels imported directly from New York, exists right here in San Francisco. You don't know how we suffered before **Miller's East Coast Delicatessen** started with the chicken soup and the matzo balls, not to mention the pastrami, the pickled herring, and the brisket (every bit as good as mine, if not better). Located at 1725 Polk St. (☎ 415-563-3542) and open daily, this is also a fine place to get sandwiches to take with you for the trip home — I wouldn't want you to go hungry.

Index of Establishments by Neighborhood

The Castro

Chow (American, $)
Home (American, $–$$)

Chinatown

Gold Mountain (Chinese/Dim Sum, $)
Lichee Garden (Chinese/Dim Sum, $)
R&G Lounge (Chinese, $)

Civic Center/Hayes Valley

Absinthe Brasserie & Bar (French, $$$)
Brenda's French Soul Food
(Breakfast/Creole, $)
Hayes Street Grill (Seafood, $$)
Jardinière (California/French, $$$$)
Zuni Café (California, $$)

The Embarcadero

Boulevard (American, $$$$)
Butterfly (Pan-Asian, $$$)
Taylor's Refreshers (Burgers, $)
Hog Island Oyster Company
(Seafood, $)
Java House (Breakfast, $)
Town's End (Breakfast, $)
The Slanted Door (Vietnamese, $$)
Yank Sing (Dim Sum, $$)

Financial District

B-44 (Spanish, $$)
City View (Chinese/Dim Sum, $)
Kokkari Estiatorio (Greek, $$$)
Plouf (French, $$)
Tadich Grill (Seafood, $$)

Glen Park

Chenery Park (American, $$)
Gialina (Pizza, $)
Le P'tit Laurent (French, $$)

Japantown/Western Addition

Isuzu (Japanese, $)
Mifune (Japanese, $)
1300 Fillmore (American/Southern,
$$$)
Yoshi's (Japanese/Sushi, $$$)

The Marina/Cow Hollow

A-16 (Italian, $$)
Bechelli's (Breakfast, $)
Bistro Aix (French, $–$$)
Greens Restaurant (Vegetarian,
$$–$$$)
Isa (French, $$)
La Terrasse (French, $$)
Mamacita (Mexican, $$)

Mission District

Bar Tartine (California/Mediterranean,
$$)
The Blue Plate (California, $$)
Burger Joint (Burgers, $)
Delfina (Italian, $$)
Dosa (Indian, $)
Farina (Italian, $$$)
Foreign Cinema (French/New
American, $$$)
Luna Park (New American, $$)
Pancho Villa (Mexican, $)
Pizzeria Delfina (Pizza, $)
Range (California, $$)
Taqueria Cancun (Mexican, $)
Ti Couz (Crepes, $)

Nob Hill

Uncle Vito's Pizzadelli (Pizza, $)

North Beach

Cafe Zoetrope (Italian, $)
Capp's Corner (Italian, $$)
Il Pollaio (Chicken, $)
L'Osteria del Forno (Italian, $)
Tommaso's Restaurant (Italian, $$)

Pacific Heights

Dino's Pizzeria (Pizza, $)
Quince Restaurant (Italian, $$$)
SPQR (Italian, $$)

Richmond/Sunset

Ebisu (Japanese, $$)
Katia's, A Russian Tea Room
(Russian, $)
Louis (Breakfast/Burgers, $)
Ton Kiang (Chinese, $$)

Russian Hill

Miller's East Coast Delicatessen
(Jewish, $)
Restaurant Gary Danko (French/New
American, $$$$)

South of Market (SoMa)

Ame (New American, $$$$)

AsiaSF (California/Asian, $$)
Blue Bottle Cafe (Breakfast, $)
Ducca (Italian, $$$)
Le Charm French Bistro (French, $$)
Mo's Grill (Burgers, $)
Restaurant Lulu (Mediterranean, $$)
supperclub (New American, $$$$)
Town Hall (New American, $$$)

The Tenderloin
Bodega Bistro (French-Vietnamese, $)

Union Square
Café de la Presse (French, $)
Café Mason (Breakfast, $)
Canteen (California, $$)
Colibrí Mexican Bistro (Mexican, $$)
Cortez (Mediterranean, $$$)
Dottie's True Blue Café (Breakfast, $)
Grand Cafe (Breakfast, $$$)
Shalimar (Indian, $)

Index of Establishments by Cuisine

American
Boulevard (The Embarcadero, $$$$)
Chenery Park (Glen Park, $$)
Chow (The Castro, $)
Home (The Castro, $–$$)

American/Southern
1300 Fillmore (Japantown/Western
Addition, $$$)

Breakfast
Bechelli's (The Marina/Cow Hollow, $)
Blue Bottle Cafe (SoMa, $)
Brenda's French Soul Food (Civic
Center/Hayes Valley, $)
Café Mason (Union Square, $)
Dottie's True Blue Café (Union
Square, $)
Grand Cafe (Union Square, $$$)
Java House (The Embarcadero, $)
Louis (Richmond/Sunset, $)
Town's End (The Embarcadero, $)

Burgers
Burger Joint (Mission District, $)
Louis (Richmond/Sunset, $)
Mo's Grill (SoMa, $)
Taylor's Refreshers (The
Embarcadero, $)

California
The Blue Plate (Mission District, $$)

Canteen (Union Square, $$)
Range (Mission District, $$)
Zuni Café (Civic Center/Hayes
Valley, $$)

California/Asian
AsiaSF (SoMa, $$)

California/French
Jardinière (Civic Center/Hayes Valley,
$$$$)

California/Mediterranean
Bar Tartine (Mission District, $$)

Chicken
Il Pollaio (North Beach, $)

Chinese
City View (Financial District, $)
Gold Mountain (Chinatown, $)
Lichee Garden (Chinatown, $)
R&G Lounge (Chinatown, $)
Ton Kiang (Richmond/Sunset, $$)

Crepes
Ti Couz (Mission District, $)

Creole
Brenda's French Soul Food (Civic
Center/Hayes Valley, $)

Dim Sum
City View (Financial District, $)
Gold Mountain (Chinatown, $)
Lichee Garden (Chinatown, $)
Yank Sing (The Embarcadero, $$)

French
Absinthe Brasserie & Bar (Civic Center/Hayes Valley, $$$)
Bistro Aix (The Marina/Cow Hollow, $–$$)
Café de la Presse (Union Square, $)
Foreign Cinema (Mission District, $$$)
Isa (The Marina/Cow Hollow, $$)
La Terrasse (The Marina/Cow Hollow, $$)
Le Charm French Bistro (SoMa, $$)
Le P'tit Laurent (Glen Park, $$)
Plouf (Financial District, $$)
Restaurant Gary Danko (Russian Hill, $$$$)

French-Vietnamese
Bodega Bistro (The Tenderloin, $)

Greek
Kokkari Estiatorio (Financial District, $$$)

Indian
Dosa (Mission District, $)
Shalimar (Union Square, $)

Italian
A-16 (The Marina/Cow Hollow, $$)
Cafe Zoetrope (North Beach, $)
Capp's Corner (North Beach, $$)
Delfina (Mission District, $$)
Ducca (SoMa, $$$)
Farina (Mission District, $$$)
L'Osteria del Forno (North Beach, $)
Quince Restaurant (Pacific Heights, $$$)
SPQR (Pacific Heights, $$)
Tommaso's Restaurant (North Beach, $$)

Japanese
Ebisu (Richmond/Sunset, $$)
Isuzu (Japantown/Western Addition, $)
Mifune (Japantown/Western Addition, $)
Yoshi's (Japantown/Western Addition, $$$)

Jewish
Miller's East Coast Delicatessen (Russian Hill, $)

Mediterranean
Cortez (Union Square, $$$)
Restaurant Lulu (SoMa, $$)

Mexican
Colibrí Mexican Bistro (Union Square, $$)
Mamacita (The Marina/Cow Hollow, $$)
Pancho Villa (Mission District, $)
Taqueria Cancun (Mission District, $)

New American
Ame (SoMa, $$$$)
Foreign Cinema (Mission District, $$$)
Luna Park (Mission District, $$)
Restaurant Gary Danko (Russian Hill, $$$$)
supperclub (SoMa, $$$$)
Town Hall (SoMa, $$$)

Pan-Asian
Butterfly (The Embarcadero, $$$)

Pizza
Dino's Pizzeria (Pacific Heights, $)
Gialina (Glen Park, $)
Pizzeria Delfina (Mission District, $)
Uncle Vito's Pizzadelli (Nob Hill, $)

Russian
Katia's, A Russian Tea Room (Richmond/Sunset, $)

Seafood
Hayes Street Grill (Civic Center/Hayes Valley, $$)
Hog Island Oyster Company (The Embarcadero, $)
Tadich Grill (Financial District, $$)

Spanish
B-44 (Financial District, $$)

Sushi
Yoshi's (Japantown/Western Addition, $$$)

Vegetarian
Greens Restaurant (The Marina/Cow Hollow, $$–$$$)

Vietnamese
The Slanted Door (The Embarcadero, $$)

Index of Establishments by Price

$

Bechelli's (Breakfast, The Marina/Cow Hollow)
Bistro Aix (French, The Marina/Cow Hollow)
Blue Bottle Cafe (Breakfast, SoMa)
Bodega Bistro (French-Vietnamese, The Tenderloin)
Brenda's French Soul Food (Creole, Civic Center/Hayes Valley)
Burger Joint (Burgers, Mission District)
Café de la Presse (French, Union Square)
Café Mason (Breakfast, Union Square)
Cafe Zoetrope (Italian, North Beach)
Chow (American, The Castro)
City View (Chinese/Dim Sum Financial District)
Dino's Pizzeria (Pizza, Pacific Heights)
Dosa (Indian, Mission District)
Dottie's True Blue Café (Breakfast, Union Square)
Gialina (Pizza, Glen Park)
Gold Mountain (Chinese/Dim Sum, Chinatown)
Hog Island Oyster Company (Seafood, The Embarcadero)
Home (American, The Castro)
Il Pollaio (Chicken, North Beach)
Isuzu (Japanese, Japantown/Western Addition)
Java House (Breakfast, The Embarcadero)

Katia's, A Russian Tea Room (Russian, Richmond/Sunset)
Lichee Garden (Chinese/Dim Sum, Chinatown)
L'Osteria del Forno (Italian, North Beach)
Louis (Breakfast/Burgers, Richmond/Sunset)
Mifune (Japanese, Japantown/Western Addition)
Miller's East Coast Delicatessen (Jewish, Russian Hill)
Mo's Grill (Burgers, SoMa)
Pancho Villa (Mexican, Mission District)
Pizzeria Delfina (Pizza, Mission District)
R&G Lounge (Chinese, Chinatown)
Shalimar (Indian, Union Square)
Taqueria Cancun (Mexican, Mission District)
Taylor's Refreshers (Burgers, The Embarcadero)
Ti Couz (Crepes, Mission District)
Town's End (Breakfast, The Embarcadero)
Uncle Vito's Pizzadelli (Pizza, Nob Hill)

$$

A-16 (Italian, The Marina/Cow Hollow)
AsiaSF (California/Asian, SoMa)
B-44 (Spanish, Financial District)

Bar Tartine (California/Mediterranean, Mission District)

Bistro Aix (French, The Marina/Cow Hollow)

The Blue Plate (California, Mission District)

Canteen (California, Union Square)

Capp's Corner (Italian, North Beach)

Chenery Park (American, Glen Park)

Colibrí Mexican Bistro (Mexican, Union Square)

Delfina (Italian, Mission District)

Ebisu (Japanese, Richmond/Sunset)

Greens Restaurant (Vegetarian, The Marina/Cow Hollow)

Hayes Street Grill (Seafood, Civic Center/Hayes Valley)

Home (American, The Castro)

Isa (French, The Marina/Cow Hollow)

La Terrasse (French, The Marina/Cow Hollow)

Le Charm French Bistro (French, SoMa)

Le P'tit Laurent (French, Glen Park)

Luna Park (New American, Mission District)

Mamacita (Mexican, The Marina/Cow Hollow)

Plouf (French, Financial District)

Range (California, Mission District)

Restaurant Lulu (Mediterranean, SoMa)

The Slanted Door (Vietnamese, The Embarcadero)

SPQR (Italian, Pacific Heights)

Tadich Grill (Seafood, Financial District)

Tommaso's Restaurant (Italian, North Beach)

Ton Kiang (Chinese, Richmond/Sunset)

Yank Sing (Dim Sum, The Embarcadero)

Zuni Café (California, Civic Center/Hayes Valley)

$$$

Absinthe Brasserie & Bar (French, Civic Center/Hayes Valley)

Butterfly (Pan-Asian, The Embarcadero)

Cortez (Mediterranean, Union Square)

Ducca (Italian, SoMa)

Farina (Italian, Mission District)

Foreign Cinema (New American/French, Mission District)

Grand Cafe (Breakfast, Union Square)

Greens Restaurant (Vegetarian, The Marina/Cow Hollow)

Kokkari Estiatorio (Greek, Financial District)

Quince Restaurant (Italian, Pacific Heights)

1300 Fillmore (American/Southern, Japantown/Western Addition)

Town Hall (New American, SoMa)

Yoshi's (Japanese/Sushi, Japantown/Western Addition)

$$$$

Ame (New American, SoMa)

Boulevard (American, The Embarcadero)

Jardinière (California/French, Civic Center/Hayes Valley)

Restaurant Gary Danko (French/New American, Russian Hill)

supperclub (New American, SoMa)

Part IV
Exploring San Francisco

The 5th Wave   By Rich Tennant

In this part . . .

*N*ow you get to the main course. This part tells you about the landmarks and neighborhoods that define San Francisco to the world. And you know what? Most of them are worthy of their star billing.

How do you take in everything? That depends on how much time you have. If you have only a day or two, a guided tour may be the best way of at least seeing, if not savoring, the sights. Or you can pick and choose from a list of a few places to explore, spend some quality time at each, and plan to come back to the city another time to catch the rest. If you have three or more days to wander, take a look at my suggested itineraries for an idea of how to absorb as much of the city as possible.

Don't forget the shopping opportunities while the pleasure of browsing in one-of-a-kind stores is still possible. An entire shopping chapter awaits, and it's filled with suggestions for finding interesting clothes, gifts, and foods that you won't see in your local mall. Leave room in your suitcase — it'll be heavier on the trip home.

You'd think it would be enough for me to help you plan your trip to San Francisco, a marvel among big cities, but no . . . I toss in a few extra treats for your dining and sightseeing pleasure. Chief among them are trips to the gorgeous Napa and Sonoma valleys, where the sights and scents of grapes and olives act like a restorative. Closer still is Berkeley, a microcosm of Northern California life that revolves around the university and a vibrant dining scene. Finally, nature boys and girls will have a veritable field day hiking, kayaking, or seeking the perfect cracked crab in the quaint hamlet of Half Moon Bay.

Chapter 11

Discovering San Francisco's Best Attractions

. . . .

In This Chapter

▶ Finding the most popular attractions in San Francisco

▶ Breaking into Alcatraz

▶ Riding the cable cars

▶ Crossing the Golden Gate Bridge

▶ Indulging history, architecture, sports, and nature lovers

▶ Taking a guided tour by land or sea

. . . .

Something is bringing you to San Francisco. Perhaps you've been overcome by recollections of old Rice-A-Roni commercials ("the San Francisco treat [ding ding!]") that became synonymous with cable cars. Or maybe visions of the Golden Gate Bridge spanning the icy waters of the bay are pulling you to the left coast. Are the views from your window a bit too flat? Is the thrill-seeker in you ready for the action our hills provide to drivers and passengers alike? Did you manage to schedule a week off from work, and coming to San Francisco just seemed like a good idea? Whatever your reasons for choosing this city, I don't think you'll be bored, and I know you won't be disappointed.

You may be curious to understand firsthand why this city is different from any other urban center in the United States, and why its residents are so passionate about where they live. After a few days making your way around, you may glean some of the reasons, the most apparent of which is the sheer beauty of the setting. There's more, of course. You never know what you'll see when you look carefully. Take those cable cars, for example: Sure, they're a fun ride, but as you climb aboard, observe the gripman (or gripwoman — there's one) and the other passengers, and note how the neighborhoods change as you head from Union Square through North Beach or past Nob Hill. Even watching the passersby on the pavement is an experience. I'll always remember how heads turned (and kept turning) to follow a gorgeous girl in black leather

Saving on entrance fees

Your timing has to be right, but if you're in the neighborhood, take advantage of free museum days. Entry is free to the **California Academy of Sciences** and the **Exploratorium** on the first Wednesday of every month; to the **Asian Art Museum** on the first Sunday of the month; and to the **Museum of Modern Art (MoMA)** and the **Legion of Honor** on the first Tuesday of every month. Every Thursday after 5 p.m., admission is reduced at the Asian and at MoMA, and they stay open until 9 p.m.

pants as she sashayed up Mason Street. It was certainly the first time I've ever been on a cable car that intentionally moved backward!

The following list gives you a quick reference of the features that make San Francisco, well, San Francisco.

San Francisco's Top Attractions

Alcatraz Island
Fisherman's Wharf

Hollywood movies, including *Birdman of Alcatraz, Escape from Alcatraz,* and *The Rock,* have recast what is essentially an early-20th-century ruin in San Francisco Bay into a hugely popular tourist site. Even if you're familiar with this former military fort and federal prison only from vague references to its famous prisoners — Al Capone, "Machine Gun" Kelly, Robert (the Birdman) Stroud — you'll find the self-guided tour of the cell house strangely moving. I credit this to the excellent audio guide, which includes remembrances narrated by former guards and prisoners, and to the low-key manner in which Alcatraz is presented. No attempt is made to glamorize the inmates or to condemn the system. This was a cold, isolated, maximum-security prison housing the most hardened criminals of the day, which coincidentally offered them glimpses of an enticing city, perhaps invoking longing and regret. Imagining what life here was like isn't all that difficult, but at the moment you begin to feel inklings of pity for the incarcerated, a vividly told story of an attempted prison escape reminds the listener that these inmates were, for the most part, remorseless. Before or after the cellblock tour, you're invited to view an orientation video. During fall and winter, you can tour the island itself on a walking path that begins near the ferryboat landing. (The trail is closed from mid-Feb through early Sept, during bird-nesting season.) Park rangers are around to answer questions, and they often give talks on the history of the prison and famous escapes. Bring a jacket as well as comfortable shoes for the steep walk to the cell house. A tram is available once an hour to take wheelchair users or anyone unable to make the walk up to the prison. The Alcatraz experience takes about 2½ hours, including the ferry ride.

To get the full effect of what being an inmate may have been like, try the **Alcatraz Night Tour.** The prison becomes especially sinister after the sun goes down, so use discretion before deciding to bring kids along. The tour is available Thursday through Monday only; the ferry departs at 6:10 p.m. and 6:50 p.m. (4:20 p.m. during the winter).

During the summer, you must reserve tickets far in advance for the ferry ride to the island, and tickets purchased are valid only on the date and time indicated on the ticket. Order tickets over the Web site, or call ☎ **415-981-ROCK** to buy them over the phone.

See maps p. 162 and p. 171. Pier 33, at Fisherman's Wharf for location of ferry departures. ☎ *415-981-7625.* www.AlcatrazCruises.com *or* www.nps.gov/alcatraz. *Open: Winter daily 9 a.m.–1:55 p.m.; summer daily 9 a.m.–5:25 p.m. Ferries run approximately every half-hour; arrive at least 20 minutes before sailing time. F-Market streetcar, Powell-Mason cable car (the line ends a few blocks away), or 30-Stockton bus. Admission (includes ferry and audio tour): $25 adults, $23 seniors 62 and older, $15 children 5–11. Night Tour: $32 adults, $29 seniors, $31 kids 12–17, $19 children 5–11.*

Asian Art Museum
Civic Center

The new Asian Art Museum holds one of the largest collections of Asian art in the Western world, covering 6,000 years and encompassing the cultures of Japan, China, Korea, and Southeast Asia. Housed in Golden Gate Park until 2003, the Asian gathered public and private funds to renovate the interior of the old Beaux Arts Main Library and create 37,500 square feet of exhibition space (and if that doesn't invigorate Civic Center, I'm not sure what will). Although the collection remains more than enough reason to visit, the renovation has also attracted plenty of attention. The design is by Gae Aulenti, the Milanese architect who turned the former d'Orsay train station in Paris into the popular Musée d'Orsay. The Asian is compact, and it won't take you more than a few hours to see all the galleries. **Cafe Asia** on the first floor is open from 10 a.m. for drinks and Asian-influenced dishes served cafeteria style.

Getting around and in with Citypass

Citypass (www.citypass.net) is a booklet of discounted tickets to six major attractions — the **Museum of Modern Art, Palace of the Legion of Honor** and **de Young museums, Aquarium of the Bay,** and **Exploratorium** or **Asian Art Museum,** and a **Blue & Gold Fleet Bay Cruise.** The price includes a seven-day Muni Passport, making the pass quite a bargain for those who are ambitious enough to use all the coupons; they're valid for nine days from the date of purchase. The cost is $54 for adults, $44 for kids, online or at the participating attractions.

San Francisco's Top Sights

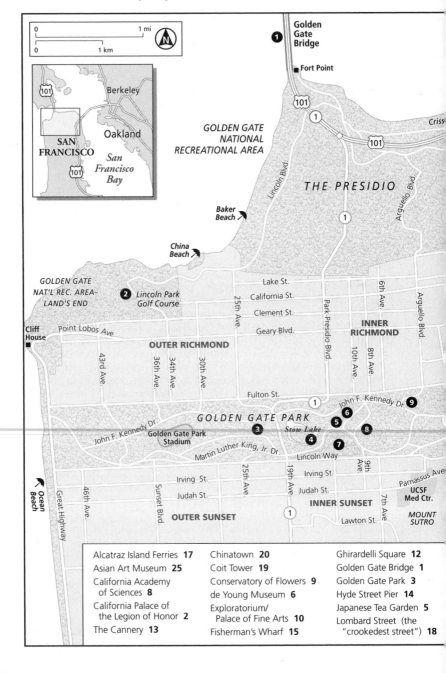

Alcatraz Island Ferries **17**	Chinatown **20**	Ghirardelli Square **12**
Asian Art Museum **25**	Coit Tower **19**	Golden Gate Bridge **1**
California Academy of Sciences **8**	Conservatory of Flowers **9**	Golden Gate Park **3**
California Palace of the Legion of Honor **2**	de Young Museum **6**	Hyde Street Pier **14**
	Exploratorium/ Palace of Fine Arts **10**	Japanese Tea Garden **5**
The Cannery **13**	Fisherman's Wharf **15**	Lombard Street (the "crookedest street") **18**

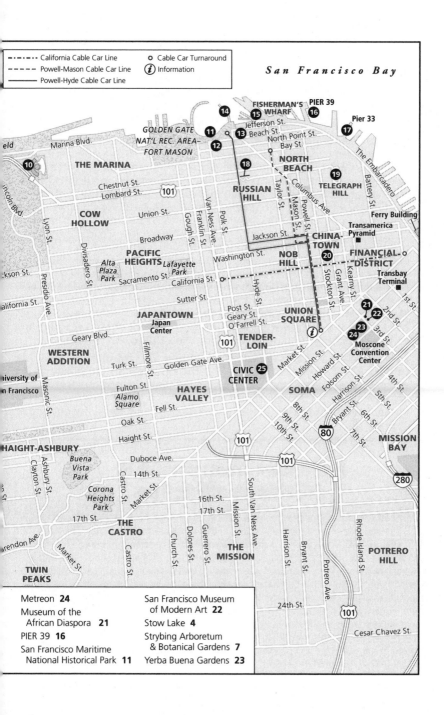

- - · - · California Cable Car Line
- - - - Powell-Mason Cable Car Line
———— Powell-Hyde Cable Car Line

o Cable Car Turnaround
ⓘ Information

San Francisco Bay

FISHERMAN'S WHARF — PIER 39
Jefferson St.
Pier 33
GOLDEN GATE NAT'L REC. AREA– FORT MASON
Beach St.
North Point St.
Bay St.
THE MARINA
Marina Blvd.
eld

Chestnut St.
Lombard St.
101

NORTH BEACH
RUSSIAN HILL
Taylor St.
Columbus Ave.
Mason St.
Powell St.
TELEGRAPH HILL
Battery St.

COW HOLLOW
Union St.
Broadway
Van Ness Ave.
Franklin St.
Gough St.
Polk St.

Ferry Building
Transamerica Pyramid

CHINA-TOWN
PACIFIC HEIGHTS
Lafayette Park
Washington St.
Jackson St.
NOB HILL
FINANCIAL DISTRICT

Alta Plaza Park
Sacramento St.
California St.
Hyde St.
Stockton St.
Grant Ave.
Kearny St.
Transbay Terminal

Sutter St.
1st St.

JAPANTOWN
Japan Center
Post St.
Geary St.
O'Farrell St.
UNION SQUARE
21
22

Geary Blvd.
Fillmore St.
TENDER-LOIN
101
23
24
Moscone Convention Center
2nd St.
3rd St.

WESTERN ADDITION
Turk St.
Golden Gate Ave.
Market St.
Mission St.
Howard St.
Folsom St.
Harrison St.
4th St.

niversity of
n Francisco
Masonic St.
Fulton St.
Alamo Square
HAYES VALLEY
CIVIC CENTER
25
SOMA
5th St.

Fell St.
8th St.
9th St.

Oak St.
Bryant St.
6th St.

HAIGHT-ASHBURY
Haight St.
101
10th St.
80
7th St.
MISSION BAY

Buena Vista Park
Duboce Ave.
14th St.
101
280

Corona Heights Park
16th St.
17th St.
South Van Ness Ave.
Mission St.
Rhode Island St.
POTRERO HILL

17th St.
THE CASTRO
Dolores St.
Guerrero St.
THE MISSION
Harrison St.
Bryant St.
Potrero Ave.

TWIN PEAKS
Castro St.
Church St.
24th St.
101

Cesar Chavez St.

Metreon **24**

Museum of the African Diaspora **21**

PIER 39 **16**

San Francisco Maritime National Historical Park **11**

San Francisco Museum of Modern Art **22**

Stow Lake **4**

Strybing Arboretum & Botanical Gardens **7**

Yerba Buena Gardens **23**

See map p. 162. 200 Larkin St., at Fulton Street. ☎ **415-581-3500.** www.asian art.org. *Muni or BART to Civic Center station. Public parking lot across the street. Open: Tues–Sun 10 a.m.–5 p.m., Thurs until 9 p.m. Admission: $12 adults, $8 seniors 65 and over, $7 students and kids 13–17, free for kids under 12. $5 every Thurs after 5 p.m. and free first Sun of the month.*

Cable Cars
Union Square/Financial District

San Francisco's most notable icon is probably the cable car. These cherished wooden cars creak and squeal up and around hills while passengers lean out into the wind, running the risk of getting their heads removed by passing buses. San Francisco's three existing lines make up the world's only surviving system of cable cars, and they are a delight to ride. The sheer joy of whizzing down a hill with the bay glistening in the foreground will linger in your memory. But these legendary icons aren't just fun — they're also a useful means of transportation. The **Powell-Mason line** wends its way from the corner of Powell and Market streets through North Beach and ends near **Fisherman's Wharf.** If you have time to ride the cars only once, this is the one I'd recommend. It will take you most of the way to Fisherman's Wharf, or, if you prefer, you can hop off when you get to North Beach. The **Powell-Hyde line,** which starts at the same intersection, ends up near the **Maritime Museum** and **Ghirardelli Square.** The somewhat less thrilling, but less crowded, **California line** begins at the foot of Market Street and travels straight up California Street over **Nob Hill** to Van Ness Avenue.

I thought I had a foolproof method of avoiding the crowds at the cable-car turnarounds (which is literally where the cars are turned around at the end of the line) by waiting 2 blocks from the Powell Street turnaround, but after forcing my visiting brother to watch as one full car after another passed us by ("And you do this professionally?" he said), my only other

From maximum prison to maximum attraction

Alcatraz Island was discovered in 1775. Taking advantage of its strategic location in San Francisco Bay, the U.S. Army began building a military fortress atop "The Rock." From 1850 to 1933, it served as a military post and army prison, housing Civil War, Spanish-American War, and, finally, civilian prisoners. In 1934, it was converted into a maximum-security prison. The prison was home to famous gangsters such as Al Capone; Robert Stroud, the so-called Birdman of Alcatraz (because he was an expert on ornithological diseases — he never kept birds on Alcatraz); and "Machine Gun" Kelly. Twenty-nine prisoners tried to escape from Alcatraz. Two made it ashore, only to be captured almost immediately, and five presumably drowned, although their bodies were never recovered. All 29 attempts are said to have failed. The prison closed in 1963, due to deterioration of the buildings and prohibitive maintenance costs. Alcatraz became part of the Golden Gate National Recreation Area in 1972.

The steel wheels tour

The famous cable cars you see going up and down the hills of downtown San Francisco were invented in 1869 by Andrew Hallidie. Hallidie saw the need for a new mode of transportation when he witnessed a horse-drawn streetcar slide backward down one of the many steep slopes that make up San Francisco's unique topography. Here's how the cable-car system works: A steel cable sits just under the street in a rail, kind of like an inside-out train rail (it's the cable that makes that clickity-clacking sound). Powered by electricity, this cable constantly runs through the rail. Each cable car has a lever that, when pulled back, closes a pincerlike "grip" on the cable. The person who pulls the lever is called a *gripper* — some would call this person a driver, but he doesn't drive, he "grips" the cable. The cable car is then attached to the cable that runs through the rail under the pavement, and the car begins to move at a constant 9 mph — the speed at which the cable is set to travel.

suggestion is to get up early to ride. (It turns out we were waiting at what the hotel doormen refer to as "Fantasy Island.") You can also try walking a few more blocks to the next stop. (Brown signs with a white cable car on them indicate stops.) Although at first it will appear that there's no room among the zillions of passengers already on the car, by magic a foothold may open up. Otherwise, go get in line with a coffee. Cars run from 6:30 a.m. to 12:30 a.m. The fare is $5 per person one-way, payable on board; Muni Passports are accepted. For more information, call Muni at ☎ 415-673-6864 or log on to www.sfmta.com. See Chapter 8 for more details, including a route map on p. 80.

Chinatown

Crowded with pedestrians and crammed with exotic-looking shops and vegetable markets whose wares spill onto the sidewalks, Chinatown is a genuinely fascinating destination. Take your time as you walk through this enclave, home to the largest Chinese population outside of Asia — it's easy to miss something. The **Dragon Gate arch** at Grant Avenue and Bush Street (just a few blocks north of Union Square) marks the entry to Chinatown. To get a more authentic experience, explore the side streets and alleys off Grant Avenue. If you stay for lunch or dinner, your adventure will take about a half-day. Walking from Union Square is the sensible way to get here, but you can also reach Chinatown by taking the 30-Stockton bus — quite an experience during rush hour. Parking is nearly impossible, but if you want to try it, your best bet is on Kearny Street under Portsmouth Square. (See Chapter 10 for dining suggestions and Chapter 12 for shopping pointers.) While you're in Chinatown, don't miss the following highlights.

The Chinese Historical Society of America is a good place to begin. A museum and research center, the Historical Society documents the fascinating story of the Chinese in California through photographs, art, and changing exhibits. Its bookstore stocks fiction and nonfiction titles on Chinese themes.

Chinatown

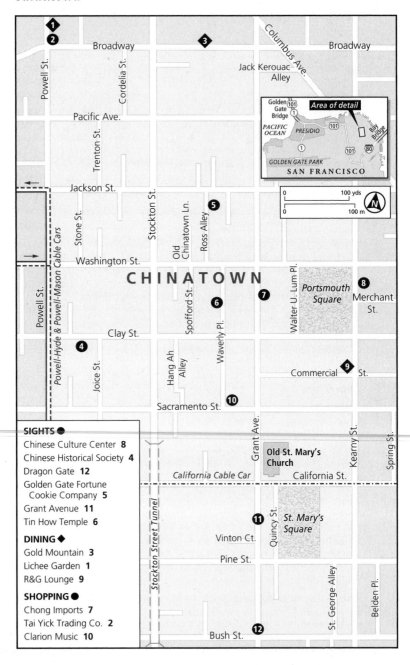

SIGHTS ●
Chinese Culture Center **8**
Chinese Historical Society **4**
Dragon Gate **12**
Golden Gate Fortune
  Cookie Company **5**
Grant Avenue **11**
Tin How Temple **6**

DINING ◆
Gold Mountain **3**
Lichee Garden **1**
R&G Lounge **9**

SHOPPING ●
Chong Imports **7**
Tai Yick Trading Co. **2**
Clarion Music **10**

See map p.166. 965 Clay St. ☎ 415-391-1188. www.chsa.org. *Admission: $3 adults, $2 seniors, $1 children 6–17; free first Thurs of the month. Open: Tues–Fri noon to 5 p.m., Sat 11 a.m.–4 p.m.*

Tin How Temple, one of the oldest Chinese temples in the United States, is dedicated to the Goddess of Heaven, protector of fishermen. The temple is open to the public, but please keep in mind this is an active house of worship. Be prepared to climb a narrow staircase to the top floor, and make an offering or buy some incense on your way out.

See map p. 166. 125 Waverly Place, off Clay Street between Stockton and Grant streets. No phone. Admission: Free. Open: 9 a.m.–4 p.m. daily.

Golden Gate Fortune Cookie Company is a working factory where you can buy bags of fresh, inexpensive almond and fortune cookies (in chocolate or vanilla). You may find the cramped quarters somewhat claustrophobic, but watching rounds of dough transmogrify into cookies is fun.

See map p. 166. 956 Ross Alley, between Jackson and Washington streets near Grant Avenue. No phone. Admission: Free. Open: Daily 10 a.m.–7 p.m.

Portsmouth Square, a park above the Portsmouth Square parking garage on Kearny Street between Washington and Clay streets, marks the spot of the original settlement of San Francisco and is the site of the first California public school, which opened in 1848. A compact but complete playground attracts the neighborhood preschoolers and, in the morning, elderly Chinese people practice their tai chi exercises. The landscape includes comfortable benches, attractive lampposts, and young trees. The distinctly San Francisco view includes the **Transamerica Pyramid** looming above the skyline. The garage below is a good place to know about if you're driving. Interestingly, the garage's fourth floor is most likely to have empty spaces, because in Cantonese, the word for *four* sounds like the word for *death*. Superstitious Chinese won't park there.

The pedestrian bridge over Kearny Street leads directly into the third floor of the Hilton Financial District, where you'll find the **Chinese Culture Center.** A gift shop leads to the gallery, where changing exhibits may feature photographs from pre-earthquake Chinatown, Chinese brush painting, or embroidered antique clothing and household items. The center also offers two-hour docent-led heritage walks for groups of 4 or more by reservation; $18 adults and $10 kids under 12.

See map p. 166. 750 Kearny St. ☎ 415-986-1822. www.c-c-c.org. *Admission: Free. Open: Tues–Sun 10 a.m.–4 p.m.*

Coit Tower
Telegraph Hill (near North Beach)

Erected in 1933 with funds bequeathed to the city by Lillie Hitchcock Coit, this 210-foot concrete landmark is visible from much of the city. But everyone needs to take a closer look to see the beauty of the tower. The décor inside features dramatic murals inspired by and commissioned during the Great Depression. Take an elevator to the top for panoramic views of the city and the bay. This diversion will probably take about 30 minutes from start to finish.

See map p.162. Atop Telegraph Hill. ☎ *415-362-0808. Take the 39-Coit bus, or walk from Lombard Street where it meets Telegraph Hill Boulevard. (2 blocks east of Stockton Street). Parking: The drive up and the parking lot are always a mass of cars. Admission to top of tower: $4.50 adults, $3.50 seniors, $2 kids 6–12. Open: Daily 10 a.m.–5 p.m.*

Contemporary Jewish Museum
SoMa

The newest addition to the Yerba Buena cultural mix is the long-awaited Contemporary Jewish Museum. You can admire the dramatic Daniel Libeskind–designed building, which incorporates elements from the historic Jessie Street Power Substation, from various angles, including the patio outside Ducca alongside the Westin Market Street (see Chapter 10). An exploration of modern perspectives on Jewish culture, history, art, and ideas, it mounts temporary exhibits ranging from an examination of the writer Gertrude Stein to a sound piece commissioned and curated by musician John Zorn. Should you have a chance to visit before October 2009, be sure to stop by the StoryCorps Outpost that's been based at the museum for one year. Families with young children can pick up an art pack at the front desk that will help engage the kids as they explore the premises. Admission isn't necessary to eat at the museum's cafe or visit the gift shop. A plaza that fronts the museum is a lovely link to Yerba Buena Gardens across the street.

See map p.178. 736 Mission St., between Third and Fourth streets. ☎ *415-344-8800.* www.thecjm.org. *Take any Muni streetcar to the Montgomery Street Station or the 15-Third, 30-Stockton, 45-Union/Stockton or any Market Street bus. Admission: $8 adults, $6 seniors and students, free for kids under 19. Open: Mon, Tues, Fri–Sun 11 a.m.–5:30 p.m., Thurs 1–8:30 p.m. Closed Wed.*

Exploratorium/Palace of Fine Arts
Marina District

Scientific American magazine rates the Exploratorium "the best science museum in the world," and it's certainly an intriguing space that appeals to all ages. The hands-on exhibits explore topics such as technology, human perception, and natural phenomena. Well-written text accompanies the exhibits to enhance the learning experience. Don't worry about feeling like a science dunce if you're visiting with children; a well-informed volunteer is ready to field any questions you can't answer. Expect to spend two hours minimum exploring the museum, especially if you're traveling with kids. Allow more time, and make reservations, if you want to experience the popular Tactile Dome, a pitch-black geodesic dome that you have to feel your way through. A walk around the grounds of the **Palace of Fine Arts,** which now houses the Exploratorium but was originally built for the

1915 Panama-Pacific International Exposition, is a great way to unwind after exploring the museum. Better yet, if the weather's balmy, bring a picnic and stay awhile.

See map p. 162. 3601 Lyon St., at Marina Boulevard. ☎ **415-561-0360.** www.exploratorium.edu. *30-Stockton bus to Marina stop. Parking: Free and easy. Admission: $14 adults; $11 students, youth 13–17, and seniors; $9 kids 4–12; free kids under 4; free for all first Wed of the month; tactile dome: $17 (includes general admission) all ages. Open: Tues–Sun 10 a.m.–5 p.m.*

Fisherman's Wharf

Don't be confused when you arrive at Fisherman's Wharf and see lots of people wandering around, none of whom appear to fish for a living. This was once a working set of piers, but today it's a seemingly endless outdoor shopping mall masquerading as a bona fide destination. Some people enjoy examining the refrigerator magnets and cable-car bookends stocked in one olde shoppe after another; others, dazed in the presence of so much kitsch, plan their escape. Still, because most folks stop by the wharf for one reason or another, here's a rundown of what's there.

No matter the weather, tourists crowd **PIER 39,** a multilevel, Disneyesque shopper's dream (or nightmare). Arcades, lined with deafening video games, anchor the pier on each end. You can also find T-shirt and sweatshirt shops and plenty of fried food. Join the mob if you want to take in the views of Alcatraz visible from the end of the pier or watch the huge sea lions that loaf around on the west side of the pier (follow the barking). Catch the ferry to Alcatraz or for bay cruises as well. If you're hungry, stop by the only authentic place to eat, the **Eagle Cafe** (☎ **415-433-3689;** www.eaglecafe.com), open daily from 7:30 a.m. to 9 p.m. on the second floor. This inexpensive breakfast and lunch joint opened in 1920. If you're arriving by car, park on adjacent streets or on the wharf between Taylor and Jones streets. *Note:* The parking garage charges $6 per hour! Do your best to avoid the price gouging and don't bring a car here. Besides, taking the F-Market down the Embarcadero is much more fun (see Chapter 8).

The giant fish bowl known as the **Aquarium of the Bay** is dedicated to the creatures that inhabit the San Francisco Bay ecosystem (so don't go looking for tropical species). After a brief introduction to the underwater world, facilitated by a loquacious band of naturalists, visitors descend to a moving walkway that slowly leads through two clear tunnels surrounded by 700,000 gallons of filtered bay water. Many thousands of fish swim by, some seemingly chasing their lunch. If you've ever wanted to be practically face to face with a *Prionace glauca,* this is your big chance. The last exhibit contains touch pools, always a hit with children. Should a trip to the Monterey Bay Aquarium be in your future, you can easily skip this smaller cousin, but for something with an educational component on the wharf, this is a refreshing stop.

See map p. 171. PIER 39 Fisherman's Wharf. ☎ *800-SEA-DIVE.* www.aquariumofthebay.com. *Admission: $15 adults, $8 seniors and kids 3–11, $38 for a family ticket. Add $6 for the "Behind the Scenes" tour. Open: Winter Mon–Fri 10 a.m.–6 p.m., Sat–Sun 10 a.m.–7 p.m.; summer daily 9 a.m.–8 p.m.*

The **San Francisco Maritime National Historical Park** is a small two-story museum overlooking the bay and Alcatraz. Examining the model schooners, figureheads, and photographs illustrating the city's maritime heritage takes only 15 minutes, although children may lose interest after the first five minutes. Still, it's sweet and admission is free. The museum will be closed for remodeling, however, until mid-2009.

See map p. 162. Bathhouse Building at the foot of Polk Street. ☎ *415-561-7100.* www.nps.gov/safr.

The **National Park Service** operates a **visitor center** inside the Argonaut Hotel (see Chapter 9), which partners with the Maritime National Historical Park. Along with exhibits and an educational center, the rangers working the desk can answer questions about special events on the Hyde Street Pier.

See map p. 84. Hyde and Jefferson streets. ☎ *415-447-5000.* http://www.nps. gov/safr/planyourvisit/the-visitor-center.htm. *Admission: Free. Open: Daily 9:30 a.m.–5:30 p.m.*

If you have small children (or anyone interested in history) along, you won't want to miss touring the **USS *Pampanito*.** This submarine saw active duty during World War II and helped save 73 British and Australian prisoners of war. The family pass (for two adults and up to four children) also gets you into the **Hyde Street Pier** (see following).

See map p. 171. Pier 45. ☎ *415-561-6662. Admission: Submarine with 20-minute audio tour $9 adults, $5 seniors and students, $3 children 6–12, free for kids under 6; family pass $20. Open: Winter daily 9 a.m.–6 p.m., summer until 8 p.m.*

At the **Hyde Street Pier,** 2 blocks east of the Maritime Museum, you can roam around on a number of historic, refurbished ships. Of particular note is the ***Balclutha,*** an 1886 square-rigger with an interesting past. During the year, activities on the *Balclutha* include concerts, sea chantey sing-alongs, and children's events. Call for a schedule. Touring the vessels takes at least an hour or so.

See map p. 171. ☎ *415-556-6435. Admission: $5 adults, free for kids under 16. Pier open: Daily 9:30 a.m.–5:30 p.m.*

Ghirardelli Square, which is the site of the original Ghirardelli chocolate factory, is across the street from the Maritime Park. Granted landmark status in 1982, the series of brick buildings is home to some unique stores and restaurants, and sponsors a roster of special events, including an annual chocolate-tasting benfit in September. At the moment, the south end of the square is under construction and, in partnership with Fairmont Hotels and Resorts, will emerge as a private residence club.

See maps p. 162 and p.171. Bordered by Polk and Hyde streets to the east and west, Beach and Bay streets to the north and south. ☎ *415-775-5500.* www.ghirardelli sq.com. *Admission: Free. Open: Mon–Wed 10 a.m.–7 p.m., Thurs–Sat until 9 p.m., Sun 10 a.m.–6 p.m.*

Fisherman's Wharf and Vicinity

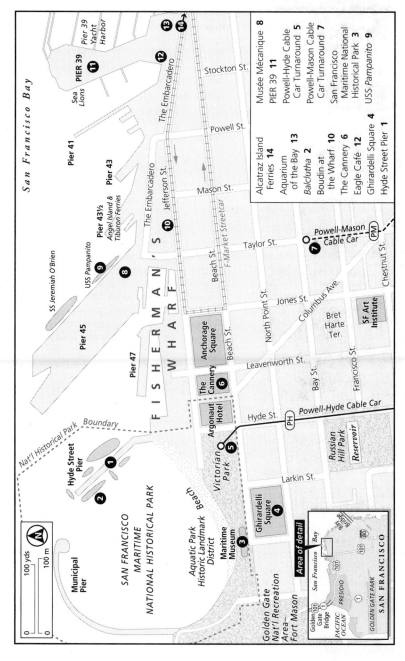

Alcatraz Island Ferries **14**
Aquarium of the Bay **13**
Balclutha **2**
Boudin at the Wharf **10**
The Cannery **6**
Eagle Café **12**
Ghirardelli Square **4**
Hyde Street Pier **1**
Musée Mécanique **8**
PIER 39 **11**
Powell-Hyde Cable Car Turnaround **5**
Powell-Mason Cable Car Turnaround **7**
San Francisco Maritime National Historical Park **3**
USS *Pampanito* **9**

Go 1 block east of Ghirardelli Square and you find what was once the largest peach-canning facility on earth. Today, the **Cannery at Del Monte Square** features shops, jugglers, musicians, and food. Visitors especially enjoy **Lark in the Morning** (☎ 415-922-HARP), a music haven with an array of early music and modern instruments. Gift shoppers of a practical bent and people with newly formed blisters will also love **Sock Heaven** (☎ 415-563-7327), which, as the name implies, sells foot coverings, in both silly and conventional patterns.

See map p. 171. At the foot of Polk Street, on the western edge of the Embarcadero. ☎ *415-556-3002. Take the Powell-Hyde cable-car line to the last stop; the F-Market streetcar; or the 19-Polk, 30-Stockton, 42-Downtown Loop, or 47-Van Ness bus. Parking: Pricey lots and garages; street parking is difficult. Admission: Free. Open: Daily 10 a.m.–5 p.m.*

Golden Gate Bridge

You can walk the bridge, bike the bridge, or drive the bridge, but whatever you do, don't miss the bridge. The quintessential San Francisco landmark spans 1$\frac{7}{10}$ miles and soars hundreds of feet above the water. Bundle up against the windy conditions, and then set out from the **Roundhouse** on the San Francisco side of the bridge lot (see "Especially for hikers," later in this chapter, for information on walking to the bridge). It can get pretty noisy, but the views can't be beat. Remember that the only way to return from the other side is on foot, so know your limits before crossing the entire bridge and finding out you're too tired to make it back. Afterward, take some time to climb below the span to see the 5-acre garden there. The 28–19th Avenue or the 29-Sunset buses deposit you across from the viewing area, right by a parking lot. If you're driving, take 19th Avenue or Lombard Street and pay attention to the sign that indicates when to exit for the parking lot. Otherwise, enjoy your drive across the bridge: There's a $5 toll upon your return to the city.

See map p. 162. Highway 101 North. www.goldengatebridge.org. *Admission: Free for pedestrians; $5 toll per southbound car. Open to pedestrians: Daily 5 a.m.– 9 p.m. on the east sidewalk.*

Golden Gate Park

Once nothing but a sand-covered tract, today's glorious Golden Gate Park features 1,017 acres of greenery and cultural attractions. San Franciscans do just about everything here, from playing soccer to sailing model yachts to throwing family reunions. On Sunday, when John F. Kennedy Drive closes to street traffic, bicyclists ride with impunity, and in-line skaters converge for dance parties. On Sundays from April through the middle of October, the **Golden Gate Park Band** plays from 1 to 3 p.m. in the **Spreckles Temple of Music,** between the new **de Young Museum** and the new **California Academy of Sciences.** A massive **Children's Playground** and a beautifully restored carousel sit just past the grand park entrance on Stanyan Street (off Waller Street). This remodeled entrance, for some reason, reduced the rather large number of street people who used to hang out there (the Haight seems to attract youthful transients and burnouts) but didn't completely eliminate the panhandling. In any event, don't let that keep you away. Another entrance at Ninth Avenue on Lincoln Way brings you to the **Strybing Arboretum** and the **Japanese Tea Garden.**

Joggers and parents pushing baby strollers make regular use of the path around man-made **Stow Lake.** It's the perfect place to take advantage of a sunny day by renting a paddleboat and having a picnic. The **boathouse** (☎ 415-752-0347) also rents bikes and in-line skates by the hour, half-, and full day. If you aren't driving, it's a bit of a walk to the boathouse, which is west of the Japanese Tea Garden on Martin Luther King Drive. It's open daily from 9 a.m. to 4 p.m.

See map p. 174. www.parks.sfgov.org. *The N-Judah Muni Metro streetcar drops you off on Ninth Avenue and Judah Street; from there it is a 3-block walk to the park. Numerous bus lines drive close to or into the park, including the 44-O'Shaughnessy, which you can catch on Ninth Avenue, the 21-Hayes, the 71-Haight-Noriega, and the 5-Fulton. You can also transfer to the 44-O'Shaughnessy from the 38-Geary bus on Sixth Avenue. Open daily. Contact individual attractions for hours and admission prices.*

California Academy of Sciences
Golden Gate Park

Always a must on the tourist trail, the rebuilt California Academy of Sciences is now a world-class destination for students of architecture, sustainability, and the natural sciences. A favored weekend haunt of San Franciscans for decades, it is not to be missed. The new building, designed by Pritzker Prize–winning architect Renzo Piano and opened in September 2008, is a marvel from top to bottom. Inside, a rain forest dome spirals up three stories, highlighting a different ecosystem on each floor. The Morrison Planetarium is back, with regularly scheduled shows featuring all your favorite stars (sorry — couldn't stop myself), and Piano recreated the African hall from the original building, only better, adding a display area at one end for African penguins. On the basement level, the aquarium includes the world's deepest coral reef, tanks filled with fish and seahorses and jellies, and a swamp with genuinely scary alligators. An early-childhood playroom, a cafe, and well-stocked gift shop make this an ideal outing for families. When you can tear yourself away from all the wonders within the walls, take the elevator to the roof. Planted with 2.5 acres of native plants tucked into coconut fiber containers, it's not merely beautiful, it's a model of energy efficiency.

See map p. 162. Hagiwara Tea Garden Dr., off John F. Kennedy Drive. ☎ **415-379-8000.** www.calacademy.org. *Admission: $25 adults, $20 seniors over 64 and youths 12–17, $15 kids 7–11, free for children under 7. Free third Wed of the month. $3 discount with Muni transfer or fast pass or bike. Open: Mon–Sat 9:30 a.m.–5 p.m., Sun 11 a.m.–5 p.m.*

The Conservatory of Flowers
Golden Gate Park

A fixture in guidebooks and tourist brochures, and nearly as recognizable as the Golden Gate Bridge, the postcard-perfect Victorian Conservatory

Golden Gate Park

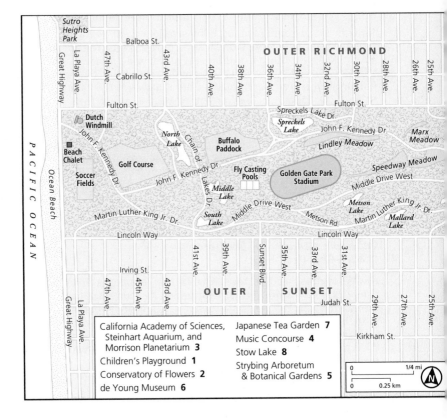

California Academy of Sciences, Steinhart Aquarium, and Morrison Planetarium **3**
Children's Playground **1**
Conservatory of Flowers **2**
de Young Museum **6**
Japanese Tea Garden **7**
Music Concourse **4**
Stow Lake **8**
Strybing Arboretum & Botanical Gardens **5**

of Flowers closed in 1995 after sustaining massive damage during a storm. Prefabricated in Ireland in 1875 and erected in the park around 1878, it reopened in 2003. Rare orchids, ferns, tropical plants, and a 100-year-old philodendron rescued from the wreckage are on exhibit.

See map p.162. Conservatory: Just off John F. Kennedy Drive, near the Stanyan Street entrance. ☎ *415-666-7001.* www.conservatoryofflowers.org. *Admission: $5 adults, $3 seniors and youth 12–17, $1.50 kids 5–11, free for children under 5. Free first Tues of the month. Open: Tues–Sun 9 a.m.–4:30 p.m.*

The de Young Museum
Golden Gate Park

San Francisco Chronicle publisher, M. H. de Young founded the city's first fine arts museum in 1895. Its eclectic permanent collection today includes American paintings as well as sculpture, textiles, African and Oceanic objects, furniture, and contemporary crafts housed in a sprawling, copper-clad three-story complex that opened in 2005. If you want to make some

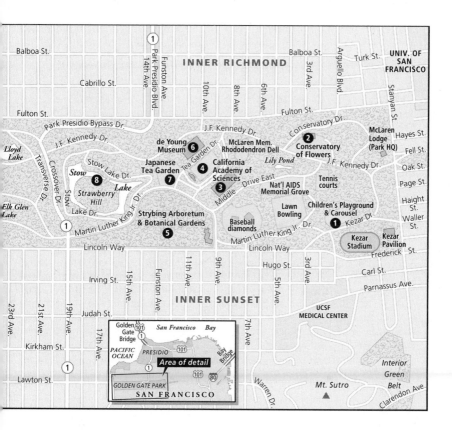

sense of the collection, consider taking one of the free docent tours offered daily at 10 a.m., 11 a.m., 1 p.m., and 2 p.m. A highlight of the building is the 144-foot tower offering unobstructed views (if the sky is clear) of the neighborhoods beyond the park and the living roof of the Academy of Sciences across the way. Access to the tower is free, even if you visit the museum. The menu at the museum's cafe (salads, sandwiches, a few mains such as steamed halibut) features local producers and seasonal produce.

See map p. 162. 50 Hagiwara Tea Garden Dr., off John F. Kennedy Drive. ☎ *415-750-3600.* http://www.famsf.org/deyoung. *Admission: $10 adults, $7 seniors, $6 students and kids 13–17, free for children under 13. $2 discount with Muni transfer or fast pass. Open: Tues–Sun 9:30a.m.–5:15 p.m., until 8:45 p.m. Fri.*

The Strybing Arboretum and Botanical Gardens
Golden Gate Park

This splendid oasis houses over 6,000 species of well-tended plants, flowering trees, and theme gardens. It is exceptionally lovely in late winter when the rhododendrons blossom and wild iris poke up in corners, and there is no more peaceful a place when it's rainy and gray outside. You can catch a free docent tour offered daily at 1:30 p.m.; I recommend it for those, like myself, who are arboreally and botanically challenged when trying to identify any but the most basic of flowers and trees. Plan to spend at least half an hour here just wandering around.

See map p. 162. Ninth Avenue at Lincoln Way, left of the tour bus parking lot by the Music Concourse. ☎ **415-661-1316**, *ext. 314, for docent tour information.* www.sf botanicalgarden.org. *Admission: Free. Open: Mon–Fri 8 a.m.–4:30 p.m., Sat–Sun 10 a.m.–5 p.m.*

Japanese Tea Garden
Golden Gate Park

Enjoying this tranquil spot, with colorful pagodas, koi ponds, bridges, and a giant bronze Buddha, you feel as though you've been transported for a moment to the Orient. Young children find this part of the park particularly memorable — they can climb over a steeply arched wooden bridge, just as I did when I was much younger and lots more limber than I am today. The Tea Garden's beauty is slightly marred by its gift shop, full of miniature license plates and other junk. Bus tours overrun this major destination during the day, so try to get here before 10 a.m. or after 4 p.m. during the summer to avoid the onslaught. You can partake of Japanese tea and snacks in the teahouse for $2.95 per person. I think the garden is worth the small admission fee, but you won't be missing anything if you pass on the tea and crackers.

See map p. 162. The garden entrance is to the left of the de Young Museum. ☎ **415-752-4227**. *Admission: $3.50 adults, $1.25 seniors and children 6–12. Open: Daily 8:30 a.m.–6 p.m.*

Lombard Street
Russian Hill (near North Beach)

Lombard Street — or, to be exact, the part of Lombard with the moniker "crookedest street in the world" — begins at Hyde Street below Russian Hill. This whimsical, flower-lined block attracts thousands of visitors each year. If you intend to drive the red-brick street (it's one-way, downhill, so take the curves slowly), go early in the morning before everyone else revs up their rentals. If you stop to take a picture from your car, you'll be holding up traffic and everyone will hate you. Instead, walk down the stairs to admire the flowers, the houses with their long-suffering tenants, and the stellar view.

See map p. 162. Between Hyde and Leavenworth streets. Take the Powell-Hyde cable-car line.

Museum of the African Diaspora
SoMa

If you walk down Third Street toward Yerba Buena Center, you can't fail to notice the multistory photo mosaic marking one of latest additions to the

South of Market culture klatch. MoAD packs quite a bit into its relatively small exhibition space. It won't take more than an hour to tour, but you'll find much to think about. Photographs, video, and some very cool interactive displays and technological touches focus on the themes of origins, movement, adaptation, and transformation in relation to Africa — and thus, in relation to our own selves and communities. Take the kids.

See map p. 162. 685 Mission St. at Third Street. ☎ *415-358-7200.* www.moadsf.org. *Take any Muni streetcar to the Montgomery Street Station or the 15-Third, 30-Stockton, or 45-Union/Stockton bus. Admission: $10 adults, $5 seniors and students, free for children under 13. Open Wed–Sat 11 a.m.–6 p.m., Sun noon to 5 p.m.*

San Francisco Museum of Modern Art
SoMa

The handsome Museum of Modern Art (MoMA) houses an impressive collection of 20th-century paintings, sculptures, and photographs. The beautiful interior exudes a warmth that makes viewing the art even more enjoyable. The exhibits, the excellent museum cafe, and the artfully stocked museum store will keep you there for a good half-day.

See maps p. 162 and p. 178. 151 Third St., 2 blocks south of Market near Howard Street. ☎ *415-357-4000.* www.sfmoma.org. *Take any Muni streetcar to the Montgomery Street Station or the 15-Third, 30-Stockton, or 45-Union/Stockton bus. Admission: $13 adults, $8 seniors, and $7 students with ID; half-price Thurs 6–9 p.m.; free for kids under 12; free to all first Tues of the month. Open: Thurs 11 a.m.–8:45 p.m., Fri–Tues 11 a.m.–5:45 p.m.; closed Wed and major holidays; open at 10 a.m. during the summer.*

Yerba Buena Gardens and Center for the Arts
SoMa

This 22-acre complex is a microdestination in a setting once known for nothing but parking lots and derelicts. It includes a collection of galleries showing a rotating exhibition of contemporary visual and performance art by local artists, lovely gardens, a stage for dance troupes (including ODC/San Francisco and Smuin Ballets/SF), and a film/video theater. Interactive amusements include an ice-skating rink, a bowling alley, a children's garden and carousel, and an arts/technology studio for older kids. An unrelated entertainment behemoth in a separate building across the street — the **Metreon** — houses restaurants, shops, an IMAX theater, games, and multiplex movie screens. If you take in all that Yerba Buena Center has to offer, you can easily spend the entire day in this area. Parking is expensive; use public transportation if possible.

East of the carousel you can find the enclosed, light-filled, **Yerba Buena Ice-Skating Rink** and the 12-lane **Bowling Center** (☎ 415-820-3532; www.skatebowl.com). Public skating session times vary, so phone before trekking over. Admission is adults $8, seniors $5.50, and children under 13 $6.25. Skate rental is $3. The Bowling Center is open Sunday through Thursday 10 a.m. to 10 p.m., until midnight Friday and Saturday. Admission for adults is $4 per game or $25 an hour; Sunday through Thursday night

Yerba Buena Gardens

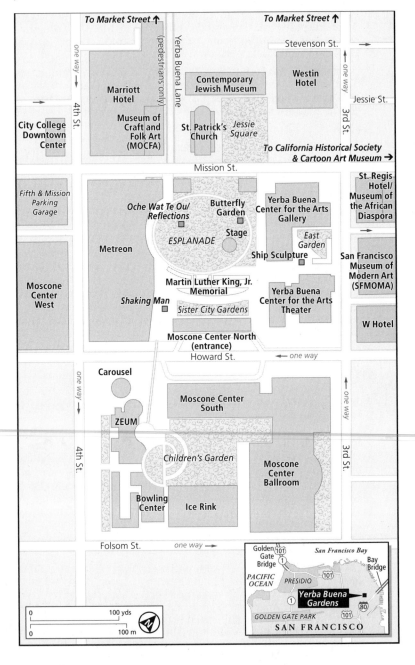

and weekend afternoons it's $5.50 per game or $30 an hour, and Friday and Saturday night it's $7 per game, $35 an hour.

Wednesday from 7:15 to 9:15 p.m. is free skate-rental night.

Zeum (☎ **415-820-3320**; www.zeum.org) is a wonderful art/technology center with hands-on labs that give visitors the opportunity to create animated video shorts with clay figures; learn about graphics, sound, and video production in the second-floor studio; and interact with the gallery exhibits. The center is rare in that it's the only attraction specifically designed for older kids and teens that delivers some intellectual stimulation and doesn't rely on video games. Even your standard-issue bored adolescent would find it difficult not to succumb to a Zeum offering. It's open Tuesday through Sunday 11 a.m. to 5 p.m. in the summer; Wednesday to Friday 1 to 5 p.m., weekends 11 a.m. to 5 p.m. during the school year. Admission is $8 for adults, $7 for seniors and students, $6 for kids 3 to 18. *See map p. 178. 701 Mission St., between Third and Fourth streets.* ☎ *415-749-2228 or 415-978-ARTS (box office).* www.yerbabuenagardens.com. *Take a streetcar to the Powell or Montgomery Street station, or take the 14-Mission or 15-Third bus, among others.*

The Metreon
SoMa

Noisy and lit like a Vegas casino, the Metreon is four stories of glass and brushed metal, enclosing a handful of shops and cafe along with the interactive game arena, a favorite with the city's teenagers and young adults. On the third floor are 15 movie screens and the city's first IMAX theater. A West Coast outpost of New York's Tavern on the Green is scheduled to open on the fourth floor in late 2009. *See maps p. 162 and p. 178. Mission at Fourth Street.* ☎ *800-METREON.* www.west field.com/metreon. *Open: Daily 10 a.m.–10 p.m.*

Finding More Cool Things to See and Do

Just because you've visited the top sights doesn't mean you've seen it all. This section offers ideas on how to entertain children and teens, how to get a taste of San Francisco history and more than a taste of art, where to take your hiking shoes, where to grab a bike, and much more.

Especially for kids

San Francisco has enough family activities to exhaust even the most energetic clan. Along with those I list in this section, consider an afternoon at the ballpark (see "Especially for sports fans," later in this chapter), which has an exciting play area just for kids that's open whether or not the Giants are in town. The easy walk to Fort Point (see "Especially for hikers," later in this chapter) appeals to kids as well, because it takes in the Golden Gate Bridge and incorporates a cool Civil War–era fort they can explore.

The best Web site for finding out what's available for children is **GoCityKids** (www.gocitykids.com). The well-maintained calendar of events mines what's going on in and around the city.

The **San Francisco Zoo,** Sloat Boulevard and 45th Avenue (☎ 415-753-7080; www.sfzoo.org), has been renovating like mad, ridding itself of old-fashioned cages and exhibits, and embracing animal conservation. You'll find an African Savanna exhibit and Lemur Forest; an innovative, noteworthy primate center; a historic merry-go-round; an expanded children's petting zoo; and — this is the clincher — a sizable children's playground near the Sloat Boulevard entrance. Stroll the more than 65 acres to see the animals, and then park your tired body on a bench within yelling distance and let the under-10 members of the family climb to their heart's content. Zoo admission is $11 for adults, $8 for seniors and kids 12 to 15, $5 for kids 3 to 11, free for babes under 3, and free the first Wednesday of each month. The zoo is open daily from 10 a.m. to 5 p.m. To get there, take the L-Taraval Muni streetcar.

Another kid-pleaser, the **Musée Mécanique,** Pier 45 at the end of Taylor Street (☎ 415-346-2000; www.museemecanique.org), contains a fantastic collection of lovingly restored and maintained mechanical marvels that were the forerunners of pinball machines. Among the treasures, you can try your hand at World Series Baseball, have your fortune told, and giggle wildly with Laughing Sal, all for a quarter a pop. The museum is near PIER 39. Admission is free, but bring along a roll of quarters. The museum is open Monday through Friday from 10 a.m. to 7 p.m., Saturday and Sunday from 10 a.m. to 8 p.m. To get there, take the F-Market streetcar or the Powell-Mason cable car.

China Beach has picnic facilities and awe-inspiring views of the Golden Gate Bridge. It's also one of the few safe swimming beaches in town, but the water is chilly, so designing sand castles and picnicking are better activities. The 29-Sunset bus stops at 25th Avenue and El Camino del Mar. From there, walk about 6 blocks north to the beach.

San Francisco has no shortage of parks and playgrounds in nearly every neighborhood, but they do range in quality. In the Nob Hill/Russian Hill area, **Lafayette Park** is appealing for its small but nicely equipped and fenced-in playground, walking paths, and views. It's on Clay Street between Washington, Laguna, Gough, and Sacramento streets. Take the 1-California or 12-Folsom-Pacific buses to get there. You have to make a little effort to reach **Mountain Lake Park,** which is close to the Richmond District side of the Presidio on Lake Street (between Eighth and 12th avenues), but this is one of the best parks in town for the entire family. The playground is two-tiered; the street-level half is for the under-6 set, while the bottom half is fun even for young-at-heart teens. Hiking trails and a small beach make this spot even more attractive. To get there, take Muni bus 1AX, 1BX, or 28–19th Avenue.

Young Performers Theatre (YPT) at Fort Mason presents children's plays most weekend afternoons, starring members of the YPT acting

The Zoo and Lake Merced Area

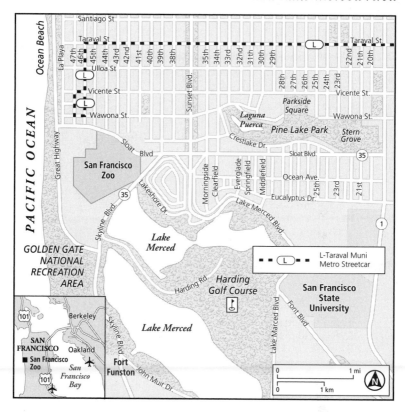

classes. The performances are most suitable for kids under 11. You can find a schedule of events on the Web (www.ypt.org). Tickets are $7 for kids and $10 for adults. Make reservations by phoning YPT at ☎ 415-346-5550. The theater is in Room 300, Building C, at Fort Mason. To get there, take the 22-Fillmore, 30-Stockton, or 42-Downtown bus.

Especially for teens

The South of Market neighborhood works well as a teenage playground encompassing Yerba Buena Gardens, the Metreon, and many places to shop. From here, it's a quick walk to Market Street, where you can catch the N-Judah Muni streetcar to Haight-Ashbury. After your kids have seen Haight Street, they've seen it all.

The **Cartoon Art Museum,** 655 Mission St., between Second and Third streets (☎ 415-227-8666; www.cartoonart.org), takes the funny papers seriously. Exhibits in the museum's five galleries, a half-block from Yerba Buena Gardens, trace the history of cartoon art from political jabs to underground comics. Temporary shows highlight individual artists such as Edward Gorey and forms such as television cartoon animation. The museum shop has a sophisticated selection of books for enthusiasts. Admission is $6 for adults, $4 for seniors and students, and $2 for children 6 to 12. The first Tuesday of the month is "pay what you wish day." The museum is open Tuesday through Sunday from 11 a.m. to 5 p.m. To get there, take any streetcar to the Montgomery Street station and walk a block east to Mission Street.

San Francisco Centre, on the corner of Market and Fifth streets, is a nine-story mall containing many familiar names beloved by teenage girls, including a huge **Nordstrom** department store. Next door is a 357,740-square-foot Bloomingdale's (and that's a lot of hangers), the anchor tenant at the humongous new Westfield Centre. Your young shopper may be just as happy exploring the stores around Union Square (see Chapter 12), and at least there you'll get a little fresh air on your way in and out of the revolving doors.

Teenagers adore the **Metreon** because the technology stores contain all the latest widgets, some of which they can audition. When they tire of gawking at stuff, the video games in the TILT arcade can occupy as many minutes as you'll allow or they can pay for. And after you've had enough, you can coax them away from the flashing screens with promises of food at one of the many cafes.

Zeum was designed for 8- to 18-year-olds and is staffed by savvy teens. Even recalcitrant 15-year-olds can find something engaging to do here, whether or not they admit it.

 I saved the best for last; take your teen to Haight Street for some shopping (and shock) therapy. The N-Judah streetcar deposits you a few blocks south of Haight, and it beats parking. One of the best music stores in town, **Amoeba Records,** is at 1855 Haight St. (☎ 415-831-1200). Both the used and new clothing stores here — in particular **Villains,** 1672 Haight St. (☎ 415-626-5939) — stock the coolest stuff around. I don't mean to make too much of the street scene, but youthful runaways and poseurs do congregate in this neighborhood, and it can feel equally attractive, poignant, and scary to adolescents. At the very least, you'll have something interesting to talk about on the ride back to your hotel.

Especially for history buffs

In this case, you'll have to settle for fairly recent history, given that not a whole lot was happening around here until the Gold Rush. The next major event was the 1906 earthquake.

One of the historic sites related to the earthquake that you can visit is at the corner of Market and Kearny streets: **Lotta's Fountain** (given to the city in 1875 by popular entertainer Lotta Crabtree). This gold-painted landmark served as a community bulletin board where people left notes for missing family and friends after the disaster.

To find out about San Francisco's rise during the quest for gold, take the free Gold Rush City walking tour offered by City Guides on Sunday at 2 p.m. and Wednesday at 11 a.m. Meet by the Transamerica Pyramid at Clay and Montgomery streets. The walk encompasses **Jackson Square** (Jackson and Montgomery streets), a landmark admired for its many restored Gold Rush–era brick warehouses. Call ☎ **415-557-4266** for details.

The **Cable Car Museum** explains everything you'd want to know about our antique road warriors, through photographs, models, actual cable cars, and a close-up look at the mechanisms that make them click. The museum is inside the cable-car barn, 1201 Mason St., at Washington Street (☎ **415-474-1887**; www.cablecarmuseum.com). Admission is free, and the museum is open daily, April through September 10 a.m. to 6 p.m., and October through March until 5 p.m. To get there, take the Powell-Mason or Powell-Hyde cable-car lines.

Mission Dolores, 16th and Dolores streets (☎ **415-621-8203**; www. missiondolores.org), is a fine example of Mission architecture, and the oldest building in the city. This is the sixth of the 21 missions founded under the auspices of Franciscan missionary Junipero Serra and built by Native Americans. Services were first held on the site a few days before the Declaration of Independence was signed. A $1 self-guided audio tour takes 40 minutes. Admission is free, but donations are gratefully accepted; the mission is open daily from 9 a.m. to 4 p.m., and in the summer until 4:30 p.m. To get there, take the J-Church streetcar, which stops 1 block east.

The **Wells Fargo History Museum** is at 420 Montgomery St., at California Street (☎ **415-396-2619**; www.wellsfargohistory.com/museums). Wells Fargo opened one of its first offices on this site in 1852, ready to handle business generated by the Gold Rush. Among the displays are mining equipment, an antique stagecoach, and gold nuggets. Be sure to try out the telegraph machine on the first floor, especially if you have kids in tow. The museum is open weekdays from 9 a.m. to 5 p.m., and admission is free.

Especially for art lovers

The **Legion of Honor,** Lincoln Park between Clement Street and 34th Avenue in the outer Richmond District (☎ **415-750-3600**; www.famsf. org), exhibits an impressive collection of paintings, drawings, decorative art, and one of the world's finest collections of Rodin sculptures, including an original cast of *The Thinker.* The grounds around the **Palace of the Legion of Honor,** as the building is known, are a draw as well. Admission is $10 for adults, $7 for seniors over 65, $6 for children 13 to 17, and free for children under 13, and free on the first Tuesday of the month. The museum is open Tuesday through Sunday from 9:30 a.m. to 5:15 p.m. To get there, take the 38-Geary bus to 33rd Avenue, and then transfer to the 18–46th Avenue bus for a ride to the museum entrance.

Union Square from Grant Avenue to Mason Street and Geary to Post Street is home to a number of fine-arts dealers. Of note are the **Art Exchange Gallery** (☎ 415-956-5750) and **Toomey Tourell** (☎ 415-989-6444; www.toomey-tourell.com), both in the canvas-rich building at 49 Geary St., at Grant Street, as well as the **John Berggruen Gallery,** at 228 Grant St., between Sutter and Post (☎ 415-781-4629; www.berggruen.com). The galleries close on Monday.

First Thursdays is a program sponsored by the San Francisco Art Dealers Association to get people inside member galleries. They open on the first Thursday of the month at 49 Geary St., serving wine and maybe a little cheese from 5:30 to 7:30 p.m. For a list of participating galleries, call ☎ 415-921-1600.

Combine a walk along the Marina with a tour of the galleries at **Fort Mason Center** (☎ 415-345-7575; www.fortmason.org). They include the **Museo ItaloAmericano** and **SFMoMA's Artists Gallery,** which displays original art for sale and for rent. The galleries are fairly small but often have quirky exhibits. Wandering around Fort Mason is a good way to round out your excursion. The **Museo ItaloAmericano** charges a small admission fee, but the Artists Gallery is free. Open daily from 8 a.m. to midnight. To get there, take the 30-Stockton, 47–Van Ness, or 28–19th Avenue bus, which run nearby.

Especially for architecture lovers

When you visit the **Alamo Square Historic District,** you may feel a touch of déjà vu. It's the subject of the famous photograph of the Victorian row houses. The "painted ladies," which front the San Francisco skyline, are a magnet for photographers, probably on a daily basis. You'll find this historic block between Steiner, Scott, Hayes, and Grove streets, west of the Civic Center. The 21-Hayes bus takes you right there from Market and Hayes streets.

The **Haas-Lilienthal House** (☎ 415-441-3000; www.sfheritage.org), an 1886 Queen Anne Victorian, is open to the public for one-hour tours on Wednesday and some Saturdays from noon to 3 p.m. and Sunday from 11 a.m. to 4 p.m. Located at 2007 Franklin St., at Jackson Street, this is the only local example of a home from this period that's open to the public. To get there by bus, take the 12-Folsom, the 27-Bryant, the 42–Downtown Loop, the 47–Van Ness, the 49–Van Ness/Mission, or the 83-Pacific. Admission is $8 for adults, $5 for seniors 65 and older and for children under 12.

You may also want to check out the **San Francisco Public Library,** 100 Larkin St. (☎ 415-557-4400; http://sfpl.lib.ca.us), between Grove and Fulton streets. Natural light streams in from a five-story atrium skylight and windows that encircle the stacks. If you have kids along, browse the children's section. The library even has — gasp! — a gift shop. Take any Muni streetcar to the Civic Center station and walk a block west on Grove Street.

While you're in the Civic Center neighborhood, drop by the refurbished **City Hall** on Van Ness Avenue, between McAllister and Grove streets. The 1915 building has never looked better. Not only did the structure get a seismic retrofitting (de rigueur in this earthquake-prone town) and a good cleaning, but the dome and ornamental balcony railings were regilded, creating an impressive landmark and adding golden highlights to the view. The rotunda is breathtakingly beautiful and worth going through the metal detectors to view.

For more architectural wonders, check out the walking tours later in this chapter.

Especially for bicyclists

If your reflexes are good and you have a reliable helmet, try touring San Francisco from the seat of a two-wheeler. You can rent bikes and helmets from quite a few locations around town.

For a ride in beautiful Golden Gate Park, stop by one of the nearby bike stores, such as **Avenue Cyclery,** 756 Stanyan St. (☎ **415-387-3155;** www. avenuecyclery.com), or **Wheel Fun** at Stow Lake (☎ **415-668-6699**), inside the park. The **Bike Hut** at South Beach, on the Embarcadero at Pier 40 (☎ **415-543-4335;** www.thebikehut.com), is the place to find high-quality bikes to pedal along the waterfront. It's open Wednesday through Sunday (unless it is raining) from 10 a.m. to 6 p.m. Rentals are a mighty reasonable $5 an hour or $20 per day. And if you're considering a bike trip across the Golden Gate Bridge, the nice guys at **Blazing Saddles** (☎ **415-202-8888;** www.blazingsaddles.com) — in North Beach (1095 Columbus Ave.), at the Powell/Hyde cable car turnaround (2715 Hyde St.), and at Fisherman's Wharf (Piers 41 and 43½) — will provide you with all the information and encouragement you need. The equipment for kids and adults is shiny and well maintained. Rentals cost $7 to $11 an hour or $28 to $68 a day and include helmets, locks, front packs, rear racks, maps, and advice. Three-hour guided bike tours are also available at $65 per person, including a return ticket on the ferry.

Pedaling across the Golden Gate Bridge into Sausalito, where you can eat, look around the arty, touristy town, and then return by ferry, can be good fun; in truth, you don't really need a chaperone. The **Blue & Gold Fleet** (☎ **415-705-8200;** www.blueandgoldfleet.com) and **Golden Gate Ferry** (☎ **415-923-2000;** www.goldengateferry.org) depart the Sausalito ferry dock at least half a dozen times a day. Call for a schedule. One-way Blue & Gold Fleet fares are $9 for adults and $5 for children 5 to 11; one-way Golden Gate Ferry fares are $7.10 for adults, $3.55 for children 6 to 18 (under 6 free), and $3.55 for seniors. The 9-mile ride to Sausalito can be challenging, partly due to the windy conditions and partly due to the other bicyclists you're competing with for space.

For more information on biking in the area, contact the **San Francisco Bicycle Coalition** (☎ **415-431-BIKE**), or browse the Web site at www. sfbike.org.

Golden Gate National Recreation Area

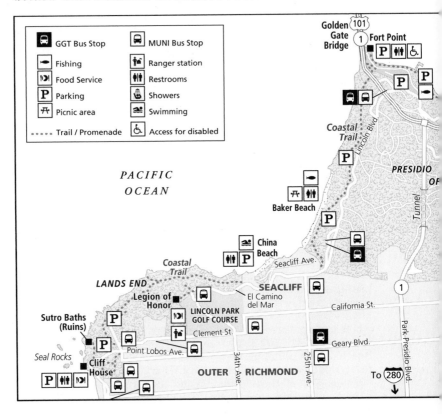

Especially for hikers

A surprisingly good amount of hiking opportunities await in the city, in the Presidio, along the bay, through Golden Gate Park, and along the Pacific Coast. Committed hikers should head to the Marin Headlands for the best trails and views. Muni runs a bus (76–Marin Headlands) from downtown to the Headlands parking lot on Sunday and holidays. Check www.sfmta.com for a schedule and route information.

Angel Island, a federal and state wildlife refuge that is the largest of San Francisco Bay's three islets, is 8 miles from San Francisco and accessible only by ferry (a 20-minute journey) or private boat. Plan to spend the entire day on the island if you decide to go during the week — the ferry departs San Francisco sometime after 10 a.m., and the only return trip departs sometime after 3 p.m. (The schedule changes seasonally.) On weekends, you have a choice of four return trips. You can bring a picnic or get something at the small store and cafe that operate near the dock. Check out the beautiful 12 miles of hiking trails, climb up Mt. Livermore

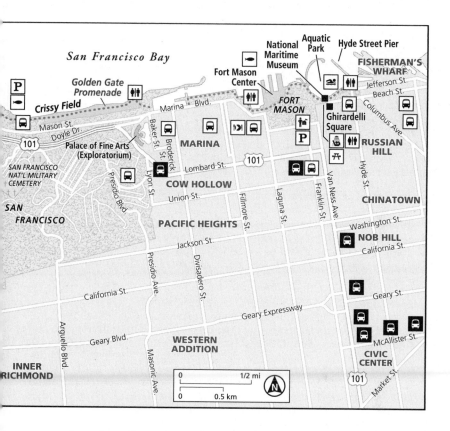

for yet another spectacular view of the Golden Gate Bridge, or take the one-hour tram tour past the historic sites, including the former immigration station, which has undergone renovation and should be open for tours by the time you read this. Mountain-bike rentals are also available on Angel Island, but only during the spring and summer. Call **Blue & Gold Ferry** (☎ **415-705-8200**) for a current ferry schedule. Round-trip fares are $15 for adults and $8.50 for children 6 to 12. For recorded information about the island, call ☎ **415-435-1915.** Ferries leave from Pier 41 in Fisherman's Wharf.

Crissy Field (☎ **415-561-7690** general information or 415-561-7752 for weekend workshops and classes; www.crissyfield.org) is a national park made up of 100 acres between the bay and the Presidio. The park features a tidal marsh, sheltered picnic area, bike path, walking trail, cafe, bookstore, and education center. It's a beautiful spot; an easy, flat walk; and wheelchair accessible. Begin with a visit to the Crissy Field Center. Ask for an activity book for a self-guided walk, or join one of the interpretive hikes offered most weekends. Stop at the Warming Hut at

---

A short history of Angel Island

Originally a Miwok Indian hunting and fishing ground, Angel Island was a harbor for Spanish, British, and Mexican ships at various times beginning in 1775. Before the Civil War, the U.S. government turned the island into a military base, remnants of which are still visible. Between 1910 and 1940, Angel Island was a detention center mainly for Asian immigrants, which earned it the nickname "Ellis Island of the West." The immigration station at China Cove is open for tours and provides a poignant glimpse into an era when anti-Asian and anti-immigration policies placed hundreds of Chinese in forced detention for weeks, months, and sometimes years. Poems carved into the walls of the barracks by lonely, isolated detainees were rediscovered in 1970 and inspired the ongoing preservation effort by the California legislature.

---

the western end of the park by the fishing pier for a snack and some inspired gift shopping. Foodies will be suitably impressed to discover that the cafe menu was developed with input from Alice Waters, of Chez Panisse fame. The 28–19th Avenue, 29-Sunset, and 43-Masonic buses stop nearby.

Fort Point (☎ 415-556-1693), which dates from 1857, lies under the Golden Gate Bridge at the tip of the peninsula. Along with Civil War–era cannons, it boasts surfers who appear to be risking their lives much more than the soldiers once stationed here did. From the Hyde Street Pier, take the easy 3½-mile stroll along the paved Golden Gate Promenade, which hugs the coast as it passes through the Marina Green and Crissy Field. Or take the 28–19th Avenue or 29-Sunset bus to the Golden Gate Bridge and climb down from the viewing area to a short trail leading to the premises. You can take a self-guided audio tour of the fort if you like, then backtrack to the Hyde Street cable-car turnaround, where you can hop on a cable car to Union Square. Fort Point is usually open Friday through Sunday from 10 a.m. to 5 p.m., but phone first to check.

If you're a hiking novice or walking with kids, the **Coastal Trail** to the Cliff House probably isn't the hike for you. It's rigorous and can be dangerous. The trail head, a bit east of Fort Point, is well marked. Heading south, the trail parallels the Pacific Ocean through the Presidio.

You can see small beaches below the trail on this hike, but if you're tempted to feel sand beneath your toes, follow the marked paths to get there. Don't climb over any rocky cliffs; the land here isn't stable enough to guarantee your safe return.

When you reach Baker Beach, about 1½ miles from Fort Point, be prepared for the nude sun worshippers, if there is any sun. As you continue on the trail, you'll pass the Lobos Creek Water Treatment Plant. From there it's a short way to El Camino Del Mar, a street leading through Sea

Cliff, a fancy residential neighborhood. At the end of El Camino Del Mar, you'll pick up the trail near the Lincoln Golf Course. If you continue along this trail, with the land and the views rewarding your every step, eventually you'll arrive at the **Cliff House,** which has been serving refreshments to visitors since 1863. It has one casual and one fancier restaurant plus a bar, all with the views that keep tourists as well as locals enthralled. Prices are high, so if you're on a budget or prefer beer to wine, keep walking down the Great Highway until you reach the **Beach Chalet** restaurant and brewery (☎ **415-386-8439;** www.beachchalet. com). After lunch, you can return toward the Cliff House and catch the 38-Geary bus at La Playa and Balboa Street, or continue to Judah Street and take an N-Judah streetcar downtown.

Named in honor of Sierra Club founder and conservationist John Muir, 553-acre **Muir Woods** in Marin County is what's left locally of the red-wood forests that once dominated the coast of Northern California. Although not as sizable as Redwood National Forest farther north, these old-growth redwoods are beautiful, and a range of trails suits hikers of all levels. From the Golden Gate Bridge heading north toward Point Reyes, take the Stinson Beach/Highway 1 exit west and follow the signs. Parking is limited, so set out early in the day on weekends or go during the week. Muir Woods Park is open from 8 a.m. until sunset. For additional information, call ☎ **415-388-2595.**

Especially for sports fans

The San Francisco Giants Major League Baseball team opened the fabulous, 40,000-seat **AT&T (formerly Pac Bell, formerly SBC) Park** stadium on the bay in April 2000. The ballpark is sweet — sightlines are clear, you don't freeze to death the way you did at Candlestick, the food is pretty good, and home runs splash into the bay. Season-ticket holders hold the best seats, but buying bleacher tickets to any but the most sought-after games (Giants versus Dodgers contests, for example) shouldn't be impossible, because they're sold only on game days. To purchase regular tickets or tickets from season-ticket holders unable to make it to a particular game, log on to the Web site (www.sfgiants.com) before you arrive, or call ☎ **877-473-4849** to charge tickets by phone. Transportation to the ballpark is simple — take Muni to the Embarcadero Station and transfer to the King Street extension. In or out of season, the stadium is open for 75-minute tours daily except game days at 10:30 a.m. and 12:30 p.m. Admission is $10 adults, $8 seniors, and $6 kids under 13.

The San Francisco 49ers play at **3Com Park.** Home games have been sold out for years, but if you want to try your luck, the ticket office number is ☎ **415-656-4900.** Scalpers sell tickets, which are often counterfeits, outside the park. The best method of transport to the park is Muni bus. The 9X–San Bruno Express bus leaves from Sutter Street near Union Square; the 28X–19th Avenue bus runs along 19th Avenue; and the 47X–Van Ness cruises Van Ness Avenue.

Checking out sports on the Web

In addition to the following specific sites, where (in most cases) you can purchase tickets online, swing by the Bay Area's general sports site at www.bayinsider.com.

✔ **Golden State Warriors:** www.nba.com/warriors

✔ **Oakland A's:** www.oaklandas.com

✔ **Oakland Raiders:** www.raiders.com

✔ **San Francisco 49ers:** www.sf49ers.com

✔ **San Francisco Giants:** www.sfgiants.com

You can also head across the bay to watch Oakland's professional teams play. For information on schedules and availability, and to order tickets, visit the sites listed in the "Checking out sports on the Web" sidebar.

 Getting seats to home games isn't impossible, but you have to use some creativity. A terrific source for last-minute concert and sports tickets (as well as lots of other things) is the Web site www.craigslist.org. Craig Newmark, an actual person who lives in San Francisco, created the Web site in 1995, and it quickly became a community asset. Craigslist is now nationwide, and it's free to use.

Golfers have a great selection of public courses on which to play, including gorgeous (and inexpensive) **Lincoln Park** (☎ 415-221-9911; www.lincolnparkgc.com), **Harding Park** (☎ 415-664-4690; www.hardingpark.com), and the **Presidio Golf Course** (☎ 415-561-4661; www.presidiogolf.com). The links in the Presidio opened to the public in 1995, although the 18-hole, par-72 course was originally built in 1895. Both Harding Park and the Presidio have restaurants and pro shops, and there's a putting green at the Presidio.

Seeking Some Spiritual Pursuits

San Franciscans aren't merely a hedonistic group of left-wing freethinkers, despite what you may have heard. As a matter of fact, most pray on a daily basis. Sometimes they pray for a parking space, but mostly they thank God that they live in San Francisco.

 Arrive a half-hour early to claim a seat at the 9 a.m. Sunday services (an hour early for the 11 a.m. services) at **Glide Memorial United Methodist Church,** 330 Ellis St. (☎ 415-674-6000; www.glide.org). The Rev. Cecil Williams, a genuinely great man, lets the multiethnic gospel choir do most of the sermonizing, and they're wildly effective. A cross-section of friendly San Franciscans packs the pews, clapping, singing, and celebrating. It's church, it's theater, and it's amazing.

Grace Cathedral, the magnificent Episcopal Church at the top of Nob Hill, 1100 California St., between Taylor and Jones streets (☎ **415-749-6300;** www.gracecathedral.org), has an outdoor stone terrazzo labyrinth that may promote a meditative moment. It's open to visitors daily, anytime. You can rent a labyrinth audio tour, complete with walking music provided by the Grace Choir, at the gift shop.

Old First Presbyterian Church, 1751 Sacramento St., at Van Ness Avenue (☎ **415-474-1608**), sponsors a concert series leaning heavily toward the classical that's low cost and high quality. You can call for a list of upcoming events or check the Internet (www.oldfirstconcerts.org). Getting from downtown to the church is a snap on the California Street cable-car line.

Completed in 1970, **St. Mary's Cathedral,** 1111 Gough St., between Ellis and Geary (☎ **415-567-2020;** www.stmarycathedralsf.org), is worth a look for its modern architecture and soaring interior space. Inside, be sure to lift your eyes toward heaven to admire the cross-shaped skylight.

Going for Garden and Park Respites

San Franciscans cherish the city's open spaces. If you know where to look, you'll find little parks and secret gardens in some unlikely places. At the end of Market Street in the Embarcadero, two simple gardens grace the seventh floor of **One Market Plaza.** Elevators to the gardens are in the Spear and Steuart Street lobbies. Upon exiting, walk toward the bay; you'll find two patios surrounded by well-tended expanses of lawn and flowers overlooking a classic bay view.

If you've stopped by City View on Commercial St. (between Montgomery and Kearny streets) for a dim sum lunch (see Chapter 10), you'll be steps away from a tiny pocket park maintained by the 505 Montgomery building landlord. The benches and tables at **Empire Park** often fill with people taking a breather from the office.

At **Rincon Center** (corner of Mission and Steuart sts.) you'll find a courtyard garden with benches sitting among a generous array of ornamental hedges, azaleas, and seasonal plantings. You can get a snack inside and enjoy it in the garden. A few blocks away, at 100 First St., you'll find the award-winning second-floor garden in the **Delta Tower,** which is a lush respite from the madness of the Transbay Terminal and Mission Street. The black granite and green glass fountain sculpture provide a soothing counterpoint to the street traffic. **Yerba Buena Gardens** features willow trees, a sweep of bright-green lawn, and a variety of blossoms. Behind the gardens' 22-foot waterfall is a memorial to Martin Luther King, Jr., featuring a series of glass panels etched with quotations from his speeches and writings.

Levi's Plaza, between the Embarcadero and Sansome Street, consists of the company's multiple buildings and two plazas separated by Battery Street. The centerpiece of the hard plaza is a fountain you can walk through on paving stones — a big favorite with kids. The soft plaza across the street is really a park with fir trees and grass. The company displays letters and products in a visitor center at 1155 Battery St., open weekdays from 9 a.m. to 6 p.m. and Saturday from 10 a.m. to 5 p.m.

Cross the plaza to Sansome Street and look for the bottom of the Filbert Steps, a steep staircase that rises to Montgomery and Filbert streets. Around the midpoint of the stairway, you'll find a sight so profoundly San Francisco that you'll immediately understand what all the fuss is about. This is the **Grace Marchand Garden;** its roses and ferns add a wild elegance to the hillside. The residents don't like the tourists who clog the steps, especially on weekends, but that's the price they have to pay for living next to a minor landmark. In any case, this is a garden to admire from outside the wooden fence only.

Seeing San Francisco by Guided Tour

I used to feel self-conscious about taking a guided tour in a new city. Many travelers, myself included, shy away from the idea of being herded on and off large buses like curious sheep. But I've finally embraced my inner tourist and learned to appreciate organized outings. Actually, guided tours are a sensible way to get your bearings in an unfamiliar place. You may not have much time to explore on your own and may want to catch the major sights in one day. Or perhaps you have difficulty getting around, or you don't want to drive. Maybe you need an overview to find out what interests you in San Francisco, or you're traveling alone and want some company.

Fortunately, you can find almost as many varieties of guided tours as there are varieties of people in San Francisco. Not all of them have you peering out a dirty bus window at some landmark while straining to hear the muffled voice of your guide over the microphone (or, worse, an out-of-date tape). In San Francisco, guided tours happen on foot and ferry-boats as well as on buses and even zebra-striped Land Rovers. They cover special interests as well as the major sights. If you think a tour listed in this chapter is for you, visit the Web site, call the company or individual guide for a brochure, or ask your hotel to send you information. Most tours require advance reservations.

Hotels generally have preferred companies that they recommend for bus tours. The hotel often gets a small kickback for every reservation, so it may not have your best interests in mind. If you favor one tour company over another, book it yourself or request that company specifically when you speak to the concierge. Don't leave the decision up to the hotel.

The bus stops here: Touring on wheels

If you want to be sure you at least catch a glimpse of San Francisco's major attractions, orientation tours may be just the ticket. Some tour operators spiff up the menu with motorized cable cars or double-decker buses, whereas other companies use lower-profile minibuses that appeal to visitors who don't want to stand out in a crowd.

Be advised that not all trips are narrated by the bus driver; some just have recorded commentary. I don't recommend these audio tours. The sound quality is miserable, and some of the information is outdated, such as the part about the prices of the houses you pass on the tour. Be sure to ask whether the commentary is recorded or live before you book your tour.

Gray Line Tours (☎ 415-434-8687; www.sanfranciscosightseeing. com), the big kahuna of the tour industry, schedules a number of orientation tours around the city and beyond in red double-decker buses, motorized cable cars, and smaller vans. The deluxe 3½-hour city tour (tickets: $44 for adults, $42 seniors, $22 for children 5–11) hits the highlights — Twin Peaks, Mission Dolores, the Cliff House, Golden Gate Park, the Golden Gate Bridge — and there's an option to tack on a bay cruise.

Tower Tours (☎ 415-345-8687; www.towertours.net) is popular with many San Franciscans with visiting relatives because the company uses sleek minibuses that carry only about two dozen people. Tower's 3½-hour city tour stops at the same sites as Gray Line's buses. The cost is $47 for adults, $45 seniors, and $26 for children 5 to 11.

Fire Engine Tours (☎ 415-333-7077; www.fireenginetours.com) are not for people who want to avoid attention, but go ahead and suspend your dignity for an hour and 15 minutes while heading for a ride across the Golden Gate Bridge. Tour guide Marilyn Katzman, a tap dancer and former child actress, quits talking, singing, and leading cheers only when required by law. As the shiny 1955 Mack Fire Truck drives past various sights — the Octagon House, the Presidio Pet Cemetery, Union Street — Marilyn tosses out historical facts and figures mostly relating to fires and the nice folks who put them out. Although this tour doesn't include a good part of the city, you will see the famous skyline from a vantage point across the bridge and have an extremely fun time. Pick up the tour outside the Cannery on Beach Street. Tickets are $45 for adults, $35 for teens 13 to 17, and $25 for kids under 13. Reservations are advised. Tours run Wednesday through Monday at 1 p.m., unless it rains. Phone for a schedule.

The Urban Safari (☎ 415-282-5555 or 1-866-MYSAFARI; www.theurban safari.com), under the guidance of überguide and Land Rover aficionado Daniel Oppenheim, can mimic a somewhat conventional city tour or completely devolve into a freewheeling, wacky adventure.

Basically, *Bwana* Daniel is up for anything, and he'll mine every ounce of his imagination to design a minimum four-hour outing to your specifications, exact or inexact. Throw him a theme and he'll come back with a plan, or choose from a menu of ideas on his Web site. Pith helmets, animal crackers, and leopard-print fleece blankets provide additional ambience. Prices, which include a meal, lots of extras, and hotel pickup, are $100 per person for groups of four and $75 for each additional person in the same group.

Doing it yourself (and saving money) on Muni

Stopping at every other corner and having a driver who doesn't give much, if any, commentary may not seem like the ideal let's-get-to-know-the-city excursion. But a do-it-yourself tour by Muni bus has its advantages. The outing will cost you only a few dollars and no more than three transit hours. This approach lets you come and go at your leisure — if you decide 25 minutes at Golden Gate Park isn't enough, who cares if the bus leaves? You can always catch the next one. These "orientation" tours are not for anyone who requires a great deal of comfort, however — city buses are, after all, creaky and well worn.

Ask for a free transfer when you board the bus. With the transfer, you can disembark whenever you like and catch another bus or a Muni streetcar at no additional charge (within 90 minutes). Transfers are not valid on cable cars, however.

Muni tour #1: Painted ladies and Pacific Heights

Here's a tour that introduces you the famous Victorians on Alamo Square, Japantown, Fillmore Street shopping in Pacific Heights, the Marina, and Chinatown. Board the 21-Hayes bus at Market and Powell streets (and remember to ask for a transfer). Exit on Steiner Street, at one side of Alamo Square. When you've gotten your fill of the painted ladies, walk a block east to Fillmore Street and look for the 22-Fillmore. That bus runs toward the bay through Japantown and continues up toward Pacific Heights. All kinds of shops line Fillmore Street, and they become swankier as you pass California Street. The bus eventually crosses Union Street and ambles through the Marina District. Exit as close as possible to Chestnut Street, where you can catch the 30-Stockton. See the following tour for a description of a ride on this bus back to Union Square. If you don't stop for breaks (which sort of defeats the purpose), expect to spend two hours on this route.

Muni tour #2: Traveling on the west side

Another do-it-yourself tour takes you around the western perimeter of the city. From any downtown Muni station (Powell Street is closest to Union Square), catch the L-Taraval or N-Judah streetcar, each of which travels through some well-kept residential neighborhoods. Get off at Sunset Boulevard in the outer Sunset District. On Sunset Boulevard, at Taraval Street or Judah Street, depending on which streetcar you rode, pick up a 29-Sunset bus going to the Presidio (*not* to California and 25th Avenue, which doesn't enter the former military base). The spectacular views on this part of the ride include the Pacific Ocean and the Golden Gate Bridge. In fact, the bus stops by a viewing area where you can get off the bus and walk across the bridge and back if that's on your to-do list. The ride also includes a look at a pet cemetery inside the Presidio.

The 29-Sunset terminates at the transit center in the Presidio, but you can then catch the 43-Masonic bus nearby. It takes you down Lombard Street and over to Chestnut Street in the Marina district. From there, the 30-Stockton meanders along Chestnut over to Van Ness Avenue, and then travels down Van Ness to North Point Street, close to Aquatic Park and Ghirardelli Square. The route then goes through North Beach and Chinatown, then back to Union Square. Alternatively, you can walk to PIER 39 and catch the F-Market streetcar for a ride down the Embarcadero and up Market Street. Allow three hours without breaks.

Tooling around town

The latest and greatest DIY driving tour comes in the form of three-wheel, two-passenger **Trigger Scooter** cars fitted with global positioning systems and a 45-minute audio component that doubles as a tour guide. The bright yellow theme park escapees are a hoot to drive but are strictly for use in the city — for safety reasons, you can't take them over the bridges. Rent a Trigger through **GoCar Rentals** (☎ **800-914-6227** or 415-441-5695; www.gocartours.com) for $49 the first hour, $39 for the second, and $29 an hour after that up to five hours, with a maximum daily charge of $175. The company has two locations (you can pick up and drop off at either): 321 Mason St., at O'Farrell Street, near Union Square (open: 9 a.m.–6 p.m. daily), and 2715 Hyde St., at Beach Street, near the cable-car turnaround (open: 8 a.m. to dusk daily). If you have a youngster along for the ride, I guarantee he or she will be talking about it for years to come.

Two if by sea: Touring by boat

Boat cruises provide a view of the city from an unusual vantage point and are the only way to experience the bay in all its glory. You have quite a few options for riding the waves, one of which is the commuter ferries. Ferries pick up passengers from Fisherman's Wharf (Piers 41 and 43½) and the Ferry Building.

The Blue & Gold Fleet (☎ **415-705-5555;** www.blueandgoldfleet.com) operates ferries to and from Marin County. This is also the only company that will take you to Alcatraz Island. Blue & Gold's one-hour bay cruise (tickets: $22 for adults, $18 for seniors and kids 12–18, $14 for kids 5–11) sails under the Golden Gate Bridge; past Sausalito, Angel Island, and Alcatraz; and then back to Fisherman's Wharf. This tour will be a satisfying, if brief, encounter with the bay. Check the Web site for discounts on tickets.

Red and White Fleet (☎ 415-673-2900; www.redandwhite.com) offers an identical bay cruise with the added option of an open-air double-decker bus tour around the city. The one-hour cruise alone is $22 for adults and $16 for youths 5 to 17; with the bus, it's $44 adults and $28 youths.

You want something a little more exciting than a ferry? Try sailing on *The Ruby* (☎ 415-861-2165; www.rubysailing.com). This 60-foot steel sloop, which holds about 30 passengers, skims the whitecaps in the bay daily on a lunch cruise from 12:30 to 3 p.m. and an early-evening sail with hors d'oeuvres from 6 to 8:30 p.m. The cost is $40 per person (including food); beer and wine are available at an additional cost. Kids under 10 are $20. Reservations are necessary. *The Ruby* docks by the ramp at the foot of Mariposa Street at Third Street. The 22-Fillmore or 15-Kearny bus drops you off a block away.

Hornblower Dining Yachts (☎ 888-467-6256; www.hornblower.com) let you sup as you sail on dinner and weekend brunch cruises around the bay. Cruises last from one-and-a-half hours for brunch to three hours for the nightly dinner/dance. The food is hotel-like, but this is a festive way to dine — surrounded by superb views. Dinner rates per person are $94 Sunday and Tuesday through Thursday, $104 Friday, and $114 Saturday. Weekend brunch cruises cost $72. Kids are half-price. Reservations are required.

The bright yellow amphibious vehicles you may see bouncing around bayside neighborhoods belong to **Bay Quackers San Francisco Duck Tours** (☎ 415-431-3825; www.bayquackers.com). The 80-minute tours leave every two hours beginning at 10 a.m. from the Anchorage Mall at Fisherman's Wharf and end up in the bay motoring around McCovey Cove. If you time it right, you could enjoy an unusual view of a Giants baseball game. It's most definitely an entertaining ride, and the water portion lasts just long enough to see the views but not get bored. Tickets are $35 adults, $32 seniors and students, and $25 kids 3 to 12; $100 buys a family ticket for two adults and two children.

Taking a walk on the wild side: Walking tours

Friends of the Library sponsor **City Guides walking tours** (☎ 415-557-4266; www.sfcityguides.org). You may choose from 26 different tours, all free! All you have to do is pick the tour that interests you and show up at the proper corner on time. You can get an insider's view of Chinatown, admire beautifully restored Victorian homes on the Landmark Victorians of Alamo Square tour, or explore the haunts of the original forty-niners on the Gold Rush City walk. "Rising Steel: Two Centuries of San Francisco Architecture" takes place on two Sundays each month; given the amount of construction going on, it's a great walk for anyone fascinated with urban buildings. Tours run about two hours on average. Highly recommended!

The Victorian Home Walk (☎ 415-252-9485; www.victorianwalk.com) combines a bus excursion with a walking tour through a number of cele- brated neighborhoods. During the 2½-hour tour, you see an array of houses in areas that prohibit tour vans from entering. The guide prom- ises the walk isn't strenuous. The cost is $20. Tours leave daily from Union Square at the corner of Powell and Post streets.

San Francisco Architectural Heritage conducts a Pacific Heights walk (☎ 415-441-3000 for reservations; www.sfheritage.org) on Sunday at 12:30 p.m., beginning at the Haas-Lilienthal house. The two-hour tour through the swanky neighborhood costs just $8 for adults and $5 for seniors and children under 12.

HobNob Tours (☎ 866-851-1123; www.hobnobtours.com) gives you the lowdown on Nob Hill while pointing out the highlights of one of the city's more significant 'hoods. Sure, the gossip and scandal provided are on the historic side, but it's still fascinating. The two-hour tours begin in the Fairmont Hotel lobby weekdays at 10 a.m. and 1:30 p.m. and cost $30 per person.

Eating your way through San Francisco

Shirley Fong-Torres, a local writer and personality, has been operating Chinatown food tours for over 20 years. The 3½-hour walk manages to demystify the exotic rather irreverently. It includes running commentary about the history of this fascinating neighborhood and stops at an artist's studio, a one-room temple, a market, an herbal shop, and a tea company, where you're treated to a tasting. Shirley's company, **Wok Wiz Chinatown Walking Tours & Cooking Center,** 654 Commercial St., between Kearny and Montgomery streets (☎ 415-981-8989; www. wokwiz.com), schedules the tours daily at 10 a.m. The cost — $40 for adults, $35 for kids under 11 — includes dim sum lunch.

North Beach is the other popular neighborhood for food walks, and guide Tom Medin (☎ 415-665-0480 or 888-358-8687; www.sffoodtour.com) shows it off on his **Local Tastes of the City** tour. Tom's on a personal mis- sion to elevate your taste buds, and he figures the best way to do that is by introducing you to the neighborhood's butchers, bakers, and cof- feemakers. First stop is Caffe Roma for a perfect cappuccino or espresso, and then it's one bakery/chocolate shop/delicatessen after another. Bring a doggy bag. The three-hour tour — all easy walking —starts daily at 10 a.m. and 1 p.m. The cost is $59 adults, $39 youths 12 to 18, and $15 kids 8 to 11.

There's lots more to chocolate than milk and dark, so if you're curious about the history as well as the myriad flavors produced and sold around town, all will be revealed on **Andrea Nadel's Gourmet Walks** (☎ 800-979-3370; www.gourmetwalks.com). The three-hour tour begins at the Ferry Building. You'll be sampling yourself silly from there to Union Square. Tickets are $48 and for sale online or by phone. Tours run

Wednesday through Saturday. On Sunday at 2 p.m., for $72 per person, the tour includes stops at a few wine bars that pair vino with chocolate. Naps not included.

Seeking out special-interest tours

Learn all there is to know about gay and lesbian history from the Gold Rush to the present day while **Cruisin' the Castro** (☎ **415-255-1821;** www.cruisinthecastro.com). Tours meet at the rainbow flag on the corner of Market and Castro streets, Tuesday through Saturday at 10 a.m. Reservations are necessary. The cost for the two-hour walk is $35 adults and $25 kids 3 to 12.

The **Precita Eyes Mural Arts Center,** 2981 24th St., near Harrison Street (☎ **415-285-2287;** www.precitaeyes.org), a not-for-profit arts center, features more than 70 murals (including the very colorful Balmy Alley) on the Mission District walking tours it sponsors. The 6-block walk departs Saturday and Sunday at 1:30 p.m. from the center. The cost is $12 for adults, $8 college students with ID, $5 for seniors and youths 12 to 17, and $2 for children under 12. A slightly shorter walk leaves from **Café Venice,** 3325 24th St., near the 24th Street BART station, on Saturday at 11 a.m.

Someday, no one's gonna care where Janis Joplin or members of the Grateful Dead crashed back in the day, but while you still have your memories (or memory, as the case may be) check it out on the **Haight-Ashbury Flower Power Walking Tour** (☎ **415-863-1621;** for tickets call 800-979-3370; www.haightashburytour.com). The two-hour walk — a combination of hippy lore and Victorian appreciation — begins at 9:30 a.m. on Tuesday and Saturday, 2 p.m. on Thursday, and at 11 a.m. on Friday for a mere $20 per walker. If you have your own group of at least four, you can inquire about alternate days and times.

An easy way to explore the redwood groves of Muir Woods (see "Especially for hikers," earlier in this chapter) is with Sierra Club guide Tom Martell of **Tom's Scenic Trail Walking** (☎ **415-381-5106**). He'll pick you up (and drop you off) at your hotel, provide a picnic lunch, and drive up to six adventurers to the lovely redwoods just beyond the Golden Gate Bridge for a 2- to 4-mile hike. Cost for the 3½-hour walk with lunch is $50.

Chapter 12

Shopping the Local Stores

. . . .

In This Chapter

▶ Locating San Francisco's big-name shops and specialty boutiques

▶ Discovering the main shopping neighborhoods

▶ Hunting down bargains

. . . .

*A*lthough most people think of Union Square as the hub of San
Francisco shopping — and for good reasons — the downtown area
has plenty of competition. Nearly every San Francisco neighborhood
boasts a thriving "Main Street" of locally owned boutiques, cafes, and
bookstores. You can find unique arts and crafts, clothing stores that
eschew chain-mentality fashion, independent booksellers, even housewares havens that reflect the style of the local clientele. Shopping in San
Francisco is never mundane. Depending on where you head, you can try
on a different attitude as easily as a different outfit.

Surveying the Scene

If you know where to look, you can do some very interesting shopping
around here. Oh, plenty of people complain about the city being
Starbucked and Gapped to death, but they aren't looking beyond the
obvious retail centers. Not all the entrepreneurs in San Francisco are
franchisees or part of some conglomerate — some are actually opening
boutiques with a personal stamp. In particular, check out Valencia Street
for postmodern street wear and décor; Hayes Street for shoes, clothing,
and mod furnishings; Sacramento Street for contemporary clothing,
antiques, and kids' clothes and furnishings; upper Grant Street for local
designers; upper Polk Street for home furnishing and decoration design
trends; and Haight Street for vintage, mod, and skateboarding gear.

You'll find that stores are generally open Monday through Saturday from
10 a.m. to 6 p.m. and Sunday from noon to 5 p.m., even on many holidays. Shops around Fisherman's Wharf tend to stay open later, as do
most department stores.

Sales tax in San Francisco is 8.5 percent, added at the cash register. You
don't have to pay the sales tax if the store ships something out of state
for you, but shipping can cost as much as or more than the tax, unless
you're purchasing a very expensive item.

San Francisco Shopping

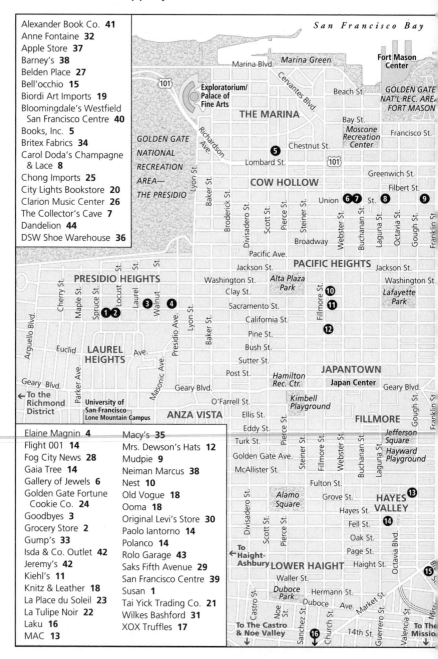

Alexander Book Co. **41**
Anne Fontaine **32**
Apple Store **37**
Barney's **38**
Belden Place **27**
Bell'occhio **15**
Biordi Art Imports **19**
Bloomingdale's Westfield San Francisco Centre **40**
Books, Inc. **5**
Britex Fabrics **34**
Carol Doda's Champagne & Lace **8**
Chong Imports **25**
City Lights Bookstore **20**
Clarion Music Center **26**
The Collector's Cave **7**
Dandelion **44**
DSW Shoe Warehouse **36**

Elaine Magnin **4**
Flight 001 **14**
Fog City News **28**
Gaia Tree **14**
Gallery of Jewels **6**
Golden Gate Fortune Cookie Co. **24**
Goodbyes **3**
Grocery Store **2**
Gump's **33**
Isda & Co. Outlet **42**
Jeremy's **42**
Kiehl's **11**
Knitz & Leather **18**
La Place du Soleil **23**
La Tulipe Noir **22**
Laku **16**
MAC **13**

Macy's **35**
Mrs. Dewson's Hats **12**
Mudpie **9**
Neiman Marcus **38**
Nest **10**
Old Vogue **18**
Ooma **18**
Original Levi's Store **30**
Paolo Iantorno **14**
Polanco **14**
Rolo Garage **43**
Saks Fifth Avenue **29**
San Francisco Centre **39**
Susan **1**
Tai Yick Trading Co. **21**
Wilkes Bashford **31**
XOX Truffles **17**

San Francisco Bay

Fort Mason Center

Marina Blvd. *Marina Green*

Beach St. *GOLDEN GATE NAT'L REC. ARE. FORT MASON*

Exploratorium/ Palace of Fine Arts

THE MARINA

Bay St.
Moscone Recreation Center Francisco St.

Chestnut St.

GOLDEN GATE NATIONAL RECREATION AREA— THE PRESIDIO

Lombard St.

Greenwich St.

COW HOLLOW

Filbert St.

Union St.

Broadway

Pacific Ave.

Jackson St. **PACIFIC HEIGHTS** Jackson St.

PRESIDIO HEIGHTS

Washington St. *Alta Plaza Park* Washington St.

Clay St.

Lafayette Park

Sacramento St.

California St.

Pine St.

LAUREL HEIGHTS

Bush St.

Sutter St.

Post St. *Hamilton Rec. Ctr.* **JAPANTOWN**

Japan Center

Geary Blvd.
← To the Richmond District

University of San Francisco Lone Mountain Campus **ANZA VISTA**

Kimbell Playground

O'Farrell St.

Ellis St.

FILLMORE

Eddy St.

Jefferson Square

Turk St.

Hayward Playground

Golden Gate Ave.

McAllister St.

Fulton St.

Alamo Square Grove St. **HAYES VALLEY**

Hayes St.

To ←Haight-Ashbury **LOWER HAIGHT**

Fell St.

Oak St.

Page St.

Haight St.

Waller St.

Duboce Park Hermann St.

Duboce Ave.

To The Castro & Noe Valley ↓

Church St. 14th St.

To The Mission ↓

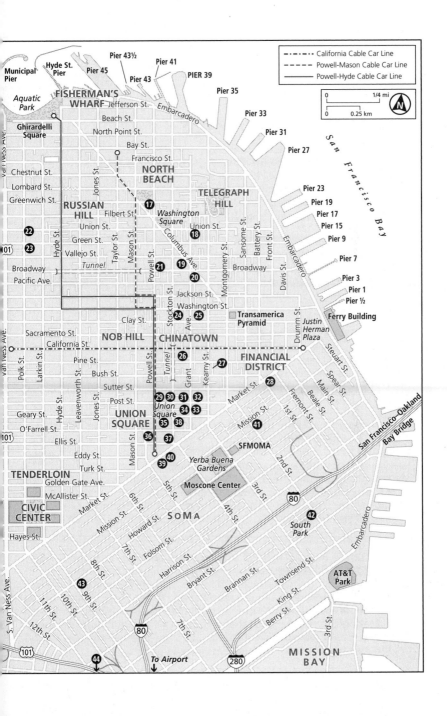

The worldwide chain-store invasion, unfortunately, has not passed by San Francisco. In fact, we accept the blame for the Gap frenzy — the headquarters is near the Embarcadero — and if you see a Pottery Barn or a Gymboree in your midst, well, those companies originated in the Bay Area as well. But you can find plenty of unique emporiums that will bring some excitement to the chase. Here's a short list of great places.

Checking Out the Big Names

Gump's, in Union Square at 135 Post St., between Kearny Street and Grant Avenue (☎ 415-982-1616; www.gumps.com), is famous for its Asian antiques, silver, and china, as well as for longevity — it's been in business since 1861. Anyone who receives a gift from Gump's will shower impressed thanks on the giver because of the name itself. It's open Monday through Saturday from 10 a.m. to 6 p.m., Sunday noon to 5 p.m.

Looking for the perfect place for one-stop shopping? Then head over to **Macy's West** on Union Square, at Stockton and O'Farrell streets (☎ 415-954-6271). At 700,000 square feet, this eight-story glass-fronted fashion behemoth is bigger than some towns. It's open Monday through Thursday and Saturday 10 a.m. to 9 p.m., Friday until 7 p.m., and Sunday from 11 a.m. to 8 p.m.

The **Original Levi's Store,** 300 Post St. (☎ 415-501-0100; www.levisstore.com), is a showcase for more than 501s — you'll see some wild designs stitched onto jackets and jeans. One corner of this three-story monument to denim is dedicated to alterations, in case your shrink-to-fits still need a nip or tuck. It's open Monday through Saturday 10 a.m. to 8 p.m., and Sunday 11 a.m. to 7 p.m.

The brandalicious **Apple Store** on the corner of Stockton and Ellis streets (☎ 415-392-0202; www.apple.com/retail/sanfrancisco) schedules a roster of workshops for current and future Mac users and has Internet access on the premises. Between this place, the Virgin Megastore across the street, and Niketown a few blocks north on Post Street, you could lose your average teen for a few hours. It's open Monday to Saturday from 10 a.m. to 9 p.m., and Sunday from 11 a.m. to 7 p.m. A second, less frenetic branch is at 2125 Chestnut St. (☎ 415-848-4445).

Bell'occhio, 10 Brady Street, off Market Street between 12th and Gough streets (☎ 415-864-4048; www.bellocchio.com), has long been a favorite with decorators, wedding planners, and sophisticated shoppers searching for elusive bits of European flavor. Hidden in an alley off Market Street, this bewitching little shop stocks cunning decorations, French ribbons, Mariage Frères tea, imported face powder, and odd finds the owner discovers on her travels. To get there, take the F-Market streetcar to Civic Center. It's open Tuesday through Saturday 11 a.m. to 5 p.m.

Polanco, a bright gallery featuring crafts and artwork from Mexico, is at 393 Hayes St. (☎ **415-252-5753;** www.polanco.ypguides.net). This block in Hayes Valley also has a few terrific clothing and home-décor shops, so if you're in the neighborhood, it's worth a side trip. The gallery is open Tuesday through Saturday 11:30 a.m. to 6:30 p.m., and Sunday 1 to 6 p.m.

Dandelion, 55 Potrero Ave., at Alameda (☎ **415-436-9500;** www. dandelionsf.com), isn't a store you'll find by accident. To reach its out-of-the-way location close to the Design Center, south of Market Street, you have to have heard about this place from a devoted customer. The owners seem to be magnets for beautiful objects. Their prices are very fair, their taste impeccable. The 9–San Bruno bus from Market and Ninth streets can take you right here. It's open Tuesday through Saturday 10 a.m. to 6 p.m. Famed *San Francisco Chronicle* journalist Herb Caen's columns often mentioned his favorite clothing store, **Wilkes Bashford,** 375 Sutter St., between Stockton Street and Grant Avenue, near Union Square (☎ **415-986-4380;** www.wilkesbashford.com). San Francisco's natty former mayor, Willie Brown, purchases his Brioni suits here. The store sells sophisticated clothing for women as well. It's open Monday through Saturday 10 a.m. to 6 p.m., and Thursday to 8 p.m.

For CDs, vinyl (remember that?), and an in-depth selection of previously owned music, head to the cognoscenti shop at **Amoeba Records,** 1855 Haight St. (☎ **415-831-1200;** www.amoeba.com), in the musically famous neighborhood of the same name. Open Monday through Saturday from 10 a.m. to 10 p.m., and Sunday from 11 a.m. to 9 p.m.

When those cognoscenti stroll down Haight Street, they often wear really cool clothes from **Rolo,** a locally grown retailer with three locations around town. The flagship store, which carries street wear for men and women, is south of Market at 1235 Howard St. (☎ **415-431-4545;** www.rolo.com). It's open Monday through Saturday from 11 a.m. to 8 p.m., and Sunday 11 a.m. to 7 p.m.

Market Street continues its upward trajectory (at least from Fifth Street toward the Bay) with the opening of the humungous **Bloomingdale's,** centerpiece of the new Westfield San Francisco Centre next to the older one (where Nordstrom is located) on Fifth and Market streets. Along with all the usual suspects one expects to find in an upscale mall, this one also has a day spa on the fifth floor, a gourmet grocer in the basement, movie theaters, and dining establishments with good pedigrees, including **Out the Door,** the takeout operation of the Slanted Door (see Chapter 10).

Going to Market

Farmers market aficionados will find Saturday at the **Ferry Building** at the foot of Market Street more than satisfying. The majority of producers bring organically grown foodstuffs to the Ferry Plaza Farmers Market (see Chapter 10), and you'll discover unusual varieties of fruits and vegetables, including heirloom tomatoes in season. The perfume of the salt air, aroma of ripe fruit, and whiff of lavender wafting past your nostrils are deeply pleasurable; combined with the bay views, a busker playing standards on his saxophone, and a plethora of tastes, the scene is magical. Inside the building, permanent shops, most of which are open seven days a week, stock everything you'd need for a feast plus all kinds of tempting items, including books, chocolates, olive oil, kitchen necessities, wine, and imported packaged foods. If you find yourself hungry, the **Slanted Door** (see Chapter 10) is here, or you can sit down at the **MarketBar** (☎ **415-434-1100;** www.marketbar.com) on the east end, visit **Taylor's Refreshers** (see Chapter 10) for fast food I heartily approve of, or attempt to get a counter seat at the excellent **Hog Island Oyster Bar** (see Chapter 10). For a break, relax at the **Imperial Tea Court** (see Chapter 10), where you can try exotic leaves and get a lesson in the art of tea.

Discovering the Best Shopping Neighborhoods

Looking for that perfect little doodad for Aunt Hermione? Or do you just like to browse and see what catches your fancy? Following is a rundown of the city's best shopping areas, with a few highlights in each. Happy hunting!

Union Square

You're never far from a department store in this neighborhood. From one spot in the middle of Union Square, you can see **Neiman Marcus** (☎ **415-362-3900;** www.neimanmarcus.com), on Stockton and Geary streets (open: Mon–Sat 10 a.m.–7 p.m. [until 8 p.m. Thurs] and Sun noon to 6 p.m.), and **Saks Fifth Avenue** (☎ **415-986-4300;** www.saksfifth avenue.com), on the corner of Powell and Post streets (open: Mon–Sat 10 a.m.–7 p.m. [until 8 p.m. Thurs] and Sun 11 a.m.–6 p.m.). Then there's the **Original Levi's Store** (see "Checking Out the Big Names") on Post and Stockton, a new candy-box-like **Barney's** on the corner of Stockton and O'Farrell streets (☎ **415-268-3500;** open: Mon–Sat 10 a.m.–7 p.m., Sun 11 a.m.–6 p.m.) and **Macy's** (see "Checking Out the Big Names") everywhere else. Ah . . . shopping!

A half-block north of Neiman's on Stockton Street is designer-shop-lined Maiden Lane. There's also a back entrance to **Britex Fabrics** (☎ **415-392-2910;** www.britexfabrics.com), probably the best-stocked notions and fabric store in the country (open: Mon–Sat 10 a.m.–6 p.m.). The front door is at 146 Geary St.

Parallel to Stockton eastward is Grant Street. One of the stores here is also one of my favorites in the world: **Anne Fontaine,** 118 Grant St. (☎ **415-677-0911;** www.annefontaine.com; open: Mon–Sat 10 a.m.–6 p.m.; Sun noon to 5 p.m.). If you appreciate gorgeously made and tailored white blouses (plus a few other nonwhite must-haves), you'll be one wide-eyed consumer. Walk another block east and 2 blocks north and watch for tiny **Belden Place** (www.belden-place.com), between Bush and Pine streets (see Chapter 10). Delicious little restaurants line the alley, and any one of them makes a satisfying place to stop for a meal. At lunchtime on fair days, Belden, which is closed to auto traffic, fills with cafe tables, giving the street a partylike atmosphere.

Chinatown

Chinatown is known for amusing trinkets and inexpensive clothing. But most of the souvenirs sold in the shops that line Grant Avenue are not the must-haves you come to San Francisco seeking. If you venture off Grant Avenue, however, shop to your heart's content in Chinese herbal shops with strange remedies and unique jewelry stores full of jade of varying quality. The merchants in the less touristy stores don't always speak English, and they may seem less than friendly, but don't let that stop you from looking around.

 Be careful when shopping for jewelry in Chinatown, especially on Grant Street. A relative of mine, who is a pretty savvy buyer, thought she was purchasing some aquamarine earrings that turned out to be glass. Get a second opinion if possible before plunking down serious money.

 The "going-out-of-business" signs you see taped to the windows of several Chinatown stores are nearly as old as the grandmothers walking about with babies tied to their backs. These stores have been running their farewell sales for years. Don't expect any bargains.

If you can't tear yourself away from Grant Avenue, the best place to find inexpensive (or expensive) gifts and housewares is **Chong Imports,** 838 Grant Ave., in the Empress of China building between Clay and Washington streets (☎ 415-982-1432; www.chongimports.com). This basement-level treasure house stocks a little of everything. It's open daily from 10 a.m. to 9 p.m.

At the **Clarion Music Center,** 816 Sacramento St., near Grant Avenue (☎ 415-391-1317; www.clarionmusic.com), check out the amazing instruments, including traditional Chinese instruments like moon-shaped guitars, plus Chinese lion dance masks. It's open Monday through Friday from 11 a.m. to 6 p.m., and Saturday from 9 a.m. to 5 p.m. Call for a Friday night world concert series schedule.

Tai Yick Trading Company, 1400 Powell St., at Broadway (☎ 415-986-0961; www.taiyick.com), sells teapots, dishes, lamps, porcelain and pottery vases, and statues at reasonable prices. The owners are helpful and friendly, and native San Franciscans swear that this is the best store of its kind in town. It's open daily from 9:30 a.m. to 6:30 p.m.

Legend has it that fortune cookies were invented at the Japanese Tea Garden in Golden Gate Park. If you want to watch the production process, head to the **Golden Gate Fortune Cookie Company** in Chinatown (see Chapter 11). The cookies make wonderful gifts to take back home. The factory is at 956 Ross Alley, between Jackson and Washington streets near Grant Avenue. It's open daily from 10 a.m. to 7 p.m.

Haight Street

The scruffiness of this area bothered me when I lived nearby in the early '80s, but I've changed, and so has the neighborhood. Clothing is the big draw for shoppers, whether vintage or cutting edge, and you'll see apparel and shoes for all ages and stages. In particular, look for **Behind the Post Office,** 1510 Haight St. (☎ 415-861-2507), for accessories from local designers; **Kids Only,** 1608 Haight St. (☎ 415-552-5445), for your flower child; **Ambiance,** 1458 Haight St. (☎ 415-552-5095), for pretty dresses, stylish shoes, and somewhat retro handbags; and **Villains Vault,** 1653 and 1672 Haight St. (☎ 415-864-7727 or 415-626-5939), for street wear and shoes. Most stores on Haight Street are open from 10 a.m. to 7 p.m. daily.

North Beach

North Beach is more than just a food-and-drink mecca — you can find all sorts of curiosities and clothing off Columbus Avenue. The section of Grant Avenue (completely different from the street of the same name in Chinatown) from Union to Greenwich streets has a more Continental accent, with stylish boutiques for clothes and accessories. Among the finds — and there are many — head to **Knitz & Leather,** 1429 Grant Ave. (☎ 415-391-3480), for handmade sweaters and leather jackets (open: Tues–Sat 11 a.m.–7 p.m. and Sun noon to 5 p.m.). **Old Vogue,** 1412 Grant St. (☎ 415-392-1522), is a better-organized and higher-quality vintage shop than most of those on Haight Street. **Ooma,** 1422 Grant St. (☎ 415-627-6963), displays the goods of local designers.

You don't need to comb Italy for ceramics when you can shop at **Biordi Art Imports,** 412 Columbus Ave., at Vallejo Street (☎ 415-392-8096; www.biordi.com). You'll find the most beautiful hand-painted Majolica dishes and serving pieces nearly too pretty to use. It's open Monday through Saturday from 9:30 a.m. to 6 p.m.

City Lights Bookstore, 261 Columbus Ave. (☎ 415-362-8193; www.citylights.com), is famous for its Beat Generation roots, but it's also a book fiend's paradise. The first all-paperback bookstore in San Francisco, this city institution dates to 1953, when Beat poet Lawrence Ferlinghetti opened it. At the time, most people thought hardcover books were superior to paperbacks in terms of both content and paper quality. Ferlinghetti challenged that attitude and made great literature available to everyone. The San Francisco Board of Supervisors has designated the store a cultural and architectural landmark, assuring a long and happy life for the building. Ferlinghetti's brainchild is also on its way to becoming a national historic site. It's open daily from 10 a.m. to midnight.

Admirers of chocolate can wedge themselves into **XOX Truffles,** 754 Columbus Ave. (☎ **415-421-4814;** www.xoxtruffles.com), a tiny store devoted to nickel-sized truffles in a huge assortment of flavors. These bites of bliss are all handmade under the direction of a handsome French chef, who removed himself from the rigors of the restaurant world to bring pleasure to us chocoholics. Open Monday through Saturday from 9 a.m. to 6 p.m.

Union and Chestnut streets

In a survey, one out of four visitors to San Francisco had plans to visit Union Street between Fillmore Street and Van Ness Avenue in the Marina district. Folks who love wandering in and out of specialty shops will think they've hit pay dirt. Muni buses 22-Fillmore, 41-Union, 42–Downtown Loop, and 45-Union/Stockton all run on Union Street.

Carol Doda, who shaped a career out of her chest long before implants were considered accessories, runs a lingerie shop, **Carol Doda's Champagne and Lace,** at 1850 Union St. (☎ **415-776-6900**). She carries bras in regular and hard-to-find sizes, plus lots of other fun things. It's open daily from 12:30 a.m. to 6:30 p.m., Sunday until 5 p.m.

Cover yourself with beautiful adornments crafted by local artists at **Gallery of Jewels,** 2101 Union St. (☎ **415-929-0259;** www.galleryof jewels.com), open Monday through Saturday 10:30 a.m. to 6:30 p.m., and Sunday 11 a.m. to 6 p.m. You'll find unique pieces of jewelry as well as purses and hats on occasion.

Because man apparently does not live by cashmere alone, you may be interested in perusing the **Collectors Cave** at 2072 Union St. (☎ **415-929-0231;** www.thecollectorscave.com). It displays all kinds of new and old comic books, action figures, and sports cards for serious and not-so-serious collectors. It's open Tuesday through Sunday from 10 a.m. to 6 p.m.

Mudpie, 1694 Union St. (☎ **415-771-9262**), sells children's expensive clothes and gifts. The downstairs saleroom, where everything is half-price, slightly alleviates sticker shock. It's open Monday through Saturday 10 a.m. to 6 p.m., Sunday 11 a.m. to 5 p.m.

Another highly attractive, healthy shopping area is **Chestnut Street** in Cow Hollow, which draws highly attractive, healthy locals with plenty of discretionary cash. Neither Chestnut nor Union Street, a few blocks south, has been able to fight off the invasion by some of the more ambitious chain stores, but local neighborhood and merchant groups are vigilant enough to keep them at a minimum. Muni bus 30-Stockton or 43-Masonic will get you to Chestnut Street.

On the western end of Chestnut is a local independent, **Books, Inc.,** 2251 Chestnut St. (☎ **415-931-3633;** www.booksinc.net), which has a broad inventory of reading material for the entire family. It's open daily 9 a.m. to 10 p.m., Friday and Saturday until 11 p.m.

Pacific Heights

The tony neighborhood of Pacific Heights offers shoppers Fillmore Street, which is chock-full of clothing boutiques and other cool places to shop. Between Jackson and Sutter streets, you won't be able to put your credit card away.

Kiehl's manufactures high-end, high-quality cosmetics and hair products for men and women. Its shop at 2360 Fillmore St. (☎ **415-359-9260;** www.kiehls.com) is open Monday through Saturday 10 a.m. to 7 p.m., Sunday 11 a.m. to 6 p.m.

Nest, 2300 Fillmore St., at Clay Street (☎ **415-292-6199;** www.nestsf.com), is yet another home store, but one that carries many old French decorative items, including quilts and linens. It's open Monday through Friday 10:30 a.m. to 6:30 p.m., Saturday until 6 p.m., and Sunday 11 a.m. to 6 p.m.

You don't see many milliners left in the world, so a visit to **Mrs. Dewson's Hats,** 2050 Fillmore St. (☎ **415-346-1600;** www.mrsdewsonhats.com), is a must if your chapeau is a little tattered. This place is home to the "Willie Brim," a fedora named after former Mayor Willie Brown. It's open Tuesday through Saturday from 11 a.m. to 6 p.m., and Sunday noon to 4 p.m.

Polk Street

The stretch of road from Filbert to Broadway on the Russian Hill end of Polk Street has blossomed into a hot spot for dining and shopping. Along with a second location for **Nest** (see the preceding section), two little shops for the home, **La Place du Soleil,** at 2356 Polk St. (☎ **415-771-4252;** open: Tues–Sat 11 a.m.–6 p.m., Sun noon to 5 p.m.), and **La Tulipe Noire,** at 2418 Polk St. (☎ **415-922-2000;** open: Tues–Sun 11 a.m.–7 p.m.), will seemingly transport you to the fourth arrondissement.

Sacramento Street

Some exclusive antiques shops as well as some of the best secondhand stores in town operate in the section of Sacramento Street between Spruce and Divisadero streets in Presidio Heights. The 1-California bus takes you within 1 block of Sacramento Street.

Elaine Magnin Needlepoint has a shop at 3310 Sacramento St. (☎ **415-931-3063;** www.elainemagnin.com) and is the place to go if you wield a mighty needle and are seeking some new patterns. It's open Monday and Saturday 10 a.m. to 4 p.m., Tuesday and Wednesday until 5 p.m., and Thursday and Friday until 6 p.m.

If you want to see what the swells have cleaned out of their closets (the locals are going to hate me for this), head to **GoodByes,** 3464 Sacramento St., between Walnut and Laurel streets (☎ 415-346-6388; www.goodbyessf.com). This consignment shop is the place for gently worn men's and women's clothing. It's open Monday through Saturday from 10 a.m. to 6 p.m., Thursday until 8 p.m., and Sunday from 11 a.m. to 5 p.m. A second store for women only is across the street (☎ 415-674-0151).

Two uniquely stylish women's clothing shops are **Susan,** 3685 Sacramento St. (☎ 415-922-3685), and the **Grocery Store,** 3625 Sacramento St. (☎ 415-928-3615). Specializing in European fashion designers, they allow you a look at the latest. Both stores are open Monday through Friday 10:30 a.m. to 6:30 p.m., Saturday 10 a.m. to 6 p.m.

Hayes Street

Naming the hippest shopping street in the city would be difficult, but if forced, I'd have to say Hayes Street. Start at Grove and Gough, where you'll find the expanded **MAC** (Modern Appealing Clothing) store at 387 Grove St. (☎ 415-863-3011; open: Mon–Sat 11 a.m.–7 p.m., Sun noon to 6 p.m.). From there, head 1 block south to Hayes Street and start walking toward the Pacific. You'll find a wealth of stuff here for all facets of your life — unless you live like a Spartan or a monk, in which case you may want to stop at the **Gaia Tree,** 575 Hayes St. (☎ 415-255-4848; open: Mon–Tues 10 a.m.–7:30 p.m., Wed–Sat 10 a.m.–8 p.m., Sun noon to 6 p.m.), for a yoga mat or maybe a facial or a massage. See, there's just no escaping commerce. For things you needed to buy before you got on the plane, stop at **Flight 001,** 525 Hayes St. (☎ 415-487-1001), which sells those little spray bottles of Evian so you won't dry up on the flight home. If your feet hurt, stop in one of the many shoe stores here, including **Paolo Iantorno,** 524 Hayes St. (☎ 415-552-4580), which sells beautiful Italian-made creations for men and women. The shop also stocks gorgeous handbags. Besides regular weekday hours, many of the stores on these blocks are open Sunday afternoon.

Valencia Street

In the last decade or so, Valencia Street in the Mission District has been developing into the shopping district for those who eschew the mainstream. The blocks from 19th to 23rd streets still hold plenty of storefront churches and used-appliance dens, but the cafes and restaurants from the first wave of gentrification now accompany sellers of youthful fashions, local art, and goods for the home. Of note is **Paxton Gate,** 824 Valencia St. (☎ 415-824-1872; open: Mon–Fri noon to 7 p.m., Sat–Sun 11 a.m.–7 p.m.), part entomological display, part garden store, but neither description does this place justice. Almost next door is **City Art** (☎ 415-970-9900; open: Wed–Sun noon to 9 p.m.), a co-op gallery featuring San Francisco artists and photographers. Across the street is a publishing company that collaborates with artists, **Little Otsu,** 849 Valencia St. (☎ 415-255-7900; www.littleotsu.com). Tables here are strewn with graphic novels, edgy comics, stationery, and interesting T-shirts, among other gifty items. And don't pass by **Encantada Gallery of Fine Arts,** 904 Valencia St. (☎ 415-642-3939; open: Tues–Sun noon to 6 p.m., until 8 p.m. Fri–Sat), which has a wonderful collection of Mexican art and pottery, as well as a changing exhibit of paintings and mixed media. One of my favorite local women's clothing designers, **Dema,** has a store and workshop at 1038 Valencia St. (☎ 415-206-0500). Dema's patterns and colors are spirit raisers. My favorite beret was fashioned at **Laku,** 1089 Valencia St. (☎ 415-695-1462; open: Tues–Sat 11:30 a.m.–6:30 p.m., Sun noon to 5 p.m.), which also sells handmade, fanciful slippers for babies and big people, jewelry, and Japanese-inspired accessories. From downtown, use BART, exit at the 24th Street Station, and walk 1 block west. Most of the Valencia Street shops close on Monday.

Hunting for bargains in SoMa and beyond

The discount manufacturers based South of Market (SoMa) have made bargain shopping in San Francisco a popular pursuit. The area between Townsend and Bryant streets and Second and Fourth streets is great for bargains.

The hip retailer Rolo has a sale outlet, **Rolo Garage,** at 1301 Howard St., at Ninth Street (☎ 415-861-1999). It's open Monday through Saturday from 11 a.m. to 7 p.m., and Sunday noon to 6 p.m.

Two worthwhile stores are off Second Street, between Bryant and Brannan streets, in South Park — a little sub-neighborhood south of Market, once infamous for ties to the dot.com industry. **Isda & Co. Outlet,** 28 South Park (☎ 415-512-1610; open: Mon–Sat 10 a.m.–6 p.m.), carries fashionable women's wear suitable for the office and after-hours at great prices. **Jeremy's,** 2 South Park (☎ 415-882-4929; open: Mon–Sat 11 a.m.–6 p.m., Sun until 5 p.m.), is filled with last season's markdowns, returns, and display items from department stores and some famous names.

Did your son outgrow his sneakers yesterday? Did you? You're gonna go wild in the **Skechers USA** outlet in the Mission, at 2600 Mission St. (☎ 415-401-6211). It's open Monday through Saturday 10 a.m. to 8 p.m., Sunday 10 a.m. to 7 p.m. If you or someone in your party needs something dressier, dance over to the **DSW** near Union Square, 111 Powell St. (☎ 415-445-9511). It's open Monday to Saturday 9:30 a.m. to 9 p.m., Sunday until 8 p.m.

Other favorites

Knitters in the know will find their way to **Noe Knit,** 3957 24th St. (☎ 415-970-9750; www.noeknit.com), open Monday through Thursday 11 a.m. to 8 p.m., and Friday to Sunday 11 a.m. to 6 p.m.; it's within walking distance of the J-Church Muni line's 24th Street exit. The Noe Valley neighborhood also abounds with good places to eat. For every sort of knitting accessory and a huge selection of gorgeous yarns, make a pilgrimage to **ImagiKnit,** 3897 18th St., in the Castro (☎ **415-621-6642;** www.imagiknit.com). Open Monday through Saturday 11 a.m. to 6:30 p.m., and Sunday 11 a.m. to 4 p.m., this truly is a knitter's paradise.

An excellent independent bookseller can be found just south of Market Street, not far from Yerba Buena Plaza. **Alexander Book Co.,** 50 Second St. (☎ **415-495-2992;** www.alexanderbook.com), has three floors of well-chosen books to peruse, and the staff is knowledgeable and helpful.

You can locate chocolate nearly everywhere, but only one store will satisfy your craving for information *and* sugar. **Fog City News,** 455 Market St. (☎ **415-543-7400;** www.fogcitynews.com), doesn't merely sell international papers and a full selection of magazines. It also carries chocolate bars from around the world that have been carefully vetted by the owner. You can talk chocolate here and be taken very, very seriously.

Index of Stores by Merchandise

Rolo (SoMa)
Rolo Garage (SoMa)
Saks Fifth Avenue (Union Square)
Susan (Sacramento Street)
Villains Vault (Haight Street)
Wilkes Bashford (Union Square)

Computers
Apple Store (Union Square;
Marina/Cow Hollow)

Edibles
Ferry Building (Embarcadero)
Fog City News (Financial District)
Golden Gate Fortune Cookie Company
(Chinatown)
Imperial Tea Court (Embarcadero)
XOX Truffles (North Beach)

Fabric/Yarn
Britex Fabrics (Union Square)
Elaine Magnin Needlepoint
(Sacramento Street)
ImagiKnit (The Castro)
Noe Knit (Noe Valley)

Gifts
Biordi Art Imports (North Beach)
Chong Imports (Chinatown)
The Collectors Cave (Union/Chestnut
streets)
Dandelion (SoMa)
Ferry Building Marketplace
(Embarcadero)
Flight 001 (Hayes Street)
Gump's (Union Square)
Little Otsu (Valencia Street)

Hats
Laku (Valencia Street)
Mrs. Dewson's Hats (Pacific Heights)

Home Décor and Housewares
Bell'occhio (Civic Center)
La Place du Soleil (Polk Street)
Nest (Pacific Heights)
Paxton Gate (Valencia Street)
Tai Yick Trading Company
(Chinatown)

Jewelry
Gallery of Jewels (Union/Chestnut
streets)

Lingerie
Bloomingdale's (SoMa)
Carol Doda's Champagne and Lace
(Union/Chestnut streets)

Luggage
Flight 001 (Hayes Street)
Macy's (Union Square)

Music
Amoeba Records (Haight Street)
Clarion Music Center (Chinatown)

Shoes
Ambiance (Haight Street)
Bloomingdale's (SoMa)
DSW (Union Square)
Macy's (Union Square)
Neiman Marcus (Union Square)
Paolo Iantorno (Hayes Street)
Saks Fifth Avenue (Union Square)
Skechers USA (SoMa)
Villains Vault (Haight Street)

Chapter 13

Following an Itinerary: Four Great Options to Make Your Day

● ●

In This Chapter

▶ Making the most out of three to five days

▶ Showing the kids a good time

▶ Taking a food-lover's holiday

● ●

*V*isitors naturally want to pack as much as possible into a sightseeing trip, in case they don't have a chance to return. Having been in that position myself, I've come to the conclusion that travel isn't pleasurable if all you do is run around checking off sights as if you're grocery shopping. My idea of a good time is visiting one or two important sights in a day (or sometimes just walking past the front portal and waving) and then finding somewhere to sit and watch the world pass by. (I must admit that I felt foolish for missing the Eiffel Tower on my first visit to Paris — and I was in the neighborhood.) You may prefer a compromise between these approaches, in which case I suggest you decide in advance what you *must* see, and then fit in whatever else you can based on how much time and energy you have.

On that note, the following suggested itineraries are intended for first-time visitors who want to catch as much as possible without completely exhausting themselves or their companions. I've packed in a lot, but you can pick and choose (or completely ignore) parts of each.

San Francisco in Three Days

Three days is barely enough to "get" San Francisco, so I'm going to keep you within the city limits for the entire time. The following list takes you step by step through the city.

✔ **Day 1:** Find Market Street and catch one of the historic **F-Market streetcars** (see Chapter 8) heading toward PIER 39 and Fisherman's Wharf. If you haven't eaten breakfast, stop off first at **Café Mason** or **Dottie's True Blue Café** (see Chapter 10). If it happens to be Saturday, exit at the **Ferry Plaza Farmers Market** (see Chapter 10). A few local restaurants — **Hayes Street Grill** (see Chapter 10) and **Rose Pistola** — have booths where you can eat your morning meal, or you can make yourself quite happy with coffee and fresh pastries from **Frog Hollow Farms** inside the building. When you reach **PIER 39,** greet the sea lions (follow the barking) and continue to the end of the pier for a dead-on view of Alcatraz Island. Walk to **Aquatic Park** to complete a tour of **Fisherman's Wharf** (see Chapter 11). You'll pass the **Hyde Street Pier** and the **Maritime National Museum** — pop in if you like ships — as well as **Ghirardelli Square.** On Bay Street, catch a 30-Stockton bus to Chestnut Street. If it's not too soon to shop or eat, **Mamacita** (see Chapter 10) is a great choice for Mexican food. The bus ends up at Beach Street, and your task is to walk from the **Palace of Fine Arts,** through Crissy Field and the Presidio, to the **Golden Gate Bridge.** Follow the joggers along the bay; there's a path. The 29-Sunset bus will also take you there and back. End the afternoon around **Union Square,** window shopping along Stockton and Sutter. Change your clothes, then go to the **Top of the Mark** (see Chapter 10) for an aperitif and a grand view. For dinner, see what's cooking on **Belden Place** (see Chapter 10). If you still have a bit of steam left, drop by **Biscuits and Blues** (see Chapter 16) for a musical nightcap.

✔ **Day 2:** This day starts early with another transportation highlight. Fling yourself on a **Powell-Hyde cable car** (see Chapter 8) for the brief ride to Lombard Street. Walk down the staircases on either side and, heading north, find the **San Francisco Art Institute** at 800 Chestnut St. Inside the campus, follow the signs to the cafe for breakfast or a snack (Mon–Fri only). This is a funky place with unobstructed views of the bay and a menu of sandwiches, bagels, and vegetarian entrees priced for starving artists. Follow Filbert Street to **Washington Square Park** in North Beach, a modest pocket of green with plentiful benches on the perimeter and the twin spires of Saints Peter and Paul's Church solidly cutting into the sky to the north. Park yourself on a bench, maybe with a latte in hand from **Caffe Roma** (see Chapter 10). Then stroll around North Beach if you like, or walk up Grant Avenue past Union Street and follow the signs to **Coit Tower** (see Chapter 11). From there, return to North Beach for a leisurely lunch at **L'Osteria del Forno** or **Cafe Zoetrope** (see Chapter 10), or pick up a sandwich at one of the delis and have a picnic of sorts in **Portsmouth Square** (above the parking garage on Kearny Street between Washington and Clay; see Chapter 11), a short walk away. Spend the afternoon exploring **Chinatown** (see Chapter 11). If you're in the mood for Chinese cuisine for dinner, see Chapter 10 for suggestions. Then head back to North Beach for a performance of *Beach Blanket Babylon* (see Chapter 15).

✔ **Day 3:** Enjoy a walk in the park — **Golden Gate Park** (see Chapter 11) — where you can row a boat on Stow Lake, hunt for bison, and smell the flowers in the **Strybing Arboretum.** Find lunch over on Ninth Avenue and then stroll down Irving Street, a typical neighborhood shopping block. Alternatively, exit the park on Stanyon Street and take in Haight-Ashbury, also a typical neighborhood — for San Francisco. In the afternoon, a trip to the **San Francisco Museum of Modern Art** (see Chapter 11) finishes the artistic portion of your vacation. Take a rest stop in **Yerba Buena Gardens** (see Chapter 11), across the street. Then dine around **Union Square** if you're ambitious enough to see an 8 p.m. show at ACT or another theater. Otherwise, hail a cab and head to a Mission District restaurant such as **Delfina** or **Foreign Cinema** (see Chapter 10), and pretend you're a local. Night owls can finish the evening at a salsa dance club such as **El Rio,** or hang out with the hipsters at the **Make-Out Room** (see Chapter 16).

San Francisco in Five Days

For a four- or five-day trip, you can add the following days to the itinerary in the preceding section.

✔ **Day 4:** By now, you've already covered a fair portion of the city; it's probably time to hug a tree (you *are* in Northern California, after all). Rent a car or take a guided tour (see Chapter 11) and cross the Golden Gate Bridge into **Marin County.** Hike **Muir Woods** in the morning (take the Stinson Beach exit) and have lunch near Muir Beach at the English Tudor–style **Pelican Inn,** at the end of Muir Wood Road at Highway 1 (☎ **415-383-6000;** www.pelicaninn.com). The inn is a short walk from the beach, which lies below a hikable hill. Stop in **Sausalito** on your way back to the city for ice cream or just a walk along the bay front — the San Francisco skyline is quite the sight, but Sausalito itself, though postcard pretty, is quite touristy. In the evening, eat dinner in Japantown at **Mifune** in the Japan Center for noodles, **Isuzu** for sushi or tempura, or **Yoshi's,** if you want to splurge (see Chapter 10 for each). See what's playing at the Sundance Kabuki cinema on Post and Fillmore streets.

✔ **Day 5:** This may be the morning to get in your trip to **Alcatraz Island** (see Chapter 11) or to trek to the **Palace of the Legion of Honor** (see Chapter 11) for another dose of culture. For lunch, try the **Tadich Grill** (see Chapter 10), the oldest restaurant in California (although it's been in its current location only since 1967). The menu of favorites, such as lobster thermidor, accompanies a side of local history and an active bar. Then spend the afternoon catching up on shopping, or stroll down to Pier 5 near the Ferry Building (east of Broadway), where you can hang out on benches and watch skateboarders or just admire the view. In the evening, splurge on a fancy dinner — **Ame** and **Quince Restaurant** are two good choices (see Chapter 10).

San Francisco for Families with Kids

How to keep the kids engaged and happy (for example, not asking what time it is, what they're doing tomorrow, and when they're eating) depends on their ages and interests. Here's a list to meet any need:

✔ **For families with little kids:** A day around **Golden Gate Park** is ideal. The **Japanese Tea Garden** is memorable, and the **California Academy of Sciences** is a must. You can't miss with a bike ride or the paddleboats around Stow Lake, and youngsters with energy to spare will gravitate toward the big, imaginatively designed playground. When lunch beckons, you can feed the family reasonably at **Park Chow** (see Chapter 10) on Ninth Avenue, just a block from the park entrance. The **zoo** (see Chapter 11) is a logical alternative for a morning's activity as well; it's easy to reach on a streetcar and, on your return downtown, you may head to **Yerba Buena Gardens** for lunch and a spin on the merry-go-round. If a quieter afternoon seems like a better idea, consider a **ferryboat ride** to Sausalito and back (see Chapter 11).

✔ **For families with slightly older progeny:** Spend a delightful day taking the cable car to **Fisherman's Wharf** (see Chapter 8), where PIER 39 holds sway, with its many shops and video games. You can avoid the scene, if you prefer, with strategically timed tickets to **Alcatraz** (see Chapter 11); think about bringing along sandwiches or snacks, because most of the food around the pier is overpriced and underwhelming. If you can stave off starvation until your return from solitary confinement, hustle everyone over to **North Beach** on the Mason-Powell cable car and eat at **Il Pollaio** (see Chapter 10). **Chinatown** is convenient to North Beach, and kids love browsing in the shops. For dinner, **Lichee Garden** (see Chapter 10) is a good family-style Chinese restaurant, or you can eat at one of the North Beach eateries such as **Tommaso's Restaurant** (see Chapter 10).

✔ **For families with kids of varied ages:** Yerba Buena Gardens (see Chapter 11) is a godsend. Teens are usually more than happy to hang out in **Metreon's game room** and at **Zeum,** while younger siblings can ride the merry-go-round and then run around the gardens. Skating or bowling works for everyone, and food options within walking distance are plentiful. For a step above the center's offerings, **Restaurant Lulu** (see Chapter 10) is an excellent choice for dinner.

San Francisco for Foodies

You could spend a week honing your talents in the kitchen at **Tante Marie's Cooking School** (☎ 415-788-6699; www.tantemarie.com), and that would certainly qualify you as a foodie. Or you could imitate my friend Bev, who flies up from Los Angeles on a regular basis to raid

North Beach for supplies, and then orders huge meals at the restaurant of the moment. Because the cooking classes run from 10 a.m. to 4 p.m., and 6 to 10 p.m., let's make like Bev for a day instead.

Wake up and smell the cappuccino and a raisin roll at a local favorite, **Caffe Greco,** 423 Columbus Ave., in North Beach (☎ 415-397-6261). While you sip, make a mental note of how much room you have in your suitcase for imported Italian delicacies, then walk a block to **Molinari Delicatessen** (see Chapter 10). If you have some way of refrigerating fresh sausages and cheese, you can take better advantage of the selection here. If not, consider ordering a sandwich to go for later. Drop by **Liguria Bakery** (see Chapter 10) for a sheet of pizza focaccia, which will make you the envy of your fellow airplane passengers on the ride home. If you need a new pizza stone, go to **A. Cavalli & Co.,** 1441 Stockton St. (☎ 415-421-4219), which sells Italian cards and maps as well as cooking utensils.

Don't miss immersing yourself in San Francisco's cultural diversity by eating as much dim sum as possible and stocking up on the wealth of ingredients available in the ethnic enclaves. Bev's favorite, **Mayflower** in the Richmond District, 6255 Geary Blvd. (☎ 415-387-8338), makes fine dumplings and won't be mobbed like the dim sum places in Chinatown (few tourists venture this far out on Geary Boulevard). After lunch, walk or take a bus north down Clement Street, 1 block west of Geary, and stop by **Green Apple Books,** 506 Clement St., to peruse a sizable selection of used cookbooks. You can find many produce, fish, and meat markets along Clement, as well as housewares stores. **May Wah,** 547 Clement St., is worth a look, as is **Kamei,** 606 Clement St. If you're serious about eating, you'll probably be ready for a snack or at least coffee by this time. Bev fights for parking on Valencia Street in order to down an espresso at **Ritual Coffee** while musing over *taquerías.* Fortunately, **Pancho Villa** (see Chapter 10) tosses together a steak and prawn quesadilla that is unparalleled for quality and price. It's in the Mission District, where you'll also want to visit **La Palma,** 2884 24th St., at Florida Street (☎ 415-647-1500), for fresh tortillas, dried chilies, and other Mexican cooking essentials. Make your way to 18th and Dolores Street for ice cream that'll have you talking to yourself at **Bi-Rite Creamery** (☎ 415-626-5600). Request one scoop of salted caramel and one of malted vanilla with peanut brittle and milk chocolate. Finally, catch the J-Church to the Embarcadero and enter the Ferry Building. Find **Ferry Plaza Wine Merchant** (☎ 415-391-9400), sit down at the bar, and have a tasting. For dinner, consider a Mission District destination such as **Range** (see Chapter 10) or a high-end experience such as **Restaurant Gary Danko** (see Chapter 10). If you have another day, or you're ready for more, see Chapter 14 for additional dining destinations.

Chapter 14

Going Above and Beyond San Francisco: Three Day Trips

*I*f you have the time to spare, or want to break up your trip with a glimpse of other parts of Northern California, here are three fabulous day trips that will show you some of the region surrounding San Francisco.

Day Trip #1: Berkeley

As you approach Berkeley, a mere 20 minutes over the Bay Bridge, you'll know you aren't in San Francisco anymore. The weather is an immediate giveaway — although the temperature isn't dramatically different, San Francisco's ever-present summer fog disappears. Berkeley is also smaller, and much of its cultural life revolves around the University of California at Berkeley (UCB) campus. One thing the cities have in common is a devotion to fine dining. In fact, one excellent reason to visit Berkeley is to eat a great meal.

Getting there

You can use BART to reach Berkeley, but taking a car is better. Most people drive over the Bay Bridge and follow the signs to Highway 80. The exits include Ashby Avenue, University, and Gilman. If you intend to begin your day on Fourth Street (see "Shopping delights" later in this chapter), take the University Avenue exit. If the University is your first stop, an alternate route is Highway 24, exiting on scenic Claremont Avenue. Claremont intersects College Avenue, which leads directly to the campus while avoiding the less handsome flatlands of Berkeley.

Berkeley

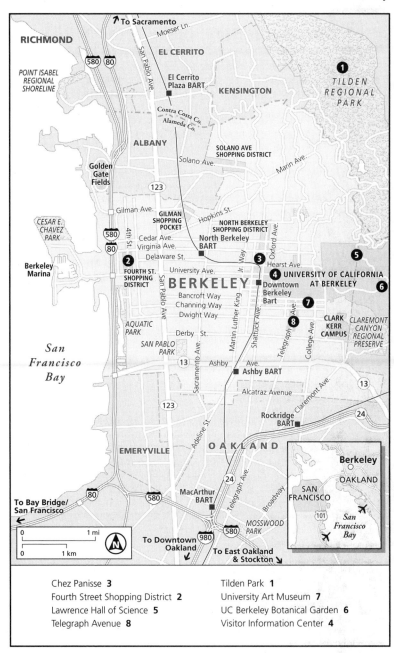

Chez Panisse **3**
Fourth Street Shopping District **2**
Lawrence Hall of Science **5**
Telegraph Avenue **8**

Tilden Park **1**
University Art Museum **7**
UC Berkeley Botanical Garden **6**
Visitor Information Center **4**

If you visit on a Thursday, you get free admission to UCB museums and the botanical garden.

Seeing the sights

To my mind, an ideal day in Berkeley revolves around lunch or dinner at **Chez Panisse** (see "Dining locally" later in this chapter). The food is as close to perfect as food gets. If your reservation is for dinner, you can easily spend your time shopping on **Fourth Street** (see "Shopping delights" later in this chapter), walking around **Tilden Park,** and seeing what's up at the UCB campus. If you've made lunch reservations, tour UCB in the morning and hike in Tilden Park or check out the merchandise on **Telegraph Avenue** or Fourth Street in the afternoon.

The attractive, active campus of **University of California at Berkeley** is the biggest sight in Berkeley, so to speak. The **Visitor Information Center** is at 101 University Hall, 2200 University Ave., at Oxford Street (☎ **510-642-5215**). You can join a free 10 a.m. campus tour from the center Monday through Friday. Weekend tours leave from the Campanile at 10 a.m. Saturdays and 1 p.m. Sundays.

Other notable UCB stops include the **Hearst Museum of Anthropology** (☎ **510-642-6271**; http://hearstmuseum.berkeley.edu; open: Wed–Sat 10 a.m.–4:30 p.m., Sun noon to 4 p.m.; admission: free; tours $5 adults, $2 children under 18); the **Berkeley Art Museum** at 2621 Durant Ave. and 2626 Bancroft Way (☎ **510-642-0808**; www.bampfa.berkeley.edu; open: Wed–Sun 11 a.m.–5 p.m.; admission: $8 adults, $5 seniors, students and children, free the first Thurs of every month); and the 307-foot-tall Campanile, or **Sather Tower,** in the center of campus, where you can take an elevator to the top for excellent views of Berkeley and the bay (open: daily; admission: $2 adults, $1 seniors, free for kids under 18).

Above the campus in the lush hills is the **UC Berkeley Botanical Garden,** 200 Centennial Dr. (☎ **510-643-2755**; www.botanicalgarden.berkeley.edu; open: daily 9 a.m.–5 p.m.; admission: $7 adults, $5 seniors 65 and older, $5 juniors 13–18, $2 kids 5–12, free first Thurs of the month). It features 13,000 plants, including cactus and rose gardens. It's a good place for an easy hike. Farther up the road, the kid-friendly **Lawrence Hall of Science** (☎ **510-642-5132**; www.lawrencehallofscience.org; open: daily 10 a.m.–5 p.m.; admission: $11 adults; $9 seniors, students, and children 7–18; $6 kids ages 3–6) brings science up close and personal. This is an excellent hands-on museum that has activities for kids from 3 to 12.

Shops, cafes, and well-stocked bookstores surround the campus. To get a sense of Berkeley street life, walk along **Telegraph Avenue** from Bancroft to Ashby, and get your fill of cappuccino, street vendors, psychic readers, and the occasional weirdo.

Shopping delights

Close to the University exit off I-80 is **Fourth Street,** a mecca for shoppers from all over the Bay Area. It started out small, with a few outlet stores and a popular diner, and over the years developed into a full-fledged destination for fashion, food, and home décor. Begin by oohing over the gorgeous accessories for home and garden at the **Gardener,** 1836 Fourth St. (☎ **510-548-4545;** www.thegardener.com; open: Mon–Sat 10 a.m.–6 p.m., Sun 11 a.m.–6 p.m.), and keep heading on down the block.

Dining locally

Each of these restaurants is a great place to dine, and Chez Panisse is definitely a destination eatery.

Bette's Oceanview Diner
$ AMERICAN

You can sit down here for a homey breakfast or lunch featuring tender baked goods, tasty salads, and Bette's famous pancakes. Expect crowds and a long wait on weekends. Next door, Bette's sells takeout sandwiches, salads, and desserts to impatient hungry people.

1807 Fourth St., Berkeley. ☎ *510-644-3230.* www.worldpantry.com/bettes/home.html. *No reservations. Main courses: $4.95–$12. MC, V. Open: Mon–Fri 6:30 a.m.–2:30 p.m., Sat–Sun 6:30 a.m.–4 p.m.*

Café Rouge
$–$$ MEDITERRANEAN

Fourth Street neighborhood residents don't have many reasons to stray. Everything you need is nearby, including a lovely meal at this French-style bistro opened by a Chez Panisse kitchen alumnus. Meat eaters will be charmed by the menu (go admire the butcher counter in the back), while mollusk fans can turn to the oysters. Desserts shine as well.

1782 Fourth St., Berkeley. ☎ *510-525-1440.* www.caferouge.net. *Reservations advised. Main courses: $16–$36. MC, V. Open: Mon 11:30 a.m.–3 p.m., Tues–Thurs 11:30 a.m.–9:30 p.m., Fri–Sat 11:30 a.m.–10:30 p.m., Sun 10 a.m.–9 p.m.*

Chez Panisse Restaurant and Café
$$$–$$$$ CALIFORNIA/FRENCH

Alice Waters, the owner of Chez Panisse, is an icon in the food world, respected for adhering to her vision of food as a gift we give daily to our loved ones (including you) and for serving beautifully constructed dishes. Eating here is one of the nicer things you'll do for yourself. Dinner downstairs is $55 to $90 prix fixe, depending on the night. The cafe is moderately priced, comparatively speaking, but expect to spend a lot more than you think prudent for lunch. It's worth it.

1517 Shattuck Ave., Berkeley. ☎ *510-548-5525.* www.chezpanisse.com. *Advance reservations a must for dinner in the restaurant; recommended for dinner in the cafe. Main courses: $55–$90 prix fixe downstairs; $18–$26 in the cafe. AE, DISC, MC, V. Open: Restaurant Mon–Sat, first seating 6–6:30 p.m., second seating 8:30–9:30p.m.; cafe Mon–Thurs 11:30 a.m.–3 p.m. and 5–10:30 p.m., Fri–Sat 11:30 a.m.–3:30 p.m. and 5–11:30 p.m.*

Day Trip #2: Half Moon Bay

A scenic 30-mile drive south on Highway 1 past the tiny hamlets of Moss Beach and El Granada brings you to **Half Moon Bay,** a coastal agricultural town with unequivocal appeal to nature lovers, beachcombers, and wildlife watchers. Originally inhabited by the Costanoan Indians, then deeded to early Spanish settlers, it's a center of floriculture, commercial fishing, and tourism — although the charming village has not given way to all things touristic. It keeps the brand names outside of town. Given Half Moon Bay's proximity to the big city, a day trip couldn't be easier, but to feel as if you've had a little country escape, you'll want to spend the night.

Deciding when to visit

When planning your trip, remember that you'll be on the coast. If it's foggy in San Francisco, it'll be foggy here, too. If possible, avoid summer weekends and their traffic on the roads south. Also check ahead to make sure that Highway 1 through Pacifica is open (rockslides at Devil's Slide are a regular problem, especially in wet weather). October brings crowds for the pumpkin festival, so skip weekends around Halloween unless you have kids along and are in the market for squash. The best times to view seasonal flora and fauna in the area are:

- ✔ **Wildflowers:** February through July
- ✔ **Elephant seals:** Pups arrive December 15 through March
- ✔ **Bird-watching:** Late fall and early Spring
- ✔ **Gray whales:** Late December through early April

And another word of advice: Wear layers. The weather in Half Moon Bay is often chilly and sometimes foggy in the summer.

Getting to the Shore

The scenic route from San Francisco involves a drive toward the Pacific Ocean (take Geary Boulevard to Ocean Beach and turn left). Look for Highway 35 south, which will link up to Highway 1. Otherwise, take Highway 280 or 101 south to Highway 92 west. Depending on traffic, the drive will take around 40 minutes.

Half Moon Bay Coastside

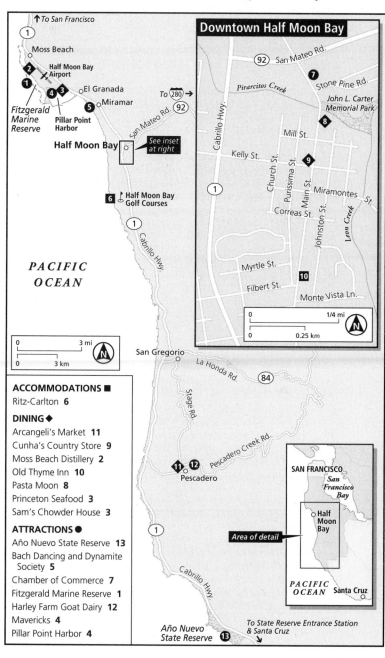

ACCOMMODATIONS ■
Ritz-Carlton **6**

DINING ◆
Arcangeli's Market **11**
Cunha's Country Store **9**
Moss Beach Distillery **2**
Old Thyme Inn **10**
Pasta Moon **8**
Princeton Seafood **3**
Sam's Chowder House **3**

ATTRACTIONS ●
Año Nuevo State Reserve **13**
Bach Dancing and Dynamite
  Society **5**
Chamber of Commerce **7**
Fitzgerald Marine Reserve **1**
Harley Farm Goat Dairy **12**
Mavericks **4**
Pillar Point Harbor **4**

Seeing the sights

The town of Half Moon Bay itself is worth a stroll — there's a good bookshop, art galleries, and many gift shops. The **Spanishtown Historical Society** preserves the former name of the village and publishes a self-guided walking tour booklet that costs $3.50 at the Chamber of Commerce, 520 Kelly Ave. (☎ **650-726-8380**).

Four miles north on Highway 1 is **Pillar Point Harbor,** where you'll find the whale-watching boats (book through **Huck Finn Sportfishing,** ☎ **650-726-7133;** www.huckfinnsportfishing.com); sea kayak rentals and tours from **Half Moon Bay Kayak Co.,** 1 Johnson Pier (☎ **650-773-6101**); and unspoiled views from the piers and pathways. During the season, boats at the dock sell live crabs that you can have boiled and cracked at the harbor (see "Dining Locally," below). You can also begin the **Coastside Trail** hike from the harbor heading south. It takes you past beaches and stunning vistas.

Bird-watching and tide pooling are favorite activities in the area; apparently 20 percent of all North American bird species make **Pillar Point Marsh,** between the harbor and Mavericks (the famous surfing spot), a regular stop on their migratory route. At low tide, take the California Street exit west off Highway 1 in Moss Beach and head for the **Fitzgerald Marine Reserve** (☎ **650-728-3584**), where you'll likely find hermit crabs and starfish hanging about.

Although you will be competing for space with fellow travelers on the weekends, there are two compelling reasons to do so. Saturday and Sunday are the only days **Harley Farms Goat Dairy,** 205 North St., Pescadero (☎ **650-879-0480;** www.harleyfarms.com), is open to the public. It offers two-hour afternoon tours by appointment only ($20 per person). Located about 15 minutes south on Highway 1, this is the home of the friendliest goats on the planet (there's a one-year waiting list for the babies) and a fine example of a sustainable, community-oriented family farm. If you can't make the tour, you can always visit the farm shop (open: daily). As long as you're in tiny Pescadero, stop by **Arcangeli's Market,** 287 Stage Rd. (☎ **650-879-0147**), to pick up a round of artichoke bread. It's 2 miles inland off Pescadero Road.

The second reason to deal with the traffic is to spend Sunday afternoon at a very popular **Bach Dancing and Dynamite Society** concert. A long-standing tradition, the music, which veers toward all forms of jazz, starts at 4:30 p.m. Buy tickets (from $30) at the door. The venue is located at **Douglas Beach House,** 311 Mirada Rd., Half Moon Bay (☎ **650-726-4143;** www.bachddsoc.org).

Elephant seals and sea lions favor **Año Nuevo State Reserve** (☎ **800-444-4445**), a 27-mile drive south of Half Moon Bay. Most of the year visitors are allowed to stroll about unsupervised, but from December through March, when the seals are birthing their pups, tours are guided and are by reservation only.

The coast has beaches aplenty, and you'll probably see surfers out there with the sea lions, but swimming is not advised because it's not safe.

Dining locally

Favorites in the area include the **Moss Beach Distillery,** 140 Beach Way, Moss Beach (☎ 650-728-5595; www.mossbeachdistillery.com) and the newer **Sam's Chowder House,** 4210 N. Cabrillo Hwy., El Granada (☎ 650-712-0245; www.samschowderhouse.com) for fish and views. For a gourmet lunch or dinner, don't pass up a local treasure, **Pasta Moon Ristorante,** 315 Main St., Half Moon Bay (☎ 650-726-5125; www.pasta moon.com). The informality of this attractive Italian restaurant suits the town, and the cuisine is some of the best locally grown food around. The bread and toothsome pastas are made on premises; the roasted beet salad with Harley Farms shaved ricotta will turn even beet loathers into beet lovers; the clam chowder is the most flavorful I've ever tasted. If you wish to take advantage of Dungeness crab season, from November through June — and why think twice about that, I ask — you can choose a couple of live crabs right off the boats in **Pillar Point Harbor** for around $4 a pound. Take them up to the nice people at **Princeton Seafood,** 9 Johnson Pier (☎ 650-726-2722), who will cook, crack, and clean them for around $2 per crab. Pick up bread and accompaniments at **Cunha's Country Store,** 448 Main St., Half Moon Bay (☎ 650-726-4071), before driving to the harbor.

Spending the night

If you'd like to turn your day trip into an overnight, here are two excellent options. For more hotel or B&B choices, contact the **Half Moon Bay Coastside Chamber of Commerce** (☎ 650-726-8380; www.halfmoon baychamber.org).

Old Thyme Inn
$$–$$$$ Half Moon Bay

Half Moon's Bay shops and restaurants are only a couple of blocks from this beautifully maintained 1898 Princess Anne Victorian bed-and-breakfast. It's a convenient, comfortably intimate place. Romantics should request the Garden Room, with its four-poster canopy bed, double whirlpool tub, and fireplace. All rooms boast cushy feather beds. Breakfast is ample and delicious; you'll want to walk it off on the Coastal Trail, then return in time for late afternoon wine and cheese. Rick and Kathy, the amiable yet discreet owners, are a great source of local information.

779 Main St., Half Moon Bay. ☎ *800-720-4277 or 650-726-1616. Fax: 650-726-6394.* www.oldthymeinn.com. *Rack rates: $155–$355 double. AE, DISC, MC, V.*

The Ritz-Carlton
$$$$ Half Moon Bay

It doesn't get any prettier or more deluxe than this Ritz, a cliffside desti-nation resort and spa surrounded by two golf courses and the ocean. The oceanview rooms are premium, but at this price point, there's no reason not to go all the way. Lounging by the fire pit on the deck in an Adirondack chair, listening to the lone bagpipe player bidding farewell to the waning sun, will not be an inducement to go into town. The nice thing about this hotel is that it takes care of all your needs — assuming your needs include spa treatments, really good food, and staring out over the water toward the horizon.

One Miramontes Point Rd., Half Moon Bay. ☎ *800-542-8680 or 650-712-7000. Fax: 650-712-7070.* www.ritzcarlton.com/hmb. *Rack rates: $329–$429 double. AE, CB, DC, DISC, MC, V.*

Day Trip #3: The Wine Country

About an hour's drive north of San Francisco is gorgeous Napa Valley, America's most celebrated wine-producing region. Less than 30 miles from end to end, this fertile area brims with world-class wine-tasting rooms, excellent restaurants, and marvelous resorts and inns.

Just to the west of Napa Valley along Highway 12 is Sonoma Valley. Peaceful, quieter, and somewhat less tourist-oriented, Sonoma Valley is equal to its neighbor as a grape-lover's paradise. Although both valleys are vacation destinations, many visitors arrive for a day of wine tasting and then turn around and head back to San Francisco. That's not the ideal way to get the most out of this bucolic piece of earth. If at all possi-ble, stay a few days to relax and renew before heading back to tackle the big city.

Planning a visit to the Wine Country

Earlier in this book, I warn you against renting a car during your stay in San Francisco. In this section, I recant — for your Wine Country trip, anyway — because the best way to tour is by car. If you don't want to drive, you can join an organized tour. But if you want to spend a night or two in Sonoma or in one of the towns near Napa, or if you want to visit smaller, less commercial wineries than those the tour companies choose, you'll need to drive yourself.

Getting to the Wine Country

Of the two possible routes, the faster one is across the San Francisco–Oakland Bay Bridge (I-80). The more scenic path crosses the Golden Gate Bridge and meanders up through Marin County on U.S. 101. For the return trip, from Napa, I highly recommend taking I-80 rather than U.S. 101 over the Golden Gate Bridge, especially if you're traveling on a weekend. But to get back from Sonoma, use the Golden Gate Bridge.

The Wine Country

If you decide to go the Bay Bridge route to Napa, drive east over the bridge (I-80) and then north to the Napa/Highway 29 exit near Vallejo. Highway 29 is the main road through Napa Valley. The trip takes approximately 70 minutes.

If you decide to go over the Golden Gate Bridge, continue on U.S. 101 north to Novato, where you need to pick up Highway 37 east. Then, if you're interested in a pleasant drive and aren't in a big hurry, take Highway 121 (the Sonoma Highway) north toward Sonoma and east to Napa, if that's your destination, where you'll end up on Highway 29. If Sonoma is your destination, take Highway 12. Make sure to have a map handy. This drive takes about 90 minutes.

Contact the **Napa Valley Conference & Visitors Bureau,** 1310 Napa Town Center, Napa, CA 94559 (☎ **707-226-7459;** www.napavalley.com), for maps to help get you on your way.

Picking the best time to visit

The most popular seasons for touring Napa and Sonoma valleys are summer and fall. The summers are hot in Wine Country, which is one reason it's a favorite with fog-bound San Franciscans. September and October are extremely busy due to the *crush,* or grape harvest, when the sweet aroma of *must* (crushed grapes) fills the air.

Wine Country is delightful any time of year. In the winter, restaurants aren't jammed and traffic is light. Spring is beautiful and still relatively uncrowded. However, if the forecast calls for rain, I recommend you save this trip for another time. If you do plan to visit Wine Country during summer or autumn, make lodging reservations early.

You'll meet with a lot more traffic and tourists on weekends than on weekdays. Also, Golden Gate Bridge traffic heading north on Friday afternoons and south on Sunday afternoons is amazing, and I don't mean that in a positive way. Let the guys with weekend plans sit and stew on 101. Go while everyone else is at work.

Looking out for your safety

Although you may taste wines all along the 35-mile route through Napa and on the scenic roads through Sonoma, the rules of drinking and driving (and common sense) still apply. All those sips add up more quickly than you think. Every tasting room has containers for spitting out the wine so you can taste without actually letting it go to your head.

Highway 29 is dangerous, even if you're not drinking. This two-lane thoroughfare through Napa Valley has been the scene of many accidents, especially at night.

Taking an escorted Wine Country tour

A good option if you don't feel comfortable driving, or if you're on a tight schedule, is a one-day Wine Country tour. On these six- to nine-hour tours, you can usually visit two to three wineries and have lunch in a picturesque village. The downside of a tour like this is that you won't see some of the great wineries that aren't part of the tour itinerary, you won't have time to relax in places that catch your eye, and you may not be able to choose where you want to eat.

But if you're interested in the escorted tours, you have two main options: a tour that starts in San Francisco or a tour that starts in the Wine Country. Here are a few good tours that leave from San Francisco:

- ✓ **The Great Pacific Tour Company** (☎ **415-626-4499;** www.great pacifictour.com) picks you up at your San Francisco hotel and delivers you back after tastings at two Sonoma wineries, a picnic lunch, and a tour of Domaine Chandon, a sparkling wine producer in Napa. The cost, including lunch, is $95 for adults, $93 for seniors, and $83 for children 5 to 11.

✔ **California Wine Tours** (☎ **800-294-6386;** www.californiawine tours.com) offers several Wine Country outings from Napa and Sonoma, and one originating in San Francisco. Customers take the 8:55 a.m. ferry to Vallejo, where a limo meets them for a six-hour excursion that includes five diverse wineries, including V. Sattuoi, where you can picnic. The price is $89 per person, not including round-trip tickets on the ferry, taxes, or tips.

✔ **Tower Tours** (☎ **866-345-8687;** www.towertours.net) takes you to Napa and Sonoma valleys for the day, with stops at three wineries and lunch in Yountville or the town of Sonoma, with a little time to shop. The charge is $67 for adults, $63 for seniors, and $46 for children 5 to 11.

And here are some of the best tours originating in the Wine Country:

✔ **Wine Country Jeep Tours** (☎ **800-539-5337;** www.jeeptours.com) will plan a custom three- to four-hour winery tour that can include some off-road trailblazing and a picnic lunch. The cost is $75 per person, plus $25 each for each additional hour.

✔ **Napa Winery Shuttle** (☎ **707-257-1950;** www.wineshuttle.com), a small, family-run enterprise, gets my vote for value and flexibility. You and your shuttle driver plan the itinerary, although the company does have some favorite wineries it likes to show off. The price is $60 per person for the day — approximately 10 a.m. to 4 or 5 p.m.

✔ The **Napa Valley Wine Train** (☎ **800-427-4124** or 707-253-2111; www.winetrain.com), like a gourmet restaurant on wheels, choo-choos 36 miles through the valley, from the town of Napa to the village of St. Helena and back. Prices for lunch, Sunday brunch, and dinner tours start at $89. These tours primarily involve dining and admiring the gorgeous scenery. Two trips that include stops at a winery are the Grgich Hills Private Winery Tour and Tasting, a luncheon ride that costs $113 per person, and the Domaine Chandon Winery excursion at $128 per person. Onboard the train is a wine-tasting car with an attractive bar and knowledgeable host. The three-hour tours depart from the train station at 1275 McKinstry St. in downtown Napa. You must make reservations for the train. If you don't want to drive to Napa, for $148, **San Francisco Sightseeing Gray Line** (☎ **888-428-6937** or 415-558-9400; www.graylinesan francisco.com) will bus you to and from your hotel to the wine train station in Napa for the excursion.

Mapping out your winery journey

A single day in Wine Country can't do the area justice and will leave you wanting more. But if that's all the time you have, plan to visit no more than three to four wineries, one before lunch and two or three after, followed by a late-afternoon snack or an early dinner.

If you spend two days and a night, you'll have the chance to do some other enjoyable activities such as checking out **Copia** and the new **Oxbow Market** (see "Napa excursions" later in this chapter), biking down a sleepy road, or taking a spa treatment. You could also cut down on your winery visits the first day and take advantage of whatever your inn has to offer, such as a swimming pool, a garden walk, or just some peace and quiet. On your second day, have a substantial breakfast and consider one of the 11 a.m. reservation-only winery tours, such as the one at **Benziger.** To occupy any extra time you may have in your schedule, there's always **outlet shopping** in Napa and along Highway 29 past St. Helena.

Creating a wine-tasting itinerary isn't easy, because there are so many vineyards to choose from. The wineries suggested in this chapter are great for first-time tasters, because they make a special effort to accommodate visitors. These vineyards offer some combination of tours, exhibits, and extra-friendly staffs. But there are plenty more vineyards to choose from, so get a map of the area and, time permitting, explore those back roads.

Touring the wineries on your own

For wine-tasting newbies, the first winery you visit should be one that offers an in-depth tour, so you can familiarize yourself with the wine-making process. If you're traveling from north to south, **Sterling Vineyards** in Calistoga is a good bet, as is **Robert Mondavi Winery** in Oakville. In Sonoma, the tram operators at **Benziger Family Winery** are both knowledgeable and accessible.

If you're already somewhat of a connoisseur, ask your local wine merchant to suggest smaller wineries that you may enjoy.

Napa Valley is home to more than 380 wineries (Sonoma has around 250), some owned by corporations and others by individuals so seduced by the grape that they abandoned successful careers to devote themselves to *viticulture* (the cultivation of grapes). Although there's no correlation between the size of a winery and the quality of the product — which has more to do with the talents of the *vintners* (winemakers) and variables such as weather and soil conditions than with size — the bigger wineries offer more to visitors in terms of education and entertainment.

You can greatly enhance your knowledge of wine by tasting correctly — and what better classroom than a French-style château smack in the middle of a vineyard? Remember that wine appreciation begins by analyzing color, followed by aroma, then taste. You do this with your eyes first, then your nose, then your mouth. Don't be shy about asking questions of the person pouring — he or she will cheerfully explain all, because the more you discover about the product, the more likely you are to become a steady customer. And that makes everybody happy!

Becoming a wine connoisseur: The basics

Cabernet sauvignon, pinot noir, and zinfandel grapes (grown for red wines), and chardonnay and sauvignon or fumé blanc grapes (grown for white wines), are the most prominent grape varieties produced in the area. Telling the difference between them takes a great deal of knowledge. Each one of these varieties contains identifiable flavors and aromas you can only begin to recognize through careful sipping.

Reading the label on the bottle is the best way to tell the difference between cabernet and pinot. The label identifies the type of grape used if the wine contains at least 75 percent of that variety, as well as other bits of information. The appellation of origin indicates where the grapes were grown. The label may state that the grapes were grown in either a viticulture area, such as the Carneros region of Napa Valley, in a certain county, or just in the state itself. Check the vintage date, which explains when at least 95 percent of the grapes were crushed. Many wines taste better aged, and some years produce better grapes than others.

You won't be able to get a deal on wine that you purchase directly from the wineries. They sell their wines at the full retail price so as not to undercut their primary market, the wine merchants. If you can't get a particular vintage at home, most wineries may be able to mail-order it for you (depending on the laws in your home state).

Wineries in Napa Valley

Wineries in Napa (less so in Sonoma) are developing new ways to market wine tasting as an educational and culinary event — and an expensive one at that. In what I think is an effort to eradicate the notion that this is a great way to cadge free alcohol, most wineries charge at least a nominal tasting fee, and many promote sit-down food and wine pairings for real money. Rubicon Estate (formerly Niebaum-Coppola) is a case in point; you can't even drive onto the property without paying $25 per adult at the gate, just so they know you *really, really* want to be there (the fee covers a tour and five tastes). Wine tasting has become very serious business in these parts.

Start in Calistoga and work your way down the valley along Highway 29 to make your return to San Francisco a bit shorter. But don't take this drive on a summer weekend. The bumper-to-bumper traffic on Highway 29 will ruin your day.

Wine tasting do's and don'ts

When you taste wines, keep in mind the following suggestions and you'll fit right in — even if it's your first time:

- **Before the pour, sniff your glass.** It should have a clean aroma.

- **Do not pour the wine yourself.** Winery staff will pour it for you.

- **Taste wines in the appropriate order.** Whites first, reds second, and dessert wines last.

- **Swirl the wine to coat the inside of the glass.** Swirling introduces more oxygen and helps open up the wine flavors and aromas.

- **Smell the wine.** Notice the different aromas — spice, fruit, flowers.

- **Take a sip and cover the back of your tongue with the wine.**

- **Taste, then spit.** Wine tasting is one of the few sports where spitting is not only allowed, it's encouraged. (Just make sure you hit your target, a bucket, or some other container available for this purpose.) Tasting, then spitting, is also a nifty way to sample many wines without becoming cloudy-headed.

- **Do not bring a bottle of wine from one winery into another.**

Beaulieu Vineyard

At this well-regarded, hospitable establishment, the vintners pass out glasses of sauvignon blanc as you walk in, to get you in the mood. After you've enjoyed a glass, you can take a free half-hour tour of the production facility, open daily from 11 a.m. to 4 p.m. Each tasting thereafter is $5, or $25 for five delicious reserve vintages.

1960 St. Helena Hwy. (Highway 29), Rutherford, CA 94573. ☎ *800-264-6918 or 707-967-5230.* www.bvwines.com. *Open: Daily 10 a.m.–5 p.m.*

Clos Pegase

The official tour takes only about 30 minutes and begins at 11 a.m. and 2 p.m. You can spend the rest of your time at this winery joyfully studying the art collection, walking around the sculpture garden, or picnicking on the vast lawn. You need to reserve a picnic table, but reservations aren't required for the complimentary tour. Wine tasting is $2.50 for current releases and $2 each for reserve wines.

1060 Dunaweal Lane (between Highway 29 and the Silverado Trail), Calistoga, CA 94515. ☎ *800-726-6136 or 707-942-4981.* www.clospegase.com. *Open: Daily 10:30 a.m.–5 p.m.*

Napa Valley

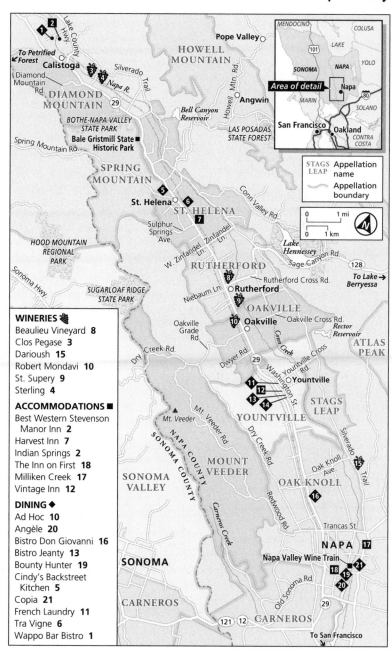

WINERIES
Beaulieu Vineyard **8**
Clos Pegase **3**
Darioush **15**
Robert Mondavi **10**
St. Supery **9**
Sterling **4**

ACCOMMODATIONS ■
Best Western Stevenson
  Manor Inn **2**
Harvest Inn **7**
Indian Springs **2**
The Inn on First **18**
Milliken Creek **17**
Vintage Inn **12**

DINING ◆
Ad Hoc **10**
Angèle **20**
Bistro Don Giovanni **16**
Bistro Jeanty **13**
Bounty Hunter **19**
Cindy's Backstreet
  Kitchen **5**
Copia **21**
French Laundry **11**
Tra Vigne **6**
Wappo Bar Bistro **1**

Darioush

A Persian palace (think *Persepolis*) in Napa? No, you haven't had one too many, you've found Darioush. This eye-catching — to say the least — building, clad in travertine stone mined in Iran, opened in 2004; the winery has been producing since 1997. Tastings cost $20 for a flight of five wines. If it's available, try the 2004 signature Chardonnay, which has an amazing pear-ish, creamy consistency from start to finish. A wine and cheese tasting ($50) starts daily at 2 p.m. On Friday, Saturday, and Sunday at 11 a.m., you can indulge in a two-hour tasting and tour of Darioush Khaledi's private wine cellar, including tidbits whipped up by his chef ($125 per person).

4240 Silverado Trail, Napa, CA 94558. ☎ *707-257-2345.* www.darioush.com. *Open: Daily 10:30 a.m.–5 p.m.*

Robert Mondavi Winery

Mondavi was the first winery to conduct public tastings, and it continues to take pride in educating people about wine. Tours range from the daily 75-minute To Kalon option at $25 a pop (☎ **888-RMONDAVI**, ext. 82001, for same-day reservations) to the $100 Harvest of Joy, which includes a three-course lunch. For fees ranging from $15 to $115, you can benefit from seminars on grape growing, essence tasting, and wine and food pairing. Reservations are required for tours and seminars. During July and August, you can catch a Saturday evening concert. The shows sell out quickly, so call ☎ **888-769-5299** or visit Mondavi's Web site for a schedule and tickets.

7801 St. Helena Hwy. (Highway 29), P.O. Box 106, Oakville, CA 94562. ☎ *800-RMONDAVI or 707-226-1395.* www.robertmondavi.com. *Open: Daily 10 a.m.–5 p.m.*

St. Supéry

Find out about aromas common to certain varietals with the self-guided interactive tour featuring "SmellaVision." You'll also hear about growing techniques at the winery's demonstration vineyard. Have $15 on hand for the tasting fee. On weekends, you can get a half-glass of the really good stuff in the Divine Wine room (the reserve tasting room) for $20.

8440 St. Helena Hwy. (Highway 29), Rutherford, CA 94573. ☎ *800-942-0809.* www.stsupery.com. *Open: Daily 10 a.m.–5 p.m.*

Sterling Vineyards

Arrive at this hilltop winery by aerial tram and swoon over the spectacular vista. The $20 ($10 for under 21s) ticket price includes wine tasting. After you reach the winery, take the self-guided tour that leads you through the entire operation and into the tasting room, where the friendly staff serves wine at tables rather than at a bar. For grander palates, a $45 reserve tasting and guided tour starts at 11 a.m. daily. Plan on spending at least one hour here.

1111 Dunaweal Lane ½ mile east of Highway 29), P.O. Box 365, Calistoga, CA 94515. ☎ **800-726-6136** *or 707-942-3349.* www.sterlingvineyards.com. *Open: Daily 10:30 a.m.–4:30 p.m.*

Sonoma Valley includes the towns of Sonoma, Glen Ellen, and Kenwood and is a bit less popular than Napa Valley because of its smaller size. Day-trippers may enjoy the relaxed, more intimate atmosphere of Sonoma Valley. You can drive here in just over an hour, tour a few wineries, shop, have a great meal, and be back in the city — traffic willing — in time for dinner. You may choose to spend the night, in which case you can find many B&Bs and hotels, plus a few resorts sprinkled around the country roads.

Enter the Sonoma Valley on Highway 121, then turn north on Highway 12. This path takes you directly into the charming town of Sonoma. (If you want to go directly to Glen Ellen, take Highway 116 instead.)

This tour includes stops at some smaller wineries that are too delicious to miss; all provide a little wine education and tastings. You'll see country roads bedecked by acres of grapes, old oaks, and flowers. And although the destinations are noteworthy, the drive alone is splendid.

Arrowood Vineyards & Winery

Arrowood is an intimate, high-end, somewhat exclusive winery with small production but national distribution. You need an appointment for daily 40- to 90-minute tours, which cost $20 to $30. Call a day or two in advance. If you don't care for a tour, you can still sit on the verandah overlooking grapevines and mountains and try some great wines. The tasting fee is $3.

14347 Sonoma Hwy., Glen Ellen, CA 95442. ☎ **800-938-5170** *or 707-938-5170.* www. arrowoodvineyards.com. *Open: Daily 10 a.m.–4:30 p.m.*

Benziger Family Winery

Tractor-pulled trams take visitors up the flower-lined path of this 85-acre ranch on a 45-minute tour ($15 per adult; $5 under 21; reservations required). The winery, owned by the Benziger family since 1981, is near Jack London State Historic Park. The tram operators enthusiastically explain how vines work, how insects are controlled, and how the sun and soil together affect the taste of the wine. You can choose from two tasting opportunities: $10 for six tastings of that day's vintners' choices, or $15 for reserve wines.

1883 London Ranch Rd., Glen Ellen, CA 95442. ☎ **888-490-2739.** www.benziger. com. *Take Highway 12 to Arnold Drive and turn left on London Ranch Road. Open: Daily 10 a.m.–5 p.m.*

B. R. Cohn Winery

Cohn's tasting room, gift shop, and picnic area flanked by olive trees are just down the road from Arrowood. Tasting fees are a modest $5 for current releases and $10 for limited release wines, including the signature 2002 Olive Hill Estate Cabernet. Along with the wines, some of which are available only at the winery, the olive oil produced here is of the highest quality and makes a great gift. Friendly staff members who are happy to talk wine and olives preside over the relaxed tasting room. Doobie Brothers music plays on the speakers and is available in the gift shop because owner Bruce Cohn is their manager.

15000 Sonoma Hwy., Glen Ellen, CA 95442. ☎ *800-330-4064.* www.brcohn.com. *Open: Daily 10 a.m.–5 p.m.*

Moon Mountain Vineyard

A long drive up the mountain rewards visitors with stunning views and some delicious organic estate wines available only on-site. The tasting room is inside a turret, too intimate to accommodate the busloads that reach more accessible wineries. You'll have a chance to ask questions while touring the tank room and caves or tasting the Bordeaux-style offerings. Fellow tasters are likely to be serious wine students who have sought out one of the less ostentatious yet sophisticated wineries in either Napa or Sonoma. The tasting fee is just $10. You must make an appointment to visit.

1700 Moon Mountain Rd., Sonoma, CA 95476. ☎ *707-996-5870.* www.moon mountainvineyard.com. *Take Highway 12 toward Glen Ellen. Moon Mountain Road is between Agua Caliente and Madrone roads. Open: Tues–Sat 10 a.m.–4 p.m. by appointment.*

Robledo Family Winery

The modest tasting room, comfortably furnished with handsome pieces from Michoacan, Mexico, epitomizes the old-fashioned American success story. Reynaldo Robledo, Sr., who arrived in the valley as a 16-year-old migrant worker, combined hard work and a gift for nurturing grapevines into ownership of three vineyards, a vineyard management company, and this winery. His children are actively involved in the business, and you'll meet at least one behind the bar, pouring tastes of their estate Sauvignon Blanc, Pinot Grigio, Pinot Noir, and Merlot. A small producer, Robledo sells the majority of its bottles directly to consumers through its wine club or at the winery.

21901 Bonness Rd., Sonoma, CA 95479. ☎ *707-939-6903.* www.robledofamily winery.com. *Take Arnold Drive and turn on Highway 116 toward Petaluma. Open: By appointment Mon–Sat 10 a.m.–5 p.m., Sun 11 a.m.–4 p.m.*

Taking advantage of other fun stuff in the valleys

Wine Country offers many other activities besides wine tasting. If you're staying overnight, be sure to check out the following sites, sports, and downright sumptuous pleasures in Napa and Sonoma.

Sonoma Valley

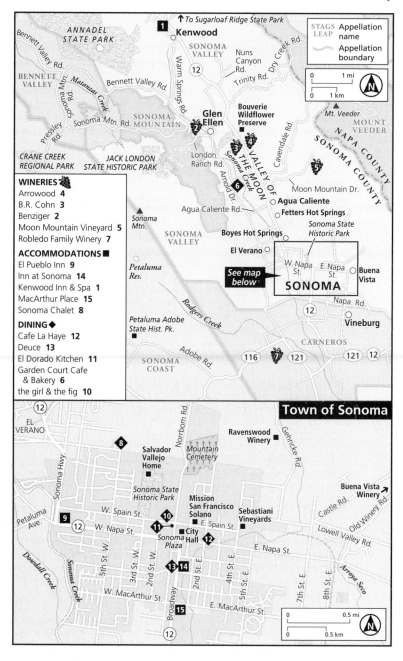

WINERIES
- Arrowood **4**
- B.R. Cohn **3**
- Benziger **2**
- Moon Mountain Vineyard **5**
- Robledo Family Winery **7**

ACCOMMODATIONS ■
- El Pueblo Inn **9**
- Inn at Sonoma **14**
- Kenwood Inn & Spa **1**
- MacArthur Place **15**
- Sonoma Chalet **8**

DINING ◆
- Cafe La Haye **12**
- Deuce **13**
- El Dorado Kitchen **11**
- Garden Court Cafe & Bakery **6**
- the girl & the fig **10**

STAGS LEAP · Appellation name
— Appellation boundary
0   1 mi
0   1 km

To Sugarloaf Ridge State Park
Kenwood **1**
SONOMA VALLEY
Nuns Canyon Rd.
Trinity Rd.
Dry Creek Rd.
Warm Springs Rd.

ANNADEL STATE PARK
Bennett Valley Rd.
BENNETT VALLEY
Bennett Valley Rd.
Matanzas Creek
Sonoma Mtn. Rd.
SONOMA MOUNTAIN
Glen Ellen **2**
Bouverie Wildflower Preserve
Mt. Veeder
MOUNT VEEDER
NAPA COUNTY
SONOMA COUNTY

Arrowood **4**
London Ranch Rd.
VALLEY OF THE MOON
Cavendale Rd.
Moon Mountain Dr.
5
6

CRANE CREEK REGIONAL PARK
JACK LONDON STATE HISTORIC PARK
Agua Caliente Rd.
Agua Caliente
Fetters Hot Springs
Sonoma State Historic Park

Sonoma Mtn.
SONOMA VALLEY
Boyes Hot Springs
El Verano

Petaluma Res.
See map below
W. Napa St.
E. Napa St.
Buena Vista
SONOMA
Napa Rd.

Rodgers Creek
12
Vineburg

Petaluma Adobe State Hist. Pk.
Adobe Rd.
CARNEROS
SONOMA COAST
116 **7** 121
121 12

Town of Sonoma

12
EL VERANO
Norrbom Rd.
Ravenswood Winery
Gehricke Rd.
8
Salvador Vallejo Home
Mountain Cemetery
Sonoma Hwy.
Sonoma State Historic Park
Mission San Francisco Solano
Sebastiani Vineyards
Buena Vista Winery
Castle Rd.
Old Winery Rd.
Petaluma Ave.
9
12
W. Spain St.
E. Spain St.
Lowell Valley Rd.
W. Napa St.
10
11
Sonoma Plaza
City Hall
12
E. Napa St.
Dowdall Creek
Sonoma Creek
5th St. W.
3rd St. W.
2nd St. W.
Broadway
13 14
2nd St. E.
4th St. E.
5th St. E.
7th St. E.
8th St. E.
Arroyo Seco
W. MacArthur St.
E. MacArthur St.
15
12
0   0.5 mi
0   0.5 km

Napa excursions

Copia: The American Center for Wine, Food, and the Arts, 500 First St., Napa (☎ 707-259-1600; www.copia.org), opened in 2001 and quickly became one of the valley's must-see attractions. Copia celebrates the finer things in life in a modern museumlike setting, but it's neither solemn nor overly reverential. One permanent exhibit, an interactive presentation on the role of food and wine in American society, is accessible and amusing. In addition, there's a state-of-the-art theater for concerts, lectures, and films. Copia offers a full roster of wine and food courses year-round, and a 500-seat concert terrace overlooking the Napa River, surrounded by orchard and organic gardens, provides warm-weather amusement. A fine restaurant, Julia's Kitchen (open: Mon–Sat 11:30 a.m.–3 p.m., Sun 11 a.m.–3 p.m. for brunch, and daily 5–9:30 p.m.), wine bar, and, of course, a gift shop round out the experience. Check the Web site for programming during your trip, and try to take in an exhibit, a class, a concert, or a meal — all four if time allows. Check the Web site for prices; general admission is free. Open daily 10 a.m. to 5 p.m.

Next door to Copia is the **Oxbow Public Market,** 610 First St., Napa (☎ 707-226-6529; www.oxbowpublicmarket.com), an upscale development spearheaded by the same fellow who project-managed San Francisco's Ferry Plaza market. Open daily from 9 a.m. to 6 p.m. (restaurants stay open later), it sells produce outside and prepared foods, wine, cheeses, and gourmet gifts inside. Of particular note, especially for people who can't eat gluten, is **Pica Pica,** a vendor specializing is Venezuelan maize breads filled with your pick of good stuff such as fried plantains, skirt steak, cheese, smoked ham, and black beans. It's the future of fast food, I imagine. **Oxbow Wine Merchant** takes the place of a day's worth of winery visits: You can sit at the bar, order a flight of wine from a vast list, add a variety of cheeses and a charcuterie plate, and never see the need to move again. Finish up by tottering over to the **Three Twins** organic ice cream counter (look for a very long line). Sure, this ice cream will ruin your desire for just about any other ice cream in the world, but I'd be remiss if I didn't mention it.

Art turns up in the most unexpected places, but none more so than the **di Rosa Preserve** (☎ 707-226-5991, ext. 25; www.dirosapreserve.org). This is a 217-acre indoor/outdoor gallery 6½ miles west of Napa on Highway 121. It displays more than 2,000 works amid meadows, hanging from trees, and throughout the former winery. Rene di Rosa, a former journalist and viticulturist, owns the property. Guides conduct one-hour introductory and 2½-hour tours Tuesday through Saturday (reservations required); admission is $10 and $15. Admission and tours are free on Wednesday! Soaring over the vineyards under a colorful balloon, with just a few other souls sharing your basket, is a breathtaking experience. **Bonaventura Balloon Company of Napa Valley** (☎ 800-FLY-NAPA or 707-944-2822; www.bonaventuraballoons.com) is one of Napa's most trusted operators, with a range of packages from $198 per person. Or call **Napa Valley Aloft, Inc.** (☎ 800-944-4408 or 707-944-4408; www.nvaloft.com), which offers early-morning lift-off, a preflight snack, and a postflight brunch with bubbly. However, at $225 to $325 per person (depending on the number of people and the extras you choose), you may decide to keep those feet on the ground.

If you want to join the many bicyclists you see pedaling Napa's scenic roads, **St. Helena Cyclery,** 1156 Main St., St. Helena (☎ **707-963-7736;** www.sthelenacyclery.com), will set you on the Silverado Trail for $10 per hour or $30 per day. **Getaway Adventures BHK** (Biking, Hiking, and Kayaking), 1117 Lincoln Ave., Calistoga (☎ **800-499-BIKE** or 707-942-0332), runs day trips with lunch and winery tours.

Wind down after a busy day with a mud bath. People have been immersing themselves in Calistoga mud for more than 150 years, but if you're prone to claustrophobia, get a massage only. You can reserve a tub and a follow-up massage at **Dr. Wilkinson's Hot Springs Resort,** 1507 Lincoln Ave. (☎ **707-942-4102;** www.drwilkinson.com); **Indian Springs Resort and Spa,** 1712 Lincoln Ave. (☎ **707-942-4913;** www.indianspring scalistoga.com); or **Calistoga Spa Hot Springs,** 1006 Washington St. (☎ **707-942-6269**). A mud bath and 50-minute massage is $200 at Indian Springs, and you get use of the pool.

Hop on the city of Napa's free downtown trolley for a 40-minute tour or a ride to Copia (see listing above), the local outlet mall, or other stops. Trolley routes and times vary by day. Monday through Wednesday trolleys run every 45 minutes from 11 a.m. to 7:53 p.m. Thursday through Saturday, two trolley loops operate every 30 minutes: The Red Loop runs from 11 a.m. to 7:57 p.m., and the Green Loop runs from 11:15 a.m. to 8:12 p.m. On Sunday the trolley runs every 45 minutes from 11 a.m. to 7:53 p.m. Find a trolley stop at First and Main streets. Call ☎ **707-255-7631** for more info.

Sonoma activities

Massage therapists abound in the valley, many of them well trained at the **California Institute of Massage and Spa Services,** 772 W. Napa St. (☎ **707-939-9431**), near the Sonoma Plaza. This is not a fancy facility, but the treatment rooms are comfortable, clean, and quiet. A 60-minute therapeutic massage is currently $80.

Olives are also an important crop in Wine Country, and olive oil tastings have become a popular activity. You can debate the merits of various extra-virgin olive oils at the **Olive Press,** 24724 Arnold Dr. (☎ **800-965-4839;** www.theolivepress.com), which shares digs with the Jacuzzi Family Vineyards Winery. The press runs 24 hours between October and February. Watch the process from the tasting room while sampling award-winning olive oil and browsing olive-themed merchandise.

Jack London State Historic Park, 2400 London Ranch Rd. (☎ **707-938-5216;** www.jacklondonpark.com), is where the prolific author of *The Call of the Wild* lived before his death in 1916 at age 40. You can walk on trails to the ruins of Wolf House, London Lake, and Bath House, and visit the recently restored cottage, which displays first editions of London's works and some of his and his wife's personal memorabilia. It's a gorgeous place for a hike. Open daily from 9:30 a.m. to dusk. The park charges a $6-per-vehicle entrance fee.

The **Goodtime Touring Co.** (☎ **888-525-0453** or 707-938-0453; www.good timetouring.com) meets customers off the Sonoma Plaza to embark on guided 4½-hour picnic/winery rides for $125, which includes lunch and tasting fees. Bike rentals alone are also available for $25 to $45 per day.

If you have an intense interest in food, sign up for a three- to four-hour class at **Ramekins,** 450 W. Spain St. (☎ **707-933-0450;** www.ramekins. com), a small B&B and culinary school next to the General's Daughter restaurant. During the day, take in the demonstration classes; then in the evening, glean culinary tips from some major Bay Area chefs. Students have lots of opportunities to sample the goods with a few glasses of wine. Call for a catalog. You can register over the phone, in person, or on the Web.

Spending the night

Although country inns and bed-and-breakfasts interspersed with spas and motels dot both valleys, supply and demand keep room rates and occupancy on the high side. Even if you plan to look for a hotel in San Francisco at the last minute, you need to make reservations in the Wine Country as far in advance as possible, especially for stays between May and October. Most lodgings have a two-night minimum on the weekends during the high season. The good news: Parking is free at all the accommodations I list in this section.

Here is a breakdown of what the dollar signs represent in the following hotel listings (Note: This is a slightly different scale from San Francisco proper.):

- ✔ $: Under $150
- ✔ $$: $151 to $225
- ✔ $$$: $226 to $300
- ✔ $$$$: Over $300

Finding a substantial, well-prepared meal won't be as hard as finding a room, although you still need to make reservations. Some great chefs have settled their lives and businesses around the valleys, perhaps realizing that well-to-do tourists and urbanites with second homes love to eat out. Eating out is also one of the few evening activities in Wine Country — there's not much else to do after 10 p.m.

Contact the **Napa Valley Conference & Visitors Bureau,** 1310 Napa Town Center, Napa, CA 94559 (☎ **707-226-7459;** www.napavalley.com), for information on accommodations.

The **Sonoma Valley Visitors Bureau** is on the Sonoma Plaza at 453 First St. E. (☎ **707-996-1090;** www.sonomavalley.com). It keeps an availability sheet listing hotel, B&B, and motel rooms in case you didn't make reservations.

In Napa Valley

Best Western Stevenson Manor Inn
$–$$$ Calistoga

Situated just east of town, this pleasant motel offers great value in an expensive neighborhood. Rooms are motel basic, boosted a notch by fireplaces or whirlpool tubs, cable TV, fridges, coffeemakers, and hair dryers, as well as on-property extras including a pool, hot tub, sauna, and steam rooms. Guest rooms with two queen-size beds won't crowd the family, and kids under 12 stay free.

1830 Lincoln Ave. (west of Silverado Trail), Calistoga. ☎ *800-942-1112. Fax: 707-942-0381.* www.stevensonmanor.com. *Rack rates: $115–$240 double. Rates include continental breakfast. AE, CB, DC, DISC, MC, V. Check the Web site for Internet-only discounts. Guests get 10 percent off services at a nearby spa.*

Harvest Inn
$$$–$$$$ St. Helena

Rooms in this Tudor-inspired complex are light, attractive, comfortable, and roomy enough for a family. Two pools and two Jacuzzis sit in lovely gardens against a dramatic backdrop of mountains and vineyards. Lots of little luxuries help justify the price, including feather beds, fireplaces, CD players, and VCRs. The midvalley location is central to everything.

1 Main St., St. Helena. ☎ *800-950-8466 or 707-963-9463. Fax: 707-963-4402.* www.harvestinn.com. *Rack rates: $259–$599 double; $399–$675 suite. Rates include continental breakfast. AE, DC, DISC, MC, V.*

Indian Springs
$$–$$$$ Calistoga

Each of these comfortable, old-fashioned bungalows has a kitchen with a refrigerator and microwave, and picnic tables and barbecue grills are nearby. *Surreys* (bikes with bench seats and awnings) and Ping-Pong tables for guests to use enhance the resortlike atmosphere. Lounge chairs surround a warm, Olympic-size mineral pool. The spa, which is in a 1913 bathhouse, offers a full range of services with experienced practitioners. Booking a bungalow in the summer isn't easy, but try edging out the families who come here year after year by calling 48 hours ahead to find out whether you can get in on a cancellation. Rooms in the lodge just aren't as delightful.

1712 Lincoln Ave., Calistoga. ☎ *707-942-4913. Fax 707-942-4919.* www.indian springscalistoga.com. *Rack rates: $185–$315 double studio or 1-bedroom; $280–$410 2-bedroom; $600–$825 3-bedroom. MC, V.*

The Inn on First
$$$–$$$$ Napa

Downtown Napa has a good selection of B&Bs in converted Victorians, and this family-run inn is among the best. It's a smart choice for couples seeking a little romance who also want a location that's close to restaurants and whatever nightlife is available. The Inn on First has a total of ten individually designed TV-free rooms, five in the mansion and five in a slightly more private new building in the garden. The focal points are the cushy beds and in-room Jacuzzis (heart-shaped in the Poppy suite), just so you understand in what direction you're headed. In the heat of the summer, a more resortlike hotel with a pool would probably be preferable, but in snuggling weather, the Inn on First provides nearly everything you need.

1938 First St., Napa. ☎ *866-253-1331.* www.theinnonfirst.com. *Rack rates: $250–$399 double. Rates include full breakfast. MC, V.*

Milliken Creek Inn & Spa
$$$$ Napa

Cushy, chic, and romantic, the airy, large rooms in this intimate inn resemble photos out of *Metropolitan Home.* No luxury is overlooked, from Frette bed linens and L'Occitane bath products to candlelight turndown service. The 3-acre creekside gardens are equally stunning and private; you'll find it difficult to tear yourself away, although many excellent small wineries await along the Silverado Trail.

1815 Silverado Trail, Napa. ☎ *888-622-5775 or 707-255-1197. Fax: 707-942-2653.* www.millikencreekinn.com. *Rack rates: $400–$650 double. Rates include breakfast and afternoon wine and cheese. DC, MC, V.*

Vintage Inn
$$$–$$$$ Yountville

This big, attractive French-country inn is near some of the finest restaurants in the valley. Decorated in French Renaissance style, rooms are clustered throughout the lovely flowering grounds and are equipped with fireplaces, fridges, Jacuzzi tubs, and coffeemakers. Tennis courts and a heated pool make this a comfortable miniresort, good for couples exploring the area. Spa services are available next door at the Villagio, the sister inn. Check for specials and packages, which can make this a relative bargain.

6541 Washington St., Yountville. ☎ *800-351-1133 or 707-944-1112. Fax: 707-944-1617.* www.vintageinn.com. *Rack rates: $295–$665 double. Rates include continental champagne breakfast and afternoon tea. AE, CB, DC, DISC, MC, V.*

In Sonoma

El Pueblo Inn
$–$$$ **Sonoma**

Here's a lovable, way-better-than-average motel almost within walking distance of the Sonoma Plaza, and very well located for touring. Family-owned and -run, it has a really nice vibe and very comfortable, spacious rooms in the buildings closest to reception. (The corner units there have fireplaces.) Guest rooms in the original two-story building in the back are less expensive, and bathrooms are older and smaller. A pretty garden and pool sit next to a shaded patio and fitness room; it could get noisy in the summer, because the property is right along Highway 12. If I had the kids along, I'd stay here without question. And if I was seeking affordable lodgings, ditto.

896 W. Napa St., Sonoma. ☎ *800-900-8844 or 707-996-3651.* www.elpwebloinn. com. *Rack rates: $120–$299 double. Rates include continental breakfast. MC, V.*

Inn at Sonoma
$$–$$$ **Sonoma**

This attractive member of the Four Sisters Inns chain offers terrific value. Public and guest rooms are graciously decorated and smartly maintained, and rates include a generous breakfast, afternoon happy hour, and cookies. With just 19 rooms, the Inn at Sonoma offers as much attention as you require from the staff. Booking a room in summer will take planning, because this is a popular destination for wedding parties. Less than 2 blocks from the Sonoma Plaza, the location makes walking to dinner a simple treat. For romantic occasions, I'd prefer a more secluded and luxurious hideaway such as the Kenwood Inn or Milliken Creek; otherwise, a room here more than satisfies.

630 Broadway, Sonoma. ☎ *888-568-9818 or 707-939-1340. Fax: 707-996-5227.* www. innatsonoma.com. *Rack rates: $165–$270 double. Rates include full breakfast, afternoon wine, and bike rentals. MC, V.*

Kenwood Inn and Spa
$$$$ **Kenwood**

If price is no object, or you want an all-out splurge, this gorgeous inn — reminiscent of villas on the Italian Riviera — is my pick over any hotel in either valley. The faux-painted buildings appear almost miragelike as you drive up the Sonoma Highway, the pale yellow stucco blending into the landscape on a sunny day. When you step inside, you'll have no desire to leave. Rooms are fitted with wood-burning fireplaces, feather beds, and sensuous fabrics, and the facilities — an inviting saline pool, a separately situated Jacuzzi, cozy bar and cafe (for guests only), and spa rooms that overlook vineyards — guarantee a feeling of sublime, luxurious seclusion.

10400 Sonoma Hwy., Kenwood. ☎ *800-353-6966 or 707-833-1293. Fax: 707-833-1247.* www.kenwoodinn.com. *Rack rates: $300–$825 double. Rates include three-course breakfast. AE, MC, V.*

MacArthur Place
$$$$ **Sonoma**

This divine small hotel is a renovated Victorian connected to newer buildings. The rooms are spacious and comfy, with four-poster beds that'll make you think twice about getting up. Contented guests relax at the small, well-staffed spa where the practiced hands of a masseuse work out pre-vacation tension. Manicured gardens surround a swimming pool, and a steakhouse restaurant in the 100-year-old barn supplies room service.

29 E. MacArthur St., Sonoma. ☎ *800-722-1866 or 707-938-2929. Fax: 707-933-9833.* www.macarthurplace.com. *Rack rates: $299–$399 double; $375–$499 suite. Rates include continental breakfast. AE, MC, V.*

Sonoma Chalet
$$–$$$ **Sonoma**

Although all you see from this Swiss-inspired farmhouse inn are mountains and the ranch next door, it's less than a mile from the Sonoma town square. Antiques and collectibles decorate the three delightful, spacious cottages. Inside the farmhouse, the upstairs rooms have private facilities, while the two downstairs rooms share a bathroom. The simple and delicious breakfast includes fresh pastries.

18935 Fifth St. W., Sonoma. ☎ *800-938-3129 or 707-938-3129.* www.sonomachalet. com. *Rack rates: $125–$225 double. Rates include continental breakfast. AE, MC, V.*

Dining in the valleys

Wine tasting certainly isn't the only reason to make the drive from San Francisco to Wine Country: The food here is sublime. Picking and choosing which dining rooms to include below almost hurt, but someone has to make the tough decisions. I tend to lean toward the places locals support, because tourist-oriented restaurants don't expect to see you again. (And if you're wondering why the French Laundry is missing, it's because reservations are nearly impossible to get; see Chapter 10 for one suggestion if you're in a gambling mood and feeling lucky.)

In Napa

Ad Hoc
$$ **Yountville** **AMERICAN**

This is Thomas Keller's other local restaurant, and although it doesn't carry quite the same cachet as the French Laundry, at least you can get a table here. Paying the bill won't require a federal bailout, either. Every night and at Sunday brunch, Ad Hoc serves a four-course meal family style. A typical spring menu may include frisée salad with pickled veggies, flatiron steak and shrimp accompanied by local corn, Cowgirl Creamery cheese, then beignets for dessert. Delicious, homey food combined with the wonderful atmosphere and enthusiastic staff adds up to an experience that will make a great day better. Plus, you can go home and tell everyone you ate at a Keller restaurant.

6476 Washington St., Yountville. ☎ **707-944-2487.** www.adhocrestaurant.com. *Reservations recommended. $48 prix fixe. MC, V. Open: Daily 5–9 p.m., Sun brunch 11 a.m.–3 p.m.*

Angèle
$$–$$$ Napa   FRENCH BISTRO

Napa is experiencing a major growth spurt in hotels and especially restaurants, and few have more to recommend them than this warm, casual brasserie overlooking the Napa River. Part of the historic Hatt Building development, Angèle serves typical French fare as interpreted by a chef with access to the bounty of Northern California. My perfectly cooked *pavé de boeuf haché* (yes, a hamburger) may not have been the most challenging selection, but it sure hit the spot one winter evening when a heavier meal would only have led to gout. My dining companions ate every scrap of their succulent pan-seared scallops and tender veal stew. A high level of professionalism at every turn makes this spot a standout.

540 Main St., Napa. ☎ **707-252-8115.** *Reservations recommended. Main courses: $20–$34. AE, MC, V. Open: Daily 11:30 a.m.–10 p.m.*

Bistro Don Giovanni
$$–$$$ Napa   ITALIAN/COUNTRY FRENCH

Share a pizza, some antipasti, and a bottle of chardonnay for a delightful, light Italian meal, or go all out with the porterhouse for two. This inviting place, easily the most popular restaurant in the valley for all the right reasons, attracts a crowd that gathers at tables on the porch overlooking vineyards. It's heavenly.

4110 Howard Lane (off Highway 29), Napa. ☎ **707-224-3300.** www.bistrodon giovanni.com. *Reservations recommended. Main courses: $12–$36. AE, CB, DC, DISC, MC, V. Open: Sun–Thurs 11:30 a.m.–10 p.m., Fri–Sat 11:30 a.m.–11 p.m.*

Bistro Jeanty
$$$ Yountville   FRENCH BISTRO

Much applauded around the Bay Area for its menu, authenticity, and vivacious dining room, this French bistro satisfies both the appetite and the spirit. Rustic dishes like lamb tongue and potato salad or rabbit and sweetbread ragout make up the seasonal menu. Both timid and adventurous eaters can find something to suit them, with typical bistro items such as steak frites and coq au vin also available.

6510 Washington St., Yountville. ☎ **707-944-0103.** www.bistrojeanty.com. *Reservations recommended. Main courses: $16–$38. MC, V. Open: Daily 11:30 a.m.–10:30 p.m.*

Bounty Hunter Rare Wine & Provisions
$$ Napa   AMERICAN

Foremost a wine shop, Bounty Hunter stocks a wealth of bottles to pair with the first-rate Southwestern-influenced cooking that pretty much obviates the need to ever drive Highway 29 again. Surrounded by the best wines available, your other difficult choice will be what to eat — grilled whole chicken stuffed with Tecate beer? Barbecued ribs, smoky and succulent? A plate groaning with artisan cheeses and meats? This cozy former grocery in downtown Napa knows how to elevate dining into a rousing good time.

975 First St., Napa. ☎ *707-255-0622.* www.bountyhunterwine.com. *Reservations not accepted. Main courses: $12–$45. MC, V. Open: Sun–Thurs 11 a.m.–10 p.m., Fri–Sat 11 a.m. to midnight.*

Cindy's Backstreet Kitchen
$$ St. Helena   CALIFORNIA

Cindy Pawlcyn (of Mustards Grill fame) opened this smaller, more low-key eatery in 2001. St. Helena gets its fair share of weekend wine tasters, and the way this two-story house feels like a neighborhood hangout is a testament to Pawlcyn's sensibility. A table in the garden is the ideal spot for a Cobb salad or curried chicken and something cold (there's a full bar as well as fresh juice drinks). In the evening, small plates, such as rabbit tostados or Piquillo peppers stuffed with cumin-scented beef, seem made for a local lager. Large plates include specials from the wood-burning oven, fish of the day, and steak frites that'll have you hunkered over your dish. Use one of Cindy's root beer floats, featuring house-made vanilla ice cream, to teach kids the difference between ordinary and extraordinary.

1327 Railroad Ave. (between Hunt and Adams), St. Helena. ☎ *707-963-1200.* www.cindysbackstreetkitchen.com. *Reservations recommended. Main courses: $11–$21. AE, DC, DISC, MC, V. Open: May–Oct daily 11:30 a.m.–10 p.m.; Nov–Apr Sun–Thurs until 9 p.m., Fri–Sat 11:30 a.m.–10 p.m.*

Tra Vigne
$$$ St. Helena   CLASSIC ITALIAN

This elegant (but not stuffy) restaurant is what people dream of when they dream of eating in the Italian countryside. You have a choice of where to take your meal — in the more formal dining room inside, or outside on the lovely courtyard patio (probably the better spot if the kids are with you). The Cantinetta delicatessen is the place to pick up wine and prepared foods to eat at the bar or to take on a picnic. Nearby, at 1016 Main St., **Tra Vigne Pizzeria,** a favorite with local families craving spaghetti and meatballs or thin-crusted pizzas in a more casual setting.

1050 Charter Oak Ave., St. Helena. ☎ *707-963-4444.* www.travignerestaurant.com. *Reservations recommended. Main courses: $15–$34. CB, JCB, DISC, MC, V. Open: Daily 11:30 a.m.–4 p.m., Sun–Thurs 4–10 p.m., Fri–Sat 4–10:30 p.m.*

Wappo Bar Bistro
$$$ Calistoga INTERNATIONAL

I like this pair of restaurants off the main drag for an unusual menu that spans a good part of the globe. Start an international culinary tour with spiced chickpea fritters and Vietnamese spring rolls, and then head to South America with a Brazilian seafood stew, layered with flavors, or opt for a soft landing in Italy over some tender *osso buco*. Wappo also has seating on a pretty patio that lies in between its two storefronts. A glass of white wine, the Turkish *mezze* (appetizers) plate, and a table in the warmth of a Napa Valley afternoon defines one version of happiness.

1226 Washington St., Calistoga. ☎ *707-942-4712.* www.wappobar.com. *Reservations accepted. Main courses: $14–$25. AE, MC, V. Open: Wed–Mon 11:30 a.m.–2:30 p.m. and 6–9:30 p.m.*

In Sonoma

Cafe La Haye
$$ Sonoma CALIFORNIA

This casual little cafe serves some of the best food around and, unlike many other Wine Country restaurants, makes no attempt to pretend it's in Italy or France. Plain tables and chairs are carefully set about, as if not to disturb the art that fills the walls, making La Haye's single room resemble a gallery. The menu, spare but complete, features whatever's seasonal and offers organic produce. The daily risotto is fabulous, but you can't go wrong no matter what you order.

140 E. Napa St., Sonoma. ☎ *707-935-5994.* www.cafelahaye.com. *Reservations advised. Main courses: $16–$25. AE, MC, V. Open: Tues–Sat from 5:30 p.m.*

Deuce
$$ Sonoma CALIFORNIA

With so many valley restaurants and chefs vying for attention, travelers overlook Deuce, a popular stop for county residents. In the yellow Craftsman-style house, which sits on the main road heading toward the Sonoma Plaza, you'll find especially friendly service and well-prepared food that doesn't require any translation. Lots of diners (especially those who want dessert) make do with a couple of starters, in particular the tender, crispy calamari or the irresistible lobster pot pie. For mains, the smart money is on the thick, perfectly grilled pork chop, although it's hard to pass up the cassoulet. Kids are welcome here, and the kitchen will prepare something to their liking if you ask.

691 Broadway, Sonoma. ☎ *707-933-3823.* www.dine-at-deuce.com. *Reservations advised. Main courses: $17–$24. AE, MC, V. Open: Sun–Thurs 11 a.m.–9 p.m., Fri–Sat 11 a.m.–9:30 p.m.*

El Dorado Kitchen
$$$ Sonoma CALIFORNIA

Anchoring the northwest corner of the square, EDK answers the question of where to eat in hot weather when you want to dine outside. In the winter, the restaurant's open kitchen and communal table provide a different sort of warmth. It's a joy to order a bottle of local vino, a charcuterie plate featuring house-made sausage, and another of olives and hummus. Linger over excellent steamed mussels. If you can manage another course, bacon-wrapped pork tenderloin served over garlic-enhanced polenta is a dish worthy of New Orleans' best. Desserts are also gorgeous, so plan ahead: You'll be sorry if you can't manage the ice cream sandwiches.

405 First St. West, Sonoma. ☎ *707-996-3030.* www.eldoradosonoma.com. *Reservations suggested. Main courses: $22–$29. AE, MC, V. Open: Sun 11 a.m.–2:30 p.m., Mon–Sat 11:30 a.m.–2:30 p.m., Sun–Thurs 5:30–9:30 p.m., Fri–Sat 5:30–10:30 p.m.*

Garden Court Cafe and Bakery
$ Glen Ellen AMERICAN

Get a modest plate of bacon and eggs and lunch to take out, or a tasty, filling breakfast that keeps you going most of the day. This is a completely unpretentious diner where the regulars settle back with the paper and coffee while waiting for gravy and biscuits. Atkins and South Beach dieters have lots of egg dishes to choose from — hold the house-baked breads. Well, maybe not; these are especially fine.

13647 Arnold Dr., Glen Ellen. ☎ *707-935-1565.* www.gardencourtcafe.com. *Reservations not accepted. Main courses: $4–$10. MC, V. Open: Wed–Mon 7:30 a.m.–2 p.m.*

the girl & the fig
$$ Sonoma COUNTRY FRENCH

This upscale country French bistro moved to the Sonoma Hotel a few years ago, adding outdoor dining to the delight of its admirers. The seasonal menu meets the needs of seafoodies, vegetarians, and carnivores with one or two dishes in each category. The grilled fig salad with arugula and local goat's cheese is a must when fresh figs are available.

110 W. Spain St., Sonoma. ☎ *707-938-3634.* www.thegirlandthefig.com. *Reservations advised. Main courses: $17–$25. MC, V. Open: Daily 11:30 a.m.–10 p.m.*

Part V

Living It Up after Dark: San Francisco Nightlife

"We loved Beach Blanket Babylon. It's a show featuring a bunch of people making fun of celebrities and politicians while cavorting around in big, silly hats. You know, a lot like your mother's garden club."

In this part . . .

*B*ecause San Francisco is home to such a diverse population, no single form of entertainment has come to be
associated with the city in the same way as jazz with New
Orleans or theater with New York. Instead, San Francisco
offers an eclectic mix of dance, music, performance art, theater, and opera, with plenty to choose from on any given
night. If you shun anything requiring a trip to a box office, you
can choose from plenty of bars and clubs to keep you off the
streets until the wee hours.

Even travelers with kids don't have to limit after-hours activities to dinner and a movie. A few clubs offer shows for
patrons of all ages, featuring local alternative or blues bands.
(Your kid will think you're very special.) A night at the theater
is also a great family alternative; you can usually find something that appeals to people of all ages.

Chapter 15

Applauding the Cultural Scene

. . . .

In This Chapter

▶ Finding out what's going on in town when you're here

▶ Getting tickets to concerts, theater, and other events

▶ Enjoying the major opera, ballet, theater, and classical music scenes

▶ Broadening your horizons with experimental theater and dance

▶ Dining before or after the show

. . . .

*W*hether you're up for world-class classical music or experimental theater, or pretty much anything in between, you can find it on stage in San Francisco. In this chapter, I give you the overall picture, then detail how to find out what's going on and score tickets.

Getting the Inside Scoop

Performing-arts fans can find plenty of interesting offerings in San Francisco. For drama, Broadway road companies drop into town, and our own **American Conservatory Theatre (ACT)** regularly produces works that are visually inspired and well acted. Opera is just as vibrant. Although the great Enrico Caruso never returned to San Francisco after the shock of the 1906 earthquake, plenty of other stars have aria'd their way through town, raising the local opera company to world-class heights. The **San Francisco Symphony** is in a similar league, and while I'm bragging, I'd better mention the **ballet.** It, too, is as fine a company as you'll see anywhere. But don't let the big brands sway you from trying stages outside Civic Center, including Yerba Buena Gardens, and smaller venues South of Market where experimental theater abounds.

Finding Out What's Playing and Getting Tickets

On the Web, you can check sites such as **Citysearch** (http://san francisco.citysearch.com) and the ***San Francisco Chronicle*** (www.sfgate.com) for reviews and synopses; otherwise, follow your instincts (and local recommendations) when you get here. You may stumble onto something wonderful. If you're looking for something outside the mainstream — and this is a fine place to find that — a month or so before your trip, sign up for the e-mail list Flavorpill SF (sf.flavor pill.net). The free weekly e-mail highlights the more elusive cultural events around town, including films, concerts, and theater.

Here are a few other Web sites to check out for what's happening now:

✔ www.sfbg.com: You can find the *San Francisco Bay Guardian's* complete entertainment listings online. Try this one first.

✔ www.sanfran.com: *San Francisco,* our very own monthly magazine, is chock-full of arts and entertainment information.

✔ www.sfweekly.com: This is the Web site for *SF Weekly,* a great lefty publication with provocative features, lots of local info, and reviews.

For tickets to any theater, dance, symphony, or concert performance, you can call the appropriate box office directly or head online and order with a credit card (charges are nonrefundable if, for some reason, you don't show up). Around Civic Center, **City Box Office,** 180 Redwood St., Suite 100 (☎ **415-392-4400;** www.cityboxoffice.com), sells tickets to shows playing at the Nob Hill Masonic Center, Project Artaud Theater, Herbst Theatre, and other lesser-known stages. If you arrive in town without plans, visit **TIX Bay Area** (☎ 415-433-7827; www.theatrebay area.org/tix) for half-price tickets to same-day performances (subject to a $1–$3 service charge). TIX, which is also a **BASS Ticketmaster** outlet, is on Union Square between Post and Geary streets. It's open Tuesday through Thursday from 11 a.m. to 6 p.m., Friday and Saturday until 7 p.m., and Sunday 10 a.m. to 3 p.m.

Don't buy tickets from anyone outside TIX or a box office claiming to have discounted or scalper tickets, especially to sporting events. Folks get duped all the time, forking over real cash for counterfeit tickets. Another common scam is to sell tickets to an event that has already taken place.

The concierge at your hotel can be a source for hard-to-get tickets. The larger the hotel, the more likely it is that the concierge will be successful, but in any case, it's worth asking. If he or she does manage to come through, a $5 to $10 tip is appropriate.

Surfing for performing-arts information

Check out the following sites for all your performing arts needs:

- ✔ American Conservatory Theater: `www.act-sfbay.org`
- ✔ Best of Broadway theater info: `www.shnsf.com`
- ✔ Lamplighters light opera company: `www.lamplighters.org`
- ✔ San Francisco Ballet: `www.sfballet.org`
- ✔ San Francisco Opera: `www.sfopera.org`
- ✔ San Francisco Performances: `www.performances.org`
- ✔ San Francisco Symphony: `www.sfsymphony.org`

If you're flexible about your plans for the evening, pick a show and go to the theater box office to stand in line awaiting last-minute cancellations by season-ticket holders or the release of tickets held for media or VIPs. With luck, you can land seats in the orchestra. Without luck, you'll have wasted an hour or so.

Don't be late to the theater, symphony, or opera. Curtains rise on time, and if you're late, you won't be seated until there's a break in the action.

 If you're attending a show at the Geary Theater, avoid the boxes on either side. The sightlines obscure half the stage, generally the half where the action takes place.

As for what to wear, you'll see a little of everything, from tailored evening clothes to jeans. People seem to dress up a bit more Friday and Saturday nights, especially in the orchestra seats, but your Sunday best isn't necessary.

Raising the Curtain on the Performing Arts

Cable cars will get you to Union Square theaters if you're coming from North Beach; from the Marina or Union Street, take a 30-Stockton or 45-Union/Stockton bus. If you prefer to take a cab to your lodgings afterward, walk to a big hotel to catch one. You can find a number of parking garages near Union Square. They charge at least $10 for the evening.

You can reach **Civic Center,** where the opera, ballet, and symphony perform, by any Muni Metro streetcar or any bus along Van Ness Avenue. I wouldn't walk around this area unescorted after dark to get back to the Muni station, and taxis aren't always immediately available. If you feel

San Francisco Performing Arts

American Conservatory Theatre (Geary Theatre) **10**

Beach Blanket Babylon (Club Fugazi) **2**

Curran Theatre **9**

42nd St. Moon (Eureka Theatre) **3**

Golden Gate Theatre **14**

Herbst Theatre **16**

Intersection for the Arts **22**

Lorraine Hansberry Theatre **6**

The Magic Theatre **1**

Marines Memorial Theatre **7**

New Conservatory Theatre **18**

New Langton Arts **20**

Noontime Concerts (St. Patrick's Church) **12**

Old First Presbyterian Church **5**

Orpheum **19**

Post Street Theatre **8**

Project Artaud Theatre **21**

San Francisco Ballet **17**

San Francisco Opera **17**

San Francisco Symphony **17**

Smuin Ballets/SF (Yerba Buena Center for the Arts) **13**

Ticket Outlets:
  City Box Office **15**
  TIX Bay Area **11**

West Coast Live **4**

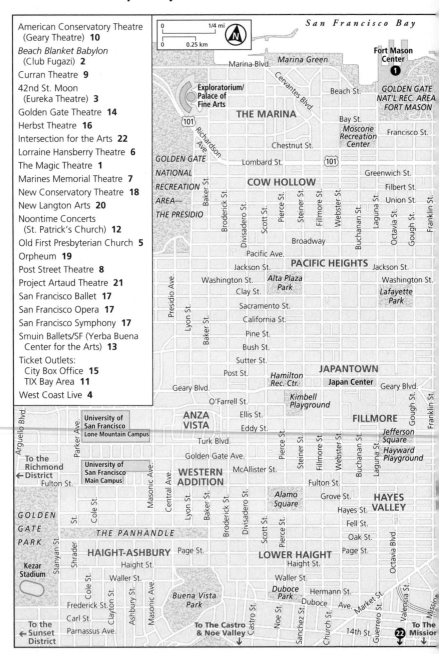

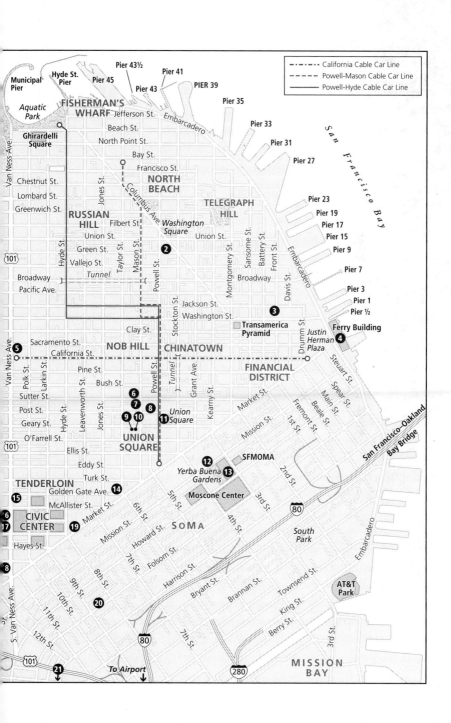

stuck, walk to one of the many nearby restaurants and ask the host to call a taxi for you. Relax, and prepare to wait awhile at the bar. If you're driving, you can park in the garage on Grove Street between Franklin and Gough streets.

South of Market and **Mission** neighborhood venues have troubles similar to Civic Center's. You can usually get to the performance by public transportation, but returning late at night by bus is less interesting (or perhaps more interesting, depending on your perspective). Again, if you're attending a show in this area, don't expect a cab to materialize afterward. Instead, walk to a nearby restaurant or bar and call. These numbers for local cab companies can help:

- ✔ **Desoto Cab:** ☎ 415-970-1300
- ✔ **Luxor Cabs:** ☎ 415-282-4141
- ✔ **Pacific:** ☎ 415-986-7220
- ✔ **Veteran's Cab:** ☎ 415-648-1313
- ✔ **Yellow Cab:** ☎ 415-626-2345

I would never seriously compare our little theater district to the Great White Way in New York, but San Francisco has a fair number of professional stages. At least ten of varying sizes cluster around **Union Square,** and experimental theaters dot the **South of Market** and **Mission** districts in converted warehouses and gallery spaces. Productions may include a musical or two, distinguished classics, and world-premiere comedies and dramas.

The **American Conservatory Theater (ACT),** the preeminent company in town, produces a wide variety of plays during its season, which runs October to June. The acting is first-rate, and the costumes and sets are universally brilliant. The choice of material ranges from new works by playwrights such as Tom Stoppard, can't-lose American chestnuts, and Shakespeare, all the way to not-quite-ready-for-prime-time dramas that still receive a careful rendering. The lovely **Geary Theater,** 415 Geary St., at Mason Street (☎ **415-749-2228;** www.act-sfbay.org), is home to ACT productions. Ticket prices range from $17 to $82, and the box office is open every day from noon until showtime (6 p.m. on nonperformance days).

Broadway hits and road shows appear down the block at the **Curran Theater,** 445 Geary St., between Mason and Taylor streets; the **Golden Gate Theater,** 1 Golden Gate Ave., at Market Street; and the **Orpheum,** 1192 Market St., at Eighth Street. All three share one phone number and Web site (☎ **415-551-2000;** www.shnsf.com), and the recorded message explains what's playing, where to buy tickets, and how to get to the theaters.

You may like your theater a little more cutting-edge. If so, check out the **Magic Theatre,** Fort Mason Center, Building A (☎ **415-441-8822;** www. magictheatre.org), where David Mamet premiered his adaptation of *Dr. Faustus.* Tickets range from $26 to $52, with great "day-of" discounts. Or try **Intersection for the Arts,** a 72-seat performance space in the Mission District at 446 Valencia St., between 15th and 16th streets (☎ **415-626-3311;** www.theintersection.org). You won't find anything traditional in the exhibits, literary series, music, or interdisciplinary works of art. Tickets cost $9 to $15.

The Magic Theatre sets aside a limited number of tickets for "Sliding Scale" Wednesdays. Prices range from $5 to $25, and reservations aren't accepted; it's first-come, first-served at the box office (open: Tues–Sat noon to 5 p.m.), cash only.

The **Lorraine Hansberry Theatre,** 620 Sutter St. (☎ **415-474-8800;** www.lhtsf.org), features dramas and musicals by black authors past and present such as Langston Hughes and August Wilson. Ticket prices are $25 to $36. If you are in town during December, don't miss the holiday gospel show, *Black Nativity.*

Another Union Square stage is tucked inside the building that houses the Kensington Park Hotel, 450 Post St. The **Post Street Theatre** (formerly Theatre on the Square) opened with the rock 'n' roll musical *Buddy: The Buddy Holly Story* and recently played host to the fabulous Dame Edna. The nearby **Marines Memorial Theatre,** on the second floor of the Marines' Memorial Club, 609 Sutter St., is similar in size and flavor to the **Post Street Theatre.** The two share a box office number and Web site (☎ **415-771-6900;** www.unionsquaretheatres.com).

Close to Civic Center, in an impressive former Masonic temple built in 1911, is the **New Conservatory Theater Center** at 25 Van Ness Ave., a half block off Market Street (☎ **415-861-8972;** www.nctcsf.org). NCT, which consists of three small theaters, presents a variety of productions throughout the year. April through August is **"Pride Season,"** during which a series of six plays with gay themes is presented. NCT also produces children's theater programming all year.

Admirers of musical theater should keep an eye out for productions by **42nd Street Moon** (☎ **415-255-8207;** www.42ndstmoon.org). The company presents long-forgotten American musicals in concert format and gives audiences an opportunity to hear delightfully clever tunes that somehow "disappeared." Check ahead for shows and dates. Productions take place at the **Eureka Theatre,** 215 Jackson St., at Battery Street in the Financial District (☎ **415-978-2787**).

Pre- and post-theater dining

You have plenty of dining choices before attending any 8 p.m. performance. After the show, however, your dining choices are more limited. On Union Square, a branch of the **Cheesecake Factory** graces the eighth floor of Macy's. It's open until 11 p.m. **Farmer Brown,** 25 Mason St., at Turk Street (☎ 415-409-3276), next to the Hotel Metropolis, serves a Southern-leaning menu featuring succulent fried chicken until midnight. If you're attending an event around Civic Center and want to eat before the show, be sure to make reservations. The **Hayes Street Grill** (see Chapter 10) originally opened to accommodate the culture crowd, paving the way for a great many more restaurants on and around Hayes Street. Down around Yerba Buena Center, **Bacar,** 448 Brannan St., between Third and Fourth streets (☎ 415-904-4100), has an extensive wine list and serves tempting small and large plates. **XYZ** at the W Hotel, 181 Third St., at Howard Street (☎ 415-817-7836), has a cafe as well as a restaurant, so you can go casual or upscale, depending on how quickly you need to eat.

Symphony and Opera

San Francisco has many venues for listening to classical music. Local papers and Web sites are your best source for event listings. You can see major groups such as the **San Francisco Symphony,** which performs in the **Louise M. Davies Symphony Hall,** 201 Van Ness Ave., at Grove Street (☎ 415-864-6000), in Civic Center. The season runs from September through July, and tickets cost $25 to $130. Also at Civic Center is the **Herbst Theater,** 410 Van Ness Ave. (☎ 415-621-6600), home to **San Francisco Performances** (www.performances.org) and other professional groups.

You can also enjoy piano and violin duos, chamber music ensembles, and singers at **Old First Presbyterian Church,** 1751 Sacramento St., at Van Ness Avenue (☎ 415-474-1608; www.oldfirstconcerts.org). These less formal concerts take place in the afternoon and evening, and tickets are a mere $9.60 to $14. The California Street cable car takes you to within 2 blocks of the church. If you're around **Yerba Buena Gardens** at lunchtime on Wednesday, head to **St. Patrick's Church,** 756 Mission St., where **Noontime Concerts** (☎ 415-777-3211; www.noontimeconcerts.org) produces half-hour concerts. These brief shows may be solo or full orchestral performances. Admission is $5. Noontime Concerts also uses the **A. P. Giannini Auditorium** at the Bank of America headquarters, 555 California St., in the Financial District. Concerts currently take place every Tuesday, but call for an updated schedule.

The **San Francisco Opera** opens its season with a gala in September and ends quietly in early January. It plays at the **War Memorial Opera House,** 301 Van Ness Ave., at Grove Street (☎ 415-864-3330), in Civic Center. Tickets run from $15 to $290. **Pocket Opera** (☎ 415-972-8934;

Civic Center

www.pocketopera.org) delivers opera to the masses in stripped-down, English-language versions that are quite entertaining and highly professional. The season begins in February and ends in June; productions take place at different locations, including the Palace of the Legion of Honor.

Dance

Plenty of classical and modern dance groups raise the *barre* in San Francisco, the **San Francisco Ballet** being the best-known company. The season runs from February to June, and performances are at the **War Memorial Opera House,** 301 Van Ness Ave., at Grove Street. Call ☎ **415-865-2000** for tickets. Prices run from $10 for standing room to over $100 for orchestra seats. Students, seniors (68-plus), and military personnel qualify for discounted same-day tickets, at $10 to $20. You can check for availability by phoning the box office.

You'll find adventurous modern dance, performance art, and theater at the **Project Artaud Theater,** 450 Florida St., at 17th Street (☎ 415-626-4370; www.artaud.org), in the Mission District. Ticket prices are $20 or less, depending on the day and type of show.

Some of the most interesting dance companies, including **Smuin Ballets/ SF,** appear on stage at the **Yerba Buena Center for the Arts,** 700 Howard St. (☎ 415-978-2787; www.ybca.org). It's easy to reach, and there are many fine restaurants in the neighborhood for pre- or post-theater supper.

New Langton Arts, a nonprofit, artist-run experimental performance space in SoMa, may have an art show, a theater performance, video pieces, or all three at the same time. Check it out at 1246 Folsom St., between Eighth and Ninth streets (☎ 415-626-5416; www.newlangton arts.org). Gallery and box office hours are Tuesday through Saturday, noon to 6 p.m.

You may not want to miss *Beach Blanket Babylon*, a San Francisco ritual. The 90-minute musical revue is known for wildly imaginative hats that seem to live lives of their own. The spectacle is so popular that even after celebrating 35 years of poking fun at stars, politicians, and San Francisco itself, the constantly updated shows always sell out. Purchase tickets ($25–$80) through TIX or by mail at least three weeks in advance (especially if you want to attend a weekend performance). You must be 21 for evening shows; minors are admitted only for Sunday matinees, when no liquor is sold. You can enjoy this spectacle in North Beach at **Club Fugazi,** 678 Green St., between Powell Street and Columbus Avenue (☎ 415-421-4222; www.beachblanketbabylon.com). You've got to see it to believe it.

It's not *A Prairie Home Companion,* but we make do with our own Bay Area radio show broadcast live on Saturday morning from 10 to noon. You can join the studio audience for host Sedge Thomson's **West Coast Live** (☎ 415-664-9500; www.wcl.org) and watch well-known writers, local personalities, musicians, and even a staff naturalist have their say (or flog their most recent masterpieces). The show broadcasts from the Ferry Building or from Berkeley — check the Web site for a schedule. Tickets are $15 in advance and $18 at the door; reservations are a good idea. The shows are entertaining, informative, and a highly enjoyable way to spend a morning.

Chapter 16

Hitting the Clubs and Bars

· ·

In This Chapter

▶ Checking out the hippest clubs and bars for live music
▶ Moving and grooving at dance clubs
▶ Aiming for atmosphere
▶ Getting a good laugh
▶ Broadening your horizons at some unique establishments

· ·

*O*ne thing I love about this city: There's no end to the good times. You can have a night at the theater, followed by a night hopping through a few bars and clubs, followed by a night listening to great jazz. There are so many places for drinking and dancing and socializing, you'll have no excuse (except maybe exhaustion) for staying in at night.

Livin' It Up with Live Music

Bars, all of which by law must close from 2 to 6 a.m., are self-explanatory. Clubs are a different story altogether. South of Market, dance clubs with different styles and names may share the same space. For example, a particular club may feature 1970s-revisited disco catering to the Velvet Elvis crowd on Friday, and then play Gothic industrial "music" for body-piercing aficionados on Monday. Take a careful look at the listings in *SF Weekly* or *Bay Guardian* to know what you're getting into. Most clubs don't get going until after 10 p.m., so plan to take cabs anywhere not within walking distance of your hotel.

Finding some cool jazz

Yoshi's Jazz Club, 1330 Fillmore St. (☎ **415-665-5600,** www.yoshis.com), which opened in 2007 in the revitalized Fillmore Heritage district near Japantown, is an offshoot of an Oakland music fixture. The San Francisco Yoshi's brings an eclectic mix of jazz stalwarts (Herb Alpert and Nicholas Payton, to name two) to town. Shows, which cater to all ages, sell out quickly. The club generally schedules two sets nightly; if you have tickets to the late show, you can enjoy a leisurely meal featuring delicious Japanese food at Yoshi's restaurant (see Chapter 10). An evening at this handsome place will be a memorable night out.

San Francisco Clubs and Bars

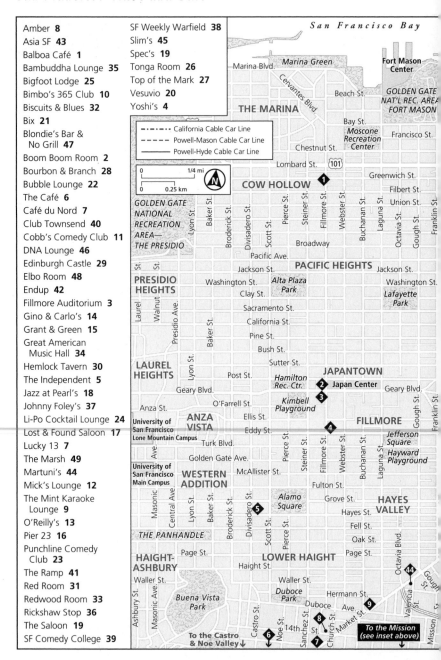

Amber **8**
Asia SF **43**
Balboa Café **1**
Bambuddha Lounge **35**
Bigfoot Lodge **25**
Bimbo's 365 Club **10**
Biscuits & Blues **32**
Bix **21**
Blondie's Bar &
  No Grill **47**
Boom Boom Room **2**
Bourbon & Branch **28**
Bubble Lounge **22**
The Café **6**
Café du Nord **7**
Club Townsend **40**
Cobb's Comedy Club **11**
DNA Lounge **46**
Edinburgh Castle **29**
Elbo Room **48**
Endup **42**
Fillmore Auditorium **3**
Gino & Carlo's **14**
Grant & Green **15**
Great American
  Music Hall **34**
Hemlock Tavern **30**
The Independent **5**
Jazz at Pearl's **18**
Johnny Foley's **37**
Li-Po Cocktail Lounge **24**
Lost & Found Saloon **17**
Lucky 13 **7**
The Marsh **49**
Martuni's **44**
Mick's Lounge **12**
The Mint Karaoke
  Lounge **9**
O'Reilly's **13**
Pier 23 **16**
Punchline Comedy
  Club **23**
The Ramp **41**
Red Room **31**
Redwood Room **33**
Rickshaw Stop **36**
The Saloon **19**
SF Comedy College **39**

SF Weekly Warfield **38**
Slim's **45**
Spec's **19**
Tonga Room **26**
Top of the Mark **27**
Vesuvio **20**
Yoshi's **4**

- ·—·—· California Cable Car Line
- ‑ ‑ ‑ ‑ Powell-Mason Cable Car Line
- —— Powell-Hyde Cable Car Line

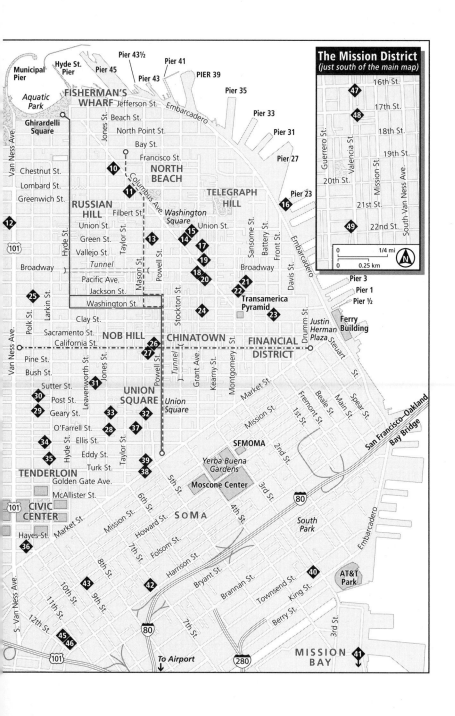

Jazz at Pearl's, 256 Columbus Ave., at Broadway (☎ 415-291-8255; www.jazzatpearls.com), showcases the 17-piece big band Contemporary Jazz Orchestra every Monday and local musicians the rest of the week. A smaller venue than Yoshi's, the room has more of a '30s supper-club atmosphere, although you'll want to eat elsewhere in North Beach. Tickets are $15 to $30. Over in the Mission, the ever-cool **Elbo Room,** 647 Valencia St., near 17th Street (☎ 415-552-7788), blasts acid jazz for a well-dressed younger crowd. On some nights, you can move to Latin and funk bands. Cover starts at $5 upstairs; downstairs the bar has a fine menu of microbrews and a couple of pool tables.

Feelin' blue: Blues bars

The **Boom Boom Room,** 1601 Fillmore St., at Geary Street (☎ 415-673-8000; www.boomboomblues.com), is open every night for dancing, cocktails, and jiving. Lines often form on the weekends, so it doesn't hurt to arrive early and sip your drink slowly. The cover charge varies depending on the night and the act; it generally ranges from free to $22. Check the Web site for an events calendar.

Follow the crowds to **The Saloon,** 1232 Grant Ave., at Fresno Street near Vallejo Street (☎ 415-989-7666), as your first stop on a walking tour of North Beach blues bars. Johnny Nitro plays here Friday and Sunday night. If you can manage to get inside, the cover is usually $4 to $5. Up the block, check out the **Lost and Found Saloon,** 1353 Grant Ave., between Vallejo and Green streets (☎ 415-981-9557). It's crowded on weekend nights; there's no cover. **Grant & Green,** 1371 Grant Ave. (☎ 415-693-9565), is the third in the North Beach blues triumvirate. No cover here, either. If you're looking for something a little less . . . real, head over to **Enrico's,** 504 Broadway, at Kearny Street (☎ 415-982-6223). Revived and remodeled in 2007, this landmark continues to book live music nightly.

During the day, **Pier 23,** the Embarcadero, at Front Street (☎ 415-362-5125), serves lunch to fashionable business executives on the patio. At night, hot local blues and funk musicians, honky-tonk pianists, or ska bands play for fans ages 21 to 70. The cover is $5 to $10 on weekends.

Catching the big-name acts

You'll want to contact the box office directly or purchase tickets from **BASS** (☎ 415-776-1999) for major musical acts. Ticket prices vary at the following clubs, depending on the performers.

The **Great American Music Hall,** 859 O'Farrell St., near Polk Street (☎ 415-885-0750; www.musichallsf.com), books everything from rhythm and blues to Cajun bands to Grammy Award–winning artists such as Bonnie Raitt. Although you'll notice the club isn't in a squeaky-clean neighborhood, safety isn't a problem because so many people are going in and out. If you're driving, use the valet in front (if available) or park in the AMC 1000 garage across the street. Take a cab home after the show if you aren't driving. You can find the club schedule and order tickets on the Web site.

It won't be the Grateful Dead, but you can find out who's playing **The Fillmore,** 1805 Geary St., at Fillmore Street, by checking out its Web site (www.thefillmore.com) or by calling the box office at ☎ **415-346-6000.** A pilgrimage here for die-hard rock 'n' roll fans really is meaningful. **The SF Weekly Warfield,** 982 Market St. (☎ **415-567-2060**), is a huge theater that books big-time musicians, mostly rock 'n' roll. **Slim's,** 333 11th St., between Folsom and Harrison streets (☎ **415-255-0333;** www.slims-sf.com), is a smaller, fairly comfortable club owned by singer Boz Scaggs, who plays here every now and then. A much bigger room that some grown-ups I know find extra palatable is **Bimbo's 365 Club,** 1025 Columbus Ave., at Chestnut Street, in North Beach (☎ **415-474-0365;** www.bimbos365club.com). It's a '30s-style ballroom with an ornate bar and an attendant in the ladies' restroom. Music varies from rock to alternative. You can check the schedule on the Web site. **Bottom of the Hill,** 1233 17th St., at Texas Street (☎ **415-621-4455;** www.bottomofthehill.com), is a 300- to 500-capacity venue that caters to nationally known indie rock acts with special appeal to the demographic that listens to college radio. This Potrero Hill club also serves bar and grill food. Smokers are allowed to puff on the patio. You can get there on the 22-Fillmore or 19-Polk bus. My sources in the music biz inform me that **The Independent,** 628 Divisadero St., between Grove and Hayes streets (☎ **415-771-1421;** www.theindependentsf.com), has the best sound system in the city and books the hottest indie and pop bands. The schedule is online; entrance runs from free with a two-drink minimum to $25.

Shakin' Your Groove Thang: Dance Clubs

The Ramp, 855 China Basin, off Third Street at Mariposa Street (☎ **415-621-2378;** www.ramprestaurant.com), is an indoor/outdoor bar/restaurant serving salads, burgers, breakfast, and perhaps the best views over the water. Between May and October you can dance to live music on the weekend; Saturday features salsa bands, and Sunday brings world music (both days 5–8 p.m.). There's no cover charge. The ultracool but friendly **Cafe du Nord,** below the Swedish American Hall, 2170 Market St., at Sanchez Street (☎ **415-861-5016;** www.cafedunord.com), is a basement-level club and restaurant that features indie bands or some type of live music almost every evening. Cover runs from $10 to $20. Some shows admit under-21 bohemians accompanied by adults. **DNA Lounge,** 375 11th St., at Harrison Street (☎ **415-626-1409;** www.dnalounge.com), may be blasting metal, gothic, hip-hop, synth pop . . . whatever . . . on different nights of the week. Cover ranges from free to $15.

Swing, salsa, tango, and ballroom dancers, and those who've never completely let go of their Ginger Rogers fantasies, can dip to their hearts'
content at **Cheryl Burke Dance,** 1830 17th St. (☎ **415-252-9000;** www.
cherylburkedance.com). You can swoop by at 8 p.m. to take a class,
and then stay for a dance party on Friday, Saturday, or alternate
Sundays, or simply arrive at 9 p.m. to trip the light fantastic. This is
strictly a social dancing venue; only snacks and nonalcoholic beverages
are available. The cover charge is $8 to $15. Already have your moves
down? The **Top of the Mark** in the InterContinental Mark Hopkins hotel,
1 Nob Hill (☎ **415-616-6916;** www.topofthemark.com), with its surround-
sound view, is one of the prettiest rooms in the city. Tables ring the
dance floor, and a six-piece band plays '40s dance tunes on Friday and
Saturday night. Cover is $5–$10 — or you can go all out and eat dinner
here, too.

Local nightlife encompasses much more than South of Market dance
halls. For a little fiesta in the Mission District, reserve a seat on **El
Voladote,** the Mexican Bus (www.mexicanbus.com), as it cruises the
dance clubs Friday and Saturday nights. The $38 ticket price includes
cover charges at three clubs. Call ☎ **415-546-3747** for reservations two
or three weeks ahead. Salsa dancing is all the rage, and the place to take
a lesson or just sit back watching expert couples heat up the expansive
dance floor is **Roccapulco,** 3140 Mission St., at Precita Street (☎ **415-
648-6611;** www.roccapulco.com). Ten dollars gets you a two-hour
lesson Monday or Wednesday at 7 p.m., or a one-hour class Friday or
Saturday at 8:30 p.m. Live Latin bands play Friday and Saturday from
10 p.m., and Mexican specialties are available to keep your energy up.
You'll want to dress the part here.

Sunday afternoons in the Mission call out for a *cerveza* on the patio at
El Rio, 3158 Mission St. (☎ **415-282-3325;** www.elriosf.com), where
they pack 'em in for salsa parties ($8 admission after 3 p.m.). The rest of
the week you might find DJs, a movie on the patio, or a benefit for an
alternative magazine, and you'll always find a mixed but congenial
crowd of locals. Usually there's no cover; for special events you may pay
around $7.

Drinking in the Atmosphere: The Best Places to Have a Drink and Mingle

San Francisco offers a special ambience. From coffee shops and dance
clubs to galleries and restaurants, there's something to appeal to every
persuasion. If atmosphere is what you're after, check out these favorites.

Joining the singles scene

The **Balboa Cafe,** 3199 Fillmore St., between Greenwich and Filbert streets
(☎ **415-921-3944**), has withstood the test of time. The bar/restaurant gets
lots of repeat customers — they come here after every divorce. In and

around the Tenderloin, patrons line up to enter the **Red Room,** 827 Sutter St., between Jones and Leavenworth streets, next door to the Commodore Hotel (☎ **415-346-7666**). Look sharp. **Bambuddha Lounge,** at the Phoenix Hotel, 601 Eddy St., at Larkin Street (☎ **415-885-5088**), combines an Asian sensibility with the desire to have a really good time eating, drinking, and checking out the people around the pool. It offers innovative cocktail fare, house music nightly, and well-regarded food. **Blondie's Bar and No Grill,** 540 Valencia St., between 16th and 17th streets (☎ **415-864-2419**), is on the sizzling Valencia Street corridor in the Mission District. The young and the restless make good use of the free jukebox. The **Make-Out Room,** also in the Mission at 3225 22nd St. (☎ **415-647-2888**), attracts a very attractive young crowd and features alternative bands (cover ranges from free to about $8).

The Mission has its own version of the Bermuda Triangle, and, if you have the stamina to investigate, you could begin the evening at **Latin American Club,** 3286 22nd St. (☎ **415-647-2732**). This bar has an unstructured feel — maybe it's the piñatas hanging from the ceiling — and you'll see lots of mid-20s to mid-30s people hanging out and drinking while they wait for things to get going at one of the nearby music clubs. Although the Make-Out Room is just across the street, walk down to Mission St. and see what's happening at **12 Galaxies,** 2565 Mission St. (☎ **415-970-9777;** www.12galaxies.com), which on some nights is a little out of this world. Live music draws the local party crowd, and not infrequently the club is the scene of theme bashes. The night I visited, the Devil-Ettes were out in full force, horns and all, for their five-year anniversary go-go blowout. Right next door is **Doc's Clock,** 2575 Mission St. (☎ **415-824-3627;** www.docsclock.com), which is the best bar in the area — according to Aiden, who checks identification at the door. He also pointed out that it has the only shuffleboard in the Mission, plus charming, articulate bartenders. For a more low-key neighborhood hang-out (with free Wi-Fi), follow your ears to **Revolution Cafe,** 3248 22nd St., at Bartlett Street (☎ **415-642-0474**). Open at 9 a.m. daily for coffee and croissants, it offers live music on weekends, when a great local crowd spills out onto the street, giving this little cafe a party vibe. Squeeze your way to the bar for beer on tap, wine, sandwiches, and snacks.

Still too fancy for you? A most solid dive bar with a huge list of beers, cheap cocktails, free popcorn, pool table, jukebox, and outdoor patio for smokers would be **Lucky 13,** 2140 Market St. (☎ **415-487-1313**), near the Castro and just off the J-Church and F-Market Muni lines. The clientele is a mixture of hipsters and couples meeting for a pre-dinner drink, but given the crowds and the lack of lighting, you may not notice.

Mixing with the sophisticates

A splendid Art Deco supper club, **Bix,** 56 Gold St., off Montgomery Street between Pacific and Jackson streets in the Financial District (☎ **415-433-6300;** www.bixrestaurant.com), will make you want to wear a bias-cut gown (or a dinner jacket, perhaps) and appear very glamorous. The food is good, too. The **Redwood Room,** at the Clift Hotel, 495 Geary St., at

Jones Street (☎ 415-929-2372), is not quite the refined place it was in my mother's day, but the clientele appears to have dropped in from a *Vanity Fair* photo shoot. The **Tonga Room** at the Fairmont Hotel, 950 Mason St., at California Street (☎ 415-772-5278), features a happy hour buffet weekdays from 5 to 7 p.m. For the price of a drink (about $7), you can enjoy hors d'oeuvres and entertainment — a tropical rainstorm hits every half-hour. Okay, okay, maybe that isn't so sophisticated, but at least the hotel's posh.

Speakeasys are back, as evidenced by **Bourbon and Branch,** a bar in the Tenderloin that requires you to make reservations online and then use a password (which arrives in an e-mail) for entry. Now, given the number of places in San Francisco delighted to ply you with liquor, you may be thinking, "Why go to the trouble?" But part of the fun of drinking here, besides the superbly concocted drinks, stylish atmosphere, and upmarket clientele, is going to the trouble of drinking here. Anyway, it's fun. Contact the bar at www.bourbonandbranch.com for reservations. And even though you aren't supposed to know this already, the address is 501 Jones St., between Geary and O'Farrell streets (☎ 415-346-1735). By the by, all those people heading through a door to the back room are taking a booze mixology class.

Heading to the local for a pint

Chief among our expat watering holes is **Edinburgh Castle Pub,** 950 Geary St., near Polk Street (☎ 415-885-4074), which offers a mix of entertainment, ranging from live music to readings to Quiz Night on Tuesday. A pool table adds to its stellar reputation. There's no cover charge. Convenient to Union Square is the fine **Johnny Foley's,** 243 O'Farrell St. (☎ 415-954-0777). If you're in the mood for bangers and mash or fish and chips, this is the place to be. It schedules live entertainment nightly. Missing Guinness? Head to **O'Reilly's,** 622 Green St. (☎ 415-989-6222), an Irish pub (no kidding) with two-toned stout and weekend brunch, as well as an authentic crowd of employed locals.

Bringing the kids along

Biscuits and Blues, 401 Mason St., at Geary Street (☎ 415-292-2583), is near the theater district on Union Square in a basement room. The all-ages venue has inexpensive food ($13–$16 entrees), and the music — by blues musicians of varied repute — is really good. If you dine here, you get the best seats in the house. Tickets are $13 to $35. I'd also check out the free jam sessions Thursday to Sunday from 3:30 to 6:30 p.m.

The **Great American Music Hall** (see "Catching the big-name acts," earlier in this chapter), allows children over 6 for some shows; call for an events calendar to see who's playing an early show. Because they offer food service, **Yoshi's** and **Jazz at Pearl's** can also accommodate minors. The same is true of **Slim's** and **Bottom of the Hill.** (See "Finding some cool jazz" and "Catching the big-name acts," earlier in this chapter.)

Laughing It Up: Comedy Clubs

I probably don't have to remind you that San Francisco is where Robin Williams got his start and where Lenny Bruce once shocked the audience at the Purple Onion by using foul language. Imagine that. Although the city is no longer the hotbed of chuckles that it was in the '70s, the comedy clubs are still packin' 'em in.

Cobb's Comedy Club, 915 Columbus Ave. (☎ **415-928-4320;** www.cobbs comedy.com), features headliners Thursday through Sunday and more eclectic shows on some Wednesday nights. Check the calendar for details. No one under 16 admitted; tickets range from $20 to $40, and there's a two-drink minimum. The **Punchline Comedy Club,** 444 Battery St., between Washington and Clay streets (☎ **415-397-7573;** www.punch linecomedyclub.com), also books local and nationally known comics nightly at 9 p.m. with a second set at 11 p.m. Friday and Saturday. These shows are open only to folks 18 and over; tickets range from $5 to $20, and there's a two-drink minimum. The Valencia Street corridor in the Mission District is one hot property, but before it was the place to be, it was the longtime 'hood of **The Marsh,** 1062 Valencia St. (☎ **800-838-3006** or 415-826-5750; www.themarsh.org), a complex of theaters devoted to developing work, performance art, storytellers, musicians, and comedians, including Marga Gomez. Monday night showcases works-in-progress, and Wednesday night features the "Rising Series." Check the Web site for more events. And because I'm a big believer in supporting the local talent (and saving a couple of bucks), laugh for less at **San Francisco Comedy College and Clubhouse,** 414 Mason St., No. 705 (☎ **415-921-2051;** www.sfcomedycollege.com). You can check out the comedians of the future on Wednesday, Friday, and Saturday night. Tickets are around $10. It's BYOB, and no liquor license means no two-drink minimum.

Defying Categorization: Unique Bars

If you smoke and drink, or drink and don't mind smoke, **Amber,** 718 14th St., around Church and Sanchez streets (☎ **415-626-7827**), is the bar for you. This is a locals' hangout with high-quality booze, a comfy lounge, and excellent lighting. **Li-Po Cocktail Lounge,** 916 Grant Ave., at Washington Street (☎ **415-982-0072**), is an authentic, dark, Chinatown dive, complete with dusty Asian furnishings, a huge rice-paper lantern, and a shrine to Buddha behind the bar. If you want to drink with professionals, head to North Beach and grab a barstool at **Gino and Carlo's,** 548 Green St., between Columbus and Grant avenues (☎ **415-421-0896**), which opens early so the regulars can get in a fortifying scotch before lunch. **Spec's,** 12 Saroyan Alley, off Columbus Avenue and Broadway (☎ **415-421-4112**), is another North Beach institution — dark and dingy, but historic.

Literary types make a pilgrimage to **Vesuvio** in North Beach, where Jack Kerouac passed the time. It's at 255 Columbus Ave. (☎ 415-362-3370), next to Kerouac Alley, where the author used to pass out.

Fancy yourself an undiscovered singing sensation? Make your way to the back room at **Martuni's**, 4 Valencia St., at Market Street (☎ 415-241-0205), where customers croon and the piano player is kind.

Champagne lovers unite in the Financial District at the **Bubble Lounge,** 714 Montgomery St. (☎ 415-434-4204). The bar has over 300 sparkling wines, plush sofas, and an array of financial-center types reminiscing over their expense accounts.

If you're around Polk Street for dinner, stop in afterward at the **Bigfoot Lodge,** a retro, log-cabin-like bar with good recorded music, a cool crowd of singles, and a wooden likeness of Bigfoot, as we imagine him to be. Find all this and more at 1750 Polk St., near Washington Street (☎ 415-440-2355). Alternatively, **Hemlock Tavern,** 1131 Polk St. at Post Street (☎ 415-923-0923; www.hemlocktavern.com), brings in two indie bands most nights to play in one of the smallest enclosed public spaces I've seen. It has another room for drinking, a pool table, and a patio for smoking. Over in Hayes Valley, you can snack on corn dogs and other foodlike products, drink, and discover what's happening in the indie music scene at **Rickshaw Stop,** 155 Fell St. at Van Ness Avenue (☎ 415-861-2011; www.rickshawstop.com). Events are scheduled Wednesday through Saturday nights, and tickets are $5 to $15 at the door.

For beer, wine, and entertainment in an atmospheric red haze, **Amnesia,** 853 Valencia St., between 19th and 20th streets (☎ 415-970-0012; www.amnesiathebar.com) is an excellent pick. You can find a calendar of events on the Web site, but my suggestion is to just show up and be surprised. The neighborhood has enough places for dinner that you can easily plan a night worth telling your pals back home about.

Stepping Out: The Gay and Lesbian Scene

In this section, I give you a short list of the many clubs and bars that cater to the gay and lesbian community. Find specific listings in the weekly entertainment guides, *SF Weekly* and *Bay Guardian,* and look for the free *Bay Area Reporter* in bookstores, cafes, and bars around town. Another well-regarded free guide is the *Gay Pocketguide,* which you can find wherever the *Reporter* is available.

The Cafe, 2367 Market St., near Castro Street (☎ 415-861-3846), is currently the place for both sexes to go dancing. It's also the place to stand in line on weekend nights. Farther into the Castro is **The Men's Room,** 3988 18th St., at Noe St. (☎ 415-861-1310). It's a neighborhood bar but welcoming to all, according to my source, Paul, who bartends at **Twin Peaks Tavern,** 401 Castro St., at Market Street (☎ 415-864-9470), an unpretentious, comfy landmark with a pleasant clientele that spans the ages. Outside of the Castro, Paul also recommends **Truck,** 1900 Folsom St. (☎ **415-252-0306;** www.trucksf.com), popular for sweet bartenders, a mellow crowd of regulars, and decent bar food. **Endup** is another gay icon, a hangout as well as a dance club. South of Market at 401 Sixth St. (☎ **415-646-0999**), it's a San Francisco institution like the cable cars or Coit Tower. Cover is $20.

To be entertained or be entertaining, try **Martuni's** piano bar (see the preceding section), which is certainly gay-friendly, but you should also make your way to **The Mint Karaoke Lounge,** 1942 Market St. in the Castro (☎ **415-626-4726**). On the weekends, the hard core come in to warm up at 4 p.m., but the show goes on seven nights a week, and it's terrifically fun. Some of the singers may cause you to drink too much to stop the pain, but others will have you raising your eyebrows in pleased amazement. Your fellow imbibers will likely be quite friendly, so I can almost guarantee that you'll have a good time. Stop off at the ATM before you arrive, because the bar accepts cash only.

Part VI
The Part of Tens

The 5th Wave   By Rich Tennant

"Oh, look. Shake it, and it fills with tiny felons trying to swim their way to freedom."

In this part . . .

Whipping up these top-ten lists was a challenge! I'm just glad I didn't have to come up with my ten favorite restaurants (too challenging) or my ten favorite parking places (the first ten available spots, wherever they are). Instead, in this part I offer you my humble opinions on the greatest views, the best pastimes in foul weather, useful/playful gifts that won't damage your credit rating, and the best ways to look less like a tourist — not that I have anything against tourists, mind you.

Chapter 17

The Top Ten San Francisco Views

....

In This Chapter

▶ Finding the best panoramas

▶ Golfing, dining, and drinking cocktails, with a view

▶ Checking out the view from Berkeley

....

*P*eople like views. That much is clear from the wrangling for a table with a view in restaurants, and from the extra tariff imposed on a room with a view, not to mention a home with a view. San Francisco is one major view, owing to all those hills. I admit to a permanent sentimental attachment to the views of San Francisco. Following are some of my favorites.

From Twin Peaks

The mother of all views — if the weather cooperates — is from **Twin Peaks,** which sits in the center of San Francisco in a residential neighborhood at the top of Market Street. The sightline encompasses the entrance to the bay and reaches all the way 'round to Candlestick Point. If you're driving, head southwest on Market Street, which becomes Portola Drive past 17th Street. The first light past Corbett Street is a right turn only; this is Twin Peaks Boulevard, the road that takes you up the hill.

 The **37-Corbett bus,** which you can catch on Market and Church streets, takes passengers near, but not all the way to, Twin Peaks. And the rest of the trip is quite a hike uphill. If you'd prefer something less strenuous and want to see one of San Francisco's beautiful "hidden" staircases, here's a tip: Exit the bus at Corbett and Clayton streets, and look for an old concrete wall on the west side of Clayton marked by a street sign that says "Pemberton." This leads to the Pemberton Stairs. You won't get to the top of Twin Peaks by climbing them, but you'll enjoy bay views in quiet, green surroundings.

From Bernal Heights Park

Look southeast from downtown and you'll spot a prominent hill with a few trees decorating the top. That's **Bernal Heights Park,** the favored dog-walking and fireworks-viewing area for the Bernal Heights neighborhood. The weather in this part of town is far superior to the weather around Twin Peaks, which can get really foggy, much to the dismay of the camera-toting folk on the tour buses. I consider the views here equally wonderful, partly because Bernal Hill is closer to downtown and the bay. The **67-Folsom bus** drives to the end of Folsom at Esmeralda. Exit and walk up the hill on any of a number of paths.

From Lincoln Park

Lincoln Park is one of the prettiest golf courses in creation, situated around the Palace of the Legion of Honor and above the entrance to San Francisco Bay at Land's End. Standing in front of the museum, you can see in the distance a snippet of downtown framed within the green branches of fir trees. From here, walk west down the street. You'll be stunned by a postcard-perfect view of the Golden Gate Bridge from a unique perspective — facing north as if you're entering the bay. Take a seat on one of the benches along the street so you can survey the vista in comfort. The **18–46th Avenue bus** stops in the museum parking lot.

From the Beach Chalet Restaurant

The waves along **Ocean Beach,** at the end of Golden Gate Park on the Great Highway, are at times soothing and at times violent enough to discourage beachcombing. In either case, you'll be as comfy as a babe in a crib if you get a table upstairs in the **Beach Chalet** restaurant (☎ 415-386-8439) overlooking the Pacific (ideally, as the sun sets). Willis Polk designed the building, and murals painted in the 1930s by the same artist who created the frescoes at Coit Tower adorn the first-floor visitor center. The restaurant is particularly popular for its menu of house-brewed beers, and it serves throughout the day and evening, starting at breakfast. If you don't want to wait for a table in the dining room (the food is so-so), you can take a seat in the bar (a much better idea) and turn toward the view, dramatic in any season. The Park Chalet part of the building looks onto, well, the park, of course. The **5-Fulton bus,** which you can pick up on Market and Powell streets, takes you to Ocean Beach, a block or so from the Beach Chalet.

Above Dolores Park

From any Muni Metro station (the Powell Street Station being the closest to Union Square), take the J-Church toward Daly City. Exit on 18th and Church streets, above Dolores Park. The city and bay views over this stretch of green on a clear day have been responsible for more than one decision to relocate to the Bay Area. After soaking in the scenery and taking a stroll through the park, walk two blocks north on Dolores Street until you reach **Mission Dolores** at 16th and Dolores streets, the oldest building in San Francisco. Top this off with an ice cream from **Bi-Rite Creamery**, 3692 18th St. (across from the park), possibly the most delicious cone in town, and certainly the most creative.

From the Top of the Mark

If you feel like having a cocktail as you drink in a view, head to the **Top of the Mark** in the InterContinental Mark Hopkins hotel, 1 Nob Hill, at California and Mason streets (☎ 415-392-3434). Sometimes it's so busy you have to wait in line at the elevator, but the city views from the tables are mesmerizing.

From the Cheesecake Factory

Union Square is a compact urban hub, immensely appealing, especially when it's crowded and bustling. Above the madding crowd, **Macy's** (see Chapter 12) has a branch of the **Cheesecake Factory** (☎ 415-397-3333) on the eighth floor. Management shrewdly included a heated patio for diners who favor a city view in all its skyscrapered glory. The restaurant is open Monday through Thursday from 11 a.m. to 11 p.m., Friday and Saturday until midnight, and Sunday from 10 a.m. to 10 p.m.

From Fisherman's Wharf

If you've skipped straight to this section, you won't know that I, like all upstanding San Franciscans, generally avoid **Fisherman's Wharf** (see Chapter 11) the way I avoid the Oakland A's. However, I recently discovered a way to escape the folks crowding the sidewalks, yet still take advantage of the views and freshly cracked crab.

The crab stands are plopped in front of their namesake restaurants along one block off Jefferson Street. Just to the left of Fisherman's Grotto #9 are glass doors marked PASSAGEWAY TO THE BOATS, the boats being what remains of the fishing fleet. Take your cracked crab, your beer, and plenty of napkins, and push through. You'll be on a pier that leads to the tiny **Fisherman's and Seaman's Memorial Chapel** on your right, with views of the bay and Telegraph Hill in front and to your left. The pier is parallel to Jefferson Street but may be gloriously close to empty even on a weekend. You can eat your crab in peace sitting on the dock of the bay, watching . . . well, you know. Close by, sea lions jump, swim, and beg in the waters below.

From Fort Point

The remains of **Fort Point,** an 1861 brick artillery fortress, occupy the land at the edge of the bay nearest the Golden Gate Bridge. I remember the first time I visited this area, because heavy fog obscured everything around me except the uppermost portion of the bridge. It was a dramatic vision. On a clear day, you'll be treated to the bridge, of course, but also to bright views of the downtown skyline and Alcatraz. The **29-Sunset bus** stops as close as the parking lot next to the bridge visitor center, a downhill walk to a particularly pretty viewpoint in the midst of eucalyptus trees. If you're up for a hike, follow the joggers past the Marina Green and through the Presidio (see Chapter 11).

From UC Berkeley Botanical Gardens

Drive to the **UC Berkeley Botanical Gardens,** high in the hills behind the campus. Find the rose garden. Beyond the plants, you can see the bay and San Francisco, small and glowing in the distance. See Chapter 14 for other ideas on what to do in Berkeley after you finish admiring the view.

Chapter 18

Ten Things to Do If It's Raining (Or Just Too Foggy)

● ●

In This Chapter

▶ Making the most of a soggy day
▶ Pampering yourself at the hot springs or spa
▶ Finding entertaining indoor activities

● ●

*S*an Francisco isn't Seattle or London by any means, but our gray days can get in the way of enjoying the city. Actually, a foggy morning is what bothers people most — fog is always cold and damp and dark. But you don't have time to grouse about the weather. You have things to do, places to see, people to meet . . . oh, you don't like getting wet? Okay. Here are a few rainy/foggy-day options.

Taking Afternoon Tea

Afternoon tea at one of the many hotels that offers it is probably the only civilized way to keep dry. Try the cozy **King George Hotel,** 334 Mason St. (☎ 415-283-4TEA; weekends only); the **Fairmont Hotel's Laurel Court,** California and Mason streets (☎ 415-772-5260); the **Palace Hotel,** Market and New Montgomery streets (☎ 415-546-5089; Sat only); or the **Ritz-Carlton,** 600 Stockton St. (☎ 415-773-6198). **Neiman Marcus** also has a lovely, traditional tea service in the **Rotunda** restaurant, 150 Stockton St. (☎ 415-362-4777), from 2:30 to 5 p.m. daily.

Checking Out Japantown

Head to Japantown and take cover inside the **Kinokuniya Building** at 1581 Webster St., between Post Street and Geary Boulevard. Although the exteriors of this and the other buildings in the area aren't much to look at, inside you can get a delicious bowl of noodles at **Mifune** (see Chapter 10), the most authentic noodle house in town. Then entertain yourself in any of a number of stores, such as **Mashiko Folkcraft** (open: Wed–Mon 11 a.m.–6 p.m.) and the **Kinokuniya Bookstore** (open: daily

10:30 a.m.–7 p.m.). If the sky still hasn't cleared, take in a movie at the **Sundance Kabuki Cinemas,** next door. Robert Redford's organization has tarted up this multiplex and tacks on an "amenities" fee to the ticket prices, but the theaters are comfortable. Another perfect way to spend a half-hour or more is getting a chair massage at **Sain Saine,** 22 Peace Plaza (☎ 415-292-3542), steps away from the entrance to the Hotel Kabuki (see Chapter 9). In the interest of research, I had two, and my shoulders have never felt so fine. Plus the price is right, at $1 a minute. An underground parking lot is off Webster Street. Muni buses 2-Clement, 3-Jackson, 4-Sutter, 22-Fillmore, and 38-Geary all drop you in Japantown.

Luxuriating at Kabuki Springs

Staying indoors can turn into a modest luxury at **Kabuki Springs & Spa,** 1750 Geary Blvd., at Webster Street (☎ 415-922-6000; www.kabuki springs.com), a most respectable communal bathhouse. You can soak your feet, have a massage, and take a steam bath. Women may use the communal bath facilities on Sunday, Wednesday, and Friday; Tuesday is coed; and men get the rest of the week. Shy people may not feel comfortable at first walking around the premises au naturel, but no one will bother you. Massages, facials, acupuncture, and other treatments are by appointment. To get here, take the 38-Geary bus. Open daily from 10 a.m. to 10 p.m.

Rock Climbing (Or Working Out) at the Touchstone Mission Cliffs Gym

Rather than let the kids climb the walls in your hotel room, take everyone rock climbing (indoors, of course) in the Mission District at **Touchstone Mission Cliffs Climbing and Fitness,** 2295 Harrison St., at 19th Street (☎ 415-550-0515), and open every day. This world-class facility caters to beginners and experts of all ages and even folks who never dreamed of making like flies. *Belay* (rope handling) classes run regularly, so you can act as assistant to your compadres and vice versa. You don't even need any special equipment — you can rent whatever is necessary (including shoes) — and there goes your final excuse. Also on-site is a gym with locker rooms and a sauna, relief for those who prefer to keep their feet on the floor.

Watching the Weather from the Cliff House

Admire the storm from the confines of the **Cliff House,** 1090 Point Lobos Ave., on the Great Highway (☎ 415-386-3330), open every day. This historic property has two restaurants, a bar, and viewing decks. The food, while rather expensive, is quite good, but what you are really shelling out for is the impressive view of Seal Rocks and the Pacific Ocean, doubly dramatic if waves are crashing about. The closest museum is the **Palace of the Legion of Honor** (see Chapter 11), another wonderful place to wait out the weather (it has a good cafe). The 18–46th Avenue bus serves both locations.

Finding Activities for Everyone at the Metreon and Yerba Buena Gardens

The **Metreon** and **Yerba Buena Gardens** (see Chapter 11) make up a one-stop rainy-day haven, particularly if you're traveling with your family. Depending on everyone's ages, you don't have to stick together for the entire day. Teens can flex their independence at **Zeum** or in the **Tilt** arcade. The elders, if they aren't needed, can shop, play pool at **Jillian's** (the large restaurant on the first floor), or even dash across the street to the **Museum of Modern Art.** Bowling and ice-skating work for everyone, and when it's time to regroup, you can see what's playing at the movies.

Defying the Weather at the California Academy of Sciences

The **California Academy of Sciences** (see Chapter 11) has returned to Golden Gate Park, and the new building is spectacular. You don't need kids along to enjoy the exhibits (although there's no kid-friendlier place in town), and with the planetarium shows, three-story rain forest, cafe, and gift shop, you may pray for drizzle. Time permitting, you can later run across the music concourse to the de Young Museum and get all your culture tourism finished in one day.

Moving to the Beat Museum

Borrow an umbrella from your hotel, head to Caffe Roma in North Beach for a sustaining espresso, then walk over to the **Beat Museum,** 540 Broadway (☎ **415-399-9626;** www.kerouac.com), to either jog your rec-ollections of the '60s or educate yourself on an era that changed San Francisco. For a modest $5 admission fee, you can sit in the eight-chair screening room and watch a documentary about the Beats; see Jack Kerouac's typewriter, manuscripts, letters, and photos; and perhaps get in on an event, such as a poetry reading. Tie-dyed goods and excellent T-shirts fill the gift shop. Open daily from 10 a.m.–10 p.m., this is cer-tainly an only-in–San Francisco way to spend an hour or two while you wait for the rain to clear.

Babying Yourself at Nordstrom

See if you can get an appointment for a manicure, a pedicure, and/or a facial at Nordstrom in the **San Francisco Centre shopping mall** at Fifth and Market streets (☎ **415-977-5102**). If you have a retinue to deal with, send them to the fourth-floor grill for lunch or a snack. You can find lots of shopping opportunities here as well, although most of the stores are your typical mall flavors. There's also a spa at the **Bloomingdale's Westfield Centre** next to Nordies, along with many more shops and restaurants.

Doing Business on a Rainy Day

A great thing to do is sit around your hotel lobby or, better yet, the glamorous lobby at the **Palace Hotel,** 2 New Montgomery St., and complain about the weather. Grab a copy of the *Chronicle* and maybe the *Wall Street Journal* for good measure. Whisper into a cellphone while gripping a cup of coffee in your free hand. Then hail a cab and dash to the nearest Internet cafe to check your e-mail: **Golden Gate Perk,** 401 Bush St. at Kearney Street (☎ **415-362-3929**), has computers if you didn't bring your laptop, and **Café de la Presse,** 352 Grant Ave. (☎ **415-398-2680**), has free Wi-Fi. The terminals at the **Apple Stores** on Stockton Street and Chestnut Street get busy, but using them is free. Anyway, if you think the rain is bad, be thankful you haven't been inundated with foggy mornings for 40 days straight. Now you know why anyone who can afford a summer house in Napa puts up with the traffic on Friday afternoon.

Chapter 19

Ten Ways to Avoid Looking Like a Tourist

In This Chapter
- ▶ Eating, shopping, and dressing like the locals
- ▶ Avoiding tourist traps

I don't understand why some people consider being a tourist so beneath them. Even my own dear husband scoffs at tourists — or people he presumes are tourists — and when we travel, he does his well-meaning best to look like a local. This generally leads to amusing misunderstandings with actual citizens, who ask him something in a language he doesn't understand, or presume he knows where he's going when he hasn't a clue. So, why live a lie, I say. If you're visiting for pleasure and have a keen interest in looking around, you're a tourist. Be proud. Wear that camera around your neck (but maybe leave the bum bag at home). Rattle a map in frustration. Ask a stranger for directions.

Otherwise, memorize the following tips.

Dress for the Weather

This is not *The O.C.* — you cannot tan here. In summer, San Francisco is foggy and cold in the morning and turns sunny in the afternoon, with temperatures in the upper 60s or low 70s. I know this because the meteorologists repeat the same forecast every morning in July and August. Dress in long pants, not shorts. Wear a sweater over your T-shirt and a jacket over both. You can always tie extraneous clothing around your waist when you enter one of our famous microclimates. In San Francisco, the temperature changes from neighborhood to neighborhood, so if you're shivering in Golden Gate Park, head to the Mission to warm up.

 September and October are the warmest months. If you look good in shorts, wear them then.

Don't Trust Your Map

Those darn hills have a way of interrupting the streets in ways that may not be apparent to the untrained eye. It may look like a straight shot from one part of town to the other, but consider the up-and-down of the steep hills. Telegraph Hill is the worst offender. If you can't go through, you'll have to go around. If you plan to walk to a particular destination, ask first at the hotel or call ahead to see if it's more advisable to take public transit or a cab.

Don't Gawk at Tall Buildings

An article in the *San Francisco Chronicle* noted that San Franciscans do not gawk at tall buildings, although I don't know if that includes sky-scrapers in other towns. The author also noted that San Franciscans are breaking their own rule and gawking like mad at the downtown ballpark. So, if you don't want to look like a tourist, don't stare at the Transamerica Pyramid — a quick glance should do — but feel free to drool while admiring AT&T Park. You'll then resemble a local who didn't buy season tickets.

Don't Eat or Shop Like a Tourist

Be picky about where you spend your time and money. Places most residents wouldn't be caught dead include the Hard Rock Cafe, any restaurant on Fisherman's Wharf, Ripley's Believe It or Not!, and the Golden Gate Bridge on a Friday afternoon.

Wait 'til You Get Back to the Airport to Buy That Delicious San Francisco Sourdough

Don't walk around with loaves of bread wrapped in plastic for the trip home. Around here we buy our baguettes for same-day consumption. Anyway, you can buy that particular brand of bread at the airport, where no one will see you.

Cross the Bridge before or after — but Not during — Rush Hour

Don't cross the Bay Bridge between 3 and 7 p.m. unless you want to be mistaken for a suburban commuter. Anyway, no one, not even a bona fide commuter, actually crosses the Bay Bridge at this time; rather, everyone sits, fumes, and occasionally inches forward. This is important to remember if you have friends in the East Bay who invite you to come over for dinner.

Don't Stare at the Locals

Don't point/gasp/shriek at the man/woman/other with the attention-getting tattoo/leather chaps/chartreuse wig, no matter how unusual he/she/it appears. That would be unseemly.

Don't Shout at People You Suspect Don't Speak English

Don't raise your voice or speak extra slowly to your waiter if you suspect he doesn't speak English. In fact, he does speak English. He's merely trying to turn your table as quickly as possible.

Do the Farmers Market Thing

Hang around the Ferry Plaza Farmers Market on a Saturday morning. Have breakfast, circle the stalls, eat all the samples, buy something non-perishable to take home. If you really want to blend in with the natives, head to the Alemany Farmers Market (off 280 South at Alemany) on a Saturday morning instead. You'll need to take a cab.

Remove Any Incriminating Evidence

Remember the plastic nametag you attached to your lapel upon entering the Moscone Convention Center? It's okay to remove it now.

Chapter 20

The Top Ten Gifts for Cheapskates

In This Chapter

▶ Bridging the gap with Golden Gate souvenirs

▶ Sweetening the return with fortune-cookie souvenirs

▶ Spreading the fruits of love with gifts of jam

I don't know about you, but buying gifts for the folks back at the ranch who know I've been on vacation is sometimes more a chore than a pleasure. Besides the fact that no one in the Western world *really* needs another T-shirt, those souvenirs add up (and subtract from my shoe allowance). Understanding, however, that some people expect a little something, here is my list of portable, fun, San Francisco–related gifts — and they're (almost) all under $10.

Playing Bridge

Not to be outdone by the museum gift shops, our own Golden Gate Bridge hawks a variety of items sure to remind your nearest and dearest of one of the wonders of the modern world. I particularly like the $6 **Golden Gate Bridge playing cards,** printed with trivia about the construction and history of the landmark. A close second is the $7 **Golden Gate Bridge kitchen towel,** the gift of choice from thrifty shoppers like my cousin Irene. If you run out of time and can't get to the gift shop, you can purchase these things online at http://store.goldengate.org.

Riding High

Everyone loves refrigerator magnets, right? So take an F-Market streetcar to the Embarcadero, locate the streetcar museum (see Chapter 11) and take home a $4.99 die-cut historic magnet that possibly resembles the very car you rode in on Market St. Or take home all six models and thrill the relatives.

Smelling Salts

The Ferry Building Marketplace is full of places to find great gifts, especially on Saturday, when the Ferry Plaza Farmers Market is running at full tilt. Behind the building, look for the Eatwell Farms booth and check out the $8 jars of **lavender salt** or **rosemary salt.** They smell divine and add extra oomph to salads and roasts. Your friends who cook will be most impressed.

Bringing Good Fortune

The biggest producer of fortune cookies in town is **Mee Mee Bakery,** 1328 Stockton St., between Broadway and Vallejo streets in Chinatown (☎ **415-362-3253;** www.meemeebakery.com). Hand over $10.25 and you can delight someone with a **giant fortune cookie.** Okay, at roughly 5 inches in diameter, maybe it's not an actual giant, but it's still fairly large. Mee Mee also sells bags of chocolate- and strawberry-flavored fortune cookies for $6.75 per pound, and almond cookies for $4.75 per pound. If you want to splurge on something more creative, for about $25 per 100 cookies, the bakery will put your own custom fortunes inside the crispy little devils.

Lighting the Way

Intellectuals and all your friends who belong to book clubs will be thrilled to receive anything from **City Lights,** San Francisco's iconic bookstore. For those keeping to a budget, check out the very cool $8 **black-and-white posters** featuring the North Beach storefront, or Jack Kerouac and Neal Cassady looking rather James Deanish.

Writing Clearly

You can't have too many postcards, but picking them out can be stressful. After all, postcards are like greeting cards — they say something about the person who spent 20 minutes deciding between the one with the cat and the one depicting Einstein. Save time and give your friends a book of **30 San Francisco postcards** featuring the photographs of Michal Venera. At $9.95, this is a deal. Find *San Francisco 30 postcards* at the **Chronicle Books Metreon Store,** 101 4th St. (☎ **415-369-6271**).

Spilling the Beans

You may not believe this, but B.S. (before Starbucks), people in the Bay Area were drinking strong, delicious coffee! And many continue to do so. They purchase it at any of a number of **Peet's Coffee & Tea** stores, including the ones in the Ferry Building (see Chapter 10), in the Russ Building at 217 Montgomery St., and at 2156 Chestnut St. in the Marina. A gift your coffee-loving pals will truly appreciate is **a pound of Peet's French Roast,** my husband's favorite — the stuff is so strong it can bench-press the competition. At $11.95 per pound, it crosses the cheapskate limit, but not by much. Besides, it's worth it.

Ringing Your Bell

Useless ornaments . . . ah, where would commerce be without snow globes, pewter models, and plastic barista figurines? Well, San Francisco can supply its fair share, and at the top of my list is a spiffy **tin cable car.** A mere $8.75, this little beauty actually moves using friction, and ting-a-lings like the real thing while skittering over the linoleum. These are among the many fine doodads available online and at the **Cable Car Museum** gift shop, 1201 Mason St. (☎ 415-474-1887; www.cablecar museum.org). Admission to the museum is free. It's open every day from 10 a.m. to 5 p.m.

Nibbling Bliss

San Francisco has long attracted chocolate makers to its shores, not for any reason I know of. Ghirardelli started things off, followed by Joseph Schmidt (of the beautiful truffles), and most recently by a former doctor and a former winemaker who together produce some serious dark chocolate under the Scharffen Berger label. Free one-hour tours of the handsome brick factory, at 914 Heinz Ave., Berkeley (☎ 510-981-4050; www.scharffenberger.com), are offered by appointment daily from 10:30 a.m. to 3:30 p.m. for people 10 and older. Scharffen Berger sells two gifts that I, for one, would be genuinely pleased to receive: the $10.50 **folio box filled with a dozen squares of chocolate in four different flavors,** and the $7 **rectangular acrylic package of a dozen 5-gram squares** (the 70 percent cacao bittersweet, if you're wondering).

Spreading the Love

Twelve bucks for a small jar of jam? Berkeley's June Taylor does not make ordinary preserves from ordinary fruit, and her divine products created from organic fruit in small batches do not sell for chicken feed. And that's why an 8-ounce jar of her **white nectarine conserve** or **tangerine marmalade** (among many flavors that will cause your bread to sit up and take notice) is such a thoughtful and extravagant offering. Buy June Taylor's jams at the Ferry Plaza Farmers Market on Saturday or at Boulette's Larder in the Ferry Building.

Quick Concierge

* *

Fast Facts

American Automobile Association (AAA)

The office at Sutter and Kearny streets in Union Square provides maps and other information for members traveling by car. Call ☎ 800-222-4357 for emergency service or ☎ 415-565-2012 for general information.

American Express

The office is at 455 Market St., at First Street (☎ 415-536-2600), open Monday through Friday from 8:30 a.m. to 5:30 p.m., Saturday from 9 a.m. to 2 p.m.

Area Codes

The area code for San Francisco is **415**; for Oakland, Berkeley, and much of the East Bay, **510**; for the peninsula, generally **650**.

ATMs

ATMs are easy to find, especially downtown but also on any main business corridor.

Baby sitters

Your hotel concierge can probably arrange for a baby sitter. Otherwise, try American Child Care Service (☎ 415-285-2300; www. americanchildcare.com). Its rates are $20 per hour with a four-hour minimum plus $20 agency fee.

Camera Repair

Discount Camera, 33 Kearny St. (☎ 415-392-1180; www.discountcamera.com), is convenient to Union Square and it sells and repairs photographic equipment. It's open from 8:30 a.m. to 6:30 p.m. Monday through Saturday and 9:30 a.m. to 6 p.m. Sunday (for sales only, no repairs).

Convention Center

The Moscone Convention Center, 747 Howard St., between Third and Fourth streets (☎ 415-974-4000), is within easy walking distance of the Montgomery Street Muni and BART stations.

Credit Cards

To report a lost or stolen card, contact Visa at ☎ 800-336-8472; American Express at ☎ 800-221-7282; MasterCard at ☎ 800-307-7309; Discover at ☎ 800-347-2683; or Diners Club at ☎ 800-234-6377.

Dentists

For 24-hour referrals, call the San Francisco Dental Society (☎ 415-421-1435).

Doctors

Saint Francis Memorial Hospital, 900 Hyde St., between Bush and Pine streets (☎ 415-353-6000), offers 24-hour emergency-care service. The hospital's physician-referral service number is ☎ 415-353-6566. Your hotel can also contact on-call doctors. Before receiving any treatment, check with your health insurance company to find out how to handle emergency treatment when you're out of your provider area.

Earthquakes

California will always have earthquakes, most of which you'll never notice.

However, in case of a significant shaker, you should know a few precautionary measures. When you're inside a building, seek cover; do not run outside. Stand under a doorway or against a wall and stay away from windows. If you exit a building after a substantial quake, use stairwells, not elevators. If you're in a car, pull over to the side of the road and stop — but not until you're away from bridges, overpasses, telephone poles, and power lines. Stay in your car. If you're out walking, stay outside and away from trees, power lines, and the sides of buildings. If you're in an area with tall buildings, find a doorway in which to stand.

Emergencies

Dial ☎ **911** from any phone for police, an ambulance, and the fire department.

Hospitals

San Francisco General Hospital, 1001 Potrero Ave. (☎ 415-206-8111), accepts uninsured emergency patients, but the wait can be long and uncomfortable. The patient referral and assistance number is ☎ 415-206-5166.

Hot Lines

In case of emergency, here are a few numbers to have at hand: Poison Control Center, ☎ 800-876-4766; Rape Crisis Center, ☎ 415-861-2024; Family Service Agency, ☎ 415-474-7310.

Information

The San Francisco Convention and Visitors Bureau is in the lower level of Hallidie Plaza, 900 Market St., at Powell Street (☎ 415-391-2000).

Internet Access and Cafes

You can check your e-mail at Golden Gate Perk, 401 Bush St. (☎ 415-362-3929), or Quetzal Internet Café, 1234 Polk St. (☎ 415-673-4181).

Liquor Laws

You can't drink or purchase alcohol legally if you're under 21. All clubs, bars, supermarkets, and liquor stores require ID from anyone who looks younger than 30 (try not to be offended if you don't get carded). Bars don't serve liquor from 2 a.m. to 6 a.m.

Maps

The visitors bureau (see "Information" earlier in this section) has maps of the city. AAA members can stop by the office (see "AAA" earlier in this section).

Newspapers/Magazines

The major papers are the morning *San Francisco Chronicle* and the afternoon *San Francisco Examiner.* They are available at sidewalk kiosks and boxes. The free weekly *San Francisco Bay Guardian* includes excellent events listings. Find it in cafes and in sidewalk boxes around the city. *San Francisco* magazine is the monthly city magazine. You can find it at newsstands everywhere.

Pharmacies

Walgreens has taken over the city, and you should be able to find one almost anywhere. Call ☎ 800-WALGREEN for the address and phone number of the nearest store. Around Union Square, Walgreens is at 135 Powell St. (☎ 415-391-4433), open Monday through Saturday from 7 a.m. to midnight and Sunday from 8 a.m. to midnight, but the pharmacy keeps shorter hours. A branch on Divisadero Street at Lombard Street has a 24-hour pharmacy.

Police

Call ☎ **911** from any phone. No coins are needed. The non-emergency number is ☎ 415-553-0123.

Post Office

Dozens of post offices are located all around the city. The closest to Union

Square is in Macy's department store, 170 O'Farrell St. (☎ 800-275-8777).

Radio Stations

Find KQED, our National Public Radio affiliate, at 88.5 FM. KCBS 740 AM broadcasts news and sports.

Restrooms

Dark-green public bathrooms are on the waterfront at PIER 39, on Market Street near the cable-car turnaround on Powell Street, and by the Civic Center. The restrooms cost 25¢ and are clean and safe. Also try hotels, department stores, museums, coffeehouses, and service stations. Restaurants usually let only patrons use their bathrooms.

Safety

Walking around alone late at night is never a good idea. San Francisco is relatively safe, but it still has its share of muggings and more heinous crimes. Areas to be particularly careful in include the Tenderloin; the lower Haight; the Mission District anywhere between 16th and 24th streets east of Mission Street; lower Fillmore Street; and South of Market, particularly Sixth and Seventh streets. Keep your wallet in an inside coat pocket, and don't carry around wads of cash. Try to avoid using ATMs at night.

Smoking

Smoking is illegal in bars, restaurants, and public buildings, which is why you see so many well-dressed people loitering on the sidewalk during their coffee breaks.

Taxes

A sales tax of 8.5 percent is added to all purchases except snack food. The hotel and parking garage tax is 14 percent.

Taxis

Outside of Union Square, expect to have trouble hailing a cab on the street; you'll have to call for one instead. Try Yellow Cab (☎ 415-626-2345), Veteran's Cab (☎ 415-648-1313), Desoto Cab (☎ 415-970-1300), or Luxor Cabs (☎ 415-282-4141).

Time Zone

California is on Pacific Time, three hours behind New York.

Transit Information

Calling ☎ 415-817-1717 connects you to all transit organizations.

Weather Updates

While in town, turn to one of the news stations on the radio (try KCBS 740 AM). Otherwise, www.sanfrancisco.city search.com lists comprehensive forecasts.

Toll-Free Numbers and Web Sites
Airlines
Major U.S. airlines
(*flies internationally as well)

Alaska Airlines/Horizon Air*
☎ 800-252-7522
www.alaskaair.com

American Airlines*
☎ 800-433-7300 (in U.S. and Canada)
☎ 020-7365-0777 (in U.K.)
www.aa.com

Continental Airlines*
☎ 800-523-3273 (in U.S. and Canada)
☎ 084-5607-6760 (in U.K.)
www.continental.com

Delta Air Lines*
☎ 800-221-1212 (in U.S. and Canada)
☎ 084-5600-0950 (in U.K.)
www.delta.com

Frontier Airlines
☎ 800-432-1359
www.frontierairlines.com

Hawaiian Airlines*
☎ 800-367-5320 (in U.S. and Canada)
www.hawaiianair.com

JetBlue Airways
☎ 800-538-2583 (in U.S.)
☎ 080-1365-2525 (in U.K. and Canada)
www.jetblue.com

Midwest Airlines
☎ 800-452-2022
www.midwestairlines.com

Northwest Airlines
☎ 800-225-2525 (in U.S.)
☎ 870-0507-4074 (in U.K.)
www.nwa.com

Southwest Airlines
☎ 800-435-9792 (in U.S., U.K., and Canada)
www.southwest.com

Ted (part of United Airlines)
☎ 800-225-5561
www.flyted.com

United Airlines*
☎ 800-864-8331 (in U.S. and Canada)
☎ 084-5844-4777 in U.K.
www.united.com

US Airways*
☎ 800-428-4322 (in U.S. and Canada)
☎ 084-5600-3300 (in U.K.)
www.usairways.com

Virgin America*
☎ 877-359-8474
www.virginamerica.com

Car Rental Agencies

Advantage
☎ 800-777-5500 (in U.S.)
☎ 021-0344-4712 (outside of U.S.)
www.advantagerentacar.com

Alamo
☎ 800-GO-ALAMO (800-462-5266)
www.alamo.com

Avis
☎ 800-331-1212 (in U.S. and Canada)
☎ 084-4581-8181 (in U.K.)
www.avis.com

Budget
☎ 800-527-0700 (in U.S.)
☎ 087-0156-5656 (in U.K.)
☎ 800-268-8900 (in Canada)
www.budget.com

Dollar
☎ 800-800-4000 (in U.S.)
☎ 800-848-8268 (in Canada)
☎ 080-8234-7524 (in U.K.)
www.dollar.com

Enterprise
☎ 800-261-7331 (in U.S.)
☎ 514-355-4028 (in Canada)
☎ 012-9360-9090 (in U.K.)
www.enterprise.com

Hertz
☎ 800-645-3131
☎ 800-654-3001 (for international reservations)
www.hertz.com

National
☎ 800-CAR-RENT (800-227-7368)
www.nationalcar.com

Payless Car Rental
☎ 800-PAYLESS (800-729-5377)
www.paylesscarrental.com

Thrifty
☎ 800-367-2277
☎ 918-669-2168 (international)
www.thrifty.com

Appendix: Quick Concierge **293**

Major Hotel & Motel Chains

Best Western International
☎ 800-780-7234 (in U.S. and Canada)
☎ 0800-393-130 (in U.K.)
www.bestwestern.com

Courtyard by Marriott
☎ 888-236-2427 (in U.S.)
☎ 0800-221-222 (in U.K.)
www.marriott.com/courtyard

Crowne Plaza Hotels
☎ 888-303-1746
www.crowneplaza.com

Econo Lodges
☎ 800-55-ECONO (800-552-3666)
www.econolodge.com

Four Seasons Hotels and Resorts
☎ 800-819-5053 (in U.S. and Canada)
☎ 0800-6488-6488 (in U.K.)
www.fourseasons.com

Hilton Hotels
☎ 800-HILTONS (800-445-8667) (in U.S. and Canada)
☎ 087-0590-9090 (in U.K.)
www.hilton.com

Holiday Inn
☎ 800-315-2621 (in U.S. and Canada)
☎ 0800-405-060 (in U.K.)
www.holidayinn.com

Hyatt Hotels and Resorts
☎ 888-591-1234 (in U.S. and Canada)
☎ 084-5888-1234 (in U.K.)
www.hyatt.com

InterContinental Hotels & Resorts
☎ 800-424-6835 (in U.S. and Canada)
☎ 0800-1800-1800 (in U.K.)
www.ichotelsgroup.com

Marriott Hotels
☎ 877-236-2427 (in U.S. and Canada)
☎ 0800-221-222 (in U.K.)
www.marriott.com

Omni Hotels
☎ 888-444-OMNI (888-444-6664)
www.omnihotels.com

Residence Inn by Marriott
☎ 800-331-3131
☎ 800-221-222 (in U.K.)
www.marriott.com/residenceinn

Sheraton Hotels & Resorts
☎ 800-325-3535 (in U.S.)
☎ 800-543-4300 (in Canada)
☎ 0800-3253-5353 (in U.K.)
www.starwoodhotels.com/sheraton

Westin Hotels & Resorts
☎ 800-937-8461 (in U.S. and Canada)
☎ 0800-3259-5959 (in U.K.)
www.starwoodhotels.com/westin

Where to Get More Information

Area tourist information offices

San Francisco Convention and Visitors Bureau

P.O. Box 429097; 900 Market St., San Francisco, CA 94142-9097 (☎ 415-391-2000; www.onlyinsanfrancisco.com).

Call or write the Convention and Visitors Bureau if you'd like to receive a nifty booklet with lots of useful information, including maps and a calendar of events. Of course, the slant is toward the advertisers, so take those glossy ads lightly. There is a $3 mailing charge. If you have a fax and a touch-tone phone, use the toll-free number for automated 24-hour fax service and "fast facts."

Napa Valley Conference and Visitors Bureau

1310 Napa Town Center, Napa, CA 94559 (☎ 707-226-7459; www.napavalley.com).

This is the second-busiest visitor center in California, which says something about either our fondness for wine or the beauty of the area (or both). The bureau will send you a free brochure and a list of hotels on request; for $10 (plastic accepted), it will mail you a 120-page magazine, suggested itineraries, and a handsome map of the area.

Information on the Web

www.sanfrancisco.citysearch.com

A comprehensive, regularly updated site devoted to all things San Francisco, including arts, entertainment, dining, and attractions, with links to the hotel reservation network.

www.sfbg.com

The *San Francisco Bay Guardian* site with event listings and the lowdown on nightlife.

www.sfgate.com

The *San Francisco Chronicle* Web site. Read all about it.

www.iglta.org

A Web site for gay and lesbian travelers.

www.sanfranmag.com

The Web site for *San Francisco* magazine. Includes dining recommendations and timely entertainment suggestions.

www.gocitykids.com

The Web site for families wondering what to do. Lots of helpful info; membership fee.

Print resources

Frommer's San Francisco

This guide covers all 46 square miles in great detail, including background on the sites, personalities, and neighborhoods that make San Francisco "everybody's favorite city."

Frommer's San Francisco from $90 a Day

For the budget-minded traveler who doesn't want to compromise the quality of the experience, this guide offers advice on the best values and free and almost-free things to see and do.

Frommer's Irreverent San Francisco

A pocket-size guide that's funny and informative; offers unusual and eccentric experiences (as well as information on hotels, restaurants, accommodations, and attractions) in the City by the Bay.

Frommer's Memorable Walks in San Francisco

This guide covers 12 easy-to-follow walking tours through San Francisco's most charming neighborhoods. Includes detailed maps.

Frommer's San Francisco Day by Day

Small but packed with information, this heavily illustrated guide outlines 23 itineraries custom designed to take one day each. Includes detailed maps.

Index

See also separate Accommodations and Restaurant indexes at the end of this index.

General Index

• Numerics •

• A •

BUSINESS, CAREERS & PERSONAL FINANCE

Accounting For Dummies, 4th Edition*
978-0-470-24600-9

Bookkeeping Workbook For Dummies†
978-0-470-16983-4

Commodities For Dummies
978-0-470-04928-0

Doing Business in China For Dummies
978-0-470-04929-7

E-Mail Marketing For Dummies
978-0-470-19087-6

Job Interviews For Dummies, 3rd Edition*†
978-0-470-17748-8

Personal Finance Workbook For Dummies*†
978-0-470-09933-9

Real Estate License Exams For Dummies
978-0-7645-7623-2

Six Sigma For Dummies
978-0-7645-6798-8

Small Business Kit For Dummies, 2nd Edition*†
978-0-7645-5984-6

Telephone Sales For Dummies
978-0-470-16836-3

BUSINESS PRODUCTIVITY & MICROSOFT OFFICE

Access 2007 For Dummies
978-0-470-03649-5

Excel 2007 For Dummies
978-0-470-03737-9

Office 2007 For Dummies
978-0-470-00923-9

Outlook 2007 For Dummies
978-0-470-03830-7

PowerPoint 2007 For Dummies
978-0-470-04059-1

Project 2007 For Dummies
978-0-470-03651-8

QuickBooks 2008 For Dummies
978-0-470-18470-7

Quicken 2008 For Dummies
978-0-470-17473-9

Salesforce.com For Dummies, 2nd Edition
978-0-470-04893-1

Word 2007 For Dummies
978-0-470-03658-7

EDUCATION, HISTORY, REFERENCE & TEST PREPARATION

African American History For Dummies
978-0-7645-5469-8

Algebra For Dummies
978-0-7645-5325-7

Algebra Workbook For Dummies
978-0-7645-8467-1

Art History For Dummies
978-0-470-09910-0

ASVAB For Dummies, 2nd Edition
978-0-470-10671-6

British Military History For Dummies
978-0-470-03213-8

Calculus For Dummies
978-0-7645-2498-1

Canadian History For Dummies, 2nd Edition
978-0-470-83656-9

Geometry Workbook For Dummies
978-0-471-79940-5

The SAT I For Dummies, 6th Edition
978-0-7645-7193-0

Series 7 Exam For Dummies
978-0-470-09932-2

World History For Dummies
978-0-7645-5242-7

FOOD, GARDEN, HOBBIES & HOME

Bridge For Dummies, 2nd Edition
978-0-471-92426-5

Coin Collecting For Dummies, 2nd Edition
978-0-470-22275-1

Cooking Basics For Dummies, 3rd Edition
978-0-7645-7206-7

Drawing For Dummies
978-0-7645-5476-6

Etiquette For Dummies, 2nd Edition
978-0-470-10672-3

Gardening Basics For Dummies*†
978-0-470-03749-2

Knitting Patterns For Dummies
978-0-470-04556-5

Living Gluten-Free For Dummies†
978-0-471-77383-2

Painting Do-It-Yourself For Dummies
978-0-470-17533-0

HEALTH, SELF HELP, PARENTING & PETS

Anger Management For Dummies
978-0-470-03715-7

Anxiety & Depression Workbook For Dummies
978-0-7645-9793-0

Dieting For Dummies, 2nd Edition
978-0-7645-4149-0

Dog Training For Dummies, 2nd Edition
978-0-7645-8418-3

Horseback Riding For Dummies
978-0-470-09719-9

Infertility For Dummies†
978-0-470-11518-3

Meditation For Dummies with CD-ROM, 2nd Edition
978-0-471-77774-8

Post-Traumatic Stress Disorder For Dummies
978-0-470-04922-8

Puppies For Dummies, 2nd Edition
978-0-470-03717-1

Thyroid For Dummies, 2nd Edition†
978-0-471-78755-6

Type 1 Diabetes For Dummies*†
978-0-470-17811-9

* Separate Canadian edition also available
† Separate U.K. edition also available

Available wherever books are sold. For more information or to order direct: U.S. customers visit www.dummies.com or call 1-877-762-2974.
U.K. customers visit www.wileyeurope.com or call (0) 1243 843291. Canadian customers visit www.wiley.ca or call 1-800-567-4797.

INTERNET & DIGITAL MEDIA

AdWords For Dummies
978-0-470-15252-2

Blogging For Dummies, 2nd Edition
978-0-470-23017-6

**Digital Photography All-in-One
Desk Reference For Dummies, 3rd Edition**
978-0-470-03743-0

Digital Photography For Dummies, 5th Edition
978-0-7645-9802-9

**Digital SLR Cameras & Photography
For Dummies, 2nd Edition**
978-0-470-14927-0

**eBay Business All-in-One Desk Reference
For Dummies**
978-0-7645-8438-1

eBay For Dummies, 5th Edition*
978-0-470-04529-9

eBay Listings That Sell For Dummies
978-0-471-78912-3

Facebook For Dummies
978-0-470-26273-3

The Internet For Dummies, 11th Edition
978-0-470-12174-0

Investing Online For Dummies, 5th Edition
978-0-7645-8456-5

iPod & iTunes For Dummies, 5th Edition
978-0-470-17474-6

MySpace For Dummies
978-0-470-09529-4

Podcasting For Dummies
978-0-471-74898-4

**Search Engine Optimization
For Dummies, 2nd Edition**
978-0-471-97998-2

Second Life For Dummies
978-0-470-18025-9

**Starting an eBay Business For Dummies,
3rd Edition†**
978-0-470-14924-9

GRAPHICS, DESIGN & WEB DEVELOPMENT

**Adobe Creative Suite 3 Design Premium
All-in-One Desk Reference For Dummies**
978-0-470-11724-8

**Adobe Web Suite CS3 All-in-One Desk
Reference For Dummies**
978-0-470-12099-6

AutoCAD 2008 For Dummies
978-0-470-11650-0

**Building a Web Site For Dummies,
3rd Edition**
978-0-470-14928-7

**Creating Web Pages All-in-One Desk
Reference For Dummies, 3rd Edition**
978-0-470-09629-1

**Creating Web Pages For Dummies,
8th Edition**
978-0-470-08030-6

Dreamweaver CS3 For Dummies
978-0-470-11490-2

Flash CS3 For Dummies
978-0-470-12100-9

Google SketchUp For Dummies
978-0-470-13744-4

InDesign CS3 For Dummies
978-0-470-11865-8

**Photoshop CS3 All-in-One
Desk Reference For Dummies**
978-0-470-11195-6

Photoshop CS3 For Dummies
978-0-470-11193-2

Photoshop Elements 5 For Dummies
978-0-470-09810-3

SolidWorks For Dummies
978-0-7645-9555-4

Visio 2007 For Dummies
978-0-470-08983-5

Web Design For Dummies, 2nd Edition
978-0-471-78117-2

Web Sites Do-It-Yourself For Dummies
978-0-470-16903-2

Web Stores Do-It-Yourself For Dummies
978-0-470-17443-2

LANGUAGES, RELIGION & SPIRITUALITY

Arabic For Dummies
978-0-471-77270-5

Chinese For Dummies, Audio Set
978-0-470-12766-7

French For Dummies
978-0-7645-5193-2

German For Dummies
978-0-7645-5195-6

Hebrew For Dummies
978-0-7645-5489-6

Ingles Para Dummies
978-0-7645-5427-8

Italian For Dummies, Audio Set
978-0-470-09586-7

Italian Verbs For Dummies
978-0-471-77389-4

Japanese For Dummies
978-0-7645-5429-2

Latin For Dummies
978-0-7645-5431-5

Portuguese For Dummies
978-0-471-78738-9

Russian For Dummies
978-0-471-78001-4

Spanish Phrases For Dummies
978-0-7645-7204-3

Spanish For Dummies
978-0-7645-5194-9

Spanish For Dummies, Audio Set
978-0-470-09585-0

The Bible For Dummies
978-0-7645-5296-0

Catholicism For Dummies
978-0-7645-5391-2

The Historical Jesus For Dummies
978-0-470-16785-4

Islam For Dummies
978-0-7645-5503-9

**Spirituality For Dummies,
2nd Edition**
978-0-470-19142-2

NETWORKING AND PROGRAMMING

ASP.NET 3.5 For Dummies
978-0-470-19592-5

C# 2008 For Dummies
978-0-470-19109-5

Hacking For Dummies, 2nd Edition
978-0-470-05235-8

Home Networking For Dummies, 4th Edition
978-0-470-11806-1

Java For Dummies, 4th Edition
978-0-470-08716-9

**Microsoft® SQL Server™ 2008 All-in-One
Desk Reference For Dummies**
978-0-470-17954-3

**Networking All-in-One Desk Reference
For Dummies, 2nd Edition**
978-0-7645-9939-2

**Networking For Dummies,
8th Edition**
978-0-470-05620-2

SharePoint 2007 For Dummies
978-0-470-09941-4

**Wireless Home Networking
For Dummies, 2nd Edition**
978-0-471-74940-0

OPERATING SYSTEMS & COMPUTER BASICS

iMac For Dummies, 5th Edition
978-0-7645-8458-9

Laptops For Dummies, 2nd Edition
978-0-470-05432-1

Linux For Dummies, 8th Edition
978-0-470-11649-4

MacBook For Dummies
978-0-470-04859-7

**Mac OS X Leopard All-in-One
Desk Reference For Dummies**
978-0-470-05434-5

Mac OS X Leopard For Dummies
978-0-470-05433-8

Macs For Dummies, 9th Edition
978-0-470-04849-8

PCs For Dummies, 11th Edition
978-0-470-13728-4

Windows® Home Server For Dummies
978-0-470-18592-6

Windows Server 2008 For Dummies
978-0-470-18043-3

**Windows Vista All-in-One
Desk Reference For Dummies**
978-0-471-74941-7

Windows Vista For Dummies
978-0-471-75421-3

Windows Vista Security For Dummies
978-0-470-11805-4

SPORTS, FITNESS & MUSIC

Coaching Hockey For Dummies
978-0-470-83685-9

Coaching Soccer For Dummies
978-0-471-77381-8

Fitness For Dummies, 3rd Edition
978-0-7645-7851-9

Football For Dummies, 3rd Edition
978-0-470-12536-6

GarageBand For Dummies
978-0-7645-7323-1

Golf For Dummies, 3rd Edition
978-0-471-76871-5

Guitar For Dummies, 2nd Edition
978-0-7645-9904-0

**Home Recording For Musicians
For Dummies, 2nd Edition**
978-0-7645-8884-6

**iPod & iTunes For Dummies,
5th Edition**
978-0-470-17474-6

Music Theory For Dummies
978-0-7645-7838-0

Stretching For Dummies
978-0-470-06741-3

Get smart @ dummies.com®

- Find a full list of Dummies titles
- Look into loads of FREE on-site articles
- Sign up for FREE eTips e-mailed to you weekly
- See what other products carry the Dummies name
- Shop directly from the Dummies bookstore
- Enter to win new prizes every month!

* Separate Canadian edition also available
† Separate U.K. edition also available

Available wherever books are sold. For more information or to order direct: U.S. customers visit www.dummies.com or call 1-877-762-2974.
U.K. customers visit www.wileyeurope.com or call (0) 1243 843291. Canadian customers visit www.wiley.ca or call 1-800-567-4797.